Queer
Kinship

THEORY Q A series edited by
Lauren Berlant, Lee Edelman, Benjamin Kahan, and Christina Sharpe

Queer Kinship

Race, Sex, Belonging, Form

TYLER BRADWAY AND
ELIZABETH FREEMAN, EDITORS

Duke University Press Durham and London 2022

Library of Congress Cataloging-in-Publication Data
Names: Bradway, Tyler, [date] editor. | Freeman, Elizabeth,
[date] editor.
Title: Queer kinship : race, sex, belonging, form / Tyler Bradway
and Elizabeth Freeman, editors.
Other titles: Theory Q.
Description: Durham : Duke University Press, 2022. | Series:
Theory Q | Includes bibliographical references and index.
Identifiers: LCCN 2021053879 (print)
LCCN 2021053880 (ebook)
ISBN 9781478016021 (hardcover)
ISBN 9781478018650 (paperback)
ISBN 9781478023272 (ebook)
Subjects: LCSH: Queer theory. | Kinship—Political aspects. |
Gays—Family relationships. | BISAC: SOCIAL SCIENCE /
LGBTQ Studies / General | SOCIAL SCIENCE / Anthropology /
Cultural & Social
Classification: LCC HQ76.25 .Q3745 2022 (print) |
LCC HQ76.25 (ebook) | DDC 306.76/6—dc23/eng/20220124
LC record available at https://lccn.loc.gov/2021053879
LC ebook record available at https://lccn.loc.gov/2021053880

Cover art: Clifford Prince King, *Communion*, 2019.
Courtesy of the artist and STARS, Los Angeles.

Contents

vii   *Acknowledgments*

1   Introduction: Kincoherence/Kin-aesthetics/Kinematics
TYLER BRADWAY AND ELIZABETH FREEMAN

QUEERING LINEAGES

25   01. Kinship beyond the Bloodline
JUDITH BUTLER

48   02. The Mixed-Race Child Is Queer Father to the Man
BRIGITTE FIELDER

71   03. World Making: Family, Time, and Memory among
Trans Mothers and Daughters in Istanbul
DILARA ÇALIŞKAN

KINSHIP, STATE, EMPIRE

95   04. In Good Relations: Native Adoption, Kinstillations, and
the Grounding of Memory
JOSEPH M. PIERCE

119   05. Queering the Womb: Surrogacy and the Economics of
Reproductive Feeling
POULOMI SAHA

138   06. Beyond Family: Kinship's Past, Queer World Making,
and the Question of Governance
MARK RIFKIN

159   07. Ecstatic Kinship and Trans Interiority in Jackie Kay's *Trumpet*
AQDAS AFTAB

180   08. Marielle, Presente: The Present and Presence in
Marielle Franco Protests

JULIANA DEMARTINI BRITO

KINSHIP IN THE NEGATIVE

203   09. Akinship

CHRISTOPHER CHAMBERLIN

227   10. Against Friendship

LEAH CLAIRE ALLEN AND JOHN S. GARRISON

248   11. Kidless Lit: Childlessness and Minor Kinship Forms

NATASHA HURLEY

269   12. Till Death Do Us Kin: Sworn Kinship and Queer
Martyrdom in Chinese Anti-imperial Struggles

AOBO DONG

291   Epilogue: How Did It Come to This? Talking Kinship with
Kath Weston

KATH WESTON, ELIZABETH FREEMAN, AND TYLER BRADWAY

303   *References*

333   *Contributors*

339   *Index*

Acknowledgments

We would like to thank, foremostly, the authors whose work appears in this volume. They worked creatively and faithfully during a pandemic that changed all of our lives, and we could not have asked for better colleagues. We are also indebted to the staff at Duke University Press for their professional expertise, commitment to academic scholarship, and kindness. Bethany Qualls provided essential help in formatting and preparing the manuscript for submission, and we thank her profusely.

Tyler Bradway would like to thank Jen Lightfoot for her endless care, insight, and ability to make me laugh. Thank you to Caroline Levine, Jennifer Spitzer, and Laura Davies for feedback and encouragement throughout the process. Thanks also to the SUNY Cortland English Department, particularly my chair, Andrea Harbin, and former chair, Matt Lessig, who were supportive of this project in crucial ways. It is difficult to express my profound admiration for Elizabeth Freeman as a writer, thinker, editor, and collaborator. I am grateful to you for believing in this project, for your generosity throughout every stage of its development, and for everything you've taught me about how kinship sustains us in and across time.

Elizabeth Freeman would like to thank Candace Moore for her magnanimous support, especially during the final stages of the preparation of this manuscript. I'm grateful, as well, to Ken Wissoker for his long-haul faith in my work. I owe the University of California at Davis, especially Interim Dean Ari Kelman, Advisor to the Dean Claire Waters, Personnel Director Jenni Mattheis, and the Department of English, an enormous debt for the time and resources that they have afforded me to coedit this manuscript. My friends, especially those who drew close during the summer of 2020, have taught me everything there is to know about kinship: you know who you are. And Tyler Bradway has been a dream collaborator—on point at all times, patient, ethical, and generous beyond compare.

The editors express their gratitude to the following institutions and individuals for their generous financial support of this book. At SUNY Cortland: President Erik Bitterbaum and the Haines Fund and Dean of Arts and Sciences Bruce Mattingly. At UC Davis: the Office of Research Publication Assistance Fund.

TYLER BRADWAY AND ELIZABETH FREEMAN

Introduction
Kincoherence /
Kin-aesthetics /
Kinematics

Queer theory has always been a theory of kinship. Think, for example, of the centrality of the Oedipal family—with its closeted urges, taboos, and perverse identifications—to Sigmund Freud and queer uptakes of psychoanalysis; of Michel Foucault (1990) tracing the deployments of alliance as they laminate onto the deployment of sexuality; or of the origins of private property that Friedrich Engels (1902) discovers within the social form of the bourgeois nuclear family, understood as contingent by him and by sexuality studies. Inspired by yet deeply critical of these accounts, so many of the foundational texts of queer studies devote themselves to what we might call "kinship theory." We see this project, for example, in works by Gayle Rubin (1975, 1984), Adrienne Rich (1980), Eve Kosofsky Sedgwick (1985), Hortense Spillers (1987), Gloria Anzaldúa (1987), Judith Butler (2002), and Kath Weston (1991). Kinship theory—as practiced in queer, feminist, and critical race studies—contests structuralist accounts of kinship, particularly as the latter naturalize the mutual imbrications of heteronormativity, patriarchy, white supremacy, and Western imperialism. This project endures in scholarship over the past decade or so by Elizabeth Freeman (2007, 2019), Richard T. Rodríguez (2009), David L. Eng (2010), Mark Rifkin (2011), Sharon P. Holland (2012), Juana María Rodríguez (2014), and Adele Clarke and Donna Haraway (2018), among others. At the same time, kinship theory weaves critique with imagination to dream belonging other-wise. Indeed, queer theory rewrites kinship as a bodily practice rather than a cultural substrate (Freeman 2007), composed through ephemeral encounters such as sex, friendship, and activism (Berlant and Warner 1998; Dean 2009; Freeman 2010; Roach 2012), pointing beyond heteronormative organizations of intimacy, care, desire, and even reproduction (Muñoz 2009; Franklin 2013; Rodríguez 2014; Lewis 2019). Here, kinship names a radical and open-ended field of relational experimentation. In short, the problems and the promises of kinship animate queer theory even when they have not been named as such.

Of course, queer theory frequently eschews the idiom of "kinship." More often, theorists prefer terms such as *relationality*, *belonging*, *intimacy*, and *sodality*. These terms are typically used in lieu of kinship, as important qual-ifiers to a notion of kinship modeled on the heteronormative nuclear fam-ily, or in contradistinction to theories and vernacular understandings of lesbian and gay families as sites of everyday solidarity and long-term se-curity (see Weston 1991).[1] To be sure, queer scholarship, including our own, has found great promise in such diffuse and poststructural grammars for sociability. Yet the expansiveness of "queer belonging" may also risk evacu-ating the historical specificity of kinship as an idiom of state power, white supremacy, and Western modernity. To put this bluntly, we find ourselves asking a simple question: if everything is kinship, what isn't?[2]

Thus, although we share the ethos behind calls to "forget family" (see Halberstam 2007), we also note the intractability of kinship as an ideol-ogy, a material relation, an affective structure, and a narrative frame for conceiving, organizing, and living relationality in the contemporary mo-ment. In this respect we draw inspiration from Judith Butler's claim, ar-ticulated in conversation with Gayle Rubin (1994, 87), that there is "some value in holding on to the term 'kinship' precisely in order to document that shift in the way in which the social life of sexuality is reconfigured and sustained." The idioms of kinship make perceptible the mobile grounds of sexuality's social life as well as its vital intersections with Indigeneity, race, and ethnicity. Indeed, insofar as *queerness* denotes an excess or perceived deficiency in relation to the normative family, the term always includes and indexes racialization (Cohen 1997). Our goal is not to foreclose queer experi-ments in belonging beyond kinship, then, but rather to understand their complex relationships to the historical, ontological, and epistemological violence that kinship engenders.

However, the trouble with kinship is that we do not always know where we stand in relation to it. This is because the idioms of kinship are not simply riven with ideological ruses waiting to be exposed; they are also invested and bound up with desire, fantasy, and affect. Indeed, as Butler notes elsewhere, the desire for the state to legitimize one's relationships within its extant terms represents a wish to become "socially coherent" (2004, 116). To think through the interleaving relations of queerness and kinship, then—the kinship of queerness, the queerness at the heart of kinship—means confronting what we call their (kin)coherence, their (k)incoherence. As a concept, *kincoherence* fuses the mutually constituting and complicating forces, desires, practices, relations, institutions, and forms that render kinship a horizon of violence and possibility. It recognizes that there is no theory of kinship without desire, and it foregrounds what we take to be kinship's salutary promise for queer theory and its attachment to problems of social legitimacy and sexual dissidence. Kincoherence traces, theorizes, and engages kinship's fraught and overdetermined nature: our desire to forget kinship and the apparent impossibility of doing so, queer kinship's creative experimentation with relationality, and its ongoing imbrication with entrenched idioms of ancestry, descent, and family.

By placing kincoherence at the center of queer kinship theory, we are fascinated by relationality's *durability* as much as its immanence. After all, kinship does not exist without extension over time (see Freeman 2007). Kinship promises. Kinship endures—or, as Butler (2017) argues, its grounding in duration is exposed precisely when it fails. It is strangely futural and retrospective, moving in queer temporalities and through corporeal uptakes. Kinship must be reproduced materially (see Stevens 1999), and this reproduction also makes possible forms of kinship that multiply beyond those we inherit, beyond those that appear to be fixed (think of informal terms such as "ex-stepmother," or "brother-out-of-law"). At the same time, the categories of kinship exist beyond the individuals occupying them (see Sahlins 2013). We cede ourselves to the roles of engroupment, violently or joyously, with resignation or with desire, or both and neither. Claude Lévi-Strauss and Freud notwithstanding, kinship lacks a center: it is diffuse and mobile, a *doing* (Bourdieu 1977) that we discover in a vast web of relationality that crosses "official" and uncodified social bonds alike. In this volume alone, kinship appears as interdependency (Butler), ecstasy (Aftab), fantasy (Hurley), memory (Pierce), performance (Brito), oath (Dong), decision making (Weston), care (Çalışkan), anonymity (Allen and Garrison), contract (Saha), racialization (Chamberlin), reproduction (Fielder), governmentality (Rifkin), and so on.

As these examples suggest, kinship happens simultaneously on the terrain of kinetics, or forces acting on existing mechanisms of inclusion and exclusion, *and also* on aesthetics, or the principles of artistic and symbolic organization.[3] For this reason, we advocate kin-aesthetics as a core methodology for queer kinship theory. As a philosophical term, *kin-aesthetics*, containing not only *kin* but also *kinetics* and *aesthetics*, concerns itself with how processes of *figuration*, whether they take place as social practice or in imaginative texts, de-form and re-form the categories and genres by which we experience our relationships. Kin-aesthetic activities make and unmake the social field. Kinship needs kin-aesthetics because kinship is a symbol system as well as a set of practices. But kin-aesthetic practices are not epiphenomenal to a deeper and invariant structure of kinship; neither are they simply a floating discourse untethered from the material relations and conditions of belonging. Rather, kin-aesthetics are the site of kinship's renewal, transformation, and extension beyond the present. This is why so much depends on the details of a ritual or the dramatics of an exchange. Of course, one queer performance does not remake an entire social system. Yet the kin-aesthetics of kinship materialize and renew both bodies and social ties in ways that grant "a future, but one with an uninevitable form" (Freeman 2007, 299). In short, *kinship needs form*. Form—by which we mean principles of ordering that crisscross and interarticulate extant structures and their possible dismantling or reconfiguration—makes the symbolics and phenomenology of kinship move.[4]

Wherein lies the queerness of kin-aesthetics? Here is one illustration, though surely not the only possibility: Leo Bersani's (Dean et al. 1997, 6) notion of a "correspondence of forms" in which visual, aural, and other resonances across things situated in disparate spaces can give rise to new relations, new solidarities. This is not the same as identification or fantasies of likeness because the rhymes are always between a subject and the part objects through which the *imago* finds itself decomposed and recomposed. These relational moments do not just re-form the subject; they offer new social imaginaries. Bersani turns, we might say, from the form of the family, the family tree or kinship diagram that has led to coercive inclusions and murderously violent exclusions as well as fundamental misrecognitions, to "families of forms" (14). Formalism, or figuration, becomes for Bersani a mode of self-extension, self-accretion, movement outward toward others, and eventually of "some other kind of sociality" (9). In conversation with Bersani, Kaja Silverman notes how such an approach to form "rethink[s] the relational in terms of design" or in terms not only (or not even) of "mothers, fathers, lovers, etc., but also [of] line, shape, composition, color" (9)—in short, of aesthetics. Implicit here is a notion of figuration itself—not only the figures articulated or exchanged within a specific form—as a site for the creation or recreation of relationality.

In their shared attunement to kin-aesthetics, queer theory and kinship theory have much to contribute to ongoing debates about formalism and the politics of aesthetics (see, for example, Rancière 2004; Wolfson and Brown 2006; Marcus and Best 2009; Doyle and Getsy 2013; Levine 2015; Ngai 2015; Amin, Musser, and Pérez 2017). Binding *kin, kinetic,* and *aesthetic* into *kin-aesthetics* highlights how kinship and art are both, as social practices, bound up with the work of the body; they work on and through the materiality of the body. If kinship constitutes a mode of corporeal dependency (Freeman 2007, 298), it depends on the aesthetic to reorganize, renew, and otherwise transform the body's relational horizons. Likewise, and as with sexuality, aesthetic objects move in time: they circulate and in these movements transmit, as Natasha Hurley (2018) argues, vestigial social histories that simultaneously afford possibilities for reimagining the lifeworld of queerness itself. The aesthetic is thus central to the history of sexuality and to the deployments of alliance and affinity alike. Indeed, as anthropological studies of so-called fetish objects and gifts demonstrate, kinship extends itself through the aestheticization of objects that are taken to be metonymic of particular social bodies (Taussig 1993; Viveiros de Castro 2009). The kin-aesthetic thus foregrounds how form is a technology that a social body uses to replicate, remake, and extend itself through time, both backward and forward, as Brigitte Fielder's contribution to this volume makes especially clear.

It may be tempting to think that kin-aesthetics can release us from the binds of kinship, into a queer field beyond or after kinship. Yet we take seriously Butler's warning, sounded in her contribution to this volume, to resist a certain *kinship idealism* (40). This requires us to avoid a simple dichotomy between queerness and kinship in which the former is detached from its temporal and historical entwinement, and even complicity, with the exclusions, violences, and abandonments of kinship. But perhaps more importantly, we resist an idealism that presumes heteronormative kinship's stability and sovereignty, thereby ignoring how the concept of kinship depends on "possibility of [its] disruption" (Butler 2017, 4). If a certain breach haunts the very core of kinship, as Butler contends, then it may not be so easy to categorically distinguish relational forms as straight or queer, conservative or radical, fixed or transient. Certainly, this means that queerness emanates from the heart of kinship and that kinship circulates through bodies of queerness and queer theory alike. But it also demands a *relational formalism* (Bradway 2021), attuned to the queer temporalities of social figuration and the bonds it tethers and unravels. Relational formalism tracks the *unfoldings* of belonging in and across time; it understands intimate bonds as a meeting ground of the social and the psychic, the political and the affective. In this way, it grasps the *kincoherence of kin-aesthetics*—the potential, that is, for the symbolic and material practices of kinship to bind and unbind us—and the *kin-aesthetics of kincoherence*—the figural mediation of relationality and the formal configurations that it takes.

Even as this collection makes evident the durability of kinship as a concern for queer theory, we wish to orient this concern within a new context— namely, the kincoherence of belonging in the contemporary moment, shaped as it is by the intellectual and sociopolitical contexts of Trumpism and neoliberalism, gay marriage and anti-immigrant xenophobia, homonationalism and boomerang babies, and Black Lives Matter and COVID-19. We contend that queer theory needs kinship theory to understand and respond to the kincoherence that infuses the present.

Why Kinship Now? On Kincoherence

We turn to kinship in a queer moment. On June 26, 2015, the *Obergefell* decision effectively authorized same-sex marriage within the United States, expanding kinship law and policy to include couples consisting of two people legally defined as men or two people legally defined as women. Ten days earlier, Donald Trump had announced his campaign for the presidency, invoking anti-immigrant xenophobia and promising to brutalize immigrants with the full power of a white nationalist state. The Trump administration kept its promise. Building on existing precedents established under Obama and Bush, Trump expanded and intensified the detention, separation, and unmaking of migrant families. In the supposedly bright afterglow of *Obergefell*, we are witnessing the emergence of a new vocabulary for negating kinship and new apparatuses for rendering migrants kinless, with dire consequences. For example, children violently separated from their parents were legally reclassified as "unaccompanied" minors, as if they had arrived alone (Bump 2018). In another example, Trump sought to deny birthright citizenship to the children of undocumented immigrants based on a reinterpretation of the Fourteenth Amendment (Davis 2018). Undoubtedly, the history of the state is bound up with a history of fungible kinship: from transatlantic slavery and settler colonialism through Chinese exclusion and Japanese internment, the state materializes its power to exclude and exploit by rewriting who does and does not count as kin. This moment is not exceptional in that lesbian and gay kinship (along with whatever forms of transgender and bisexual kinship are intelligible under the rubric of "same-sex marriage") is vested with the authority of the state in the form of the *domestic couple*—domestic in the dual sense of homed and conferred with citizenship. It is this form that was denied to enslaved people and Chinese immigrants, forcibly imposed on Indigenous North Americans, and disrupted during Japanese internment. And it is this form that justifies the shredding of migrant relationalities, which are associated with mobility, contingency, temporary housing, lack of documentation, and perverse extensivity (i.e., racist fantasies of "anchor babies" and misuses of family reunification policy). Queer kinship theory, as it variously intersects with trans theory and critical race theory, writes from within the nexus of these fraying and tethering bonds.

Currently, migrant families understood as potentially in need of state resources are disaggregated into vulnerable masses subject to state surveillance, detention, and even torture, whereas gay and lesbian individuals understood as potentially capable of sustaining themselves without state aid are given the resources to pool their property and pass it on, a form of flourishing. Yet neoliberalism's winnowing of social life to the individual has substantially eroded the material support for even heteronormative (or homonormative) kinship.[5] The nuclear household, ideologically and legally sacrosanct, is unsustainable even for many of the straight, white, middle-class families of whom it has become iconic, precisely because of the way market forces have superseded other ways of organizing care and dependency: squeezed by rent and debt, increasing numbers of people live with their parents (Picchi 2016), with their adult children, in combinations of monogamous-dyadic couples and roommates, or with other families (Fry 2018)—not to mention the rise in people renting out parts of their living spaces via Airbnb. Other chrononormativities (Freeman 2010) of the middle-class family, such as entering a stable profession, buying a home, reproducing, and retiring, are consequently disrupted as well. Figured as pathological dependency, the co-residence of parents and adult children, along with the accompanying refusal or inability of young adults to get jobs, buy homes, and/or form families, gives rise to stigmatized cultural narratives about "bad kin" who refuse to grow up, such as the "Peter Pan millennial" (Shaputis 2004). Yet such narratives are also symptomatic of a broad queering of the chrononormative plots that structure heteronormativity. Indebted and/or unemployed individuals, often unwillingly queered by economic precarity, "grow sideways" (Stockton 2009): they cannot come of age or mark their coming out, as it were, through a separation from and subsequent reproduction of the family.

In brief, even as more and more of the denizens of late capitalism are forced into familial or family-like structures of privatized dependence or interdependence as the social safety net shrinks, neoliberal privatization and the debt economy have furthered the dissolution of the heteronormative nuclear family, a dissolution that began under industrialization (see D'Emilio 1983). Even for US citizens, then, kinship is increasingly disestablished from the state even as the state simultaneously expands a very few relational forms and economic arrangements that it will recognize under the aegis of kinship. Although neoliberalism intensifies this dialectic, it is not new. On the contrary, this tension underpins the formation of the white supremacist state as it destroys the kinship ties of migrants and Black, Indigenous, and people of color (BIPOC) and confers citizenship on only white heteronormative organizations of belonging.

At the time of this writing, the COVID-19 pandemic has made the queer chrononormativity of contemporary kinship dramatically apparent while simultaneously pointing up the significance of kinship as a horizon for social theory and public health policy. As we all know by now, COVID ruptured chrononormativities of education, labor, healthcare, sex, and courtship, among many other social rhythms and rituals. The mourning of graduations, weddings, summer vacations, and in-person instruction was often louder than the mourning of the hundreds of thousands killed by the virus. As chrononormativity foundered, new kin-spatialities became salient: the household, for example, took on increasing focus as a unit of social analysis, indexing the space of quarantine, a scene of likely transmission, a unit where bodies breathe in proximity to one another. So did new kin-temporalities: the household became rezoned around fourteen-day increments of self-quarantine after potential exposure, and its horizon stretched onward to an uncertain "end" of the pandemic, which, as we write, might or might not arrive. Households became supplemented with pods, "quaranteams," bubbles, and other small social units that attempt to balance the risks of contagion against the need for interaction (Schumaker

2020); new COVID-related "safe-sex" guidelines emerged to structure eroticism around the dangers of respiratory contagion (NYC Health 2020).

We might even say that COVID has made kinship—or the refusal and denial of kinship—visceral in ways that supersede its usual coding in terms of blood and phenotypic resemblance. As Amber Jamilla Musser (2020) argues, the corporeality of sweat, inspired by the anxiety and uncertainty wrought by COVID, makes apparent "complex forms of affective connection and the persistence of metabolism and transformation." Attending to the specifically racialized ecologies of sweat and breath that justify white supremacist refusals to count Black people as members of the human family, Musser observes that the anxiety of the pandemic "activates specters of black death, possibilities of black love and care, and knowledge of black forms of survival" (Musser 2020). Indeed, if COVID reanimates the state's genocidal passivity in the face of HIV/AIDS as well as the shouldering of care and dependency by queer kin, it also indexes the genocidal sovereignty of anti-Blackness. As Musser points out, the pandemic disproportionately affects Black people and people of color; it is part of and intensifies the already oppressive atmosphere of anti-Blackness, racialized state violence, and racial capitalism that undergirds social life and, according to Christopher Chamberlin's contribution to this volume, kinship itself in the United States. This entwinement was made especially clear in the aftermath of George Floyd's murder by police on May 25, 2020, which sparked mass protests for Black Lives, for Black Trans Lives, for defunding and abolishing the police and prisons, and for redistributing the resources of the state in ways that support the preservation, care, and flourishing of social life.

We see queer kinship across these experiments in sociality and affinity. Absent state investment in the care of dependents, people create new ways of sharing resources and caretaking, such as the communities of care among disabled queers of color described in Leah Lakshmi Piepzna-Samarasinha's (2018) *Care Work: Dreaming Disability Justice*, which have now, under COVID, extended to neighborhoods and networks of people who do not identify as disabled or as people of color, although they certainly include networks of both such constituencies (see also Spade 2020 and Samuels and Freeman 2021). Or they draw upon older models such as the intergenerational or extended-family household (Roberts 2010), the dormitory (Bowles 2018), or hot-bedding (sleeping in the same bed in shifts, originally a military practice that has gained attention in England and Australia; see Hind [2006]). In the contemporary moment, many of our assumptions about heteronormative kinship thus no longer hold, and as D'Emilio (1983) once suggested, perhaps such moments of contradiction create opportunities for imagining the politics of belonging more queerly.

Yet the radical promise that queer forms of belonging offer—a promise we take seriously—paradoxically emerges from contemporary kinship's intensifying significance and insignificance to the state. This dialectic becomes evident only when we understand recent conflicts over kinship—the Supreme Court's gay marriage decision, the border patrol's separation of migrant families, neoliberalism's dependence on the very privatized structures of caretaking that are being eroded by a trickle-up economy—not as isolated from one another but *part of a vast renegotiation of the forms that belonging may take*. This is why it is imperative for queer theory to think *with*—which does not mean supporting, but attending to—the discourses of kinship, and of family in particular, which remain at the heart of the state's biopolitical management of social belonging: its investment and divestment of specific forms of relationality with power, resources, and authority. For example, Elizabeth Povinelli's (2002, 2006) work clarifies the degree to which Indigenous populations must still make claims to land based on patriarchal genealogical kinship, even as non-Native LGBTQ rights must be articulated through a language of romantic intimacy that showcases love, affinity, and choice. Moreover, as work by Jennie Livingston (1990), Marlon Bailey (2013), and others on queer ballroom culture and its accompanying "house" system of mutual support has clarified, the kinaesthetics of kinship can actually *reconfigure* social life. For example, Bailey's work shows how the language of mothers, fathers, and children in ballroom life produces a model of "platonic parenting" in which adult sexuality and the mentoring of younger or less experienced people are separated for the purposes of creating a stable "home" life, a model that straight cisgender people might take as salutary for raising children. Therefore, kinship is kincoherent: fungible and intractable, disestablished and sanctioned, dispersed and consolidated, its idioms simultaneously symptomatic and performative, sedimented with historical forces and yet capable of cracking open new fault lines in the social body.

The Kin(d)ness of Strangers: Queer Theory and Kinship Theory

Kincoherence, and indeed much of this volume as a whole, thus recasts some of the most important debates in the field around queer relationality and temporality. Among the most prominent has been the ongoing reflection on the "anti-social thesis." In broad strokes, some (Bersani 1987, 1995; Edelman 2004) understand queerness as a negation of identity, belonging, and even the social itself. For anti-social theorists, queerness is a "corrosive force" (Edelman 2004, 26) that momentarily dissolves a symbolic order that solders us to fantasies of the future. It is no coincidence that figures of kinship, such as "The Child" or "The Family," are key sites of critique for anti-social queer theory; the fantasy of the future condensed in and codified through kinship figures merely reproduces the heteronormative strictures of the present and the past. At its best, these theorists contend, queer theory embraces the relentless, untranscendable, and undeniable drive that disturbs all figurations and stabilizations of social order. By contrast, others (Muñoz 2009; Freeman 2010; Rodríguez 2014) see a different possibility in queerness: they see potentiality, in fact, as a queer force continually unleashed by the friction of bodies, temporalities, and affects. For these theorists, the social is not so much an *order* as an unfolding practice that fails to reproduce itself just as often as it succeeds. From those failures, queerness leaks out on all sides, rearranging and recalibrating the social in frequently surprising and always richly embodied ways. Kinship plays an important role in this "queer hypersociability" (Freeman 2019) precisely because it is a site to glimpse the emergence of new relational forms.

All too often these two modes—anti-social and hypersocial—have been placed at odds, conceived as irreducibly opposed in their approaches to pessimism or optimism, drive or desire, history or temporality (see Berlant and Edelman 2014). Yet we contend that kincoherence necessarily draws energies from both queer negation *and* proliferation. This is because, as Butler suggests, "there seems to be no way to think the bonds of kinship without understanding first what breaks them. *That breakability is the bond*" (Butler 2017, 21, emphasis ours). Therefore, even the dissolvent corrosions of queerness also coagulate. Kincoherence illuminates the simultaneous unbinding and multiplying of relational forms; it understands these forms as emerging within and through the social and the historical (understood as embedded and embodied) while stressing that they are not fully determined by them, either; it stays alert to the desires, fantasies, and imaginary longings that weld our attachments to kinship and our kinship attachments; yet it also embraces fantasy as a densely social scene with many affordances for queer belonging just waiting to be tapped.

Thus conceived, kincoherence affords a new vantage point for debates over the history of sexuality (Traub 2013). As Rubin notes in the 1994 interview with Butler about kinship that we cited earlier, Foucault's account of the "deployment of sexuality" has often been misread as a displacement of the "deployment of alliance" (Rubin [1994] 2011, 297–98). As Foucault (1990, 116) contends, it is not that modern regimes of biopolitical regulation replace older structures of kin-based power but that one is "superimposed" on the other, the two "turning about one another" (113) in an ongoing, complex dance. Thus, as Butler and Rubin note in this conversation, it is not a question of kinship *versus* sexuality but of their intimate and mutually enforcing relations to each other and, we would add, to the racializing effects of dominant kinship law and symbolics. The dance of sexuality and alliance with race continues in the present, with moves that Foucault may not have anticipated. Indeed, the phrase "the deployment of affinity" (Freeman 2002, x) allows us to think about emergent biopolitical logics of sexuality and kinship that overlay those so persuasively mapped by Foucault, from the flourishing of new languages of relationality untethered from family (Facebook friend, monogamish, play partner, etc.) that are bound up with new modes of capital, such as affinity marketing and data mining, to the hardening logic of blood ancestry, mapped by DNA and genomes and commodified as the essence of kinship.

As well as clarifying the dialectic of alliance and affinity, Rubin and Butler's ([1994] 2011) conversation proleptically speaks to queer theory's contemporary meditations on methodology. Indeed, Rubin calls for an anthropologically inspired relation between empiricism and theory that anticipates Heather Love's *Underdogs* (2021) on queer deviance and the social sciences and Kath Weston's remarks in her interview for this volume. Accordingly, even as many of the works in this volume are indebted to poststructural theories of language, our collection furthers a long-standing dialogue between queer theory and the social sciences, especially anthropology, and owes a debt to important texts such as Weston's (1991) *Families We Choose*, Collier and Yanagisako's (1987) *Gender and Kinship*, Schneider's (1984) *A Critique of the Study of Kinship*, Franklin and McKinnon's (2001) *Relative Values: Reconfiguring Kinship Studies*, and Sahlins's (2013) *What Kinship Is—And Is Not*.

Kinship theory, in turn, provokes new questions about methodology for queer theory because kinship theory refuses or queerly eludes sequential orderings. As Rubin and Butler ask, what comes first, the material arrangements of kinship (Lévi-Strauss) or the psychic or symbolic ordering of them (Freud and Lacan)? Rather than answer this question, we note that the quandary itself tells us something important. For Rubin and Butler, two different notions of "intractability" emerge, the structure of language for Butler ([1994] 2011, 282) and the long durée of social phenomena for Rubin

(283). These are crucially also questions of temporality. For Butler, the entrance into language depends upon gendered differentiations that "persist" (282) beyond rearrangements of family structure and gender roles. Rubin agrees that "the kind of social change we are talking about takes a long time, and the time frame in which we have been undertaking such change is incredibly tiny" (283), and that "the imprint of kinship arrangements on individual psyches is very durable" (283). Rubin sees the social terrain of "sexual conduct" as precisely where the binary-gender model that structures psychoanalytic accounts of language, the unconscious, and kinship falls apart or gets "convoluted" (294): in historical time, as opposed to the time of the unconscious, the social life of sexuality and gender *moves*. It is kinematic, if by this we might reference theories for converting one kind of motion into another, here the movement of the psyche into social movements and vice versa.

Perhaps the most iconic kinematic of queer kinship is the movement away from oppressive families of origin toward alternative structures of belonging that may offer intimacy, care, eroticism, and dependency in other forms: throuples, friendships, cousins, mentors, companionate marriages, nesting partners, roommates, queer platonic partnerships, fuck buddies, and so on (Weston 1995). In their contribution to this volume, Leah Claire Allen and John S. Garrison powerfully critique this paradigmatic narrative; they stress racialized and other exclusions that haunt figurations of queer kinship often seen as utopian, such as the liberal appropriation of "chosen family" and queer friendship. Yet queer kinematics are not exhausted in the move away from normative kinship; they also arise in movements within, across, and between it, which queer theory has often failed to see as a consequence of overlooking trans experiences and of centering whiteness.

Indeed, trans and trans of color theory has theorized movement, *transition*, within, across, and between putatively normative structurings of gender without assimilating those movements to a telos of gender normativity (Snorton 2017; Gill-Peterson 2018). On the contrary, trans theory emphasizes the *relational* structures that enable trans communities to survive, nurture one another, share knowledge—including knowledge that enables transition—and to resist medicalizing discourses that stigmatize and police gender nonconformity. Hence, white trans and trans of color kinships are especially important to this volume, for they press back against queer theory's long-standing tendency to conceive of queer fluidity through trans embodiment. Aqdas Aftab's and Dilara Çalışkan's contributions move our attention instead toward trans relationality, particularly as it manifests in affective kinematics that flourish in the shadows of colonialism, police violence, medical stigmatization, and trauma. As their essays show, the affective kinematics of trans kinship do not move in one direction—toward shame or pride, melancholia or ecstasy—but lead to altogether different choreographies for how affect creates trans bonds.

However, kinship's kinematics cannot be understood only as creative appropriations or redirections of normative kinship assumed to be fixed and static. On the contrary, the state has its own kinematics of kinship, evident in its forced dispossession of BIPOC kinship ties, production of kinlessness, and imposition of white supremacist logics of belonging. This is why we insist on the intimacy of kinlessness and kinematics, and on the necessity of thinking through queer kinship theory and critical race theory together.

Kinlessness and Kinematics: Critical Race Theory and Kinship Theory

The foundational structuralist, poststructuralist, and empiricist studies of kinship have too often overlooked the kinematics of kinship: the way that those whose natal and affinal ties are destroyed nevertheless create compensatory psychic and social structures. In particular, much of kinship theory has failed to understand the legacies of chattel slavery, settler colonialism, and immigration restriction in the United States as crucial sites of kincoherence in way we detail below. These are the histories from which queer-of-color critique, queer Indigenous studies, and BIPOC queer theory have emerged. Even as mainstream kinship theory has proceeded without much attention to the destruction and forced reconfiguration of families of color, these fields understand kinship as central to the structural position of BIPOC in particular as queer, regardless of the actual arrangement of BIPOC households (Spillers 1987; Cohen 1997; Ferguson 2004). At the same time, these theories and epistemologies track how BIPOC and other queer-of-color communities convert the destructive energies of racism, colonialism, and imperialism into mobile collective practices and systems of meaning (Stack 1983; Muñoz 1999; Shah 2001).

Most foundationally, perhaps, kincoherence and anti-Blackness are deeply entwined in the production of Black people as kinless. In Black studies, for example, Orlando Patterson's (1982) groundbreaking book *Slavery and Social Death* introduced the idea that enslaved people, rather than being killed outright, were reduced to the status of the subhuman precisely through the sundering of their natal kinship ties: torn from their birth families, renamed, barred from legal marriage, with no rights over their children, they had neither legal nor symbolic kin. Focusing especially on generationality, Patterson writes that "slaves differed from other human beings in that they were not allowed freely to integrate the experiences of ancestors into their lives, to inform understanding of social reality with the inherited meanings of their forebears, or to anchor the living present in any conscious community of memory" (5). Hortense Spillers (1987), in an essay central to queer critical race theory and intersectional kinship studies alike, beautifully and uncompromisingly lays bare the paradoxes of this social death in the United States. She reminds us that slavery in the United States not only made the enslaved kinless and therefore genderless but also granted them one negative inheritance: in the doctrine of *partus sequitur ventrem* adopted as law by the 1662 Virginia colony and by other colonies soon afterward, children's status as free or enslaved followed the condition of the mother. *Partus* legitimated the rape of enslaved Black women by white men, producing mixed-race, enslaved children. In other words, racial stigma was the one "property" transmitted by enslaved parents to their children, along a matriarchal line. Even after slavery had formally ended, mixed-race people of African ancestry were categorized as Black via the "one drop" rule in which the great-great-grandchildren of a Black person were legally Black, even if all other relatives were white. This legacy, Spillers notes, effectively makes "Mother Right, by definition, a negating feature of human community" (80). And as demonstrated by Brigitte Fielder (2020), a staple of nineteenth-century American fiction was the ostensibly white character who learned of such Black ancestry and was "born backward" into Blackness, acquiring a surfeit of family members: the opposite side of the coin of kinlessness is what Fielder terms "kinfullness." In terms of both temporal succession and lateral relations, the denial and belated restoration of Black kin to one another made for especially acute, and often queer, kincoherence.

In Black culture, then, the negative version of queering has also had a compensatory, affirmative aspect: Spillers states that captive persons were also "forced into" patterns of "dispersal," into "horizontal" relatedness, and hence into "certain ethical and sentimental features" (75) tying them to others, engendering new forms of affinity and solidarity. And as Herbert Gutman's (1976) and Carol Stack's (1983) work on Black families and communities clarifies, racist accounts of Black kinship overlook its expansiveness and creativity. Brothers, othermothers, honorary aunties: even ostensibly heterocentric Black communities have always had a vocabulary that exceeds the state's imaginary, and in this they have much to teach queer theory. Most recently, Saidiya Hartman (2019, 227) has captured much less sanctioned Black intimacies in her book *Wayward Lives, Beautiful Experiments* in her phrase "the social poesis that sustains the dispossessed."

Indigenous people in North America and beyond have undergone a similar destruction of the relational ties that preceded colonialist invasion, a destruction that was one means of denying land sovereignty. Accounts of Native Americans as "savage" frequently relied on descriptions of their nonmonogamous sexual practices and their systems for adopting children. By the late 1870s, boarding schools were established to remove Native children from their homes and inculcate them into European American gender roles, including monogamous heterosexual marriage (Rifkin 2006, 31). As Joseph M. Pierce argues in his contribution to this volume, this practice constituted a "destructuring of the possibilities of being in good relations" (99) with Native communities: a sundering not only of existing kinship ties but also a violent displacement and dispossession of Indigenous practices and conceptions of kinship that are incommensurable with white settler ideologies. The General Allotment Act, or Dawes Act, of 1887 granted plots of stolen land back to Native American men who were "heads of household," subjecting them to federal and local inheritance law. The effect of this was "a barrier to native efforts to merge land claims through extended chains of familial belonging or to maintain ties of lineage and tribal identification through the transfer of land along alternate lines of descent or affiliation" (Rifkin 2006, 35). In other words, in Indigenous American history as in the histories of other colonized subjects, kinship law—indeed, as Rifkin forcefully argues in his essay in this volume, the deployment of "kinship" itself from Louis Henry Morgan onward—was a mode of land dispossession. To achieve citizenship, families were also required to assume the last names of the paternal head of household, contravening maternal lineage as well as installing marriage and parenthood at the center of social and individual meaning at the expense of "more collective forms of subjectivity articulated within familial idioms" (Rifkin 2006, 35). As Rifkin contends in this volume, queer theory and cultural theory have all too often failed to reckon with the imbrication of kinship with settler colonialism and liberalism's racialized social imaginary, wherein kinship is understood as private and thus dislocated from political governance (156).

Other intersections among economic exploitation, racialization, and kinship suggest the impossibility of doing queer-of-color critique without both kinship theory and queer theory. For example, the 1875 Page Act that excluded Chinese women from immigrating was predicated on the threat of Chinese women, figured as prostitutes, concubines, and polygamous wives, to white men and their families (Luibhéid 2002). As Nayan Shah (2001) demonstrates, male laborers, initially too underpaid to send for their wives and eventually prohibited from doing so, formed communities and affinities of "bachelors" that anticipate some aspects of urban white queer community. As the work of Nancy Bentley (2002), Jared Hickman (2014), and Peter Coviello (2019) clarifies, even a population as seemingly white as the nineteenth-century Mormons found their polygamous marital practices equated with a racialized "barbarism" and slavery, such that they traded polygamy for both Utah statehood and white privilege. In yet another example of racialized queerness articulated through the symbolics of kinship, contemporary Latinx populations are figured as overly reproductive drains on social services, whereas the racist figure of the "anchor baby" is used to stigmatize Latinx migrants. And even the "model minority" stereotype attaching to Asian Americans depends on the ideal of small nuclear families who invest in their children's education.

These genealogies underscore that there can be no history of queerness without an attention to the ways that kinship operates as a key site of dispossession, exploitation, and struggle for racialized and minoritized social groups. Kinship cuts across them, yet these histories are also distinct and in many ways incommensurable. But they do register how communities of color have developed their own epistemological paradigms and social practices for thinking kinship, which are articulated in the context of their being positioned as queerly aslant of normative kinship. Therefore, to make kin under the sign of kinlessness is a radical act. So too is the struggle to preserve notions, practices, and feelings of kinship that live outside, beneath, or alongside official kinship. The goal of queer kinship theory is not to make these bonds legible in the language of kinship but to register their kincoherence, to let their kincoherence trouble who and what counts as bonded, as well as to ally with them affectively, politically, and theoretically. This is why we argue it is essential that queer kinship theory remain in conversation with queer-of-color critique as well as social, historical, and anthropological research actively committed to tracing the histories of racism that shape modern kinship: the point is not to convert one to the other but to track their kinematic interrelations.

The volume dramatizes these kinematic crossings by juxtaposing scenes of kinship from a range of nations—including the Cherokee Nation, the

United States, Britain, Scotland, India, China, Turkey, and Brazil—and Indigenous, Native, and diasporic communities. By no means does this volume present an exhaustive, let alone representative, account of queer kinship or queer kinship theory across the world. Yet collectively our contributors stress the importance of foregrounding and learning from non-Western, non-European, and nonwhite ways of thinking and doing kinship that have all too often been erased, expunged, eclipsed, silenced, or misrepresented within cultural theory. In this respect, queer kinship theory rejects an older structural anthropology driven to *compare* and *systematize* kinship systems across nations and cultures. Indeed, we refuse any separation of kinship from the state and likewise from any conception of the state that fails to account for kinship as a biopolitical technology of imperialism, colonialism, and empire. And, most importantly, we understand kinship as a way of *doing relationality* that is also always a way of *thinking relationality*—kinship as embodied, aesthetic, and erotic *theory*. If the kinematics of queer kinship are global and transnational, as we insist, then queer kinship theory must be continually unsettled, provincialized, and ultimately displaced by practices of kinship that outstrip our own conceptual limitations and lineages.

Mapping the Collection

The contributors to this collection each stake their own claims about the politics of queer kinship. They draw on different methodologies, historical moments, and cultural archives. Yet they all see the intersections of queerness and kinship as a vital concern for contemporary thought. Together, their essays demonstrate the manifold ways that queer theory and kinship theory might speak to each other. Each forges a new conceptual frame for thinking the kincoherence, kinematics, and/or kin-aesthetics of queer kinship.

The first section, "Queering Lineages," builds on queer theory's foundational critique of sequential models of reproduction, mapping new ways to think kinship outside of linear genealogy. In these essays the queerness of kinship, its kincoherence, lies in temporal unfurlings that create surprising opportunities for solidarity, reproduction, memory, and responsibility. In the opening essay, "Kinship beyond the Bloodline," Judith Butler pushes back on the distinction between "real" and "fictive" kinship by reimagining the "blood tie" through the shared legacies of racialized violence enacted through kinship. Butler's essay opens up alternative temporalities for kinship that are a touchstone for the section as a whole. In "The Mixed-Race Child Is Queer Father to the Man," Brigitte Fielder explores such trajectories by looking to the Harlem Renaissance author Alice Dunbar-Nelson, discovering in her work a "racialized version of mixed-race self-begetting" (51). By attending to moments of paradoxical self-begetting, Fielder uncovers queer genealogies of interracial kinship taking place on the terrain of the aesthetic, which contest notions of racial reproduction as purely biological. Moving from the literary to the anthropological, Dilara Çalışkan's ethnography, "World Making: Family, Time, and Memory among Trans Mothers and Daughters in Istanbul," traces how trans women in Turkey transmit intergenerational memory without a linear model of inheritance. Their practices upend normative mappings of parent and child; provide modes of enduring in the face of erasure, abandonment, and systemic violence; and kinematically convert the forward movement of time into a reverse implantation of memories from "younger" to "elder" trans people distinguished not by age but by time of transition.

The essays in our second section, "Kinship, State, Empire," call for queer theory to contend with non-European modes of thinking kinship. These essays confront the intimate, if often mystified, relationship between kinship and the imperial state: the constant, kinematic transmutation of contract and status, family and nationhood or empire. In "In Good Relations: Native Adoption, Kinstillations, and the Grounding of Memory," Joseph M. Pierce, who is similarly invested in reversing normative relationships between pastness and presence, sees "kinstillatory" practices, centered on the land as "spiritual guide" and "ancestral kin," as affording decolonial notions of relationality and memory that hold out the possibility of a return to an Indigenous way of belonging "in good relation" (98). Whereas many posit queer kinship as a response to heteronormativity, Pierce argues for new attention to Indigenous models of kinship outside of settler colonial epistemologies. Poulomi Saha, in "Queering the Womb: Surrogacy and the Economics of Reproductive Feeling," juxtaposes postcolonial India's efforts to ban commercial surrogacy with the proliferation of surrogacy narratives, which figure contractual and economic relationships as intimate bonds forged through sentimentality. For Saha, queer kinship is less a mode of "romantic, utopian affiliation" than a "neoliberal jouissance" articulated through "transactional, paid labor" and irreducibly bound up with the "governing reality of the global market" (121). Mark Rifkin's "Beyond Family: Kinship's Past, Queer World Making, and the Question of Governance" is likewise invested in the question of governmentality, but he sees in Indigenous forms of relationality the prospect of queer governance, of "non-heteropatriarchal formations of belonging, decision making, and resource distribution" (138). To theorize this possibility, Rifkin disrupts the equivalence often drawn between family and kinship, demonstrating, along lines convergent with Pierce's, that Indigenous social logics are neither determined by nor analogous to neoliberal understandings of the family and the state. In "Ecstatic Kinship and Trans Interiority in Jackie Kay's *Trumpet*," Aqdas Aftab extends this section's critique of colonialism's enforcement of white normative kinship. Aftab, whose essay pulls on some of the same threads as Çalışkan's, looks to Black trans fiction to develop a "trans hermeneutic" that subverts a colonialist gaze, one that both fetishizes trans embodiment and violently reduces trans to either "medicalized dysphoria or gender deviance" (178). Instead, Aftab's trans hermeneutic discovers trans interiority as a scene of "ecstatic kinship" that enables the flourishing of decolonial and diasporic trans of color belonging across generational lines (159). Last in this section, Juliana Demartini Brito's essay, "Marielle, Presente: The Present and Presence in Marielle Franco Protests," takes kinship to the streets, tracing queer modes of assembly enabled through activists' performances of kinship. Focusing on the mass protests that emerged in Brazil in response the brutal murder of Marielle Franco, Brito puts queer theory and Latin American studies in fresh conversation and articulates a temporality for queer belonging structured around an inexhaustible desire for an impossible justice.

The essays in our final section, "Kinship in the Negative," innovate new idioms for queer belonging (or unbelonging) that put pressure on kinship as such. In this respect, they build on the important traditions of queer negativity and the anti-social thesis, yet they also move these traditions in new directions by thinking about negativity in distinctly historical and social terms. From within an Afropessimist framework, Christopher Chamberlin's "Akinship" understands the social as instituted precisely *by* the foreclosure of Black kinship under slavery and beyond it. He argues for an analytic of kinship that puts policing, a "mode of racial production" (205), at the heart of Lévi-Straussian elementary structures of kinship, insofar as anti-Black policing not only negates Black kinship (thus producing "a-kinship") but also establishes the grounds for including new forms of non-Black kinship (thus producing "akin-ship," or the proximity of anti-Black policing to even the most seemingly extensive forms of kinship). Similarly tarrying in the negative, "Against Friendship," by Leah Claire Allen and John S. Garrison, refuses the popular association of queer kinship with "chosen family," iconically condensed in narratives of friendship. Where these narratives have been fully assimilated to neoliberal mystifications of individualism, choice, and whiteness, Allen and Garrison stress the destructive and difficult nature of friendship, perhaps especially queer friendship, as a scene of exclusion, conflict, radical self-undoing, and, on the final horizon, a queer kind of solipsism. Also reimagining the anti-social thesis, in "Kidless Lit: Childlessness and Minor Kinship Forms" Natasha Hurley refocuses Lee Edelman's (2004) polemic against "reprofuturity" on nonfamilial child relationality, or social attachments to *other people's children* (251). For Hurley, childlessness provocatively turns childhood itself into the site of stranger-sociability—one might call it "stranger danger"—that queer theories of friendship have generally accorded to adults (see Roach 2012). Aobo Dong's "Till Death Do Us Kin: Sworn Kinship and Queer Martyrdom in Chinese Anti-imperial Struggles" turns the volume back to blood, this time not the false certainties of bloodline critiqued by Butler but the violent blood that Butler also invokes, here the blood of sacrifice, oath, and martyrdom. For Dong, late Imperial and early modern Chinese blood brotherhoods enact a "death-driven kinship" (278) shaped by an "ethos of collective sacrifice" (284). The logic of martyrdom subtending these practices of friendship echoes Allen and Garrison's call for a less pastoral vision of friendship than the one that has organized queer theory from Foucault's "Friendship as a Way of Life" ([1981] 1998) onward. Finally, we conclude with an interview with Kath Weston, the author of *Families We Choose: Gays, Lesbians, Kinship* (1991), a foundational text in queer kinship theory and a flashpoint for many of the essays throughout the volume. Weston reflects on the conceptual transformations that queer scholarship on kinship has made possible, particularly in sociocultural anthropology and political theory. Rather than conceive of queer kinship as a structure or form, Weston approaches queer kinship as an embedded social practice and urges the development of new theoretical idioms that account for its dramatic transformations in the twenty-first century.

Taken together, the essays in this volume remind us that kinship is at once a scene of violence—psychological, imperial, neoliberal, interpersonal—and of creativity. Kinship is a technique for exclusion and inclusion, and a set of conceptual building blocks for forms of relationality that obviate and lay bare its biopolitical work. Kinship is a domain without which we cannot think in some ways but beyond which we absolutely must think, act, and live. May these essays help kindle that fire.

Notes

1 See also theories of relationality developed by Gilles Deleuze and Félix Guattari ([1980] 1987), Bruno Latour (2005), Karen Barad (2007), Jane Bennett (2010), Donna Haraway (2016), and Elizabeth Grosz (2017), among others, and even theories of stranger relationality that inform studies of nationalism (Anderson 1983) and the public sphere (Warner 2002). Haraway's recent work (2016) notably relies on the language of kinship while radically redefining it in posthuman and multispecies terms.

2 See also Butler (2004, 126): "Kinship loses its specificity as an object once it becomes characterized loosely as modes of enduring relationship" and "the relations of kinship arrive at boundaries that call into question the distinguishability of kinship from community, or that call for a different conception of friendship" (127).

3 On "kinetic kinship," see Hayden (1995). On kin-aesthetics, see Freeman (2002). On the role of aesthetics in materializing forms of sociability that can feel like or be experienced as kinship, see Nealon (2001), Bradway (2017, 2020, 2021), Seitler (2019), and Brigitte Fielder's contribution to this volume.

4 On form as constraint and affordance, see Levine (2015).

5 On the relationship among neoliberalism, debt, and the family, see Cooper (2017).

Part I Queering Lineages

———

01 Kinship beyond the Bloodline

Although I am not a scholar of kinship, I am, like most others, interested and implicated within its terms. This is one of those topics where the researcher is part of the research if only because we all came into the world, or managed in this world, by virtue of one version of kinship or another. By this, I do not mean to imply that every infant is born into *a family*: we know that is not true. But there are some human relations, perhaps technological ones as well, that account for the emergence of a human, and whether they are known or unknown, present or absent, they contribute to the scene. We cannot assume in advance that we know what kinship is, so any generalization about it must come to terms with its historically shifting character. Not only is the very definition of kinship contested, but so too is the descriptive value of the term.

Critique of Kinship Studies

Anthropologists tend to know this problem better than the rest of us. Indeed, those ethnographic approaches to kinship that once sought to distinguish real and "fictive" modes were successfully debunked by David Schneider (1984) in his *Critique of the Study of Kinship*. For the most part, since that time we no longer accept that there is a single set of structures or relations that define kinship as a system. One reason we cannot distinguish between natural and fictive ties is that the social organization of kinship depends variably on reproductive relations. Even so, those natalist distinctions emerge all the time in public life, such as when lesbian parents are asked "Who is the real mother?" Schneider's influential critique of kinship studies did not imply that there are no systematic elements to kin relations, but only that those systemic or structural features do not suffice to establish a sense of their meaning. Indeed, because the problems with mapping kin relations as well as the structuralist approach to kinship have given way to more complicated and nuanced approaches, depending on social and affective ties, legal and nonlegal arrangements and associations. As a result, we no longer work with a consensus about what kinship is or what meanings it has for our interdependent lives. My assertion of interdependency reveals my bias or my approach, although I do not mean to imply that kinship can, or should, include all relations that we call interdependent.

Yet the idea that we do have or lead interdependent lives allows us to ask how kinship foregrounds a specific kind of dependency and interdependency, arguably distinct from friendship or from other modes of intimate association and belonging, even as it surely overlaps with them as well. We might be tempted to approach kinship as if it were an autonomous sphere, but its boundaries are precisely what both define that sphere and reveal its porosity, the sites of overlap, the indefinition. The relationship of kinship to the state, the nation, the racialization of genetic research, and to property relations makes this especially clear.

Indeed, one reason why it has become so hard to consider kinship as its own area of study is that the terms of kinship are constantly defined and regulated by state power, legal and economic systems, religious codes and laws, and traditional and emerging norms, including those produced by the legal adjudication of genetic technologies. As such, kinship is always defined in relation to these defining and constraining powers, and any effort to disembed a study of kinship from social, legal, and economic powers and institutions usually ends in obfuscation or idealization. The debates in anthropology over the structural integrity of kinship systems are to some extent mirrored in that same field's disputation of the study of culture as a separate field of study. These debates have unsettled and galvanized cultural anthropology, whose own methodology has depended historically in part on delimiting objects, relations, structures, or institutions that depended on a delimitable sphere of kinship. To cast kinship as exclusively cultural is to obfuscate the larger political and social powers that are invested in defining and regulating its operations. As a result, the approach we are now obligated to pursue may well draw from anthropology—which has, of course, changed rather significantly in the past two decades—but is pervasively interdisciplinary. And although we can, with Pierre Clastres ([1974] 1989), decide that kinship has to be analyzed primarily in relation to state power (see also Stevens 1999), it seems equally true that kinship often exceeds the terms of its political and legal regulation. That does not necessarily return us to the culturalist thesis, but it raises questions about how cultural articulations of kinship as well as social modes of experimental kinship emerge in response to forms of legal and social regulation, and sometimes manage to rearticulate the political and legal definitions themselves.

Even as Schneider (1984, 200) upended the study of kinship by suggesting that kinship itself is actually a "special custom distinctive of European culture," he continued to insist upon sexual reproduction as the structuring center of kin relations. Indeed, critics such as Kath Weston (2002) have reported on Schneider's difficulties with the idea of gay marriage. And Christopher Roebuck (2013) has trenchantly summarized Schneider's critical contribution as well as its limits. As Roebuck writes, Schneider showed how "a folk model is fixed as universal, then its components (descent, alliance, marriage, and the relationship between facts of nature and culture) are said to be discovered everywhere there is organized human life, thus proving *tautologically* that this system of knowledge is the underlining logic for all social relations. Schneider concludes that the kinship is an 'artifact of the anthropologist's analytical apparatuses . . . and does not exist in any culture known to man.' If this is the case, then kinship loses any analytic power in a comparative study of human life." Roebuck continues: "However critical of taken-for-granted facts Schneider may be in questioning the universalizing streak in kinship . . . he falls back on biological reduction. Sexual reproduction in the form of the 'breeding couple' (119) remains the ground for human relations."

Schneider's position gave way to a significant number of feminist anthropologists who tracked the variable ways that sexual reproduction could work, and others sought to move the study of kinship away from sexual reproduction as its thesis (Tsing and Yanagisako 1983). For instance, in their introduction to *Gender and Kinship*, Jane Collier and Sylvia Yanagisako (1987, 3) argued that "structural-functional" models tended to reduce kinship to reproduction as its ostensibly primary function and to the nuclear family as the primary reproductive unit. Further, they argued, "descent theory" tended to presume an invariant mother-child dyad (4). And Lévi-Straussian accounts, they continued, fail to understand how gender categories themselves are articulated in relation to structural arrangements

(5). As feminists of that period took apart some of the key presumptions of kinship studies, they came to question whether something called "the domestic sphere" could even be accepted as a social given. Schneider's cultural analysis, in their view, "provided a tool for understanding the interrelationship between kinship and other domains . . . kinship is not a discrete, isolable domain of meaning." It draws its meanings from a range of other domains, among which they include "religion, nationality, gender, ethnicity, social class, and the concept of the 'person'" (6).

However, Collier and Yanagisako's analysis was both generative and clearly limited for at least two reasons. First, it considered all those other domains determining kinship to be specifically cultural, so it could not take into account the formative effects of economic powers and state regulations on kinship or the way that national boundaries tended to be assumed; second, it continued certain heteronormative presumptions about kinship that were subsequently revised by the authors and criticized by a wide range of scholars (see, for example, Borneman 1996). Indeed, the ultimate criticism was the critique of "bloodline" itself. In *Relative Values: Reconfiguring Kinship Studies*, anthropologists Sarah Franklin and Susan McKinnon (2001, 17) consider how overdetermined notions of blood and genes secure the operation of social classifications, reducing, for instance, tribal relations to biogenetic categories. Conversely, they argue, kinship names the variable relation between nature and culture, the way in which what counts as natural and what counts as cultural shift in the service of broader forms of power. The problem is not only that ostensibly natural categories are treated as cultural but that cultural categories are also naturalized. Kinship is thus neither natural nor cultural, but rather names the specific power-bound oscillation between these categories.

In the same anthology, anthropologist Janet Carsten (2002, 30) further criticizes Schneider for defining American kinship as a blood relation, understood as the sharing of "biogenetic material." As Carsten writes, "What is remarkable in this rendering of American kinship is that blood and biogenetic substance are quite unexplored as symbols" (31). What, for instance, are the links between blood and race, she asks, implying, I presume, the frequency and intensity of the blood-mixing discourse in miscegenation debates. She makes the suggestion that biogenetic heredity may well be a symbol of American culture (31). The theoretical implication is not only that "blood" cannot stand unequivocally for a natural substance rather than a culturally symbolic one but also that cultural symbols are laid into the "material" we take to be invariant or pre-cultural. No one is denying the existence of blood when the argument is made that the discourse on blood in the context of kinships is to a large degree imaginary and overdetermined.

There are myriad historical examples that show how variably and intermittently bloodline works as a way to ground or organize kin relations, ones that have clear resonance with queer models of kinship. During the nineteenth and twentieth centuries in California, for instance, Chinese workers who were immigrating mainly to work on expanding transportation systems for the state were required to prove at the border that they had family in the United States in order to conform to provisions made for family reunification. In order to comply with this condition of entry, many Chinese migrants took on the names of people already in the United States who would vouch for them, and they have continued to bear those names for many generations (Li 1977). Indeed, the families that received these workers took them on as kin, and although sometimes the family name was no more than a ticket for workers, they very often came to belong to the extended systems of support that constituted new modes of kinship or "kinship chains." Under such circumstances, kinship was established less by lines of descent or bloodlines than by modes of belonging mediated by immigration law. Interestingly, these new modes of belonging generated new lines of descent, though not based on any kind of continuous bloodline.

Franklin and McKinnon's (2001) critique of bloodline suggests that the blood that ostensibly holds people together is a highly condensed and invested metaphor for social regulations governing inheritance and property relations. It is not that these latter were based on blood but that the idea of blood became the operative metaphor through which those social regulations operated, the site of their condensation and legitimation. It hardly mattered whether you could test for shared biogenetic material, for a socially condensed metaphor is not easy to capture and test. Yet tests are done all the time to establish the blood tie, and now, when myriad lawsuits proceed on the basis of genetic testing in order to establish paternity or race, and when the last occupant of the White House claimed that migrant children detained and separated from their parents should be reunified with them only once *genetic testing* is done, it would seem that genetic structure has replaced blood or that it is the newer meaning of the blood tie, its extracted essence (Everett 2019). Genetic results, argues Donald Trump, can expose what he calls "fake families," assuming that kinship ties not based in "blood" are simply false.[1]

Although the discovery of genetic links among people often does no more than establish genetic links, these connections are often taken as signs of kinship, if not the defining criteria of kinship itself. When this happens, genetics is collapsed into kinship. So those detained children with parents who have no genetic link to them—that is, who have adoptive or acquired parents—will not have their kin relation recognized if genetic link comes to define the bond of kinship. But the problem hardly stops here. As Patricia Williams has argued (2018), the growing power of contracts governing the reproductive process threatens to discount all "epigenetic" factors as the genome takes priority. Those include all the ways that genetic structures can be modified and passed along outside of the DNA sequence. Epigenetic factors are crucial for understanding life prospects and whether certain genes are switched on or off. For Williams, the discounting of epigenetic factors is the result of the fact that presently every aspect of the reproductive scene can be patented, subject to a lawsuit, such that genes are now property, DNA is patented, and reproduction becomes a legal problem in which DNA can be stolen, improperly used, or acquired on a fraudulent basis. One would think that the buying and selling of DNA seem to pose a problem for those who would reduce kinship to bloodline, but that is not the case. In fact, bloodlines are up for sale, but in their reduced and extracted version, as genetic material. Further, bloodlines are not hereditary: they can be commenced through a purchase. It is, Williams points out, the right of the contracting party buying sperm or paying for the services of a surrogate to establish a bloodline of their liking. So when a Black child is born to a white lesbian couple, and they sue (as happened in the case of Jennifer Cramblett and her partner; see O'Brien 2016), their claim is that they received damaged goods (assuming a white supremacist value matrix), not the product for which they had paid. In the case of a legal effort to compel a surrogate mother to terminate her pregnancy, the "fatherhood" of the male genitor is described by his lawyers as "a commissioning agent in relation to the surrogate" (Williams 2018). The surrogate has no right to give birth, for that would alienate the male genitor's property from him and constitute a misuse of that property by another. Indeed, the lawyers argued that the man should not be forced to give birth. The surrogate has no choice in this matter because she is a "service provider" and, according to the terms of the contract, she has no rights.

For Williams, the intersection of genetics and law has produced new ways for both racism and objectification to function within the intersection of genetics and law. And as always, she is concerned with the extension of how pervasively contract and commodity exchange have entered into the domain of reproductive life, especially under neoliberal conditions. For instance, the implication of her position for adoption would be to establish that right as a constitutional entitlement rather than a matter of property. One example of a constitutional argument would be that no one should be discriminated against for seeking to adopt a child on the basis of marital status. This would follow from a right to equal treatment regardless of marital status. For her, seeking constitutional protections is a better route than expanding property relations, a view, as we know, that follows from her trenchant critique of slavery as a way of casting humans as racialized property (Williams 1991).

The critique of genetic law that Williams pursues is important for us to consider for many reasons. Her work brings to light how racial meanings become encoded in kinship through the re-biologization or, perhaps we should say, geneticization of both. The reduction of the meaning of race to genetics not only removes the understanding of race as it has operated in the service of a vast history of racism but also continues that racism in a new historical form. Williams notes that even raising the question of ethics in policy meetings (such as, what does it mean to reduce a human life to its genetic material and to treat that material as property?) is regularly dismissed and suspected as an effort to block research and stand in the way of greater consumer freedom and legal protection (!). Indeed, she argues, in public policy discussion and in courts of law where reproductive contracts of various sorts are framed as property claims to DNA, those ethical considerations are considered extraneous. The genetic code operates and is acted upon by living creatures in complex environments, yet that complex interaction is refused in an effort to produce genetic material that can be patented and primed for the market. Epigenetics, defined as processes that are *not* driven by genes but that can effect their activation, have no place in the discussion of policy, and in legal determinations all that is needed to establish property rights and damage claims in relation to reproductive and kinship claims is a verification of whose property and patent that any bit of DNA material happens to be. The reduction of kinship to commodity is as swift as it is horrific.

What concerns me is that in this field of law, genetics increasingly defines and constrains the meaning of kinship. That share of blood becomes that bit of DNA, and the feminist and queer arguments about bloodline resurface in light of a new challenge from the convergence of biotechnology, race, and property. Of course, the first problem is that genes are separated from epigenetic processes, and that is already a reductive approach to genes and how they work; the second is that genetic material becomes property, thus licensing the commencement of a new "bloodline" by the property owner; the third is that the complex forms of kinship that do not seek recourse to "bloodline" for their authorization are implicitly regarded as fraudulent. For instance, the legal definition of paternity as the agent who contributes genetic material of a certain sort brackets out every cultural and social determinant of paternity at the same time that it produces genetic material as a new social symbol and fetish. This invalidates all sorts of kinship arrangements not constrained by property relations and where there is no transmission of genetic material, where sperm is donated through queer arrangements, or where pregnancy is offered in the context of friendship or kinship itself. However, perhaps most important is the way that new technologies of genetic identification, management, and patenting intersect with the extension of property law in the service of shoring up paternal rights, racial privilege, and the commodification of women's reproductive labor and de-realizing the legitimate claims of queer kinship, blended families, and acquired ties. In other words, as we argue against blood and genetics as determining criteria of kinship, we also have to ask what forms of power and exploitation these notions of blood and genetic property serve.

The proposal of the last occupant of the executive branch to use genetic testing to unify children with their parents and to expose "fake families" seeks to justify on spurious grounds the separation of migrant children from their parents as well as their detention in cruel conditions, including cages. This form of treatment is fully compatible with the exclusively genetic determination of kin relations. Nonbiologically related parents and children are invalidated, as are other forms of kin relations, including caretaking and filial or affiliative relations of various kinds. But what makes the genetic reduction of kinship compatible with the caging of children, I would suggest, is not only that it tends to focus on the genetics of sperm, the ultimate proof of both paternal ownership and prerogative, but also that it evacuates in full the social and cultural relations that go into shaping kin relations, both those chosen and unchosen. So it does not matter what the lived relations may be, the bonds formed over time and/or in consequence of an adoption, whether legally binding or *de facto*. None of the claims made on behalf of those relations serve as proof of kinship. In Trump's view, even the migrant child who displays affection, connection, dependency, or what psychoanalysts call "relatedness" through expressions of joy, rage, or relief when unifying with a parent is regarded as a potential fraud, staging those displays for another purpose.

After all, in the view from the former White House, migrants exercising their international rights to ask for asylum are all "frauds," trying to enter illegally, and they doubtless lie about many things, perhaps all things. And that means that any expression of suffering on the part of those separated, on the part of the children caged, or on the part of the parents not knowing whether they will ever be reunited with a child from whom they were brutally and inexplicably separated, be discounted: if these people are all frauds or criminals, then anything they do or say will be regarded as purely instrumental. The Trump administration's refusal of all forms of sympathy results in a defiant refusal to acknowledge that emotional bonds may be part of what defines kinship. This refusal of kinship as a practice of mutual recognition, interdependency, or attachment debunks the affective grounds for any legal argument in favor of family reunification. Indeed, the active practice of family dis-unification, the defiance of the claims of kinship, functions as a highly publicized threat to any future migrants: if you come to the United States, you will lose your children. If you come to the United States, your children will be put in cages, and both you and your child will suffer permanent separation and massive, irreversible trauma. So in this very public threat of cages for children and permanent separation from kin delivered to any and all future migrants who seek without papers to cross the southern border into the United States, we see that, in fact, the emotional bond that is dismissed is of course fully presumed and exploited. The threat of punishment makes sense only if the dire importance of that emotional bond can be assumed: if you care about your child, you will not migrate to the United States and risk caging and separation with no legal recourse. On the one hand, the reduction of kinship to genetic tie (DNA minus epigenetic factors) is one way that the government evacuates the affective character of the bond of kinship. On the other hand, that same affective tie is presumed and exploited by the exact same policy.

Even as family separation policies seek to deny the range of social and cultural forms of kinship—in fact, the generalization of the view that genetic testing alone can determine kinship would invalidate all adoptive claims—that very range is very much presumed and exploited in order to advance this policy. Bruno Perreau's (2012) important work on French nationalism shows how regulating kinship serves the purposes of reproducing the nation-state whose national and racial character is at the same time produced through regulation of its borders. In the same vein we can consider in the US context that the state, as represented by the speech acts of executive power that eventually take form as policy and law, uses the method of simultaneously denying and exploiting the ties of kinship to purify the nation of its migrants and to debunk the claims of all "false" families, including queer ones. This double-edged sword is at once a racial—or racializing—project as well as a national one, and as it reasserts the colonial power of the United States over Mexico through breaking up families and subjecting migrants to inhumane conditions, it also lets the US public know that it will wield genetic discourse, if not technology, to regulate and debunk kinship at home in favor of the most narrow heteronormative version.

Slavery: The Ghost in the Machine

I began this essay by considering how the status of kinship studies changed within the field of cultural anthropology, especially in the wake of David Schneider's important works, *A Critique of the Study of Kinship* (1984) and *American Kinship: A Cultural Account* (1980). Schneider opened up a set of criticisms that exposed some of the unexamined national and normative assumptions in kinship studies only to have his own views subject to ever sharper critique. The generative work of feminist and queer anthropologists (the vast majority of whom I have not referenced here) established a new framework for thinking about kinship, emphasizing the way that technology, national frameworks, racism, and biogenetic property rights instrumentalize the field of kinship, including the way that nature and culture are conceived and mobilized. However, the relation of kinship to slavery remains in the background in the US context even as it pervades discussions of race, property, and the rights of citizenship.

However, in Hortense Spillers's (1987) searing critique of the Moynihan Report (1965), which questioned whether African Americans were capable of "family," attention is brought to bear on the requirement imposed upon slaves to lose their original kin relations and to enter, as property and chattel, into the kinship line of the slave owner. More specifically, Spillers points out "the African female's reproductive uses within the diasporic enterprise of enslavement and the genetic reproduction of the enslaved" (74). Under slave conditions, she writes, "'kinship' loses meaning, since it can be invaded at any given and arbitrary moment by the property relations." Orlando Patterson (1982) also famously wrote about the production of "fictive kinship" through enslavement in *Slavery and Social Death*, objecting to the loss of paternal claims on the part of enslaved men. Spillers points out that kinship could not be reducible to normative conceptions of the family for a broad set of historical and cultural reasons, and that the point is not to restore patriarchal forms. Throughout her work as well, Patricia Williams alerts us to the ordering of kinship under slavery as a function of the slave owner's paternal privilege. And as Toni Morrison has reiterated throughout her fiction, slavery nullified the kin relations among slaves when the slave owner displaced the father and took his place, forcing all members of the slave family to become at once his property and his subordinate kin. Yet new forms of filiation also emerge throughout slavery and its aftermath, suggesting that there is no ahistorical way to approach the problem of kinship. The lineage that kinship carries with it can be one of slavery or forced migration. It is a combined legacy of kinship relations both lost and made. There is no other way to tell the story when displacement and enslavement are crucial turning points in the narrative. The loss of a name, a history, an archive, becomes part of the social lineage of kinship itself.

Indeed, toward the end of this essay I will consider Octavia Butler's *Kindred* ([1979] 2003), where kinship ties can be established or affirmed after the fact across generations, as the consequence of capture and enslavement that continues to reverberate throughout the present. The nullification and replacement of those ties were always part of slavery and also of colonial rule: both were systematic efforts to destroy existing kin structures to produce new forms of terrorized obedience not only to the master or ruler but also to the broader systems of power and law that authorized that domination and destruction.

We may be tempted to counter these repellent reductions of kinship by returning to anthropology in order to discover more recent ways of describing kinship that affirm the social and affective dimensions of the tie. Queer legacies of kinship depart from anthropological models at the same time that they challenge those models to understand both the political regulation of kinship ties and the deregulating powers of nonnormative kinship networks. But anthropological models are useful only if those theoretical frameworks take into account the political regulation of kinship, accepting kinship as a dense site for the regulation of race and sexuality.

Yet the desire to bring it all back to culture persists. Marshall Sahlins (2013) published a set of essays on kinship that argue for the continuing perti-nence of cultural anthropology for thinking kinship in our times. Following up on the critique of the bloodline, Sahlins defined kinship in postnatal terms, arguing in a philosophical vein that kinship can be understood as a "mutuality of being" (2). Through various ethnographic examples and philosophical theories, he sought to define kin as those who "participate in each other's existence" (ix). Kin are intrinsic to one's own being, those in whom we prove to be intrinsic as well. We do not each belong to a group, and we do not exactly belong to each other. The point is ontological: we *are* each other insofar as we participate in one another, and this kind of par-ticipation constitutes us as kin. His elaboration does not rely on anyone's role in sexual reproduction, and it surely does not assume the structure of the family. At the same time it still offers a generalization, if not a univer-salization, on the basis of a select group of examples, especially Polynesia and New Guinea. In a sense, Sahlins offers an ideal version of kinship, al-though it is based on societies that are assumed to offer up more translucid versions of kinship relations, ones based on proximity and the continuity of historical transmission, as opposed to those that characterize a more scattered industrial and postindustrial condition of late modernity. How does generalization work in his view? His is perhaps a description of what kinship has been or could be, an effort to produce a temporal and spatial disorientation within what he considers to be late modernity. The value of such an approach is clear because it prompts us to imagine the present dif-ferently through a lens that is generally disregarded or unknown. Although Sahlins elaborates at length on the ontology that should be reanimated for anthropology, I am left wondering whether what he offers is a subjunctive form of writing, one that carries a wish to have present reality embody and animate the more laudable forms of filiation and solidarity that he finds among the peoples he studies. The cultural anthropological desire persists, despite some of the trenchant criticisms of the implication of ethnographic description in colonial fantasy. In other words, Sahlins offers a compelling imaginary that may seem satisfying under certain present conditions but it exposes its limit once we take seriously the role of history—specifically, the history of violence—in the making of kinship.

Although Sahlins makes the case for cultural ontology, he is renew-ing the case for the study of culture as a relatively autonomous domain, suggesting that we might approach it not through structures but through grasping a binding and co-constitutive set of relations understood as kinship. In this way his project might be understood as a philosophical imaginary, by which I do not mean that it is false. Rather, it is a way of engaging in a hypothetical, which is something different from both historical description and political analysis. He brings forth evidence of all kinds, but in the end the claims he makes depend on the reader's willingness to enter into the language of ontology. Although his ontology seems to follow from the evidence in a narrative sequence, it turns out, I believe, to function as the framework within which the evidence is interpreted. In other word, ontology is another way of seeing kinship, a lens or framework through which to see and to describe, organizing and relating evidence within its terms.

I am in favor of aesthetic experimentations, sustained hypotheticals, political imaginaries, and critical fabulations. By these I mean forms of wishful elaboration, experiments in the possible, unrealistic projects that boldly claim their own naïveté. Such modes of theorizing can, I think, help provide a counterpoint to the exceedingly rough times we are in. By a political imaginary I don't mean a simple picture of utopia toward which we drive, but rather a way of newly elaborating relationships that would counter the ascendant tendencies to base social relations on property relations: to reanimate old and persistent racisms through new technologies, rancorous antifeminism, homophobia and transphobia, shameless greed and cruelty, the intensification of economic and social inequality, the intensification of carceral and police powers that disproportionately affects the intersecting population of people of color and migrants, and the production of increasing numbers of people living in conditions of precarity and dispossession, whether in urban centers or at the margin of the metropole. For all these reasons, it is important to find ways to think beyond the horizons that bound our current conception of reality. Philosophical and fictive experiments provide ways of interlacing both critical and creative work that help refigure with the violent history of kinship and its aspirations for interdependency, livable habitation, and enduring support. In other words, there is plenty of room for wishful thinking if it is grounded in the refusal to deny the history of violence that it seems to overcome. Imaginaries answer to our longings, but they also have a way of reflecting back the sustaining dimensions of kinship that are elided by models that have been instrumentalized in the service of violent forms of regulation.

When Sahlins claims, for instance, that in kinship, we live each other's lives and die each other's deaths, that we live in and through one another, he relies on the theory of Eduardo Viveiros de Castro (2009), who claims that kin relations allow one being to be animated by another or, indeed, to participate in a transferable anima, or soul. If within the bounds of "kinship" one person participates in another, then kin are those whose bounded selves are at the same time intrinsically related to ours—that is, ways in which we are unbounded in relation to one another. We come outside our boundaries for one another, or we find that our boundaries are already traversed by another without our knowing and long ago. No contract can grasp that relation. Every contract reduces its lived meaning. One could say that the other is "in" me, but that interiority is nothing other than a relational opening to the other (and the history of such relations as they live on in a self). We could clean up our language and make it simple by saying that we are part of one another, but that formulation imagines a compartment in myself where the other also resides or some such spatial structure in the other where I am understood to dwell. It does not really rethink the problem of the boundary. That the self is relational, according to de Castro, means that the social relations animated among kin are an intrinsic feature of each member, an animate and animating feature of what one feels. Kin live, as it were, as an animated alterity in oneself.

Although I find this to be a beautiful vision, some questions nevertheless persist. The first is how do we know where kinship starts and ends. What delimits kinship as a sphere, if it is one? Is it the case that whenever we feel this way for and with another, we are therefore kin? What about relations of love or friendship that are not kin? The second question pertains to the role of dependency. Are kin relations ways of organizing human dependency, their dependency on not only other humans but also structures, institutions, and technologies, other living beings, that support the ongoing life of the person or, indeed, a number of interrelated people? I ask this in part to draw attention to the way that kinship presupposes support; we are supported or abandoned by kin in ways that are perhaps distinct. An abyss opens in a different way when kin are not there for us, although "thereness" can be in the house, across the way, on the line, or in some other form of distance. However, the same question holds for this view as it does for Sahlins's formulation: is it the case that only in kin relations do we feel that distinctive sort of support or abandonment, or is it rather that when and where we feel those things, we know we are in the midst of a kin relation? For theorists such as Elizabeth Freeman (2007), it is dependency and support that let us know when and where kinship is happening.

I return to the issue of dependency here because relations of dependency tend to be ambivalent, and for that reason kin relations are more fraught and tenuous than Sahlins imagines them to be. The reasons for the fraughtness are at once social and psychoanalytic. Indeed, one can find oneself inhabited by someone who is kin in the way that one is inhabited by a ghost, or one can deeply fear identification with a kin member and manically seek to fend off the prospect of becoming that person. One can feel profound, even unmanageable, dependency on someone who is kin, and that feeling can be alternately blissful and absolutely enraging, causing one to resolve never to feel that sort of dependency again for fear of never being able to reassume an upright posture of independence. Kin relations are defined by actual or potential rupture even as they are often imagined to be enduring. People enter into kin relations and leave them, not only for reasons of their own choosing; this means that kin relations can change historically in profound ways and that they are not always bound by contracts. As we know, in blended or complex kinship arrangements, various kin positions can be superimposed upon one another in differentiated ways, which means that multiple figures can occupy a kin position or that multiple positions can host a number of figures: two mothers or two fathers, or more than two of each, or an array of abiding kin relations that fit neither into the established norms of mother or father role nor uncle or aunt or cousin, but that call upon new names and innovate new relational vocabularies. These extended kin relations may well inhabit us only to some degree, or they may be sites of intense ambivalence: desires for belonging or the need for flight, love, and hatred.

How then do we understand these modes of distance and negation, envy, fear, loss, guilt in light of a kin relation in which, as Sahlins claims, we participate in one another's very being? Perhaps it is exactly by virtue of that uncanny participation in one another's "being" that all those complex and unresolved feelings follow. That participation could be cannibalism or engulfment. What phantasmatic forms can that participation take? Is the idea of participation in another's being itself a fantasy, one that dates at least back to Plato's mathesis? What if another is participating in, partaking of, oneself as a consequence of an unwanted capture or invasion of one's body? What if that permeability to the other is insufferable or what if one feels quite ground down to nothing by another, yet one is supposed to be kin? I am left with two questions, one psychoanalytic and the other so-cial. The first: what would happen if Melanie Klein were set loose on Mar-shall Sahlins's theory? The second: what happens when kinship is articu-lated under forcible conditions, including rape, slavery, forced exile from war or genocide, or legal forms of torture and detention?

I have brought a psychoanalytic perspective into this consideration of kinship, but not because I think that it will tell us all that we need to know. As another illuminating and partial theory, it is useful in keeping in check a form of *kinship idealism* that would encode that wishfulness as reality, one that relies upon a set of exclusions and effacements that keep us from understanding the actual workings of kinship, its violence and conflict as well as its aspiration toward care and support. The history of kinship has to include the loss of kin relations, the loss of the status of kin under co-erced conditions, and the production of forced kinship as a ruse of power. All these histories underscore the importance of not regarding kin rela-tions as ever fully autonomous: they do not form a perfectly closed-off ob-ject of study precisely because on the one hand, they are ghosted by power and often by violence, embedded in technologies and property relations, and, on the other hand, they are capable of exceeding and confounding the very definitions within which they are said to work even as they work. One other reason kinship is not a bounded object of study or a completed cul-tural system is that forms of kinship are not already fully made and never will be; they are striated with unlived futurities. In other words, they are in the course of being made, and they involve new formations, coinage, and new legal challenges for recognition as well as new vocabularies that exceed the law.

Queer Belonging and Relationality

Within queer theory in recent years, there has been a change of focus from queer kinship to queer belonging in part because it was not always possi-ble to track modes of kinship that were not structured by childbearing and child raising, or by the institution of marriage. As the mainstream LGBTQ movement (absent the I and A, and with only passing reference to the T), especially the Human Rights Campaign, sought legal recognition for gay marriage, many others worried that other forms of filiation and belong-ing were backgrounded, if not effaced. "Queer belonging," elaborated a few years ago by Elizabeth Freeman (2007) and José Esteban Muñoz (2009), for instance, testified to the ways that the term *kinship* tends to assume modes of relatedness that are too often reliant on sexual reproduction, and efforts to de-link kinship from that obdurate frame seem forever related to it, if only in a negative or critical mode. Although clearly not following the "antisocial" trend of queer theory, those who sought to establish modes of queer belonging were in part seeking to expand the terms of kinship and in part to leave that vocabulary behind. As much as I appreciate that movement, I am not sure we can leave kinship behind not only because it is articulated for us—allowing us to adopt or questioning our legal rights—but because kinship is a site of queer coinage, of a performative re-elaboration, and the recognition of binding ties made and remade. Consider, for instance, the effort to redefine kinship by Christopher Roebuck (2013), whose work I cited earlier:

> I understand kinship as kind of doing, what might be call "practice" following Bourdieu or the "tactics of everyday life" to pull from de Certeau. . . . Kinship [is] a means through which humans go about forming a network of relations constituted by practices of obligation, support, and care with significant and beloved others as well as offering the language through which humans give meanings to these practices. Although kinship is a way of knowing and being in the world, this doing and acting is not freely formed, voluntaristically chosen, or without constitutive constraints. Thus, following [Donna] Haraway, I understand kinship as a technology for producing humans, who have the effect of a "natural relationship, of shared kind."

But what is this "shared kind"—a common anthropological trope in kinship studies—that is ostensibly produced through kinship? Roebuck rightly puts the phrase in quotation marks because it seems to refer to race and species as a shared kind. On the one hand, it seems to rule out companion species of the kind that Haraway herself defends so trenchantly in her manifesto by that name: modes of kinship that cross species and whose shared character is regularly disavowed. Second, the idea of the bounded community that forms the example from which generalizations about culture itself are derived generally relies on notions of cultural or racial homogeneity; indeed, the extent to which kinship derived from isolated or so-called primitive communities presumes an unmarked racial homogeneity is not to be underestimated, contributing as this model does to a developmental account of cultures indebted to forms of civilizational racism. Yet if we wish to move away from forms of kinship that unwittingly presume heterosexual reproduction and/or racial unity as their structuring principles, we may have to reconsider modes of kinship not only in their historical contexts but also as modes of historical transmission subject to the mandate to reproduce "like kind."

In other words, a structural model asks not only how a structure is reproduced through time but how it establishes a mode of temporality that presumes the reiteration of structure. Yet contemporary critical and queer scholarship is asking a different kind of question: how does kinship become formed and reformed through histories in which kinship is forcibly wrought and broken up, highly regulated, or compelled to conform to obligatory models? In other words, when power and violence turn out to be central features of kinship's reproduction and its new formations, what kind of tracking can we do? If we no longer assume that kinship systems are static or that they yield timeless structures, we concede not only their synchronicity but also their violent regulation and foreclosure, and the traces of that violence become interwoven with kinship itself.

Consider again Saidiya Hartman's (2007, 194) enormously important claim: "slaves were the ghosts in the machine of kinship." Christina Sharpe (2016b) has more recently interpreted that formulation this way: "Chattel slavery continues to animate the present: transatlantic chattel slavery's constitution of domestic relations made kin in one direction, and in the other, property that could be passed between and among those kin." So relations of kin are not differentiated primarily from the animal or the stranger but pass through the slave, considered as chattel, and passed among slave owners for a price or a deal. The slave is the commodity that negatively establishes relations of kin: the slave also becomes the slave owner's kin of a sort, insofar as the slave is forced to live under a new patronym that destroys and effaces prior kinship ties under legal codes regulating slavery. The institution of slavery is the ghost that haunts whatever lines of kinship can be known and drawn; the terms of kinship that survive carry the history of violent appropriation and displacement, but generally not in any way that can be mapped or narrated. After all, who really has a trackable lineage? For many, if not most, a history of effacement limns the map of trackable kinship. Slavery is the ghost in the machine of kinship, yes. If so, the machinery of slavery, the violent means by which kinship was at once destroyed and wrought, ghosts the history and study of kinship, pervading the available maps as well as the descriptions of its basic structures. Is the relation to the relative whose name one never knew in a prior generation, separated by slavery or genocide, forced migration and forcible loss, followed by decades or centuries of a shredded archive, or the trace of an absence, still kin? Is that kind of loss—ungrievable—part of the history of kinship, and does it articulate relations of kin? Can kinship even remain the name for the forms of belonging we recall and make? Or is there another name that accompanies that name: a term, in other words, for its ghost?

Kindred's Fraught Blood Tie: Unwilled Dependency

I would like, then, to turn to Octavia Butler's *Kindred* in part because the title, *Kindred*, is ghosted by kinship, but not exactly that. *Kindred* also allows us to consider kinship in light of a permeability to the violent past—in this case, the violent past of slavery that destroyed kinship and re-wrought its terms.

In *Kindred*, we are introduced to an interracial couple in an apartment in California in 1976, a year in which the civil rights movement is reverberating in the United States but also a year in which apartheid in South Africa is in the process of being overthrown. At the outset of the story, we are confronted with what would seem to be a scene of abuse. Dana, the main character, seems to have lost her arm or damaged it badly, and the police ask, "Who hurt you?" (O. Butler [1979] 2003, 9). In some ways that question remains alive throughout the novel, although it modulates slightly to "Who or what hurt you?" (44). Pain seems to motivate most of the transitions in the novel, including a transport or transfer for Dana back to the time of slavery. Indeed, pain seems to initiate the transfer from one time to another. Another time bursts into this time with pain; pain takes Dana out of the present and back into the past, which, in fact, constitutes her present. Rufus, who at the outset of the novel is the young white son of a slave owner in 1815, has called to Dana over time and space, and she finds herself responding to that call—responding involuntarily to a call from another century. She is pulled down into an unconscious state and then "wakes" into that other time. So there is time travel in this novel, but not through a machine and not, it seems, through any standard devices of science fiction that orchestrate the swift and painful shifts between time and space (Octavia Butler made clear in an interview that she does not write science fiction). Dana is back in 1815, and then she returned to her apartment, often the same day, even though months have passed when she was there, and then when Rufus calls again, she returns only to find that years have passed in the minutes or hours since having received that last call.

That call is a call from the past, to be sure. How can it be heard? It is the call of a young white boy who is in some kind of distress—there is no apparent link between them. Yet Dana is inclined to help him, even to save him. The novel starts with the police interrogating Dana with "Who hurt you?" expecting to find an abusive boyfriend in the picture. But we find that that question has an earlier version, that it is Dana who asks it of Rufus in an effort to deliver him from harm and even, as it will turn out, to save his life repeatedly. In the first such encounter, Dana narrates to Kevin, her husband, how she was transported to the time of slavery, finding there a young Rufus who was at risk of drowning. She applies modern methods of rescue on the boy who is not breathing, giving mouth-to-mouth respiration and bringing him back to life: an allegory for the making of character but also of a transgenerational memory. A very sudden, intimate, and life-saving relation among apparent strangers thus turns out to be something more. However, she is there for him, and in some sense his life now depends upon hers, so she is acting the part of kin, of support, of lifeline. We do not know at first what relation she has to this boy and why she is called across space and time to help him. And how is it that her own mind, even her move between conscious and unconscious states, facilitates this transport, this "transferal"? She arrives to the past, her own body intact and carrying whatever she is clutching: her bag and once, consequentially, Kevin himself. Of course, as a Black woman, she arrives on a plantation in Maryland as a presumed slave, and when a rifle is aimed at her head, shortly after she saves Rufus's life, she loses consciousness again and reemerges in her apartment in 1976 with Kevin, who accepts the account of what has happened without much apparent skepticism. After all, there is mud on her boots, and she had disappeared quickly, so there seems to be empirical evidence that she went somewhere and came back.

She is called back again when Rufus's own life is endangered, so there seems to be a bond, an obligation there, some entanglement of lives. Is this a bond of kinship? For some obscure reason they are connected, but she does not quite have a name for that. In fact, she doesn't have a name for the time transport. As she explains to Kevin, "I do not have a name for the thing that happened to me, and I don't feel safe anymore" (Butler [1979] 2003, 17). So the transport seems to take place through a rupture in consciousness but also a rupture in language. When she goes back a second time, Rufus is a bit older, and he explains that he "sees" her in his mind, even the room with the books in California in 1976, attesting to a trans-temporal possibility of responding to and imagining each other. They are bound across time and space, but how? And why? What we know is that the call, the response, the imagining all seem involuntary and that the transports happen on the occasion of perilous pain and near-death experiences. Even the call comes from somewhere other than the conscious mind. Something fugitive binds them, and that seems to be called a "call," and it has the power to drag Dana through time.

Dana doubts her sanity only briefly but resolves that she is in the middle of a "perfect hallucination" (Butler [1979] 2003, 28)—this might be one way Octavia Butler describes the greatness of her own story, the orchestration of time and space in this novel. "Maybe he was one of my ancestors" she wonders (28). She checks the family records and conjectures that perhaps the child Hagar of the adult Rufus and Alice is linked to her own family. It is not possible to track all the kin records, and even at the end of the novel, when Kevin and Dana return to Maryland in 1976 together to find the records, they are not fully intact. Whatever kinship this may be, it is not one for which there is clear documentation. Dana claims:

> There is nothing in him that reminded me of any of my relatives. Looking at him confused me. But he had to be the one. There had to be some kind of reason for the link he and I seemed to have. Not that I really thought a blood relationship could explain the way I had twice been drawn to him. It wouldn't. But then neither would anything else. What we had was something new, something that did not have a name. Some matching strangeness in us that may or may not have come from our being related. (29)

In any case, the "strangeness" is in them both, but also in their relationship, for after all, they are hearing and seeing across time and space. Theirs does not have to be a blood relation, but it is a trans-historical tie. A matching strangeness counters the idea of a "shared kind" tied to race as a natural kind, offering instead an inadvertent biracial history wrought from slavery. The name for this is not exactly kinship, but *Kindred*.

Yet the blood tie *does* seem to matter. Dana seems clear that she has to save Rufus in order to make sure that her family line will continue and that she herself will be born. She struggles to secure the historical condition of her own emergence. Yet it is not absolutely clear that her life depends on his. And her relation to him is not exactly instrumental or self-serving. She puts herself at risk for him, and she is pulled by feelings both unknowable and unnameable. We can call this a queer form of kinship, but that alone does not really explain the complexity. However, the context of slavery does. After all, Tom Weylin, the slave owner, comes to own the children of those who work on his plantation—in his eyes, and according to slave law, they reproduce for him, reproducing his chattel, which includes the number of slaves. He can, and does, impregnate the slave women as he wishes, can and does sell the children at his will. And in this way, whatever kin relations that exist among slaves are subject to destruction by the kin relations imposed by the slaver or the slave owner. As Orlando Patterson (1982, 19ff.) tells us, slavery exercised the power to destroy original kin relations and to produce what he calls "fictive kin" relations in their place. With this phrase, Patterson seems to reanimate the kind of kinship models that David Schneider criticizes. Perhaps Octavia Butler goes in another direction. The slave owner becomes everyone's father or "daddy," and as Alice explains, "Mister Tom own all his children" (Butler [1979] 2003, 40). They are goods, property, but also kin, his children, and although interracial marriage and miscegenation were legally proscribed under slavery, miscegenation was clearly informally rampant and protected, though not generally understood to describe the forcible reproduction of slave children through rape.

Dana understands that what she is seeing is what Patterson (1982, 5ff.) calls "natal alienation"—it does not matter who gives birth to the slave infant because that infant is now chattel belonging to the slave owner. The biological father's rights are denied as the slave owner's paternal rights are asserted. So slavery destroys and preempts Black kinship ties, but it also articulates new ties, biracial ones, generations to come that are linked by virtue of a legally violent form of sexual reproduction and that in turn are the promise of the social reproduction of slavery itself. Interestingly enough, Octavia Butler establishes a kindred relation between Rufus and Dana that is—and is not—a blood tie. I am not sure we can say that they adopt each other across generations, but I am not sure we cannot say that as well!

In sum, Octavia Butler moves away from the natalist understanding of kinship. It is the social institution of slavery that gives rise to the new ties that bind. It may very well not be possible to find the document that verifies the kinship, but it hardly matters. The tie is one that emerges from the destroyed archive, the possibility of securing the life of the other in a mode of relationality that is born, as it were, from the unaccountable history of violence enlaced with the urge to lend one's body to sustain the life of the other. The last time that Rufus appears in this story, he seeks to harm Dana, then apologizes, and she is left with a knife in her hand, contemplating whether to kill him, and finally, under duress, she sinks the knife into his side only then to wake in contemporary time with her arm apparently lodged in the wall, a part of the wall, with a final scream of pain. Perhaps he is bloodline, but perhaps not, but the pain spans the centuries, articulating a relation fraught with the need to live, the need for the other to live, and the desire to free oneself of the violent hold of this past.

Bloodline Is a Discontinuous Story

What we call a bloodline gives way to a story riddled with ruptures, and whatever ties are made are built on the basis of that discontinuity, longing for repair, persistence of the unresolved. These kinds of ties are never fully unghosted by the past. Law is part of the history and present of kinship, but it can no more secure its definition than biogenetics or patriarchal structures. Even as there is probably no way to think kinship without the law, it does not follow that the law has the last say in defining kinship. Legal ties are not the only ones that bind. Slavery and forced migration are different kinds of dispossession. Very often the patronym that we carry and awkwardly share is the mark of multiple dispossessions that could neither be reversed nor fully documented. The name that abbreviates kin relations bears a story of binding connection in a different way, even as it marks the limit of our telling of any story we might carry. It is the name for unexpected filiations, the ones some of us never imagined or predicted when, as it were, we were living within the world of the blood tie. Strange that the rule of the blood tie casts so many of our relations as secondary and fictive when it is precisely in fiction that the ruse of that symbolic order is exposed.

Note

1   See also his view that gender should be defined by biological and genetic material alone: https://www.nytimes.com/2020/06/12/us/politics/trump-trans gender-rights.html.

02 The Mixed-Race Child Is Queer Father to the Man

Alice Dunbar-Nelson's short story "The Child Is Father to the Man" plays on a queerly circular formation of kinship in which childhood begets manhood, which then begets childhood.[1] Alluding to a line from William Wordsworth's 1807 poem "My Heart Leaps Up," "The Child Is Father to the Man" suggests a queerly circular form of reproduction. Reading the temporal reversal in the notion that "the child is father," we might understand not simply an articulation of individual development or of manhood achieved via a genealogical legacy but of creative—and nonheteronormative—reproduction. Casting self making in terms of fatherhood, the child-as-father speaks to a form of queer potential that is retrospective inasmuch as it is future-looking. The child as father is a necessarily circular relation, emphasizing the *re* in *reproduction* and collapsing child and father into a single self-producing being. In this doubling of fathers, Dunbar-Nelson's story departs from earlier narratives of racial reproduction to focus on Black fatherhood (rather than motherhood) and to frame fathering itself as an act of aesthetic creation. Moreover, the aesthetic racial reproduction that Dunbar-Nelson depicts extends beyond prioritizing genealogies of whiteness and white beauty.

"The Child Is Father to the Man" is not known to have been published. The hand-corrected typescript is located in the Alice Dunbar-Nelson Papers at the University of Delaware Library, and no date is listed either on the manuscript or in the library's finding aid. Katherine Adams (2019) dates the story to 1896 or 1897, connecting its setting and the protagonist's attachment to the river and the view from it to Dunbar-Nelson's brief time spent living in Boston, during which she collected clippings about the Harvard crew team in her scrapbook.[2] Unlike much of Dunbar-Nelson's short fiction, "The Child Is Father to the Man" is explicit about its protagonist's racial embodiment, presenting an opportunity to depart from conversations about racial ambiguity in her work and to discuss instead how racial embodiment informs her characters' kinship relations.

The relationship between parent and child in "The Child Is Father to the Man" is cast in terms of inherited aesthetic value. Here is a sketch of the plot: John, the protagonist, is a smart but "ugly" boy with a soul that loves and craves beauty. John's father resents his child's ugliness and his resemblance to himself, and dies when John is young. John is raised by a poor mother, Artemisa Brown, who loves him dearly and dies soon after securing him a place working as a hotel bellhop. After his mother's death, John is distracted and loses his position, to later be hired to work as a janitor in Harold Leonard's law office after Leonard (as he is called throughout Dunbar-Nelson's text) takes a particular interest in him.[3] John eventually reunites with a woman (never named in the story) who is a former schoolmate, and they fall in love, marry, and have a child together. John is excited at the prospect of fatherhood, but when his son is born, he—like his own father—shrinks from the child because the baby so closely resembles himself.

John ultimately reassesses his child's appearance and determines to make his life beautiful. At the story's close, John tells his wife, "He has made a man out of me . . . it is late, but I will make a man of him while he is yet a child" (Dunbar-Nelson n.d., 15).[4] In a temporally circular loop, John's child allows him to craft his own manhood—as well as his son's—in an act of self making via aesthetic (re)production. John's revelation at the story's close abandons notions of beauty as a thing one embodies or possesses and instead embraces beauty as something achieved through the acts of relating and creating. Beauty becomes not something that he isn't or is but something he might reproduce in his relations—especially his kinship—to others.

Set beside Dunbar-Nelson's published work, the story adds a complex treatment of race and racial mixture. Race is not always described in definitive terms in Dunbar-Nelson's short fiction, causing some scholars to whitewash her characters and others to argue for more nuanced readings of their racialization.[5] But it is in her descriptions of racial ambiguities and ambivalences that Dunbar-Nelson's most intriguing interrogations of race appear. As scholars like Elizabeth Ammons (1992, 61) warn against characterizing Dunbar-Nelson's writing as "a misguided attempt to write around race," this recently recovered story reveals a complex treatment of race that demands consideration among increasingly nuanced scholarly accounts of nineteenth-century Black writers' representations of mixed-race characters. In "The Child Is Father" (a relatively early story) we see a deliberate casting of a mixed-race Black protagonist that makes a significant contribution to genres of African American literary mixed-race hero(in)es by authors such as Frances Ellen Watkins Harper, Charles Chesnutt, and Pauline Hopkins. Like these authors, Dunbar-Nelson departs from earlier castings of mixed-race figures as necessarily "tragic." And Dunbar-Nelson's protagonist does not have both Black and white parentage, although he bears the residual markers of mixed-race genealogy on his body of "indiscriminate" complexion. Unlike better-known writers of mixed-race protagonists, however, Dunbar-Nelson veers away from motherhood as the site for examining racial reproduction and the woman's body for exploring racialized aesthetic valuation, replacing these instead with the figure of the mixed-race Black boy as self-producing a valuable form of Black masculinity.

Some readers might take the general plot of Dunbar-Nelson's story as one of conventional heteropatriarchal fatherhood in which a man is reformed via the birth of his son. Attending to Blackness, however, complicates such a reading. Hortense Spillers (2003, 204) reminds us that "according to Daniel Patrick Moynihan's celebrated 'Report' of the late sixties, the 'Negro Family' has no Father to speak of." This is decidedly not the case in Dunbar-Nelson's story. John's father is a presence that haunts him even in death, becoming overly important to John's creative development. In this way the largely heteronormative story of reproduction and nuclear family veers away from the matriliny described in both the Moynihan Report and in popular literature depicting mixed-race protagonists, and toward one that prioritizes inherited relations of Black masculinity. Amid the obscuring of Black fatherhood in US popular media, this focus itself is inherently unconventional. Dunbar-Nelson's work—like that of many African American women writers, which has too often been plagued with either overly simplistic or overtly racist readings—requires analyses that attend to the complex nexus of race, gender, and sexuality that overwhelmingly defies (white, heteronormative) conventions and continually revises earlier Black literary tropes.

If we consider the paradox by which Black boys are often understood outside of childhood and Black men are framed as "boys"—that is, as perpetual children—we might better understand John's child-father doubling. Whereas Wordsworth, in "My Heart Leaps Up," presents children as fathers to illustrate continuity of relation to an aesthetic experience, Dunbar-Nelson does this to present aesthetic experience as an act of (re)production that reevaluates the racialized body. In Dunbar-Nelson's framing, her child-father protagonist is not simply in a position of racial degradation but is instead an expansive figure whose queer temporal relations allow for the circular occupation of both of these roles, rather than a simple linear trajectory between them. Understanding John as both child and man in this story, we must consider his relation to childhood also as one of temporal circularity. The child is thereby not simply someone (or something) he begets, but a being to whom he himself returns relationally at the story's close, though as a father. Erased from both childhood and fatherhood by white supremacist imaginings, then, Dunbar-Nelson's Black child-become-father is a figure reflecting nonnormative relations of reproduction.

This essay theorizes the specifically racialized version of mixed-race self-begetting in Dunbar-Nelson's story as a queer act of self-reproduction, aesthetic creation, and the racial performance of masculinity. John is a child, himself, at the opening of Dunbar-Nelson's story, a fact that contributes to the circularity of the child-father. Reading the "child" and the "man" of Dunbar-Nelson's title via the doublings of creation and creator also allows us to see Black writers' turn-of-the-century calls for more African American literary production or textual reproduction, metaphorized as rebirth and enacted via queer temporalities. Dunbar-Nelson's paradoxical story of self-begetting hereby locates itself in a queer genealogy of interracial kinship: it seems to argue that the mixed-race person is self-produced. Moreover, the story focuses not simply on the mixed-race Black body as created but as creative. John's relationship to aesthetic (re)production might be read as an allegory of sorts for the Black Renaissance itself. This period of aesthetic reproduction is often (though wrongly) imagined in masculinist terms, just as John figures his own reproduction in "The Child Is Father" apart from women.

In Dunbar-Nelson's story, reproduction is coupled with aesthetic creation and the power of relation and self-realization that accompanies Black creativity. I read this creativity with a mind both to queer time and to nonnormative genealogies and Black futures. My approach is similar to the way that Kara Keeling (2019) connects these concepts, drawing on Audre Lorde's discussions of creativity and power. Following Lorde's "Poetry Is Not a Luxury," Keeling connects both queer time and Black futures to embodiment, referring to bodies as "sites not only of the application of power but also of power's transvaluation or redirection" (Keeling 2019, xi). I attend to the ways that "The Child Is Father" illustrates such a transvaluation of power as it shifts attention from the aesthetic valuation of racialized embodiment to creative potential in a moment of continuing Black literary production and future-gazing. As scholars such as Caroline Gebhard and Barbara Mc-Caskill (2016) have acknowledged, the "Post-Bellum–Pre-Harlem" moment (between 1877 and 1919) upsets temporal characterizations of Black creative production oriented around Jim Crow law or the Nadir of anti-Black lynchings. This story's rejection of the aesthetic superiority of mixed-race bodies, centering of masculine reproduction, and themes of Black aesthetic rebirth and child-oriented futurity also suggest a productive temporal reorientation that allows us to view Black Renaissance literary production from Dunbar-Nelson's turn-of-the-century vantage point.

Dunbar-Nelson's Mixed-Race Aesthetic

The signifier "ugly" repeats throughout Dunbar-Nelson's story largely without clear referents, seemingly absorbing meaning but effectively evacuated of it. John's body is ugly, but ugliness is not exclusive to his particular embodiment. Ugliness also inheres in the spaces John inhabits and some of the other people around him. However, the emptiness of his particular ugliness signifies throughout the text, conveyed through repetition. Early on, we read that "he was an ugly child. There was no disputing this fact" (Dunbar-Nelson n.d., 1). The emphasis that Dunbar-Nelson gives to this characteristic seems to both solidify John's ugliness as a fact and to mitigate against aesthetic judgments on the part of other characters and Dunbar-Nelson's readers. Over the course of the story, John and others lament his ugliness, fetishize it, and overlook it, but they never erase or recharacterize this judgment. Even in John's reevaluation of his child, he recognizes the latter's beauty not as a replacement for the ugliness of his own resemblance to his father, but as an accompaniment to it. Recognizing that "there was something beautiful about it [the child], after all," we read that John "forgot that his child resembled him" (14). Here ugliness and beauty sit side by side, suggesting the arbitrariness of these aesthetic signs. This odd hybridity muddles the story's depiction of mixed-race bodies, nonnormative bodies, and even the spaces that John occupies. In whatever way we understand ugliness, however, it is perpetually accompanied by beauty. This is John's ultimate vow regarding his child: "He would surround it with care and love and beaut~~yiful things.~~" (13).[6] In this act of crafting a beautiful world for his child, John rebirths both his child's and his own relationship to ugliness and beauty.

Like Wordsworth's poem, Dunbar-Nelson's story orients readers to a kind of bodily aesthetic that itself creates a temporal loop of self-begetting, locating the roots of aesthetic pleasure in childhood. "My Heart Leaps Up," sometimes called "The Rainbow," begins with an account of aesthetic pleasure: "My heart leaps up when I behold / A Rainbow in the sky" (Wordsworth 1807, 44). Here beauty is visceral, felt bodily. The poem goes on to describe this particular pleasure's temporal consistency:

> So was it when my life began;
> So is it now I am a Man;
> So be it when I shall grow old,
>   Or let me die!
> The Child is Father of the Man; (Wordsworth 1807, 44)

The poem plays on both temporal and familial relationships that imply causality. The speaker's "heart leaps up *when*" he beholds the rainbow, a phenomenon that, though fleeting, connects the present and future. Wordsworth implies that it is not the rainbow itself that inspires, but that it enables the speaker's sustained relationship to it and establishes the continuity of his future self. The child who saw the rainbow and was moved by its beauty produces the man who will continue to derive that same aesthetic pleasure. The speaker's relationship to beauty, on a conventional time line, is linked to (or perhaps evidenced by) the continuity of that experience of beauty from childhood to adulthood.

Dunbar-Nelson's story similarly orients its notions of childhood around aesthetic experience. But as Wordsworth's narrator is born through childhood awe at a rainbow's beauty, Dunbar-Nelson's protagonist is conceived through the fraught self-loathing of his own mixed-race body, deemed ugly. Even John's mother finds him to be "an ugly child," and his "hideous" body provokes not only laughter but also rejection: his father "had resented the boy's ugliness and made his life unpleasant" (Dunbar-Nelson n.d., 2–3). These relations begin the narrative in which John ultimately begets a child of his own, a "tiny replica of himself" from whom he initially shrinks in "sorrowful disgust" (12). Although John's ugliness is described in part via the physical markers of his mixed-race body, as we shall see, the story represents his body in a complex landscape in which both ugliness and beauty are in and all around him. Moreover, as the story goes on, aesthetic value inheres not simply in bodies, objects, or places but in John's relationships to them.

The story specifically describes John's ugliness in terms of his racially amalgamated features. We read that

> his skin was an indiscriminate cross between a brick-dust red and a ginger brown. It was freckled, mottled would be the better term. His hair was a light, dirty, yellowish brown, and it was very wooly. His eyes were such a pale brown that in some lights they were yellow. Then he had the worst of negro features; flat nose, thick lips. His body was dwarfed and misshapen and his hands and feet disproportionately large. Moreover his health was poor. ~~He could not run and play and be strong in sports like other boys. He tired easily and he found sitting down always pleasanter than active exercise.~~ And into this body so hideous that it provoked laughter wherever it went, Fate had placed a delicate, refined, sensitive, ∧beauty-loving ~~sul.~~ soul (Dunbar-Nelson n.d., 1–2)

The indeterminacy of his complexion seems key to John's ugliness. The story explains that "if he had been real black or real brown, decided yellow or white, his complexion might have helped him out. But he was neither one thing nor the other" (1). John's white genealogy is visible in his light hair and eyes and freckles, but these are not markers of beauty. Still other features—hair texture, nose, lips—are markers of Blackness, framing the "worst of negro features" in seemingly anti-Black terms. But Blackness can also be beautiful in Dunbar-Nelson's story. John's mother is one of the few people whose beauty satisfies him: "She was tall ~~and~~ slim and graceful. with ~~She had beautiful~~ light brown skin, dusky eyes, regular features and a wealth of crinkly black hair" (3). Both Black and beautiful, John's mother complicates the story's rendering of ugliness as racialized. We wonder, then, if it is John's "white" features that render him ugly. Or perhaps we might read other nonnormative markers of his "misshapen" and "disproportionate" embodiment as possibly—though not necessarily—connected to his mixed-race racialization. Either way, John's body is represented as simultaneously mixed-race and ugly, and aesthetic assessments of this body seem to frame his relationships with the story's other characters, particularly John's mother, his employer and friend, and his wife. This problem of Dunbar-Nelson's depiction of an inherently ugly mixed-race character seems difficult to reconcile with an antiracist reading of the story.

Despite the complexities of the story's treatment of racialization and aesthetic assessment (a point to which I will return below), the story's treatment of race stands out among Dunbar-Nelson's better-known fiction. Situating Dunbar-Nelson's story within a longer history of representations of mixed-race figures in African American literature, we can see in Dunbar-Nelson's fascinating play with mixed-race aesthetics a drastic departure from late nineteenth-century literary castings of mixed-race characters. By the late nineteenth century, mixed-race figures had appeared variously throughout US literature, well beyond the "tragic mulatto" trope that John may initially seem to resemble. Whatever tragedy his racial mixture signals, though, it is framed by notions of aesthetic beauty rather than by ambiguities of racial belonging. John's "ugliness" marks a clear difference from representations of mixed-race girls and women in prominent nineteenth-century fiction by writers such as Lydia Maria Child, Harriet Beecher Stowe, and William Wells Brown, in which white markers of beauty were fetishized in connection with their hypersexualization. The "tragedy" of this prominent trope of racial mixture lies in assumptions about mixed-race people's unassimilability into a racially dualistic society. However, mixed-race Black people's racialization has historically followed lines of genealogical hypodescent that have most often aligned them with people who experience various forms of anti-Black oppression. This alignment is both political and genealogical: mixed-race Black people have been more readily included in Black families and communities than in white ones. This has been the case even as histories of colorism have granted certain forms of white privilege to light-skinned Black people.

Perhaps the most visible privilege of racial mixture in nineteenth-century US literature (including some African American literature) is the association of light skin with notions of beauty that continue to be dangerously and inextricably tied to white supremacist standards. African American literature (particularly African American women's literature) emphasizes the irony that this kind of aesthetic valuation (particularly when tied to the literal valuation of enslaved bodies) was also linked to the hypersexualization of mixed-race Black women. Even depictions of mixed-race Black men in prominent writing by African American writers such as Frances Harper and Charles Chesnutt focus on characters who reflect white standards of beauty (despite aligning themselves with other Black people) and exhibit superior intelligence and talent. In short, mixed-race characters overwhelmingly appeared as exceptional, never mediocre. Therefore, John's ugliness defies these norms of aesthetic valuation. His mixed-race body thus cannot be tied to the usual notions of white aesthetic value. Even with the markers of Blackness that Dunbar-Nelson tells readers might otherwise render him beautiful, the ambiguity of his appearance itself seems ugly, for "he was neither one thing nor the other."

These racial ambiguities are enmeshed with a description of his "dwarfed and misshapen" body, "disproportionately large" hands and feet, and poor health. What exactly this means is left rather vague. This reference to physical nonnormativity or disability appears only in this discussion of John's appearance. A seemingly ableist rendering of bodily nonnormativity as ugliness is unremarkable in itself.[7] But the fact that that these features are absolutely reduced to an assessment of John's body as "hideous" and eliciting laughter seems significant. In a story that has otherwise to do with John's labor and creative abilities, other aspects of his embodiment and position—racialization, disability, and even class position—are collapsed into this aesthetic assessment.

The seeming inextricability of John's mixed-race racialization, bodily proportions, poor health, and ugliness plays on historical assessments of mixed-race people as frail, sickly, or sterile. Nineteenth-century scientific racism's contradictory logics argued that mixed-race Black people benefited from white features while at other times presenting them as unnatural creations. The "tragic" genre of prominent mixed-race hero(ine) fiction (in which the protagonist usually died) problematically reinforced these notions that mixed-race Black people ought not to exist at all. Overtly racist representations of such characters positioned them as a clear threat to not only white supremacy but also the very reproduction of white people on which the white supremacist nation was dependent. Alternately, positive representations of mixed-race Black people often presented these as more palatable versions of Blackness for white racist audiences or alternately (as in the case of anti-passing fiction) focused on Black political solidarity across skin colors and despite white genealogies. These dominant tropes of mixed-race protagonists are absent from Dunbar-Nelson's story. John's racialization seems almost incidental, although the various factors of his embodiment contribute to the bodily "ugliness" so central to the story. Writers such as Charles Chesnutt would, in other turn-of-the-century renderings, respond to white supremacy by touting the benefits of racial hybridity, but Dunbar-Nelson here defies the requisite rendering of her mixed-race protagonist's beauty or excellence.[8] Instead, she relocates beauty outside essentialist notions of embodiment, racialized or otherwise, and in the empowering act of reproduction.

Although Dunbar-Nelson's story initially frames beauty and ugliness in essentialist terms, as fixed qualities of appearance or racial embodiment, her protagonist's revelation extends beyond this relation to beauty. Rather than reimagining John as beautiful or even calling him to prioritize something like "inner beauty," the narrator persists in naming and describing his ugliness. This fact produces an unavoidable paradox in the text. The "ugly" mixed-race body suggests histories of idealizing pretended racial "purity," yet the relationship of racial mixture to John's ugliness remains associative but not entirely causal. What John experiences is not a temporally consistent relationship to a "rainbow in the sky." Rather, by the story's end, it is the power of being able to create, to "make . . . beautiful" that fulfills John's desire. Beautiful rainbows and beautiful bodies are red herrings. Neither happiness nor manhood nor John's child fulfills his desire, a desire not attached to objects or bodies at all but to relations, to verbs: making, creating, becoming. These are ways of being and doing that give him purpose and fulfillment in temporal circularity that has no finite end. As the child "bade him go out and create," not only does John endeavor to shape his child's life and future, but he also proclaims that "he has made a man of me. . . . It is late, but I will make a man of him while he is still a child" (Dunbar-Nelson n.d., 15). The child whom he has begotten signifies only in the continual begetting of that child's world and John's own life, for his relation to beauty and ugliness is not dependent upon his own embodiment of them or even on his experiences of beauty and ugliness, but on his ability to produce beauty in his child's—and hence his own—world. In other words, the story prioritizes not the product of aesthetic creation but the act of creativity.

Aesthetic Relation and (Re)production

Even as beauty and ugliness appear to be attached to markers of racial mixture in Dunbar-Nelson's story, it is difficult to regard this correlation as causal. Still, the story's narrative of race and ugliness tempts readers to read John's racial mixture as essential to the story's plot. If his mixed-race body is not necessarily the thing that determines his ugliness, it does inform his relationship and access to beauty. Just as John is not alone in his ugliness, he is not entirely separated from that which is beautiful. Even as he shrinks from the ugly people and places he encounters, John's apparent ugliness does not exclude him entirely from beautiful people or people who can produce beauty. Although we read that John's mother, Artemisa, "could not disguise" the fact of John's ugliness, the story is emphatic about her beauty. When she dies, John is devastated that "the one beautiful being in the world whom he loved and who loved him, was gone" (Dunbar-Nelson n.d., 4). From the loss of his mother to the birth of his son, John's relationships to the aesthetic are structured by his relationships with other people. It is through these relationships to other people—through affinities that we might call a kind of aesthetic kinship—that John revises his own relationship to beauty.

John's own father is racially unmarked in Dunbar-Nelson's story. However, his resemblance to John suggests a similar mixed-race appearance. We learn that John "had inherited his looks from his father and his father had been disappointed, bitterly so" (Dunbar-Nelson n.d., 3). Like John's mother, his father finds his child ugly, but unlike her, he does not respond to ugliness with love. John's father "had resented the boy's ugliness and made his life unpleasant" (3). Moreover, as the story opens, John's father is dead, nothing more than "a disagreeable memory to him" (3), absent from the story's plot but not from John's memory. John's own fatherhood thus appears in the wake of his own father's absence. This framing of John's father and child works to situate him in simultaneous relation to both; in this genealogy, John doubles as both child and father. His relation to each manifests most prominently as an inheritance and begetting of ugliness that cannot be divorced from notions of racial inheritance and begetting.

That John appears first as a mixed-race Black child is significant for Dunbar-Nelson's rendering of both childhood and fatherhood. As Caroline Gebhard (2016, 336) notes, "From 1895 until at least 1901 [in other words, during the period during which "The Child Is Father" was likely written], Alice Dunbar-Nelson turned repeatedly to the figure of a Creole boy or youth." In these characters, Gebhard writes, "Dunbar-Nelson creates Creole youths who demonstrate their empathy, self-sacrifice, and creativity—the higher-order capacities rarely attributed to poor boys of color" (351). "The Child Is Father" is an interesting addition to understanding Dunbar-Nelson's writing during this time because this story similarly hinges on its protagonist's struggle with his ability to relate and to create. Most significantly, what John ultimately creates in Dunbar-Nelson's story is both the mixed-race Black child and father.

Dunbar-Nelson's empathetic representations of Creole boys mirror her ability to attend to usually denigrated and devalued Black children. In her 1922 essay, "Negro Literature for Negro Pupils," Dunbar-Nelson notes the necessity of valuing Black models of beauty: "For two generations we have given brown and black children a blonde ideal of beauty to worship, a milk-white literature to assimilate, and a pearly Paradise to anticipate, in which their dark faces would be hopelessly out of place" (Dunbar-Nelson 1922, 59). We might therefore consider "The Child Is Father" as complicating this relationship between Blackness and beauty. John's ugliness is embodied but not tied specifically to Blackness; it may even be tied to whiteness. In fact, the only people described as beautiful in Dunbar-Nelson's story are two Black women, John's mother and wife. Nor is ugliness simply a manifestation of racial mixture, even as John's ugliness is tied to his racial embodiment. As John ultimately comes to recognize "something beautiful" about his infant child, we see the locus of beauty shift away from essentialist notions of being and toward an unending process of doing.

The story ultimately revises John's relationship to the aesthetic, rejecting essentialist understandings of beauty as embodiment. That is, ugliness and beauty are points of resemblance and relation for John. His father, he, and his child share a line of patrilineal genealogy that is visible and described in terms of aesthetic assessment. But the seeming heteronormativity of this inheritance cannot explain John's shifting relations to both beauty and his child. Despite the story's heteronormative romance by which John becomes a father, a truncated and vague queer romance at the story's structural center (rather than John's marriage) reorients our understanding of his relationship to ugliness and beauty. Through John's relationship with a white friend named Harold Leonard, the aforementioned man who hires him as a janitor in his law office, we see John shift from an aesthetic object of study and valuation to a potential creator of beauty. It is this shift that allows John to reassess his child's ugliness and his relationship to him.

The intellectual friendship that springs up between the men is framed by Harold Leonard's aesthetic appreciation for John's mixed-race body, one that is nevertheless problematic. When John first goes to work for Leonard, we learn that Leonard "fell in love with John at first sight" (Dunbar-Nelson n.d., 7). But Leonard's love (at least initially) veers quickly into fetishization: "He had never seen someone so 'artistically ugly' as he expressed it, in all his life. He hired him in the same spirit in which he would have purchased a Chinese idol for his rooms" (7). Not tying John's apparent ugliness to Blackness, Leonard's assessment is a vaguer form of exoticization, which is not racially specific but seemingly transferrable across racial lines. As Leonard reduces John to an object, his initial valuation follows racist logics. But in the story's somewhat truncated account of John and Leonard's relationship, we shift sharply away from its focus on John's appearance and toward Leonard's understanding of John's interests and abilities. But when Leonard suggests other occupations that John might explore, John struggles to see his point of view: "The idea that ~~they his gifts~~ ^his life could be anything that would interest anyone ~~else~~ or be of ~~consequence~~ use anywhere amused him" (8).

It is this initial masculine companionship, as much as the act of heterosexual reproduction, through which John (re)begets both his child and himself. This point distinguishes Dunbar-Nelson's story from other stories of biological mixed-race inheritance, which overwhelmingly prioritize mother-child relationships and in which patrilineal inheritance is negligible. Of the men, Dunbar-Nelson writes that

> between the two there sprang up a^n intellectual friendship. In it master and man were forgotten. ~~It was a purely intellectual friendship~~ and they both appreciated it. It was the first time in his life that John had ~~ever~~ had anything that remotely suggested companionship; the first time that anyone had ever given him credit for anything beyond brute ideas of life. It was the first time that Leonard had ~~ever met~~ known one of the Outcast who had something within him that he could meet and understand, and he was interested. (Dunbar-Nelson n.d., 7)

Despite this description of friendship, the relationship between the two men seems more like acquaintanceship. Dunbar-Nelson gives us very little of their interactions with each other. The men are called friends, but they are not social equals. Yet there is a romantic aspect to their "companionship." While John is employed as a janitor in the office of this independently wealthy man, they share conversations about John's desire but inability to write, and John spends time listening to Leonard play the piano, "fascinated, eager" (9). Leonard's love for John also extends into the domestic realm; when John marries, Leonard "was much in evidence in the furnishing of the house, and ~~his lavish expenditure of money~~ surrounded them ~~when they were settled~~, with all that wwas artistic and ha^rmonious" (11). Theirs is an unusual negotiation of masculine power relations. In *Once You Go Black: Choice, Desire, and the Black American Intellectual*, Robert Reid-Pharr (2007, 171) recognizes "'queer' narratives that are obscured by our overprivileging of traditional scripts of racialized Oedipal rivalry." Reid-Pharr reads narratives that disrupt the pattern by which "much within the study of Black American literature and culture has been overdetermined by largely unexamined assumptions of a profound and unchanging hostility between black and white male (erotic) combatants" (171). John and Leonard's odd relationship makes a similar disruption, forgetting "master and man" in its depiction of desire and power. John is eager to compare himself to others and to judge himself harshly, but his friend is insistent upon John's "~~gifts~~," his potential to create something. Leonard's interest in John is not an obviously romantic love, which only appears later and within the bounds of heteronormative domesticity in Dunbar-Nelson's story. Rather than competition with or desire for each other, their relationship is characterized as an aesthetically oriented friendship. Leonard perceives John's desire for beauty and predicts the shift in John's relationship to beauty as something made rather than as something inhering in either himself or his child.

Absent from these scenes with Leonard is a trace of the forms of "normatively strenuous masculinity" that Gebhard (2016, 349) views as a backdrop for Dunbar-Nelson's Creole boy stories. Rather, the few paragraphs devoted to the men's relationship dwell on feeling—more specifically, Leonard's urging and John's frustration. Leonard is himself a creator of beauty. He plays the piano, and as John listens, he recognizes his friend's talent and his own eagerness for some similar form of expression. It is Leonard who encourages him and recognizes his intellect. He suggests that John teach in the South, but John tells him that his home is in Boston. Leonard tells John "you are wasting your life ~~life, your gifts~~" (Dunbar-Nelson n.d., 8). He urges John to write, to at least try. But John is a perfectionist and a defeatist. He is overcritical of his drafts, revises for perfection, and tears up his pages in disgust, "for he always could quote someone who had said the same thing and said it far better than he" (8). Always comparing his creations to the better work of others, John is continually frustrated.

Leonard's encouragement is insufficient to the task of prompting John to creative action. Although Leonard views John as an ugly and exoticized curiosity, he values his intellect and creative potential. But he does not or cannot love John. Instead, a woman from John's youth becomes yet another spark of beauty in his life, and they fall in love and marry. This woman not only loves John but also recognizes his (inner) beauty. We learn that "De^epp below his ugliness and repulsiveness she saw his soul . . . She realized ~~to the~~ fulles^t his conception of beauty and power of expression" (Dunbar-Nelson n.d., 9). When John falls in love, Leonard is interested, but disappointed. Although the woman's friends believe she is sacrificing herself to a man beneath her station, Leonard believes that John is actually the one doing this: "Any man who married, according to Leonard, was sacrificing himself" (11).

Beyond the apparent misogyny of this sentiment, we might read John's assessment of "sacrifice" as a critique of normative domesticity. One might wonder what potential opportunities John may have to forgo to meet the demands of being a husband and father.

But this commentary on marriage aligns more generally with Leonard's concerns about John's wasted potential. Regarding John's work in the law office, Leonard "felt that John ~~too, had a career which he was sacrificing~~ too was sacrificing himself (Dunbar-Nelson n.d., 11). The objects and experiences of beauty that Leonard provides John are also insufficient; they do not fulfill his desires to act, to create beauty. In assessing John's potential, Leonard's views align with that of John's wife, who "realized ~~to the fulles~~t his conception of beauty and power of expression" (9). Like Leonard, she predicts that "there was something within which only needed some power to bring it out" (11). Thus situated, John enjoys some temporary though insufficient happiness with his wife, but the birth of his child, an "ugly little thing" whose life he imagines will resemble his own as much as his body does, presents his climactic crisis.

Upon viewing his child for the first time, John "shrank back with a cry of despair" (Dunbar-Nelson n.d., 12). He flees and takes solace rowing on the river, where he thinks through the causality he attaches to this reproduction of ugliness. He wonders:

> What would that ugly little thing amount to? Would it suffer as he had suffered? Would it quail before all the ugliness in life as he had quailed? Would it be inarticulate ~~a~~ and rage within itself because it was so? Would its life too, be a barren desert of unfulfilled hopes and desires? Would it go through its childhood ~~the world~~ the world unloved, derided, ʳᵒormented'ː (13)

John realizes that he has the power to "surround [the child] with care and love and ~~beautyiful~~ things. It should be shielded from pain and it should be ~~taught early~~ trained to express whatever was within it, and it should not suffer as he had done, ~~never~~" (13). Here he realizes his own potential, his power to create a life beyond the one he has inherited. He therefore aims to provide his child with a different boyhood than his own: "His son's [boyhood days] should not be like them. He should not go skulking home every evening, half ashamed of his home, the dingy Joy street rooms. His child should be proud—" (14). Reconciling himself to his new role as father, he determines to make his child's life different from his own. John recognizes that this requires a revised relationship to creativity and to reproduction, shifting the emphasis from begetting a like, genetic body to actively molding and shaping a character in relation.

The story's climax depicts John's realization of his own creative potential. His imaginings of himself shift from the persistent descriptions of ugliness to instead read his "inadequacy" as "sheer laziness" (Dunbar-Nelson n.d., 13). This revelation amounts to an agreement with Leonard's assessment that in his position as a janitor, he is "wasting [his] life." However, John assesses his occupation in terms of his child's pride and now imagines that the child requires his creativity:

> Of ᵂʰwhat good could his artistic sense of the beautiful be to the child anxious ᵗᵒ ᵖᵒⁱⁿᵗ ᵗᵒ for something his father had done? to point to? Why he must do something, achieve something, the boy must not be ashamed of him. Some flood-gate seemed suddenly to have opened within him, and words, thoughts, ideas, sentences were rushing out. It had come to him what he must do. The boy demanded it. His lips at that moment drawing sustenance from his mother's breast, bade him go out and create. And he would do it. (14–15)

At this point, Dunbar-Nelson's story turns on John's changed relationship to beauty and (re)production. Here beauty is specifically about the aesthetic experience of creation rather than about the possession of beautiful objects or even beautiful bodies.[9] Writing on nineteenth-century African American literature, Reid-Pharr (1999, 55) notes "concern with the profound ambivalence and uncertainty of family life in relation to individual desire—particularly as that desire was actualized in and through the market." However, John's desire cannot be "actualized in and through the market," for he wishes not only to consume but to produce the beauty he craves and wants his son to have. This story's complex rendering of John's relationship to beauty and its production here touches obliquely on the relationship between desire and consumption but eschews the market in favor of the creative act itself. Much as educators and writers such as Dunbar-Nelson promoted literature as a tool for uplift, John looks to creativity rather than wealth accumulation as a strategy for intergenerational pride.

What and how, exactly, John intends to create is a point that Dunbar-Nelson leaves unexplained and perhaps undecided in her corrected manuscript. John's various attempts at creative production to this point have failed. He wonders, "Of what good could his artistic sense of the beautiful be to the child anxious to point to something his father had done?"

(Dunbar-Nelson n.d., 14). Throughout the story we read that "~~he could nei-~~ ~~ther draw nor pain~~t. . . . He could do no better in music. . . . ~~he could not~~ ~~sing~~." When John tries to play the piano, "he fled from horror at the sound of his own discords" (6). It is perhaps most earnestly that he tries to write, both before meeting Harold Leonard and later, at his urging. In concluding her story, Dunbar-Nelson returns to this possibility of literary production: "Some flood-gate seemed suddenly to have opened within him, ~~and words,~~ ~~thoughts ideas, sentences were rushing out~~" (14). We readers do not know exactly what John will now create, but we are led to believe that it will be beautiful, even by his high standards. Beauty will come to be something he does, not something he is.

As John appreciates all in his life that is beautiful—the books he reads, the river, his mother, Leonard's music, his wife—he comes to recognize beauty in his child. When he returns to his wife and child, he recognizes something he had not considered before in his assessment of the child's re-semblance to himself. He comes to notice "something beautiful" about the child, which Dunbar-Nelson tentatively calls "~~the beauty of|freshness and~~ ~~innocence~~" (Dunbar-Nelson n.d., 14). But in these relations to the world or to people, he does not shift his view of his own ugliness. Employment and intellectual companionship, love and recognition do not move John to overcome his apparent ugliness. His wife does not cause him to reassess himself any more than his employer did. But his reoriented relationship to beauty renders such overcoming unnecessary. The story's conclusion is not a triumph of beauty but the reevaluation of a bodily relationship to the aesthetic, by which I mean that John does not find beauty to be fixed in his body but learns that it can be accessed via the creative act of reproduction. In this we might conclude that John shall not—and need not—become beautiful. Instead, he reevaluates his relationship to beauty as not as one of embodiment but in terms of (re)production and potential, in creation.

Ultimately, John is not a simple reflection of the father from whom he has apparently inherited his ugliness. And the child he produces will not follow his relations to ugliness and beauty. John's relationship to his child and his relationship to ugliness and beauty extend beyond genealogical inheritance, the aesthetic embodiment of resemblance between him, his father, and/or his child. Yet John never overcomes his outward ugliness, which seems fixed throughout the text. No characters, including his wife, find his appearance beautiful. The child he begets reproduces what John finds ugly in his own features and what his own father also found ugly.

John's relation to inherited ugliness concludes not only in his resolution to create beauty but also in the queer reproduction of his own self-creation.

The Queer Fatherhood of Self-Begetting

John's transformation comes only in fatherhood, only in relation to the son who begets him anew. It is ultimately his son—or rather John's imagining of his son's desires for his action—who urges him out of complacency and prompts him to view his abilities and his relation to beauty in a new light. The story ends with John's articulation of manhood, doubled in himself and his child. Now determined to create in order to make his son proud, he kneels at his wife's side and tells her "'He has made a man of me' . . . 'it is late, but I will make a man of him while he is yet a child'" (Dunbar-Nelson n.d., 15). In truth, Dunbar-Nelson's story does not go on to reveal the future of John's transformation. Readers do not witness how his changed relationship to bodily beauty and ugliness will affect his child. We do not know what he creates. At the story's close, this child has not yet become a man, although we understand that he has, even without knowing it, made his father into one. We are left in the wake of John's declaration and in the child's infancy. In this moment of temporal collapse we do not observe change but potential. In this potential, however—rather than in some product of creation—lies John's aesthetic revelation.

The doubling of child and father in the text occurs via John's occupation of both roles. Both the child and the man of the story's title are John himself, and both are also his child. In contrast to Wordsworth's speaker, John is fathered both by his child self and by his own child, who urges him into the version of creative manhood he recognizes. In this queer genealogy, which also includes Leonard, John's own father is displaced. Biological relatedness and aesthetic resemblance—essentialist markers of valuation—are rejected in favor of John's new focus on creativity as potential. In this doubling of fathers, John is not Hortense Spillers's (2003, 232) "twice fathered" child of biological father and enslaver who "could not be claimed by the one and would not be claimed by the other." Rather, his realization of creative potential leaves him unrestricted by notions of resemblance or claiming.

As we consider the genealogical trajectories of the story, it helps to consider John's simultaneous occupation of the position of child and father as an alternative to reading his progression from child to father. Throughout the story, John is always child, always bearing the burden of his paternal resemblance, in danger of replicating this relation to his own child but also of replicating his own father in his self-assessment. John's relation to himself repeats his father's assessment and rejection before the entrance of John's child into the story. Though patrilineal, this second paternal relation is not simply heteronormative. John does not amalgamate his parents' relations to him into a form of bi-gendered or androgynous parenting. His father's disappointment is that John "had inherited his looks from his father" (Dunbar-Nelson n.d., 3). John himself bypasses his mother's love even as he laments her loss. Here (in a move that departs from much of earlier African American literature's focus on mother relations), mothers and wives seem ancillary to the relations between fathers and sons. John's mother died "because she was tired out" (3), but the loss of his mother is not the main parental presence or loss that John feels. Despite his mother's importance in his life, John cannot approach himself from her position of beauty and care. Instead, he tends toward the detachment and repulsion of his other parent, both in relation to himself and in his initial reaction to his child.

Patriliny is so overdetermined in the story that John not only becomes a father to his own son but also reprises his own father's fathering of himself. John begets a child who looks much like himself and, hence, like his own father. But this act of heteronormative reproduction is not the crux of John's transformation. In some sense, we might understand John's caregiving and creation as having the potential to reach beyond the bounds of biological reproduction.[10] The child is not the end product of John's attempts at creation but prompts his own reevaluation. In this seeming circularity of reproduction, the child does not so much beget John as allow him to—in an ultimate act of reproductive circularity—beget himself. In his renewed understanding of his son's relationship to beauty he sees an opportunity for inheritance beyond the bodily, the normatively genealogical. Although he vows to provide his child with the world of beauty that he himself lacked, this impulse does not follow a linear trajectory but a recursive one instead. We leave the story not with what John provides his child but with what he has already provided himself: the knowledge that he has the ability to reproduce beauty.

John's journey toward self-creation is not incidentally patrilineal but a deliberate coupling—and refiguring—of masculine and aesthetic reproduction. As he awaits his child's birth, "the knowledge that there was someone weaker than he who looked to him for protection made him feel for the first time almost manly" (Dunbar-Nelson n.d., 12). Whereas begetting a child makes John "almost manly," he is "made a man" and will "make a man" of his child through artistic creation. In this child-father transformation, John defies the norms of white heteronormative masculinity into which he is not inscribed via not only familial relations but also his relation to beauty. It is not coincidental that John's fathering mirrors his artistic creation.

In this way, Dunbar-Nelson's story is connected to larger aesthetic questions and metaphors for queerly gendered reproduction in African American literary history. In *Manning the Race*, Marlon Ross (2004) discusses the practice of referring to Black men as midwives—rather than fathers—of the Harlem Renaissance. Ross attributes this to "the tendency to view aesthetics and artistic culture as feminine spheres of influence" (225). In "The Child Is Father to the Man," then, Dunbar-Nelson's focus on fathering reads as not simply patriarchal but as a regendering of aesthetic engagement. Ross explains that "to say that a black man *fathered* the Harlem Renaissance seems to give too much potency to the man's role in United States culture and to the status of the renaissance itself as a bastard child of American culture" (225). Reading Eugene C. Holmes's discussion of Alain Locke's influence on the younger generation of Black creators, Ross describes the "gender-bending status of midwife to the renaissance" as simultaneously "seminal" and one involved in the "birthing," "delivery," and "nursing" labor of not only aesthetic creation but of nurturing other future creators (265). This is the fatherly role that John must take, and freed of the temporal normativity of genealogical constraints, he has the capacity to perform this role for his own child and for himself.

The circularity of John's fathering allows him to father both self and child, and it also suggests a recursive trajectory of creation and an acknowledgment of Black potential. This latter set of interests appears in Dunbar-Nelson's nonfiction as well. In a reading of Dunbar-Nelson's essay "Negro Literature for Negro Pupils," for instance, Shawn Anthony Christian (2016, 273) explains that "Dunbar-Nelson envisioned African American literature as intimately tied to a celebration of the younger generation and its potential." We read the "man" to which Dunbar-Nelson's title gestures as this potential itself: John's child is an infant, his manhood existing only in his parents' projected future. We might then ask what constitutes such manhood that might be bequeathed by a parent rather than attained oneself and that paradoxically may be reached "while . . . yet a child"? Figured as potential, manhood is not inevitable. Like the adulthood of many Black, poor children, it is not guaranteed. The man to whom John is father lives in his own hopeful anticipation and in John's newfound belief that he will be able to create the requisite conditions of love and beauty for this future man's becoming.

In this new relationship to beauty, John is made anew. His desire for beauty is not a longing for that from which he is separated but a relation to that which can be self-realized. It is this relation to beauty, as much as the product of his artistic creation, that he passes on to his child. As we regard ugliness and beauty in terms of creativity and potential rather than as simply embodied, we can better understand the climactic shift that occurs in John's own self-begetting. Unlike his own father, John determines to fill his child's life with beauty. He no longer imagines himself to be bound by determiners of embodiment or inheritance but instead commits to creativity itself. His love for his child has caused him to reflect upon his own childhood and to relocate the inadequacies that have caused him pain outside of his own body. At the end of the story, then, John dwells on not ugliness but laziness. Although this negative association of working-class Black masculinity might prompt a necessary historicist critique, John's shifting his vision of his own faults from ugliness to laziness does productively relocate aesthetic valuation in action rather than embodiment and recognize ability rather than assume incapacity.

Ultimately, the story's conclusion leaves us not with a product of aesthetic creation but with a moment of creativity. At the story's close, we never learn what John ultimately decides to write. Even as we understand his creativity to lie in the words that suddenly pour forth in his imaginings, John's revelation lies not in some final, tangible product of beauty but only in potentiality. No longer a defeatist, he does not let his failed attempts at making art overshadow his newfound enthusiasm and confidence. We cannot say whether John will be successful in this new creative endeavor, but this is surely beside the point. He has been made anew; his relationship to beauty has been fundamentally changed. The closest thing to a tangible product of creation is the/a "Man" of the story's title and John's concluding words that he will "make a man" of his son. Here, "man" resonates beyond the bodily and suggests the abstract: the production and reproduction of masculinity itself. This abstraction also represents a temporal shift. John pronounces that he will make a man of his son "while he is still a child." The simultaneous existence of "man" and "child" in this declaration blurs distinctions between adult and child and collapses time. The child/man is hybridized, pure potentiality, dwelling simultaneously in the present moment and his future.

In this shortening of time, the beauty that John will create is projected into the future, not valued in the moment at which it is to be realized but in the actions by which it is continually made and remade. This remaking of masculinity removes the aesthetic signifier from its empty vessel and replaces it with the action and determination that John can control and perpetuate beyond the aesthetic product. Creativity allows him not only access to the beauty he will produce but also the tools with which he will come to relate to future generations. As Dunbar-Nelson's story imagines its protagonist in the midst of his own rebirth, she herself wrote in a moment of burgeoning renaissance. As early as 1901, in a book review for the Boston *Colored American Magazine*, William Stanley Braithwaite (1901, 73) observed that "to my mind our race should recognize that we are at the commencement of a 'Negroid' renaissance."[11] To truly consider Black creative production—and literary production, in particular—in terms of "rebirth," we might productively reassess periodizations of African American literature and the gendering of its history. Writers such as Dunbar-Nelson, Chesnutt, Hopkins, and Paul Laurence Dunbar become more comprehensible when read in relation to both earlier and later discourses of Black literary potential and aesthetic (re)production.

Notes

1   This unpublished, undated story can be read as a hand-corrected typescript in the Alice Dunbar-Nelson Papers in the University of Delaware Special Collections.

2   I am extremely grateful to Katherine Adams and Sandra Zagarell for sharing this story with me and for their helpful discussions of the story's place in Dunbar-Nelson's oeuvre. The story is also unsigned and unattributed, bearing neither Dunbar-Nelson's name nor that of any of her pseudonyms.

3   I refer to this character as Leonard throughout my discussion because this is how his name appears throughout Dunbar-Nelson's story. However, I bristle against the power relations reinforced by referring to him by last name and the protagonist by first name, and want therefore to register that difference here.

4   Page number citations from Alice Dunbar-Nelson's short story are from the undated typescript.

5   Early scholars of her work such as Akasha (Gloria) Hull (1987) were hesitant to read racial themes in her ambiguously racialized characters. Subsequent scholarship, including that of Hull, Elizabeth Ammons (1992), Kristina Brooks (1998), Pamela Glenn Menke (2002), and Elizabeth West (2009), has discussed

racial themes in her fiction, recognizing Dunbar-Nelson's subtle "winks" to readers who might recognize certain characters' racialization as Black. Other scholars such as Thomas Strychacz (2008) have noted the subtle racialization of many of Dunbar-Nelson's "creole" characters in particular.

6 The University of Delaware Library's copy of Dunbar-Nelson's story is an original hand-corrected typescript. The strikeouts and annotated insertions that I include when quoting the text are meant to render her story as close as possible to how it appears in this manuscript. I have chosen to represent these as they appear in order to give a closer approximation to the version of the text we have, complete with these hand revisions, rather than attempt to render them in standard English or closer to normative aesthetic standards for published prose or even to make them more legible or consistent. Dunbar-Nelson's notated running word counts and spacebar corrections have been omitted. The decision to render Dunbar-Nelson's corrections and strikeouts visible is consistent with the practices of the editors of Dunbar-Nelson's other recently recovered work. See Katherine Adams, Sandra A. Zagarell, and Caroline Gebhard's (2016) special issue, "Recovering Alice Dunbar-Nelson for the Twenty-First Century." My reading of Dunbar-Nelson's text freely considers both strikethroughs and insertions as relevant parts of her story available for analysis. This approach is similar to that of scholars who read Emily Dickinson's variant words as parts of a poem's identity. See, for example, Sharon Cameron (1992).

7 On the intersections of race and disability aestheticized as "ugly" and as intertwining with histories of eugenics and segregation, see Susan Schweik (2009, 15–17, 184–204).

8 On Chesnutt's discussions and depictions of mixed-race Black people, see, for example, Stephen P. Knadler (1996).

9 The slippage with which Black people were rendered marketable objects through the slave trade also resonates in Reid-Pharr's discussion.

10 Another productive discussion of fatherhood in Dunbar-Nelson's fiction might also consider this story alongside alternatives to biological fatherhood altogether. Such a discussion would productively take up alternative parenthoods via Rosalie Riegle Troester's (1984) discussion of "othermothers," in Black feminist recognition of women whose child caregiving does not always follow genealogies of childbearing.

11 On the history of referring to a "Black renaissance," see Ernest Julius Mitchell (2010).

DILARA ÇALIŞKAN

03 World Making

Family, Time, and Memory among Trans Mothers and Daughters in Istanbul

How we think of and conceptualize memory is tightly connected with how we understand and position kinship. At the same time, how we make sense of ourselves and our families is often associated with our individual and collective memories. The social, temporal, and material networks that affect how we identify ourselves, relate to family, and conceptualize our present moment with past and future are linked to and curated within often-unquestioned, state-regulated, and surveilled relationships between kinship and memory. These dynamics, where kinship and memory are lodged in and mediated by the everyday practices of social, material, and temporal norms, create a specific "we" that controls who we are, how we make sense of our life course, and whom we can relate to.

Drawing on the narratives of women with trans experiences who live in Istanbul and often live through the state of being pushed out of this "we" because of myriad reasons based on their gender and sexuality, I turn to kinship and memory to think more critically about queer forms of relatedness. I focus on the daily experiences of mutually formed mother and daughter relationships[1] to think about practices that go beyond the deeply entrenched assumptions in which relatedness is conceptualized within the lines of (non)biology and (il)legality of kinship, and chronologically overdetermined temporalities of memory and domesticity.

Through the everyday experience of trans mothers and daughters, I discuss *memory of kinship* and *kinship of memory* together to show their multidirectional and unfixed relationality. Inspired by trans-specific experiences of navigating within time, life history, and relatedness, I identify memory of kinship through spaces and moments of "remembering" family and its time that exceed the "proper" archives of domestic subjectivities. Then I locate kinship of memory in nonnormative forms of memory transmission that do not presume the social, temporal, and material structures of familial archives and remembrance. I suggest that trans narratives and life histories invite us to explore the potential of memory and its circulation across time and space to critically engage with queer ways of relating. I position queer kinship as a collage of intimacies that do not necessarily take the presentist interpersonal human contact for granted. By demonstrating the multisited relationality between kinship and memory through experiences of trans motherhoods and daughterhoods, I call attention to the forms of relatedness that are not only legally and biologically but also socially and temporally cis/heteronormative yet can still remain largely absent from the discussions on queer kinship.

First, I focus on memories of kinship through the concepts of home, care, and familial time in the narratives of trans mothers and daughters. Second, drawing on the notion of home and temporalities of being and relating, I turn to kinship of memories to explore family formations that can be created through shared memories of individual and collective trans narratives and experiences.

I discuss shifting relationships between kinship and memory as tactics of world making within the context of Turkey, where experiences that are positioned outside of normative notions of gender and sexuality are violently erased and ignored.

Trans Experiences and Womanhoods in Turkey

In Turkey, different forms of discrimination begin once trans women's gender identities become a matter of conversation within the families that they were born into. In addition, they are often denied education and housing, are fired from jobs, and experience transphobic and homophobic violence. Many trans women are often left with sex work as one of their only options for survival. Meanwhile, experiences of trans women who sustain themselves with jobs outside of sex work or continue their education in universities are labeled as "impossible" within the larger society, which clearly highlights the association between sex work and women with trans experiences.

As a natrans[2] woman who has been trying to make sense of her gender and sexuality, I have been an active member of several LGBTI+ organizations in Istanbul since 2008. It was 2008 or 2009 when I became aware of the trans mothers and daughters for the first time. At the time, our group was working on a report about the difficulties that women with trans experiences were going through in everyday life. We were often visiting houses where trans women would live and/or do sex work together. And it was during those visits that I met with trans mothers and daughters. They were introducing each other as mother or daughter and were talking about a whole genealogy of other mothers and daughters who have lived in particular houses. In the following years I learned that some friends with whom I have been doing activism were also connected to one another through mother-daughter relationships. At the time, my main aim was to explore the mundane forms of relatedness among trans mothers and daughters. What I observed then created the foundation of my current research. Between 2012 and 2020 I had conversations with thirty-four women who have had trans experiences and identify themselves as a mother and/or daughter of another trans woman (regardless of the duration of the relationship). I conducted semi-structured interviews and collected life narratives. I also had the chance to observe many interactions where certain forms of relating with family and kinship terminologies circulated among LGBTI+s. In addition, I archived key arguments or discussions that took place on social media regarding trans forms of motherhood and daughterhood.

Mother-daughter relationships center on sharing the knowledge and memories of trans womanhoods across time and space. This creates a form of relatedness that often help trans women navigate social and institutional forms of transphobic and homophobic violence and abuse. National law in Turkey has never criminalized trans identities, but as Aslı Zengin (2016) and Ezgi Taşcıoğlu (2015) show, trans women are routinely discriminated against in criminal and civil legal systems. According to ILGA-Europe's 2020 report on how the laws and policies of countries affect the lives of LGBTI+s, Turkey was ranked as the forty-eighth among forty-nine countries within Europe (regionally).

Because of to their gender identities and sexualities, many trans mothers and daughters I had conversations with since 2012 had lost their contact with or had a minimal communication with the families that they were born into. They had to leave their hometowns and move to Istanbul (or other big cities such as Izmir, Ankara, or Antalya), if they were not already living there, for new job opportunities and to start their gender-confirmation processes. The majority of trans mothers and daughters come from families and communities in which they have had to navigate the often difficult terrain of violence and neglect (Çalışkan 2019).

As Pelin, a trans daughter in her twenties, puts it, the mother-daughter relationship brings trans women together because "to be trans means that everything is forbidden. This is forbidden, that is forbidden. Don't do this, don't do that. So, your trans mother becomes a companion to you within this society. While you are exposed to exclusion, your mother embraces you and shows you the right way to do things" (Çalışkan 2019, 264).

Most of the trans women whom I had conversations with positioned the mother-daughter relationship as "necessary" to everyday life. This was especially the case for trans women who do sex work to sustain themselves. Purple, who is a trans daughter in her early thirties, thinks that the mother-daughter relationship is essential, especially for the "young trans girls" who are considered to be "inexperienced" in sex work or the social, political, and legal aspects of trans experiences. In addition, for Rojda, a trans mother in her early twenties, this relationship shows that trans women who are "isolated from society create their own communities through bringing experienced and inexperienced ones together" (Çalışkan 2019, 264).

For many mothers and daughters, this relationship provides social, economic, and legal forms of guidance on how to contend with the challenges that individuals who are situated outside of cis/heteronormativity regularly face. Within this context, the word *experience* is often used in relation to motherhood and daughterhood, and it is important to note that "being experienced" is not directly connected to one's chronological age.[3] Unlike the taken-for-granted temporal periodization of motherhood and daughterhood in the larger society, trans mothers and daughters do not build their relationship on the biologically, legally, and socially fixed association between aging and being a mother and daughter. Within the community of women with trans experiences, "being a mother" or "being older" are often used in relation to the experience of being a trans woman in Turkey and knowing how to contend with the social, legal, and economic difficulties of being a trans woman and/or a sex worker.

In this manner, being recognized, embraced, and able "to understand the right way to do things," as many of my interlocutors have put it, plays a central role within the everyday experience of mother-daughter relationships, regardless of the chronological age difference. These relationships create social and physical spaces for women with trans experiences through practices of family making and community making, which are often questioned but too often taken for granted.

Memories of Kinship

As many scholars who work on kinship and homemaking show, intimacy and kinship are often considered private, but the process of making and sharing something intimate is significantly public. Within the context of mother-daughter relationships, I want to think about how the mundane polarization of public and private spheres within the everyday experience of family affects the intersections of trans experiences, queerness, and kinship, particularly as they relate to the institutionalized archives of intimacy, care, and familial time.

Looking at the everyday experiences of trans mothers and daughters who might share the same houses in which to live and/or to do sex work recalls Marlon Bailey's groundbreaking work *Butch Queens Up in Pumps: Gender, Performance, and Ballroom Culture in Detroit* (2013) and unfixed formations of kinship and family practices. Although gender performance can be quite central in the examples of houses in Detroit and trans motherhoods and daughterhoods in Istanbul, the understandings of house and family ties differ between the two examples. Narratives of trans mothers and daughters reveal that even though mothers can have more than one daughter at the same time, daughters who share the same mother do not necessarily create affective relatedness through sisterhood. Additionally, experiences of mothers and daughters are not always associated with the practices of being a family and living together (e.g., family dinners or taking trips together).

Similar to Joëlle Bahloul's (1996, 28) account of the remembered house as "a small-scale cosmology" that carries "the importance of the spatial idiom and of the localization of activities in memories" (Carsten 2004, 34), trans mothers and trans daughters shed light on the multiplicities of home and queer possibilities of relatedness that play with the physical, social, legal, and temporal "facts" of kinship that are assumed to be essential interiors of many homes.

Unlike normative forms of family-making practices, trans motherhoods and daughterhoods are not associated with infinitude and unconditional care. There are many different motivations and conditions that shape these relationships. For some mothers and daughters, the relationship is about social and economic solidarity; for others, its purpose is solely about the gender-confirmation processes. For some, the relationship helps them ease the everyday difficulties of sex work; for some, it is a space where identities can be recognized as they are. And for others, trans motherhoods and daughterhoods can also turn into a space where the inexperienced ones (these are almost always the daughters regardless of their chronological age) are socially and/or financially exploited by their mothers. Within this context, what most of the mothers and daughters stressed to me was the disconnection of the almost automatic associations between the concepts of motherhood/daughterhood and care. For example, while warning me not to romanticize this relationship, Türkan, who experienced trans daughterhood for several years, said:

> There is no fixed example of mother and daughterhood. For instance, there are some mothers who really care about their daughters. They protect them, don't let them start sex work right away, they don't allow them to use any drugs, they show them how to sit and behave like a real woman. They guide them in terms of transition surgeries et cetera. There are also some mothers who don't care this much but still let their daughters get connected with the trans community. Or they protect their daughters when they do sex work. Most of the time in all examples, daughters provide financial return for all this care. They help with the rent or they give the half of their daily income from sex work. But there are also really bad ones that we call *domez*, those ones are the ones that nobody really cares about. Mostly mothers take them to use them for domestic stuff. They do the cleaning and cooking in the house, serve the mother and her husbands [referring to partners of the mother]. Mothers mostly deceive them by saying, "next month we will go to the epilation" or they say "we will go clothes shopping for you" et cetera. But mostly this domez doesn't know that, that month will never come. (Türkan, interview with author, 2020)

At the end of our long conversation, in which Türkan summarized all the mother-daughter relationships that she had seen in the past, she stopped and said, "But whatever the mothers or daughters do to each other, even in its most evil version, I think this relationship is something that saves many trans women. And in overall it shows that we [trans women] create this network where we make our own homes and families."

As Lauren Berlant (1998, 283) states, "A simple boundary can reverberate and make the world intelligible; taken for grantedness of spatial taxonomies like public and private makes this cluster of taxonomic associations into facts within ordinary subjectivity." Inspired by Berlant, I propose that domesticity and social and temporal codes of intimacy that are attached to mundane practices of home are productive spaces to talk about memories of kinship within trans motherhoods and daughterhoods. Drawing on this invented dichotomy between private and public, I now turn to memories of kinship that are shaped by material and temporal aspects of domesticity and that create kinship archives about being/becoming a family.

Materiality of Memories on Domesticity: Home

The idea of home requires others to be recognized as a specific kind of relationship while making itself easily recognizable by state-sponsored forms of intimacy. According to Rosemary George (1996), homes are not neutral places. Imagining a home and its daily routines is political. The stability and unity embedded in the home are tightly attached to preestablished frames of selfhood, gender, sexuality, kinship, and ideas of citizenship. Janet Carsten (2004, 49) argues that "one important lesson to be learned from the house, then, is the significance of seemingly random and trivial observations. . . . While what goes on in houses may appear all too familiar, there is no doubt of the important messages that these everyday activities convey."

These mundane activities that turn houses into homes carry memories and histories of kinship, and they archive normative ways of relatedness and taken-for-granted linkages between the notion of home and the reification of comfort and desire. The house is inhabited by memories where "remembrance is molded into the material, physical and temporal structures of the domestic space" (Bahloul 1996, 260): our everyday lives and practices are full of rituals that are stored in the houses that surround the ways in which we make sense of our existence.

In this manner, for Mary Douglas (1991), home turns into an institution that combines order and synchrony with simple divisions of labor. Douglas invites us to investigate the surveillance dynamics that define routines such as bedtime, chores, and seating plans for dinner. Similarly, Gaston Bachelard (1958, 45) positions his study on home as the "phenomenological study of the intimate values of inside space" and argues that the home has both unity and complexity because it is made out of memories and experiences.

When discussing her "longing" for the "boring and ordinary normal life," Gugu, a trans daughter in her early thirties, focuses on the multiple meanings of "home" as follows:

> I mean I don't even know now what does home mean. Because in normal life, people have their school and then work, and their home is often the place where they have their family. I want that "boring and ordinary normal life," but I can't go back to my family home. Now, I live with my [trans] mother because I couldn't really make it on my own, and we are living together. But then a lot of people that we don't even know come to our house to fuck. Then they leave. We have other customers that my mother knows for many years, for example, when they come it is different. Because then it is a bit like we have guests, but when you have people that you don't know in your house or your bedroom then it's a bit weird. It can also be dangerous of course. . . . For me home is not really a home, but our work is in the home. Is this what they call a home office? [*laughter*] (Gugu, interview with author, 2020)

Gugu's narrative shows how trans mothers and daughters unsettle the naturalized divisions between labor: private/public or familiar/stranger. In this example we see how dwelling is a dense web of affective practices and relations among people, spaces, and things that turns the notion of home into an archive of feelings and emotional and temporal investments. Gugu's words explore the potential to unsettle and play with mundane terms and practices of kinship and their assumed memories when normative formulations of home and kinship position women with trans experiences as "undomesticatable."

Distinct binaries between private/public and familiar/stranger become palpable in Gugu's narrative when she talks about her experience of sex work. Here, looking at the narrative of Ipek (Gugu's mother) helps us understand how trans mothers and daughters unsettle the memories of sociality that are embedded in kinship practices. Though displacing and relocating highly gendered and sexualized dichotomous positionalities of private/public and appropriate/inappropriate, Ipek shows how trans mothers and daughters rescript the archives of cultural norms that are assumed to be transferred from mothers to their daughters in the larger context of Turkey:

Ipek: If you think in detail things get really weird and funny. Let me clarify. So, I am a mother, right? I mean I have people around me who call me "mother." I have a dick. So, this is the first point. Then I have daughters. Some of them also have a dick. Then sometimes we live together. I teach them what to do, how to behave, et cetera, like a real mother, right? They slowly learn how to look and behave like a real woman.

Dilara: How for example?

Ipek: I mean, for example, if you want to be a woman, you can't sit in a café and open your legs side to side. You have to use your hands carefully, more elegantly like this [*shows a feminine hand gesture by touching her face and putting her head to her side*]. My girl can't look like a random dude with a synthetic cheap wig. Anyway. Now, think about a scene where a mother with a dick [is] teaching her daughter, who also has a dick, how to get fucked by a man who also has a dick. Then you see *zero morality* [*laughter*]. The most important part is to teach how to fuck. So, it is *a bit* different than the mothers we know. Right? (Ipek, interview with author, 2019)

Trans motherhoods and daughterhoods turn their relationships and different forms of domesticities into places where presumed interconnectedness among womanhood, femininity, and motherhood/daughterhood are collectively revisited while creating terrains of belonging and recognition. Even though the homemaking practices of mothers and daughters cannot be generalized, the narratives show the role of this relationship in reconnecting with memories of kinship that push trans women away because of their gender identities and sexualities. While creating new home and kinship practices that are not solely based on the ideas of unconditional care and social, material, and temporal norms around gender and sexuality, engaging with the individual and cultural memories of performing gender and kinship through home turns domesticity into a curious site of attachments that redraw the links between household and family.

Temporality of Memories on Domesticity: Familial Time

As Bahloul (1996) shows, the daily practices of home that shed light on the links between domestic space and family time are not based on remembered events that are simply experienced by family members or the domestic community. Particular conceptualizations of memory draw the boundaries of the family and domesticity by shaping the rhythm of everyday life and the chronological lineup of family members. Parallel to the materiality of memories of domesticity discussed above, temporalities of being, being at home, and being a family ensure the division between public/private and familiar/stranger through synchronized practices that are embedded in "family life."

As scholars such as Kathryn Bond Stockton (2009) and Valerie Rohy (2017) reveal, we are continuously and constantly connected to time. From the moment we are born, we are expected to relate to preestablished chronological repertoires that surround our lives. Elizabeth Freeman (2010, 3) uses the term *chrononormativity* to refer to a state-sponsored mode of implantation and techniques "by which institutional forces come to seem like somatic facts. Schedules, calendars, time zones, and even wristwatches inculcate hidden rhythms, forms of experience that seem natural to those whom they privilege."

Within this context, the temporal sequences of a day and of one's life span are tightly connected with the question of how the mundane activities of home become routinized. These activities are also linked to gender and sexuality, which highlights that conceptualizations of home and family are not only socially and physically but also temporally constructed. Following Mark Rifkin (2017, 2), I position time "less as a container that holds events than as potentially divergent processes of becoming" to focus on how trans mothers and daughters creatively challenge not only temporality but also temporal memories of selfhood, kinship, and home.

For instance, through their personal memories, trans mothers and daughters negotiate the seemingly commonsensical conceptualizations of home within the quotidian rhythm of their households. Most of the mothers and daughters show the close relationship between trans identities and myriad experiences of "being out of sync with the ordinary" (Dinshaw 2012, 130) engagements with time. Additionally, many mothers and daughters mention the specific role of trans identity on their understanding of age and aging. Most of them provoke the temporal archives of kinship by challenging the normative notions of life span while connecting the notion of aging to social, political, legal, financial, and medical experiences of being a trans woman in Turkey.

When it comes to everyday rhythms of sex work, trans mothers and daughters demonstrate nonnormative forms of relating to the temporal choreography of the everyday that often organize families and their relationship with/in the public space through myriad mechanisms of temporal surveillance. Sex work challenges the temporal archives of domesticity when the private sphere of home becomes open to the "unknown" public, especially at night. In this manner the almost automatic association between sex work and night also creates different ways of dwelling in time. This experience not only challenges the dichotomous positioning of "private-public" that is attached to the ideal conceptualization of home and family but also the production-oriented temporality of the everyday that is categorized and "documented by the nation-state through 'coherent' linear narratives of sexed, classed, gendered and racialized embodiment" (Lau 2016, 166).

Most of the mothers and daughters that I talked with do not necessarily share the assumed temporal registers of cis/heteronormative time. For example, Pelin calls her temporal experience "trans time" (trans zaman) and explains it as follows:

> **Pelin:** I think it is about the identity first, then sometimes it is about sex work. It is very simple. Whatever we do most of the people understand that we are not normal. Sometimes they get it from our Adam's apple, sometimes from our hands, sometimes from our height, and sometimes from our voice. Then there are two options, or they make it super obvious or they make sure that you know that they know, and you start feeling weird. In either option you start feeling awkward about being in the public space during the day. I mean when it is light outside. Now I don't care, and I just do whatever I want but I spent almost seven years where I almost didn't see the sunlight.

> **Dilara:** What is the part about sex work?

> **Pelin:** So, because of all this. You can't be an ordinary, invisible person. Which means you can't find a normal job easily. Then you start doing sex work. When do you do sex work? At night. So, then all fits together you see? I often go to bed in the early morning, wake up in the afternoon and have my breakfast around 5 or 6 pm. (Pelin, interview with author, 2019)

During our conversation in 2018, Purple, a trans daughter in her late twenties, revealed the interaction between trans experience and the temporal categories that are at the center of normative and linear kinship systems: "For me growing up is about learning where to be and to know what you can do or where you can go as a trans woman" (Çalışkan 2019, 266). In another context, Yıldız, a trans mother in her early thirties, referred to her gender confirmation as a process of "being born" and "giving birth" that can take place in the same body at the same time. In some cases, trans daughters also identified themselves as "children" of their trans mothers. For example, Rojda, a trans daughter in her late twenties, defined herself as "eleven months old," stating that "to be honest, I am new. But I have learned a lot. I'm eleven months old but it is very important who your mother is. I can say that I have learned a lot in such a short period of time" (Çalışkan 2019, 267).

Trans mothers and daughters encourage us to think critically about relationships among kinship, time, and memory. They articulate new forms of social, temporal, physical, medical, economic, and legal ways of being, becoming, and relating while engaging with memories of kinship through multifarious memories of home and familial/familiar time. They curiously flirt with the inextricability of femininity, domesticity, and mothering/ daughtering. Trans mothers and daughters remind us that memories of kinship are ongoing processes that are never done or settled. They help us answer Anne-Marie Fortier's (2003, 408) question regarding "how memories of home can relocate queerness within the home without reinstating home as an originary moment."

Trans mothers and daughters reconfigure the centrality of domesticity while constantly redefining the connections between kinship and its social, temporal, and material archives. They critically engage with the intersections of temporality, archives of kinship, gender relations, class, and sexuality. In order to continue with positioning memory as a key point for the discussions on queer kinship, in the next section I move from *memory of kinship* to *kinship of memory*.

By shifting our perspective in this way, I explore the active and multidirectional relationship between kinship and memory that allows us to go beyond the understanding that presupposes the social and temporal linearity of kinship in order to talk about memory and its transmission across generations. As Jian Neo Chen and micha cárdenas (2019, 473) state, "If we imagine transness to be not about a crossing from one location to another but about a multidirectional movement in an open field of possibility, then time and its direction become more fluid." Trans narratives encourage us to be more attentive to "bodily, spatial, and temporal regimes that regulate which and how, trans people will be included in the state's vision of society and nation" (476). Following Chen and cárdenas, and trans mothers and daughters who do not necessarily make sense of being and relating through confessional, continual, and coherent organization of selfhood and life span, we see that trans and queer practices of embodiment and kinmaking can move beyond what can be captured by the regimes of the nation-state.

In order to continue discussing multidirectional relationalities between memory and kinship, in the next section I conceptualize memory as a space where familial intimacies can be formed. By tracing curious circulations of memories between trans mothers and daughters, I propose to exceed the socially and temporally presumed links between kinship and memory.

The Kinship of Memory

In their introduction to "Queer Bonds," Joshua J. Weiner and Damon Young (2011, 231) state that "queer bonds might designate shifting encounters in the borderlands of phobic interpellation, the ephemeral being together of those who find, against the backdrop of a phobic world, themselves and each other in a temporary zone where togetherness seems, for the moment, not *only* scripted by hegemonic forms of power, or *determined* by the resistance to that power. Our queer bonds are not merely a bulwark of resistance, via determinate negation, of the normative socio-symbolic order." In a very similar vein, Melike, a trans mother in her early forties, talks about the mother-daughter relationship and different experiences of being part of a "we":

> How you understand your past, present and future is about your identity. For example, I am Kurdish. Everything that I learned about our culture, our history and present is all about my identity. I make sense of today with that lens that I have. It is the same in terms of my trans identity. As a community we have been going through a lot of stuff. Our past for example is full of very political events that basically wanted to erase all of us. In that sense you get all this information in the moment when you say, "I am a trans woman." For me it was also the time when I started to live with my trans mother. We basically built our relationship on the history of trans women in Istanbul. (Melike, interview with author, 2018)

Weiner and Young's comments on the sociality of queer bonds and Melike's words on formation of the "we" explore the endless possibilities of interrupting the ongoingness of kinship through queer intimacies of inheritance. Instead of assuming the already established connection between memory transmission and kinship, I follow speculative circulations of memories of trans lives and narratives that unapologetically question the normative recipes of intergenerational transmission of memory. In the example of trans motherhoods and daughterhoods, memory turns into spaces where women with trans experiences "build" relationships through exploring trans-specific forms of relating with the past, present, and future that allow them to experiment with the normative scripts of kinship and family.

Trans History in Istanbul: 1980–2000

September 12, 1980, is still considered as one of the biggest mnemonic scars in Turkey's past. While crushing the leftist movements in multiple ways, the military junta reshaped the political landscape and fostered a market economy and a new public role for Islam. Even though the civil regime was restored in 1983, what happened between 1977 and 1983 systematically targeted and traumatized many groups that were defined as "national threats." As Lorenzo D'Orsi (2019, 648) states, the "processes of marginalization can be traced to all minority groups that conflict with the nation's dominant ethno-religious imaginary."

Trans women were (and still are) considered as a "danger" to the ideal image of the Turkish citizen. The most holy and central site of the nation, which is the "moral values of the Turkish family," was among the targets of these "national threats" that trans women supposedly posed. Most trans women who have been through these years often call the period between the end of 1970s and the beginning of 1980s a "nightmare." Belgin Çelik (2012) talks about her memories of this era in an LGBTI+ oral history project called *80'lerde Lubunya Olmak*, published by the Black Pink Triangle Izmir Association:

> It was not only the right or the left who went through hell. They were not the only ones who were tortured in the cells by soldiers, they were not the only ones who were beaten up, it was not only their honor that was offended during those times. We, trans women, also got our part. And nobody even talks about it or writes about it. We were actually the ones that went through the most brutal tortures because they [soldiers] knew that nobody was going to look for us. The left hated us, the right hated us, we were psychos in

their eyes, we were suspicious, we were risky. So, we are actually the ones that lived through that nightmare in the most brutal sense.

Similar to Belgin Çelik, scholars such as Pınar Selek also talk about the "suspicion" that was attached to the identities of trans women in the martial-law period that started in 1980. During this time the state had the right to take anyone who was found to be "suspicious" into custody. According to the narratives of those who experienced these events, this law was openly used to target trans women. For example, Bülent Ersoy, "who was the first, and for a long time only, case of public figure of publicly transitioning in Turkey" (Savcı 2018, 66), was banned from performing on stage for several years after the 1980 military coup. Following this restriction, many trans women who were sustaining themselves by performing in taverns (*pavyon*), especially in Istanbul and Ankara, were strictly banned as well. The ones who continued to perform despite the ban were taken under custody and suffered the destructive experience of torture. Even though martial law ended in 1983, the everyday experience of state-sponsored homophobic and transphobic violence continued for many years. In 1993, "the era of non-martial torture," as Ipek calls it, started for trans women who were living in Beyoğlu/Istanbul. Systemic police violence and brutal interventions against the communities of trans women who were living in this neighborhood, where the majority of trans women still live today, drastically changed their everyday life. Between the years of 1993 and 1996, Süleyman Ulusoy, the chief of the Police Department in Beyoğlu, also known as Süleyman the Hose, which comes from his specific harassment (with water hoses of different colors and shapes), openly targeted the communities of trans women who did sex work.

Pelin was in her early twenties when she was taken into custody and met with Süleyman the Hose:

> The pressure was enormous. When he [Süleyman] became the chief of the police department, our lives turned into hell. They would keep us in the cell the whole night without telling us the reason. Just before we left the police station in the morning, they were taking us to his room one by one. There were water hoses in different colors and sizes. He was making us choose one of them. He was hitting us with the hose that we chose. (Çalışkan 2019, 269)

Even though communities of trans women have not experienced the same intensity of state violence since 1997, the violence has been continuing through harassment by law enforcement and state discourse in many different ways. For instance, as I write these words in February 2021, Turkey's president openly targeted LGBTI+s by equalizing their very existence with deviance, terrorism, and national threat. As activists Eylem Çağdaş, Şevval Kılıç and Sevda Yılmaz show in their 2021 account of a series of events that focus on memories of LGBTI+s—organized by an LGBTI+ community house called Boysan's House (*Boysan'ın Evi*)—since the 1980s and 1990s we have been experiencing different ways of engaging and navigating with the cis/heteronormative regimes that try to criminalize, regulate, and control LGBTI+ narratives, bodies, and lives in Turkey. Within this context, as we lend our ears to trans-specific memories of the 1980s and 1990s while thinking about today's politics that target LGBTI+ lives, we see myriad forms of relatedness that go beyond the fixed practices of belonging, inheriting, remembering, and communicating.

Here it is important to stress the importance of the moments where collective and individual memories come together within the mother-daughter relationship. For many, like Selin, individual and bodily experiences of trans identities and collective experiences of transphobic violence would come together in the narratives of trans women who were never there to experience these events. Selin, a trans daughter in her early twenties, articulates this as follows:

> Now nothing is really like the 1980s or 1990s. For example, in the '80s soldiers were torturing them [women with trans experiences] and making it impossible for them to make any money. Or when it was 1990s, Süleyman the Hose and his team were apparently locking them in their houses and putting their house on fire so that they would all die at once. And you know what? In the middle of all this, my mother's right cheek started to sag below her chin. Apparently, it happened over a night. And why? Because during those times trans women were going to doctors that were not really different from butchers. At the time my mother had no idea this person that she went for facial feminization, actually injected baby oil on her cheeks. (Selin, interview with author, 2017)

As Selin reveals, the memories and histories of police brutality, the medical experience of gender confirmation, and sex work in the 1980s and 1990s become repertoires of remembering where mother-daughter relationships emerge.

"I Have Never Been There, but I Know!"

This is a sentence that I have been hearing from trans women every time we talk about their daily interactions with the police officers. Often, trans women refer to moments in history that they were never part of but that they carry with them as part of their identities. In "Queer Postmemory" (2019), I argue that trans mothers and daughters reveal how playing with the relationships of family, time, and memory can turn into strategies and tactics of survival and resistance. Inspired by the groundbreaking work of Marianne Hirsch on postmemory (2008), I proposed the term *queer postmemory* to discuss trans forms of temporal and social transgression that go beyond the "family memory . . . that is constituted through ongoing social interaction and communication between children, parents, and grandparents" (Erll 2011, 306).

Drawing on the work of scholars such as Marianne Hirsch (2008, 2012) and Astrid Erll (2011), I ask: can memories bring people together and form kinship relations? With this question I stress the need to go beyond the understandings of memory transmission that are often discussed within cis/heteronormative conceptualizations of family that presume social and temporal norms of kinship in order to talk about intergenerational memories.

"I have never been there, but I know," says Gamze, a daughter in her early twenties, while we talk about the differences between her and her mother's "generations." She explains:

Gamze: We met with my mother very coincidentally. I wasn't looking for a mother and later on I learned that she wasn't looking for a daughter either. Actually, we were friends but with time we started to spend a lot of time and things changed. I remember for example, during the time when we just met, she used to tell me what to do and what to avoid in relation to my [gender-confirmation] process. With time I started to do sex work and it was then that I learned a lot about her life.

Dilara: What was particular about that time that made you learn more about her life?

Gamze: Even though our age difference is not big at all, I think our generation and her generation are really different. Even though she hasn't really gone through the times of 1980s or 1990s, she was so scared about everything. She is right to feel like that. I mean if I would go to doctors [as part of the gender-confirmation processes] that were not much different than butchers or if I would live in a place where the majority of my friends would be addicted to crack or if I would be in a place where I couldn't go out as a trans woman, I would be the same. Because of these fears of hers, we were fighting a lot in the beginning because she would control everything I do. . . . But it is these fights and all the stuff that she has told me from her times brought us together. (Gamze, interview with author, 2017)

As Gamze shows, for some the process of motherhood and daughterhood develops out of friendship-like relationships. Similarly, Çiçek, a mother in her early thirties, focuses on the relationship between the circulation of individual memories and her experience with her "last trans daughter":

Çiçek: I wasn't interested in this mother-daughter thing at all. Actually, I was even thinking about it as something that is really old.

Dilara: How old for example?

Çiçek: I don't know but maybe something from the time of Hortum Süleyman [which would be the period between 1993 and 1997]. There are also some mothers that under the name of "motherhood" they exploit the new girls and I really didn't want to be associated with this type of people. But I met with Yeşim in a bar that I went to with my friends. Then we kept running into each other and started talking. Then we became really close and started to know our pasts. Without even noticing one day I realized that she was calling me "mother." (Çiçek, interview with author, 2018)

As we can see in Çiçek's narrative, there is no socially and temporally assumed understanding of motherhood that makes sense in relation to specific legal and/or medical moments such as "birth" or "adoption." Instead, as Gamze and Çiçek reveal, the process of "becoming" a mother or daughter is articulated in relation to the circulation of individual and/or collective memories between both parties and positioned as something that can happen "without noticing." Here, improvisational social and temporal rhythms of memory create potentials for different ways of being in the world with flexible and creative ways of relating to one another.

As Ruth Pearce (2018, 67) states, "Queer discontinuities within a trans lifecourse may disrupt normative assumptions about the relative accumulation of knowledge and experience amongst chronologically older and younger individuals." Trans mothers and daughters invite us to rethink "relatedness" and "queerness" and explore "a different sense of what kinship might be" (Freeman 2007, 298) when we move beyond the already established archives of "lifetime kin" that live in the times and spaces of the state, society, and nation.

The multidirectional interactive exchange between *memory of kinship* and *kinship of memory* brings trans mothers and daughters together in different ways. Trans mothers and daughters disrupt the logics of materiality and linearity that prescribe how we identify ourselves and our families, and how we define the connections between private and public life. They challenge the impulse to redeem the past through already established connections between kinship and memory.

Conclusion

What roles do discussions around queer kinship have in common when it comes to practices of self, memory, and community making/kinmaking? Do we need more critical tactics or imaginaries to make sense of the complexity of intimacies and relatedness? In the context of trans motherhoods and daughterhoods, the unpredictable and curious relationships between kinship and memory allow trans women to withstand the social, political, legal, and economic marginalization and exclusion with which they are confronted. The interaction between *memory of kinship* and *kinship of memory* shows us the importance of finding meaning through individual and communal forms of being, becoming, and belonging. This interaction takes new turns within the already established itineraries of familial intimacy and the ways in which we make sense of time and inheritance of memories. Trans mothers and daughters reveal that forming and reforming kinship is not something that we can do at once. Rather, they convincingly demonstrate how different processes of making kin are unfixed collections that challenge the normative stories of kinship and memory.

As Martin Manalansan (2019) argues, queer is fluid, and its fluidity is not about smooth transitions but how situations are messily immersed in the ideological "naturalness" of normativity. The example of trans mothers and daughters enhances the scope of discussions on queer kinship by opening spaces where trans-specific forms of relatedness do not necessarily occur because of their distance from the normative codes of gender identity and sexuality. Rather, they convincingly explore different positions of memory as a new mode of relating to oneself and one another across time and space.

Kadji Amin (2014) investigates trans subjectivities and temporalities to raise voices against politics that distort the experiences of many trans or gender-variant people. According to Amin, "An attentiveness to nonchronological, nonprogressivist temporalities of gender variance across the registers of experience, history, and geography could prove critical to contesting a normative organization of temporality and identity" (221). As we see in the narratives and experiences of trans mothers and daughters, this attentiveness could also help us reveal critical ways of engaging with normative organizations of memory and kinship.

Trans temporal/spatial ways of understanding self, gender/sexuality, family, and the everydayness of the life course open spaces for memory transmissions that are not explained or automatically made legible through invisibilized regimes of cis/heteronormativity. Lives and memories of trans mothers and daughters that cannot be read "through a simplified narrative of individuality, severed from the complication of ephemeral and contingent community" (Lau 2016, 165), reveal that forming shared lifeworlds do not necessarily promise coherency, attachment, or assumed familial care.

Trans mothers and daughters do not necessarily create new terms, but they constantly fashion alternative meanings to motherhood and daughterhood, and move the understanding of kinship from "is" to "might be." They reimagine the cis/heteronormative domains of home and family, where individuals are expected to position themselves and their memories within the chronological frame of generations. As they experiment with the norms, practices, and memories of kinship and family, trans mothers and daughters explore different forms of care and resistance. Trans mothers and daughters challenge the seemingly consistent and linear memories of domesticity and kinship, and they suggest new possibilities for memory transmission while positioning memory itself as a possibility of kinmaking/family making. Trans configurations of motherhoods and daughterhoods offer unpredictable forms of dwelling within individual and collective pasts, presents, and futures.

Through the bridges they construct between social lives across different times, trans motherhoods and daughterhoods reveal the multiplicity of and intimacies between worlds that are located or choose to stay outside of life-course expectations and assumptions. Trans mothers and daughters in Turkey show creative ways of winking at endless variations of playing with the limits of narratives, lives, and bodies that are tirelessly characterized within classed, sexed, gendered, racialized, and ableist regulations of possibility and impossibility.

Notes

My deep gratitude goes first and foremost to all trans mothers and daughters who shared their thoughts, memories, frustrations, and criticisms with a great patience. I am deeply thankful to Elizabeth Freeman and Tyler Bradway for their guidance, patience, and support. I would also like to express my appreciation to Ayşe Gül Altınay, Stef Craps, Jenny L. Davis, Jessica R. Greenberg, Marianne Hirsch, Brett A. Kaplan, Martin F. Manalansan, Michael Rothberg, and Alisa Solomon for their insightful comments in the earlier versions of my work on queer (post)memories. I am thankful to Armanc Yıldız for all the encouragement and to Izem Aral for her wonderful feedback. Last, I would like to thank the reviewers for their thoughtful remarks.

My fieldwork between 2019 and 2021 was supported by the Wenner-Gren Foundation and the Social Science Research Council.

1 Here I would like to clarify that my aim in focusing on trans motherhoods and daughterhoods is not to presume a form of relatedness that can be applied to all LGBTI+s in Turkey. It is very important to keep in mind that queer forms of relatedness are multiple, disparate, and not necessarily commensurable experiences of motherhood/daughterhood and kinmaking exist.
2 Here, instead of *cis* I intentionally use *natrans*, which is a term employed by LGBTI+s in Turkey to refer to individuals who do not have trans experiences.
3 For another example that critically discusses the relationship between chronological age and queer forms of kinmaking, see Marlon Bailey (2013).

Part II Kinship, State, Empire

JOSEPH M. PIERCE (CHEROKEE NATION)

---

04 In Good Relations

Native Adoption, Kinstillations, and the Grounding of Memory

Let us begin with a story: a beloved old woman is sick, and the only medicine that can save her is tobacco. At this time, the humans and the more-than-humans can still speak the same language, so they hold a council, and together they decide that four-legged creatures will be sent to retrieve the medicine from the Geese who had taken it south. But all these attempts end in failure, in death. Even the Mole, whose plan to sneak below ground is discovered by the Geese, is killed. Another council is called in light of this tragedy, and the tiny Hummingbird volunteers to retrieve the medicine and save the beloved old woman. The rest of the creatures are not sure that Hummingbird can accomplish this task, but they are desperate and agree to let him try. In the blink of an eye he is gone and returns with a sprig of tobacco and its seeds in his beak. The woman is saved by this medicine, and this is how the Cherokee received the gift of tobacco.[1]

This story describes creating and maintaining bonds that extend beyond the human. As with other stories in the Cherokee tradition, collaboration is central to improving the lives of all. Through speaking a common language and joining in council, the humans and more-than-humans share the responsibilities of healing, and they share in the medicines that Hummingbird brings back. It is not through human enterprise, cleverness, or determination that the old woman is saved. This is not a story about individual achievement. Rather, it reveals how a sense of interconnected, mutual belonging is at the heart of Cherokee understandings of kinship, of being in good relations.

Through our stories we understand that we are connected to all things that have been and all things that will be. We recognize and are recognized by others as part of an emergent relationality through which the bonds of accountability and reciprocity are not restricted to the imposed epistemic arrangements of the colonial order. Cherokee scholar Daniel Heath Justice (2018, 84) describes the quality of being a good relative as working "to counter these exploitative forces [of colonialism] and the stories that legitimize them, while at the same time affirming—or reaffirming—better, more generative, more generous ways to uphold our obligations and our commitments to our diverse and varied kin." In addition to Justice, scholars and activists aligned with Indigenous feminisms see their task as aiming "to free Native people from extending the power relations required by colonial regimes—which include heteropatriarchy—and to frame gender and sexuality as central to work for sovereignty and decolonization" (Driskill et al. 2011, 9). These proposals situate the urgent demands for decolonial praxis as returning to (and sustaining) our being in good relations, which necessarily requires the rejection of heterosexism, patriarchal dominance, capitalism, and anthrocentrism. In the Cherokee tradition, to be in good relations means honoring the ancestors and the future generations by making ethical decisions in the present regarding human and more-than-human kin. Like many Indigenous communities, we draw on the wisdom of the past seven generations and think about the next seven generations when making decisions. By cultivating and harnessing the shared wisdom of kin we create sustainable, mutually reinforcing relations. Or, as I would like to propose here, we create kinstillations.

The term *kinstillation* joins constellation and kin. But this neologism is not an attempt to describe a new or previously misunderstood phenomenon. Instead, it is an effort to foreground ancestral knowledge in the present. In this, I am thinking along with Cree scholar Karyn Recollet (2018, 51), who coined the word *kinstillations*, and I am arguing that resurgence, reconnection, and survivance can be enacted through kinstillatory imaginings, celestial resistance that is nevertheless grounded in Indigenous epistemologies and centered on the land as a site of perpetual memory making. Kinstillations enact our ancestral knowledge, of the stars, of our own stories of creation and of survival, in an ongoing, reflexive relationality that is nonhierarchical and ephemeral (as in everyday, quotidian). It is an ongoing act, a praxis of Indigenous refusal to acquiesce to colonial normativities (specifically, the ontological and the epistemological) in favor of land-based understandings of reciprocity. Land holds memory, even when humans forget. Land holds bodies and medicine and spirits, even when humans no longer see them. Even when colonizers destroy them, too.

Recollet (2018, 51) develops this term in a poem titled "Kinstillatory Gathering," which begins with the following lines: "Kinstillatory gathering spaces, wishful thinking through dimmed light, making meaning out of the shadows because sometimes shadow-glyphs are all that we have left as our means for time travel." This is a placing, a landing of knowledge that at the same time points to a mode of ancestral fugitivity. Here, relationality is not bound by the limits of reason or proportion—and especially not by the anthropological marking of kin on charts, genealogies, or family trees—but expands the scale of possibilities through which Indigenous communities make meaning of and through the body. This meaning making shifts from the arborescent to the constellational (the web, the network), and from the rational to the embodied. Gathering in kinstillation makes possible the resonating of bodies in relation, the reverberating, kinetic sharing of space, through which we begin to recall how to travel through time, how to speak to the shadows, how to negotiate our beings-with and beings-in-relation as a form of ongoing enactment of Indigenous sovereignty, mutuality, and care.

I hasten to add: this is not a metaphor.[2] The land is not "fictive" or "chosen" kin. Our bodies are not symbolically made of stars. We are those cosmic elements, and in recognizing ourselves as cosmologically interrelated, as connecting cross-temporally as part of an emergent and ongoing epistemological project, we maintain the bonds of reciprocity and collaboration that are at the heart of our stories.

Recollet situates this grounded/celestial knowledge as a method of time travel. This is also not a metaphor. When we look at the stars, we witness the past. Kinstillatory praxis is thus a form of transtemporality that links stories of emergence with ancestral histories and future-oriented possibilities.[3] These ways of knowing do not track onto normative timescapes but rather are always situated in iterative becoming. In other words, kinstillations invoke an ancestral futurity that is grounded in our ways of relating to the human and the more-than-human across time, space, and feeling.[4] Kinstillations are a means of living in the balance of rupture and creation. They mark us as poised across normative thresholds of intelligibility.

In a subsequent intervention, Recollet ties her own fascination with the stars to the work of Cree poet Billy-Ray Belcourt and a conversation with

Cree musician Buffy Sainte-Marie. As Recollet describes it, she and Sainte-Marie were discussing the "60s scoop" (as the theft and forced adoption of Indigenous children is known in Canada) and their shared love of stars when Sainte-Marie suggested that Recollet was drawn to the sky because it is fundamentally a space of ruptures. For Recollet, herself an adoptee, the connection between the stars and adoption is clear: "The initial rupture [was] not being able to be raised by my Cree mother" (UofT AstroTours 2017). The work of repair is about coming to terms with that loss, which is both personal and spiritual, as Recollet continues: "I've had to create a narrative to fall in love with that rupture. For me, my relationship with Indigenous knowledge is celestial because of the possibilities of falling in love with our ruptured selves" (UofT AstroTours 2017). The cosmos is a place of rupture that provides a map (a method) for living in good relations, in spite of distance. In spite of breach. In spite of the time that we will never have back, yet to which we still dream of returning. Finally, in a collaborative work written with Yup'ik dance maker Emily Johnson, Recollet and Johnson (2019, 18) reflect on the choreographies and technologies of kinmaking that orient us toward land-body-sky: "Kinstillatory describes a relational practice of being grounded when you are not of this place, and considers the possibilities of rooting/routing toward the sky. This concept also refers to falling in love with rupture to mimic the practices of supernovas exploding to expel mass/consciousness, thus providing the framework to jump scale through extending the potentials for multi-variant grounding practices."[5] Kinstillatory praxis is thus a method of negotiating the ruptures of time and space as they are felt in the body. These ruptures exceed the central tools of settler colonialism: displacement, erasure, and removal. The concept is about movement, choreography, and multiple bodies in cosmic motion. In this way kinstillations are not simply stories we tell but rather enactments of decolonial love and repair that are deeply rooted in our own bodies, epistemologies, and cosmologies.

In this chapter I am suggesting that kinstillatory practices disrupt colonial temporalities, epistemologies, and kinship models by refusing to adhere to settler demands for legibility within normative frames of recognition. I am trying to shine light on ways in which Indigenous peoples are already doing this reparative work, and ways to read back into the historical archive forms of relating based on our own understandings of being in good relations. I draw on work by queer kinship scholars and queer-of-color feminism, but this essay proposes to ground (as a verb) kinship as an ongoing method of decolonial praxis that is not limited to the psychological or the anthropological but rather lands (again, as a verb) relationality as past-present-future embodiment.

This chapter engages with a particularly fraught vector of the settler colonial regime of erasure: the removal and/or adoption of Indigenous children by white families in the United States. Boarding schools and adoption have long been used by settler states to displace Native children. As a historical and political technique of severing kinship ties and cultural memory, adoption is not an event, to paraphrase Patrick Wolfe (2006), but a destructuring of the possibilities of being in good relations. These techniques of settler displacement are deemed successful when adoptees incorporate themselves into white society. Yet as the stories and ceremonies of many Indigenous communities demonstrate, there is always a way to return and to be in good relations again.

To ground this essay, then, I give a brief history of the politics of removal and adoption of Indigenous children in the United States. I then propose an Indigenous being-in-good-relations as the basis of a reparative kinstillatory praxis and discuss a few examples of what kinstillations could look like in spite of ongoing settler colonial dispossession. These are neither abstractions nor conjectures. I have a personal stake in these debates because my father was adopted out of the Cherokee community as a newborn. I am a generation removed from the event of adoption, but I still feel its lingering effects in the present, its colonial rupture. The insistent feeling of loss and of detachment, the inability to say who our family or ancestors were, the unresolved sense of displacement and loss, were all part of my formative years. Eventually we went through the process of opening my father's sealed adoption records, reconnecting with his "biological" family, our Cherokee family, becoming citizens of the Cherokee Nation, and now continuing to build and repair kinship with them and with other relatives, ancestral, human, and more-than-human.[6] I am not describing adoption and its effects in the abstract but as part of my own lived experience, even if I was not the one adopted out. In doing so I am theorizing from my own body and from the memories it bears.

Allotment, Boarding Schools, and Adoption

Over the course of the late nineteenth and early twentieth centuries, allotment, boarding schools, and adoption emerged as three intertwined technologies of settler colonial domination. In the wake of the mid-century Indian wars, politicians and reform organizations saw these new methods of assimilation as both morally superior and less expensive than genocide.[7] It was a low bar. Although these technologies were seen by reformers as a more humane way of civilizing Indians, the end result remained the same: diminished Indigenous rights and autonomy, undermined Indigenous sovereignty.

The impetus to shift from war to assimilation came primarily from white elites who sympathized with the "plight" of the Indian and lobbied for the elimination of communally held land as the only way to fully integrate Indians into US society and thus save them from oblivion (Stremlau 2011, 71–75). According to these "friends of the Indian," the central problem that needed to be overcome was the refusal of tribes to embrace private property and patriarchal authority, thus capitalist accumulation. Rose Stremlau (2011, 75) puts this succinctly: "Reformers identified Indian families as the root of the 'Indian problem.'" The kinship practices that sustained Indigenous communities had to be eradicated in order for white normativity ("civilization") to become not just possible but inevitable. Philanthropists and politicians alike viewed kinstillations—family networks, clan membership, and other nonnuclear family arrangements—as impediments to capitalist production, assimilation, and modernity. The operative phrase during this era, "kill the Indian, save the man," is reflective not simply of the patronizing efforts of reformers but also of their shift in focus from the battlefield to the classroom.[8]

Broadly speaking, allotment aimed to replace communitarianism with individualism, savagery with civilization, kinstillations with nuclear families. The General Allotment Act, also known as the Dawes Act, was signed into law in 1887 and forced private land ownership (allotments) onto Native communities while simultaneously creating "surplus" land for sale to white settlers. Although the Dawes Act did not originally apply to the so-called Five Civilized Tribes (Cherokee, Chickasaw, Choctaw, Muscogee [Creek], and Seminole), it was amended to do so by the 1898 Curtis Act, which authorized the federal government to unilaterally dissolve tribal jurisdictions in Indian Territory and impose US legal frameworks on citizens of Indigenous nations. Along with the 1906 Burke Act, which expedited the allotment of remaining land based on blood quantum, these legislative impositions usurped Cherokee sovereignty; overlaid the language of race onto local understandings of culture, reciprocity, and belonging; and paved the way for Oklahoma statehood in 1907.

In this way allotment was a racializing regime led by federal bureaucrats who controlled how land was distributed, to whom, and under what conditions. Indian agents, as they were called, stipulated that those with higher quantum of Indian blood (i.e., "full bloods") were less capable of properly developing allotment land, which was thus held in trust for twenty-five years before returning to a male head of household with fee-simple title. Blood quantum restricted who could own property and what protections and opportunities were granted to new landowners.[9] This form of ownership was fundamentally at odds with traditional Cherokee understandings of both land tenancy and custodianship in a historically matrilocal society with matrilineal inheritance practices.[10] Granting fee-simple title was also tied to US citizenship, situating patriarchal property ownership as a precondition to civic participation under settler colonialism. Allotment made the legal dispossession of land possible by replacing kinship with the market, relations with transactions, collective land tenure with fee-simple title. Through coercive deals or outright fraud, Indian land was drastically reduced, families were dispersed and forced to relocate, and kinship bonds with human and more-than-human relatives were deliberately and insistently broken. Of the original 7 million acres held in Indian Territory before allotment, individual Cherokee citizens retained only 146,598 acres in 1971 (Stremlau 2011, 5).[11]

Like allotment, the schooling of Native children extended the same impetus toward the elimination of Indigenous peoples. Central to this operation was the idea that only by removing Indian children from their "savage" cultures, and thus limiting contact with their families and extended kin networks, could the work of "civilization" be successful. Education reformers argued that earlier models such as the on-reservation day school and boarding school were limited in efficacy because they did not have the ability to completely sever students' connection to their tribal communities (Adams 1995, 28–49). Removal from community was crucial. Thus, the off-reservation boarding school became the most important manifestation of the logics and politics of education for the assimilation of Indigenous peoples in the early twentieth century. The architect of this education system was Richard Henry Pratt, a former Indian fighter in the Plains Indian Wars. In 1875 he oversaw the transfer of seventy-two prisoners of war from Indian Territory to Fort Marion, Florida, where he honed his ideas of civilizing Indians through military-style discipline, Christianization, and economic individualization. At Fort Marion, Pratt cut the prisoner/students' hair, outfitted them with military uniforms, taught them to speak and read English, and taught them to eventually discipline themselves. The federal government viewed Pratt's work at Fort Marion as a successful experiment in civilizing Indians, and in 1879 Pratt was granted funding to open the Carlisle Indian School in Pennsylvania, where he expanded on his experience at Fort Marion. Carlisle became the prototype for the militarized boarding school for Indigenous children and was exported as a model across the United States.

While at Carlisle, Indigenous children were subjected to corporal punishment, isolation, and sexual abuse. In fact, according to Sarah Deer (2015, 70), boarding schools were "synonymous with sexual abuse and sexual exploitation on a mass scale." Some of those children returned to their communities and used what they had learned to help their tribes resist federal encroachment. Others returned traumatized and enraged. Still others did not survive the forced assimilation, the cold, the corporal punishment. There are thousands of Indigenous children buried at boarding schools. Their remains have yet to be returned.

For those who did survive, off-reservation boarding schools offered vocational training for students that was aligned with settler views of gendered propriety. Young Indian men were taught to become manual laborers on farms owned by white settlers; Indian women were taught to become "employees of white women or the boarding schools that trained them" (Lomawaima 1994, 81). This provided an additional justification for the expansion of boarding schools: not only did they provide jobs for white settlers to build the required infrastructure and later to train young Indians, but in disciplining these youths in normative gender roles and providing them vocational training, these schools also produced domestic laborers for growing economies in western states.

In addition to fundamentally altering Indigenous children's relationships with community and kin, boarding schools were also leveraged as part of the broader colonial agenda by converting youths into bargaining chips in the ongoing process of Native dispossession. As Lakota historian Nick Estes (2019) shows, children from the Oceti Sakowin (Great Sioux Nation) were specifically targeted for off-reservation education. At the behest of Commissioner of Indian Affairs Ezra Hayt, Pratt personally recruited eighty-six Lakota students, sixty-six from Rosebud Agency and twenty from Pine Ridge Agency, to form Carlisle's first class. In a chilling letter to Pratt in 1879, Hayt explained that Lakota should be sent to Carlisle "because the children would be hostages for the good behavior of their people" (cited in Estes 2019). As Estes argues, Lakota children were essentially held captive in order to pressure their tribes west of the Mississippi River to cede land to the federal government. Indian children were sent not only to learn

English or to become good workers in a settler economy, but also to force compliance to settler demands for ever more land.[12]

The theft of land and the theft of children are one and the same. Breaking up communal land holdings and breaking up communities by stealing children form part of the same multifaceted assault on Indigenous futures. This is why boarding schools, allotment, and adoption need to be seen as mutually reinforcing colonial technologies. Although they may at times have operated in distinct locations and with varying degrees of intensity for Indigenous communities, they all had (and still have) the same goal: to reduce the ability of Indigenous peoples to exist as such. According to Laura Briggs (2012, 92), "The boarding school system did explicitly what the disproportionate rates of foster care and adoption did implicitly: participate in the larger policy of termination, of the systematic extinction of tribes, communal lifeways, and communal landholding." Indeed, rather than understanding the boarding school system as a form of education, we might better comprehend it as a deracinating technology, one that aimed to substitute diverse Indigenous kinstillations with a mode of intrahuman familial belonging that was binary-gendered, heteronormative, marital-reproductive, and privatized. Its primary goal was to extinguish the knowledge and lifeways of Indigenous communities that were based on reciprocal engagement with human and more-than-human relatives.

From its beginning in 1879, the boarding school system grew, reaching its peak in the 1920s. By 1900, there were 153 such off-reservation boarding schools housing more than 17,000 students (Adams 1995, 58). As K. Tsianina Lomawaima (1994, 6) documents, "In 1931, 29 percent of Indian children in school were in boarding schools." But boarding schools became less popular after World War II, and adoption surged as the preferred method for indoctrinating Indigenous children. Again, this was about cost. The Bureau of Indian Affairs devised the Indian Adoption Project in 1958, which would privatize the adoption process and in doing so reduce federal investment in placing and caring for Native children in foster care (Jacobs 2014, 5–8). Politicians, social workers, and news outlets alike saw the nuclear family model as the only conceivable form of kinship within which a child could be raised and even proposed that Native children were losing out on the opportunity for such a (white) family life because of existing hurdles to adoption. For white Americans, Native kinstillations were not illegible. On the contrary, nonnuclear family life was hypervisible if misunderstood and was seen, precisely, as the main hindrance to successful assimilation.

Although the adoption of Indigenous children by white families became more widely accepted after World War II, the practice of removing Indigenous children from their communities and placing them in white homes has been carried out since the colonial period as a method of "education" and "civilization." In her historical study of the adoption of Indigenous children in the antebellum US South, Dawn Peterson (2017, 32) argues that "adoption became a means to address the logistical, economic, and philosophical problems generated by continental expansion." Adoption, like the off-reservation boarding school, was never simply about caring for children but was more often used as a form of political exchange, as a way to negotiate with Indigenous communities for land cessions or to eliminate the need for land holdings by reeducating Indigenous children to live as white people. This was a biopolitical program of assimilation based on white supremacist ideologies that sought a "softer" form of territorial dispossession. This benevolent logic proposed that if Indians could be educated in patriarchal domesticity and cash-crop farming, then they would no longer "need" the vast territories that they occupied in the late eighteenth century. This sense of care, of benevolent patronage, has consistently followed schooling and adoption. Even today, white families claim to have the ability to make Indigenous lives better through their supposed moral and material superiority, as was argued in the most public example of Indian child theft in recent memory: *Adoptive Couple v. Baby Girl*, better known as the Baby Veronica case.[13]

It is worth stating definitively that American Indian children have been removed from their kin and communities at rates that far exceed those of other cultural or ethnic groups in the United States. In 1976 the Association of American Indian Affairs (AAIA) estimated that between 25 and 35 percent of all Native American children in the United States had been separated from their families (Jacobs 2014, xxvi). A third of a generation, stolen. The passage of the Indian Child Welfare Act (ICWA) in 1978 was meant to stem this hemorrhaging of Indigenous children from their communities. And it did for a while. But ICWA has faced legal challenges ever since it was passed.[14] The fight for Native children is ongoing. Those opposed to ICWA usually argue that the law is based on race rather than predicated on the sovereignty of Indigenous nations as political bodies. Right-wing think tanks such as the Goldwater Institute have been challenging the law in local, state, and federal courts for years.[15] The central argument they have put forth is that the law discriminates based on race and that considering Native communities as a race therefore makes the law unconstitutional.

Indeed, the ramifications of this argument, were it to be upheld by the US Supreme Court, would have drastic effects on all of Indian law. The basis of tribal sovereignty is at stake in these ongoing legal battles. On the one hand, Indigenous peoples become a "race" only when convenient for the dispossession of children and land. On the other, arguing that Indigenous children are being discriminated against precisely because there are now legal protections in place to keep them in their communities represents a continuation of the long history of imagining that white families are inherently "better" than nonwhite families.

The work of historians such as Margaret D. Jacobs (2014), Dawn Peterson (2017), and Rose Stremlau (2011) has been invaluable not simply as a resource for understanding how adoption became a pervasive technique of settler colonial displacement but also as evidence of the agency of adoptees in disrupting settler colonialism by returning to their communities. These historiographical accounts rescue our relatives from oblivion. But these histories generally focus on the role that adoption plays within a single generation—that is, regarding the experience of adoption for the adoptee—but not subsequent generations. I want to expand on this work by analyzing adoption as a technique of dispossession that is like and that reinforces other forms of dispossession: of land, culture, language, and ultimately life. I turn to texts that illuminate the intergenerational effects of adoption as a technology of settler colonial erasure, on the one hand, and on the other as a form of resistance to the normative kinship structures that are often demanded by settler states in order for someone to return to an Indigenous community once having been adopted out. This double bind is crucial to understanding how settler colonial discourses around race, gender, and kinship are wielded by institutions ostensibly aimed at "protecting" Indigenous families. These institutions demand a form of legibility possible only by performing normative kinship at the expense of being in good relations with human and more-than-human kin. Thus, the juncture of land-based pedagogies, queer forms of attachment, and contemporary Indigenous feminisms teaches us how to imagine community resurgence and revitalization as practices embedded within expansive Indigenous conceptualizations of kinship, as kinstillations.

There has been little theoretical work about the long-term effects of the adoption of Indigenous children out of Indigenous communities.[16] In contrast, there is a wealth of important, nuanced writing on transnational and transracial adoption regarding Korean children adopted by white American families. In particular, David L. Eng and Shinhee Han's (2019) development of "racial melancholia" is provocative for how it draws on Kleinian object relations but also insists on the racial dimensions of psychoanalytic study of identification, disidentification, and disavowal by transracial adoptees. But I hesitate to begin an account of the psychic and affective dimensions of Indigenous adoption from the perspective of psychoanalysis. This is because the objects through which the psyche is structured, according to psychoanalysis, are not objects for most Indigenous peoples. Object relations simply do not apply where the epistemological basis of relationality is not channeled through the identification of a subjective-objective difference but rather through a mutually constitutive and always contextual imbrication of the material and the immaterial.

For example, the foundational work of Ihanktowan (Yankton Sioux) writer, activist, and musician Zitkala-Ša (1876–1938) provides guidance about how to sense relationality in daily life. Zitkala-Ša was sent to a Quaker boarding school as a child and taught briefly at Carlisle as an adult. Dismayed by what she saw there, she would become a staunch and eloquent critic of its pulverizing mission.[17] In her 1902 essay "Why I Am a Pagan," Zitkala-Ša describes a moment of meditation along the Missouri River, in the Yankton Sioux homeland, in which the grass, the flowers, the water that passes "are living symbols of omnipotent thought" (802). Her relationships with these symbols, which are not exactly symbols in the Western sense but material enactments of Creation, demonstrate the "subtle knowledge of the native folk which enabled them to recognize a kinship to any and all parts of this vast universe" (802). This kinship is multiscalar and transtemporal. It positions her ongoing responsibilities to more-than-human relatives as part of a sacred exchange that unfolds, emergent, enmeshed in a vast social network that existed long before her and that will endure long after she is gone. Zitkala-Ša's self-identification as pagan in this text responds to the settler denigration of Indigenous kinstillatory practices. The mode of address—defiantly asserting the self-in-relation—turns the settler demand for objectification on its head: "I prefer to their dogma my excursions into the natural gardens where the voice of the Great Spirit is heard in the twittering of birds, the rippling of mighty waters, and the sweet breathing of flowers. If this is Paganism, then at present, at least, I am a Pagan" (803).

A contemporary example is the work of Potowatomi writer and botanist Robin Wall Kimmerer, who details the lessons that our plant relatives offer as gifts. Kimmerer's *Braiding Sweetgrass* (2013) is a beautiful and poignant memoir that threads together philosophy, botany, ethics, and politics. In a chapter titled "The Honorable Harvest," Kimmerer (2013, 190) picks up where Zitkala-Ša left off: "One of our responsibilities as human people is to find ways to enter into reciprocity with the more-than-human world. We can do it through gratitude, through ceremony, through land stewardship, science, art, and in everyday acts of practical reverence." Reciprocity is at the heart of our kinstillatory praxis. To enter into reciprocity with the plants and the animals, with the spirits and the ancestors, in what Zitkala-Ša called "paganism," is, in Kimmerer's reflection, part of an ethical, honorable life that defies objectification. Kimmerer's telling of the story of the strawberry continues this reflection on reciprocal exchange. The Potawatomi call the strawberry "ode min" (the heart berry) because it grew from the heart of Skywoman's daughter, who tragically died giving birth to her twins, Flint and Sapling (Kimmerer 2013, 23). Strawberries are one of many natural gifts that sustain the reciprocal exchange upon which Potawatomi epistemologies and ethical imperatives are based. Strawberry enacts a gift economy rather than a model of property: "Gifts from the earth or from each other establish a particular relationship, an obligation of sorts to give, to receive, and to reciprocate" (25). *Braiding Sweetgrass* is full of these lessons. It narrates how, across Turtle Island, Indigenous forms of relationality are based on reciprocity rather than ownership, respect rather than objectification. I want to underscore that the subject-object difference that is crucial to Western philosophical thought, a difference that was imposed most clearly and most violently over the "ownership" of land, fails to account for the ongoing, emergent forms of relationality that are central to Potawatomi philosophy, like that of many other Indigenous peoples. Kimmerer puts this succinctly: "In Western thinking, private land is understood to be a 'bundle of rights,' whereas in a gift economy property has a 'bundle of responsibilities' attached" (28). The crucial point here is that in thinking with Indigenous forms of kinmaking we need not repeat the same objectifying logics that sustain Western thought in its drive toward taxonomical divisions, pathologization, and anthrocentrism. Indigenous kinship is not object oriented but rather constellatory, irreducible to the normativity of objectification.

But objectifying Indigenous kinstillations is the fundamental basis of settler colonialism. The process by which ancestral, more-than-human, and telluric relations are converted into objects and commodities is the point of departure for the colonial mandate of estrangement from kin that has been the abiding principle through which settlers appropriate Indigenous land. Thus, the core psychic maneuver that is required in order for settler colonialism to function is the replacement of Indigenous kinship systems by Western ontologies that are based on subject-object difference. This difference incites good/bad object relations. It makes possible the racialization of Indigenous peoples, for it lays the groundwork for the conversion of kinship into estrangement. It may be that adoption creates the conditions for bad object relations to overwhelm the subjects of adoption. Let us recall that boarding schools made settler ontologies the only channels for survival for Indigenous children. Settler ontologies preconceive Native erasure. But I want to propose something different, something grounded in our stories and memories. For Indigenous adoptees and those affected by the structures of adoption, I would like to imagine repair as moving from experiencing (bad) object relations to being in good relations. This approach can provide a more comprehensive way of connecting to our own traditions.

These contradictions are eloquently developed in Cherokee novelist Brandon Hobson's (2018) *Where the Dead Sit Talking*.[18] Set in Oklahoma in the late 1980s, the novel is narrated by the auspiciously named Sequoyah, who has been in and out of foster care for most of his adolescence. His mother is serving a jail sentence, and early in the novel Sequoyah is taken to the home of Agnes and Harold Troutt for a temporary foster placement. Although Sequoyah's adoption is not permanent, the novel draws a complex portrait of this young, conflicted character, who is seemingly unable to relate to anyone around him except for Rosemary, another Indigenous foster placement in the Troutts' home. Rosemary is Kiowa, and Sequoyah is Cherokee, and both are products of the alienation, the melancholy, of lost Indigenous kinship. In this novel adoption incites a series of incomplete approximations of bodies who never quite touch, never quite heal.[19]

The novel is spare, even chilly at times. It dwells on the psychological interest that Sequoyah takes in Rosemary, who is two years older, and on his gendered, sexual, and affective ambivalences. The feeling of adoption is everywhere, pervasive, yet never explicit in the novel. It lurks like the unresolved relationship between Rosemary and Sequoyah, who nevertheless bond over being Native. In their Indigeneity they find something like kinship; they find themselves interconnected: "As the only Indians around, we shared a culture and blood unknown to the others. We were like branches intertwined from the same tree, the same root, reaching out toward the sky to the unknown" (Hobson 2018, 69). The similes link the upper and lower worlds significant to Cherokees and other Indigenous peoples: earth and sky. Their story is both grounded and celestial in this way. They are imbricated, yearning for something else, something cosmic. Something like rupture.

Their closeness is not about solidarity. Rather, Sequoyah yearns to be Rosemary, to smell like her and to look like her. He admits that "I could almost feel what it was like to be a part of her, inside her, not stifled in my own world, not confused but certain of purpose, sitting there entranced. Maybe in a weird way I wanted to be her" (Hobson 2018, 85). The proximity between them is conjured by and through adoption, as is the affective resonance—molecular, spiritual—between their bodies that want to become one and yet cannot. They are like one another, mutually attracted by their shared pain, but are unable to dissolve into each other. Here we witness two Native children thrust into an institution, adoption, that is meant not only to domesticate them but also, precisely by doing so, to tether them to settler normativity—with its gendering, sexualizing, and racializing demands. The result is a desire for mutuality, for imbrication, that nevertheless escapes them. In their shared history with institutionalization and adoption, they are proximate, but not the same. Later in the novel Sequoyah again admits: "I wanted to grow my hair longer to be like hers. In a strange way we could pretend to be each other, though I would never mention such a thing" (187). His searching for connection leads Sequoyah to attach himself to Rosemary. She knows this and allows it, but is herself always yearning for something, somewhere, someone else, to be in the presence of someone who is like her. But hers is a frustrated search that ends in suicide. Perhaps there is no one else like her. Perhaps she yearns to exist as the absence that seems her destiny as a Native child.

In this, Pratt's "kill the Indian to save the man" again proves useful: we must constantly resurrect the murdered Indian in us as a method of decolonial resistance. To kill the Indian is the central mandate of both the boarding school and adoption. For those of us affected by the ongoing, intergenerational reverberations of that death, which is our own, it is in the presencing of absence, the doing, the enactment of self-resuscitation-in-community, that we find a way forward.

I have written elsewhere about the difficulties of narrating this return to community, which calls for a form of *becoming Native* that seems at odds with the bureaucratic demand for recognition based on filiation or cultural authenticity.[20] This is what the adoptee constitutively lacks, yet it is often required of them in order to belong to the community upon return. Faced with this double bind, I described myself as "a ghost performer of Cherokeeness. My body, out of (genealogical) time. My relationship with kin, spectral" (Pierce 2017, 64). This is the contradiction for Indigenous adoptees: in order to return to community, we must be revived, we must inhabit the unresolved, spectral place of our own not-quite-dead but nevertheless unmournable selves.

This way forward is often, as described above, a cyclical and iterative re-vivification of our own Indigeneity in the face of settler demands for death. Even when in proximity, Sequoyah and Rosemary are never quite able to reconcile their ongoing spectrality. While at school one day, Sequoyah fantasizes about hurting himself in front of the class, hurting himself to demonstrate his there-ness, his presence that is denied: "*Look, look look*, I would say. *Look: I punctured my skin with my ink pen. Look: I stabbed myself with a knife*" (Hobson 2018, 119). His body seems material, visible, only in its wounding. Sequoyah concludes: "I thought of my body as a disfigurement, with putrid flesh, the skin underneath my shirt stretched and molded into a deformation" (119). Or the body materializes only as an expression of its decomposition. This literary expression allows us to think through the affective and psychological dimensions of narrating return to community while at the same time providing a glimpse into the trauma that lingers, embedding itself into the bodies of those removed from kin.

One way of reading Hobson's Sequoyah and his inability to attach himself to Rosemary would be to see him as suffering from a psychological lack, a form of melancholia. This reading might see Rosemary as what Eng and Han (2019, 92) call, drawing on D. W. Winnicott, a "racial transitional object." This would mean viewing Rosemary as a maternal—and also racialized—figure and as such an object in which Sequoyah can project his melancholic loss. He knows that he has lost something, but he does not necessarily know what. He feels this something is important—constitutive, but he cannot bear the thought of what it means to exist alone, as separated from his mother. In this scenario, Rosemary—the only other Native person in his life—becomes imprinted with the trauma of abandonment and turned into an object of envy.

However, regarding Indigenous adoption it is not clear how the psychic structures through which kinship comes to matter within the context of settler colonial regimes of erasure distort the narrative, and especially the cosmological, bases of kinship lived as being in good relations. Thus, a second way of reading the relationship between Sequoyah and Rosemary, a way that is more aligned with the constitutive role of kinstillations in Cherokee understandings of belonging, would see Sequoyah not as cut off from mother as an object but rather separated from the practice, the embedded reciprocity, of motherhood. It would be to see his closeness with Rosemary as a desire to rebuild kinship, perhaps to mother her and be mothered by her in return. The stakes of this relationship are high. In a very real way for Cherokees, to lack a mother is to be cut off from clan membership and thus from belonging to the community. In a historically matrilineal society, to lack a mother is to lack Cherokeeness. It is not necessarily lacking the mother as a psychic object that matters but rather the lack of someone who takes on the role of mothering. It is this relation, not this object, that links Cherokees to the broader kinstillation of communal belonging.

In Tsalagi (Cherokee) the word for "my mother" is more accurately rendered in English as "the one who mothers me"—DꙞɦ (agitsi).[21] This act of mothering does not necessarily adhere to gendered or sexual norms (on the surface at least) and can be expansive enough to queerly engage with mothering across generational and historical time. In other words, mothering is not necessarily object oriented but rather depends on those whose needs are met and who reciprocate in the continual act of mothering and being mothered.[22] Instead of the subject/possessive-oriented verb forms common in English (e.g., "my mother"), Tsalagi often uses action/relation-oriented "noun-verbs" (e.g., DꙞɦ). In addition, as a polysynthetic language Tsalagi does not use gendered pronouns but relational pronouns and prefixes that do not distinguish sex. The Cherokee language embeds within it the possibility that all kinship is essentially relational rather than object oriented. Among these action-based relations, we see DꙞVꙆ / agidoda ("my dad"), GVꙆ / tsadoda ("your dad"), DꙞꟼꞜ / agilisi ("my grandmother"), GꟼꞜ / tsalisi ("your grandmother"), and so on. Rather than possession, there is a reciprocity of action in these terms. The use of "noun-verbs" such as DꙞɦ, rather than subject/possessive-oriented forms of English ("my mother"), opens up possibilities for relating outside of heteropatriarchal norms. In Tsalagi, gender and kinship are action oriented, not object oriented as they are in English. Agitsi is a role, a praxis, rather than an essential state of being. This reciprocal relationship—this kinstillatory enactment of Cherokeeness—is what Sequoyah lacks in Hobson's novel.

The question is not so much what terms we have at our disposal to describe the relationships that constitute "kinship," for the reciprocal action of intimate relationships that is essential to the enactment of kinstillations is already built into Cherokee language. The language itself and the relationships that it names are always already kinstillatory. And the action-oriented reciprocity of kinstillations provides a window on what decolonial relations could look and feel like. Our language and our stories tell us this, are this. The primary forms of attachment, in short, are not made up of hereditary (or biological) schemas but traces of mutuality that are enacted by our practicing good relations. Native epistemologies most often see kinship as relational, not necessarily as "familial." The family is a Western colonial concept that depends on the division of labor, binary gender/sex roles, and patriarchal authority. Family is colonial. Relations are Indigenous.

Kinstillatory Praxis

Michi Saagig Nishnaabeg writer Leanne Betasamosake Simpson (2017) describes relational knowledge as part of the ongoing project of radical resurgence for many Native communities. In concert with Glen Sean Coulthard, Simpson argues that settler colonialism must be understood not only as the dispossession of land but rather as an *"expansive dispossession,"* which means the "gendered removal of our bodies and minds from our nation and place-based grounded normativities" (Simpson 2017, 43). This type of multifaceted dispossession is clear to me because it is part of my family's history. It is part of the histories of so many Indigenous families.

As a Cherokee person, I relate to the dispossession of kin through the memory of the Trail Where They Cried (the Trail of Tears). I also relate to dispossession of land through the process of allotment, whereby my kin were granted individual parcels, which they subsequently lost because of a massive infrastructure project in Oklahoma that dammed the Canadian River to create Lake Eufala. Our allotment land was flooded, and we had to relocate. Loss upon loss of land, of kinship. ᎠᎩᎵᏏ (my grandmother) was also dispossessed of her language when she was forced to speak English in schools. She was forced to forget how to speak Cherokee. She was dispossessed of my father when she had to give him up for adoption. My father was thus dispossessed of his language and also his culture by that adoption. And he was dispossessed of his kin, human and more-than-human, of ceremony, of medicines and spirituality. That dispossession expands, reverberates through generations, because it is not simply land that we lost—because we do not think of it as "land" in the settler sense—but our relationship with the land, which is our kin.[23]

For those many thousands of us affected by the boarding-school system and the forced adoption of Indigenous children by white families, the issue of return to community is predicated on restoring connections to kin. It depends on learning how to unlearn the settler colonial ideas that we were taught in schools and in white families. In many cases it depends on unlearning whiteness itself. One way to do this, as I have been suggesting, is by creating or reconnecting to the kinstillations that place us within our own Indigenous communities. Building kinstillations is how I understand what Simpson (2017, 44) calls radical resurgence: "nonhierarchical relationships between land and bodies, bodies meaning the recognition of our physicality as political orders, and our intellectual practices, emotions, spirituality, and hubs of networked relationships." Refusing the hierarchical, nonreciprocal relationships that settler colonialism forces upon us is part of the radical project of resisting expansive dispossession. Reconnecting to land and to the networks, the kinstillations, that sustain us as Indigenous peoples and that link us to our spiritual and ancestral communities is the hard work we must constantly perform.

I think this, too, is survivance. As Gerald Vizenor (1999, vii) writes, survivance is "an active sense of presence, the continuance of native stories, not a mere reaction, or a survivable name." Our stories are the presencing, the enactment of, our stories. This is only tautological in the Western sense of a linear narrative or temporality. The stories that constitute the repertoire of our survivance are not simply signs but glyphs and shadows left behind that are also not merely shadows, but other bodies, bodies in formation, in doing, bodying. Vizenor continues: "Native survivance stories are renunciations of dominance, tragedy, and victimry. Survivance means the right of succession or reversion of an estate, and in that sense, the estate of native survivancy" (vii). Survivance is an open-ended harnessing of the power of Indigenous sovereignty in the fields of culture and art and everyday life that is irreducible to the linearity of settler narratives of adoption and dispossession. Survivance for adoptees and those affected by boarding schools, adoption, and forced relocation is likewise irreducible. It is a form of refusal to kill the Indian inside in favor of the "man" outside. It is a constant negotiation with our shadow selves that operate on the molecular level, on the level of the sign and the body, on the level of space-time becoming infinite and yet here, now.

Conclusion: Pleiades, Pine Tree

In *Cherokee Stories of the Turtle Island Liars' Club*, Christopher B. Teuton (2012, 234) asks storyteller Hastings Shade about the constellations, and Hastings tells him about the Bear asterism (the Pleiades):

> That's where the word *jogo* comes from. That's where they talk about the story of the boys. One of 'em, all he liked to do was dance. Not regular dance, but a stomp dance. Every time he walked out that's all he did was dance. Then you don't tell him, he'd quit on you. And soon as he got a chance he'd start dancing again. Pretty soon he had a circle with him, you know, dancing. And they kept saying, "You know, you need to quit. You don't do that all the time, just at certain times." But every chance he got he would start dancing. And *jogon* the clan itself. So one day, there was several of 'em dancing and they went out there and they got on to him. But they just kept dancing. Kept saying, "No, you all quit." Pretty soon they looked, and they began to rise. Just went on up and became Ursa, the Bear constellation. . . . There's no English translation of *Ani Jogon*. There's no English word for that. So I don't know what it is. But that's what they were called.[24]

The boys just want to dance. Their bodies rise from the earth as they practice the sacred ritual that is at the center of Cherokee ceremony, around which the sacred fire burns—the fire that is the same fire that was given to us by Creator. Their bodies together, rising, spiraling upward, like smoke from the sacred fire. In the movement of their bodies, together, they become celestial. The constellation is formed of these boys, the children who would not stop dancing, who themselves became stars. There is no English word for what these boys become, *Ani Jogon*, a constellation, star people.

In the version recorded by anthropologist James Mooney there are seven boys who liked to play rather than do their chores. When their mother punishes them by giving them stones instead of corn for dinner, the boys leave the house in protest and begin to dance. Around and around they dance until they begin to rise into the heavens. Their mother goes looking for them and manages to pull one of them down, and he strikes the ground with such force that he is swallowed up by the earth. The remaining six boys enter the heavens and become the Pleiades. In her grief the mother cries at the loss of her sons, and from her tears, in the spot where the one son had been swallowed by the earth, a pine tree grows and reaches up toward the heavens (Mooney 1995, 258–59).

Here, the son brought down to earth wants to return to his brothers, so he becomes a pine reaching toward the heavens. The sky is full of our relatives. The plants, also our kin, want to reach out and touch the heavens, which is another way of saying "to become whole again." The pine tree is celestial in this way, reaching up to reform kinship, to reattach to his brothers. This kinstillation is a form of reaching across the breach between earth and sky, between human and more-than-human, between body and spirit. This is where Hobson's (2018, 69) Sequoyah takes on new meaning: "We were like branches intertwined from the same tree, the same root, reaching out toward the sky to the unknown." This reaching is kinstillatory; it is the enactment of Cherokee stories of relation beyond the human. Sequoyah reaches toward the sky that is the same ancestral sky, the same hand turned root turned branch as Pine Tree to his brothers, the stars. The Pleiades becomes not just a symbolic marker of Cherokee culture but also a map for reconnecting across the breach of the unknown.

Of course, the Pleiades is significant to many Indigenous communities. For the Haudenosaunee it is the hole through which Sky Woman fell when she descended to earth. The story of Sky Woman falling from the heavens is crucial to how the Haudenosaunee people are descended from the stars and is an enactment of a kinstillation. When Sky Woman descends, the Swans soften her fall, the Turtle offers his back for her to land, the Muskrat sacrifices himself, bringing up earth from the depths of the ocean that will grow around her and become Turtle Island. These kinstillations teach us about collaboration and care, about reciprocity, and about the space between realms, eras, and people. They teach us of time travel, of crossing the breach.

It is tempting to describe this breach as a perpetual liminality, as the constitutive in-betweenness of being while not being. But the breach is more a feeling than a state of being, more potential than existential. It is also, if not primordially, a trace of future presence that calls from within. A beginning that has already begun. This sliding into materiality is like momentum, a force that oscillates between one thing and the next, between one thing and something else. In our constellations we make sense of the abyss of infinite space and power, the sublime unfolding of space-time into ribbons of connective tissue. The gap between Pine Tree and Star is a wound closing, a scar, like a heartbeat, like memory. We, who have always been stars, we who are starring, returning to the heavens again as that which we were. The connective tissue of celestial healing is the very fact of our material life, the possibility of quotidian transcendence. This is the repair work of kinstillatory praxis: a doing of kinship, a being in good relations.

Notes

1 This version is adapted from James Mooney (1995, 254–55).
2 Here I am following Eve Tuck and K. Wayne Yang (2012).
3 I mean "transtemporality" in the general sense of across or linked through time. However, Jacob Lau's (2016, 3) use of "trans-temporality" to index how trans bodies (and in particular trans of color bodies) exist "within and beside" normative cis temporality is not entirely absent from my thinking here.
4 I first heard the term *ancestral futurity* from artist S.J Norman (Koori of Wiradjuri descent) in 2020. The concept has been central to our collaboration as curators of the performance series *Knowledge of Wounds*, which first took place at Performance Space New York in January 2020. For more information, see https://www.knowledgeofwounds.com. Norman and I discuss *Knowledge of Wounds*, ancestrality, futurity, and Indigenous bodies in "Liminal Tension/ Liminal Gifts: SJ Norman in Conversation with Joseph M. Pierce" (2020).
5 The collaborative work between Recollet and Johnson has been crucial to my understanding of kinstillations. This understanding is both experiential and conceptual. I have participated in Johnson's *Kinstillatory Gatherings in Light and Dark Matter*, the monthly fireside gatherings at Abrons Arts Center in Lower Manhattan. In addition, Johnson was a participant and space keeper in *Knowledge of Wounds* (see note 4), and both she and Recollet continue to elaborate on these concepts.
6 For a more detailed description of my father's adoption and my family's return to community, see Pierce (2015).
7 For a concise summary, see Roxanne Dunbar-Ortiz (2014, 157–61).
8 Richard Henry Pratt uttered these words at the Nineteenth Annual National Conference of Charities and Correction, held in Denver, Colorado, in 1892. During his speech, titled "The Advantages of Mingling Indians with Whites," Pratt (1892, 46) explains his position regarding Indian survival: "A great general has said that the only good Indian is a dead one, and that high sanction of his destruction has been an enormous factor in promoting Indian massacres. In a sense, I agree with the sentiment, but only in this: that all the Indian there is in the race should be dead. Kill the Indian in him, and save the man." And if the connection between war and education was not clear, we need look no further than the title of Pratt's autobiography: *Battlefield and Classroom: Four Decades with the American Indian, 1867–1904*, which was first published in 1964.
9 Of course, all of this is complicated. Kim TallBear (2013, 55–61) and Joanne Barker (2011, 87–93) have shown how blood quantum is only part of the

story of the allotment era and argue that "blood" rules also invoke Native understandings of reciprocity and ancestral relation. Still, the allotment period was marked by increased legislation of tribal blood as a form of settler colonial management of land and identity.

10 Writing of traditional land-tenancy practices, Theda Perdue (1998, 136) notes that "women made particular plots theirs by farming them. Because the women of a matrilineage normally worked together, the land belonged to the matrilineage that used it, and through their maternal kin succeeding generations of women inherited their right to farm it."

11 This paragraph draws on my essay "Allotment Speculations: The Emergence of Land Memory" (2022).

12 Will Roscoe documents how a similar strategy was used in 1898 in Zuni Pueblo. In this case four Zuni priests were illegally arrested by the US Army and imprisoned for eighteen months, with one dying in prison. The remaining three were released on the condition that twenty-five Zuni children would be sent to a government boarding school in Albuquerque (Roscoe 1991, 116–19).

13 Adoptive Couple v. Baby Girl, 570 U.S. 637 (2013). For an excellent analysis of the case, including interviews with Cherokee Nation officials, see Rebecca Nagle's (2019) podcast This Land, episode 8, "The Next Battleground."

14 For a concise overview of recent legal challenges to ICWA, see Matthew Newman and Kathryn Fort (2017).

15 For a clear example of arguments against ICWA that construe Indigeneity as a racial category rather than as political citizenship, see the article by Goldwater Institute Vice President for Litigation Timothy Sandefur (2017/2018), titled unironically "Suffer the Little Children." For a list of the Goldwater Institute's ongoing litigation, see https://goldwaterinstitute.org/indian-child-welfare-act.

16 However, there is a growing network of advocacy groups and organizations. For more information, see the National Indian Child Welfare Association website: www.nicwa.org.

17 See Zitkala-Ša (1900), "An Indian Teacher among Indians," where she not only notes the disingenuousness of the Carlisle mission but also documents the abuse, drug addiction, and mediocrity of her white colleagues.

18 I would like to clarify that in this chapter I am conscientiously not analyzing anthropological work or personal testimony from the court hearings related to the ICWA. I am choosing to discuss the psychoanalytical framework proposed by Eng and Han in a literary work rather than apply it to real people as a way of resisting a narrative of victimization.

19 Mishuana R. Goeman (2017) reflects on a similar type of embodied response to the trauma of dislocation in Linda Hogan's novel Solar Storms. Goeman refers to the connection between the women in the Wing family as a form of embodied memory that is evidence of the violence of settler colonialism: "The traces of this history linger and fester and manifest themselves on the bodies

of Native women. Hogan's depiction of Native bodies as scarred undermines the erasure of this violence and posits these scars and embodiments as Native women's resilience, healing, and alternative conception of history and futurity" (114). Angel, the novel's protagonist, had been removed from her community after her mother violently attacked her, leaving her body badly scarred. It is no coincidence that in Hobson's novel, Sequoyah is also scarred. His mother had unintentionally burned his face with grease.

20 This paragraph draws on the arguments presented in Pierce (2017).

21 Ᏽ (tsi, pronounced "ji") is the relationship noun for "mother." Adding a pronominal prefix indicates relationality: ᎠᎩᏥ (a-gi-tsi), "she is my mother," "my mother," or, as I am suggesting, "the one who mothers me" (here, "one" does not necessarily indicate gender). For a detailed explanation of Cherokee relationship nouns, see Brad Montgomery-Anderson (2015, 144–48).

22 I would like to thank Clint Carroll and Wade Blevins for their help pointing out these nuances. I am a Cherokee language learner, and any error in translation or meaning is mine alone.

23 In her anthropological account of Cheyenne kinship, Christina Gish Hill (2017, 95) describes the interconnected web of reciprocity that is also at the heart of their mobile communities: "The plains, the Black Hills, the Missouri River, the Powder River basin, and all the important places in their homeland belong to the Cheyennes like a sister or a husband or a child belongs to his or her family. Just like a family, the exact specifications of the interactions might change over time, but the relationship remains as long as it is fed through reciprocity and continued through stories." The land, animals, plants, and ancestors are all related and connected through the maintenance of stories and ceremony. Of course, there are many examples of this across Indian Country.

24 As Hastings Shade explains later in the story, Ani Jogon, among other ancient clans, no longer exists: "The other clan that's gone is the Nuyuksuht. The Rattlesnake Clan. See, we know what those are. But that Ani Jogon, there's no know [sic] English word for them. 'Cause we don't know . . . we could sit here all day long and not figure out what. . . . 'Cause I've tried!" (Teuton 2012, 235).

_____

05 Queering the Womb
Surrogacy and the Economics of Reproductive Feeling

"Women helping women! I love it!" If Oprah Winfrey could have hidden a fertile Indian woman under each audience member's seat in her Chicago studio audience for the taping of her 2007 episode on gestational surrogacy, she might well have shouted, "You get a baby! You get a baby! Everybody is getting a baby!" Even though the episode begins with the somber teaser question of how far you might be willing to go to have a baby of your own, its affective pivot toward consumerist ecstasy in the guise of altruism comes promptly. Oprah's endorsement of the Akanksha Infertility Clinic in Gujarat became a highlight of the short-lived celebration of India's foray into reproductive medical tourism. Dr. Nayana Patel, who owns the clinic, has been featured in various documentaries on surrogacy since appearing on *Oprah*, including *Google Baby* (2009) and *Made in India* (2010). In these films, as well as her various other media appearances, Dr. Patel prominently displays icons of Oprah's seal of approval in her office as a kind of transitive endorsement, vouchsafing the feminist, magnanimous ethos of the industry. It is an ouroboros of benefit, where, as in the utopia of Harpo Studios, everyone wins.

Less than two decades later, gestational surrogacy, especially as a transnational practice, is no longer seen by a global audience as an equitable and altruistic exchange of reproductive labor for proportionate compensation. India's commercial surrogacy industry is no longer the promised land of cheap but fair assisted-reproductive technology (ART) for Euro-Americans.

This is not because the draw of safe, inexpensive, "hygienic," and, most importantly, successful gestational surrogacy has faded—we can safely say it has not. Rather, the Indian government has been moving systemically since 2013 to curtail and limit the practice: to domesticate it and to indigenize it. The recently passed 2018 Surrogacy (Regulation) Bill hopes to intervene in the industry of family making, to ensure that forms of kinship created by technologies of surrogacy are simpatico with what the state sees as "natural" forms of family. Here, kinship is made not through anonymized exchanges of money for labor but through intimate goodwill; families consist not of a single parent or two parents of the same sex but of a married, heterosexual couple and their biologically related children; there is a line between necessary and extravagant reproduction. By closing itself off to a global market of assisted reproduction, India announces itself as a new kind of parent—the paterfamilial intervention into the exploitation of its domestic labor force, a refusal to be a cheap alternative for the global North. India joins all of Western Europe, the United Kingdom, and Ireland, among other places, in the proposed commercial surrogacy ban.

As one might imagine from a multibillion-dollar industry, there is significant pushback against the Surrogacy Bill. Opponents rightly claim that by banning commercial surrogacy, the Indian state will encourage the industry to go underground, away from any potential legal regulation that might protect surrogates from exploitation. Others claim (again, rightly) that women who become surrogates *want* to do this kind of work, that this is a matter of rights and choice. South Asian feminists argue that, far from protecting poor and tribal women from exploitation in the industry—as the government claims—a blanket ban on commercial surrogacy will result in radically unfair and unstandardizable compensation and gross injustice (see Menon 2019; Qadeer and John 2009). At this juncture, when the world's second largest country, and one of the most active participants in the industry, bans a massively popular form of ART, it behooves us to inquire into the relationship between kinship and economics that underpins these new conceptions of how and why families can be made.

What the ban on surrogacy, much like the popularity of the practice, shows that is the economics—that is, very precisely, the financialized and unremunerable circulations of goods and labor under the sign of exchange—of assisted reproduction is inextricable from its affect. David Eng (2010) suggests that "queer liberalism"—which, we might say, put the *homo* in *homo economicus*—gave rise to the racialization of intimacy at the sites of financialized public queerness. The feeling of kinship is a way to make sense of affiliative structures that both defy and bend to market logics which govern the legibility of care, desire, and subjectivity. When the language of kinship is explicitly queer—whether in the intergeneration of queerness by LGBT couples or in the Indian government's regulation of this form of kinmaking away from the market toward the family—we see the pressure placed on structures of kinship to do the work of both contract and care. A delicious tension develops between rights-based discourse of LGBT politics and financialized fantasies of market exchange. Queer kinship is formed through commercial gestational surrogacy but, as this essay will argue, not as romantic, utopian affiliation. Rather, this is a queer kinship of transactional, paid labor that refuses the fantasy of individual sovereignty and containment; in other words, it is a neoliberal jouissance, the shattering of relationality into the gaping maw of the market.

Contract Tracing

Why can't we just buy babies? Polemic force notwithstanding, it is startling how vigorous a refusal that question invites. It is abhorrent, here in the bright light of post-Enlightenment reason, to endorse the possibility of purchasing another human being. We are, the specious logic of secular modern (neo)liberalism avers, self-owning, sovereign, and autonomous. Particularly in the US context, chattel slavery's specter, the structural condition in which human reproduction was itself means of production, haunts the very foundations of legal and cultural debates around everything from inheritance law to transnational adoption to gay marriage even and, especially, in the face of its disavowal.

Scholars of critical race studies have compellingly argued that contemporary biopolitics and distribution of labor in late capital derive from chattel slavery's historical condition of reproductive commodification (Hartman 1997; Roberts 1997; Weinbaum 2019; Morgan 2004; Paugh 2017). Indeed, as Dorothy Roberts (1997, 278) writes, "It is the enslavement of Blacks that enables us to imagine the commodification of human beings, and that makes the vision of fungible breeder women so real." Although this logic drives the legal apparatus of the industry and, equally, the hypercompensatory affective defense of the practice in the global North, its fundamental incongruity to the history of India in particular produces a revealing conflict in terms and possibilities. Simply put, chattel slavery does not haunt the relationship that Indian surrogates have to the practice, their labor, and its remuneration. Yet they still enter into contract by way of that history. This is the transnational paradox of kinship.

The United States insists on distancing itself from its own recent history of reproductive slavery. To that end, it writes into the very legal terms of contract the impossibility of compensation for the actual labor of reproduction, especially surrogacy, donation, and adoption. A surrogate, donor, or biological mother can be given gifts and reimbursed for living costs and other, more fungible expenses. But she cannot be paid the exertion of her labor. To do so would to be to hew too closely to the uncompensated and unreparated labors of racial slavery. Similarly, adoption and donation agreements each mandate that the terms of financial exchange are never money for human bodies and their parts. Rather, what is financialized is time; wage labor's shadow is cast across the somatics and value of reproductive biology.

Postcolonial India has its own complicated history of the relationship between reproductive labor and categories of liberal subjecthood, in part inherited from imperial biopolitical governance. Kalindi Vora (2015, 28) argues that "abstract notions of 'consent,' 'freedom,' 'choice,' and 'contract' have been produced and unequally distributed by modern liberalism and have been affirmed selectively for some through the disavowal of colonized and enslaved labor. The category of labor continues to function to write over contemporary conditions of force under other names." But reproductive labor, far from a neoliberal or colonial import, has been structurally normalized by caste and class relations for a much longer period of time. That history as powerfully shapes the regulation of surrogacy in India as anxieties around traffic in human beings, indelibly colored by the ongoing force of transatlantic slavery and its figuration of the human under law, do in America.[1] Female domestic labor—the intimate and ubiquitous work of nursemaids, ayahs, household servants—negotiates interdictions of touch and contact across class and caste while fundamentally shaping the morphology of the family. This form of labor is available to, and widely employed by, even middle-class Indians. Moreover, it is labor that many women who will be commissioned as surrogates enact. Essentializing gestational labor as commercial surrogacy elides the broad matrix of (re)productive labors that produce terms of kinship, contract, and compensation.

In this way India and America meet at the contract, the proving ground of commercial surrogacy's claims to impartial and equitable exchange across nation-states and inherited histories. Commercial surrogacy's contractual premise holds that whatever forms of exchanges may be entered into, they must begin with parties who recognize each other's sovereignty. Without this fundamental liberal truism, the practice would be impossible. Yet contract and its furious disavowal of any condition of nonsovereignty (structural or personal) cannot furnish the terms of the relationship that emerges from it. This is to say, when parties enter into the surrogacy contract, they become something to one another: relationally implicated, necessarily entangled. What contract does is far from affectively disinterested and committed to self-sovereignty; it organizes subjects into relations that are queer, intimate, and necessarily financialized.

Since India's legalization of commercial surrogacy and subsequent rise into the most sought-after site for reproductive-assistance tourism, an enormous body of feminist scholarship has emerged around the practice. These accounts, particularly rich ethnographies such as those of Sharmila Rudrappa (2015) and Amrita Pande (2014), are essential to not only understanding the form and function of the surrogacy industry but also attending to why women choose to participate.[2] In the face of critiques of the industry and claims of exploitation, I use the word *choose* purposefully. I do not believe that these women misrecognize their own desires or act against their own interests. Commercial surrogacy is never equitable; its promise of fair compensation and transparent contract is spurious at best, but too often the focus of its denunciation is the women who labor in the industry. They are seen either as dupes, victims of a system in which they are outsmarted and underrepresented, or fools, believing themselves to be fairly paid and safely employed. One need not conflate the ongoing failures of the industry with a constitutional failure of its laborers. More than diagnosing false consciousness, such critiques reproduce a now-familiar colonial trope of perpetual subaltern victimhood. It is clear in accounts by surrogates that they are not simply exploited pawns. They act toward their own benefit in the constrained conditions of their own lives, as all our lives are in some regard always constrained. Should these women have financially lucrative, safe, and abundant options? Absolutely. But neither in this essay nor in general do I suggest that critiquing commercial surrogacy is aligned to, or in cahoots with, the project of rescuing postcolonial women from the grips of their own failed choice.

This essay inquires into individual and relational subjects that are made from surrogacy. I recognize the deeply unequal and dangerous conditions of commercial surrogacy in India and understand that women choose to do this labor for valuable and legible reasons. However, I turn from the question of individual agency to surrogacy's disavowed dependence on contract. It is precisely where property and ownership cannot be uttered aloud that the language of gift, kinship, and altruism appear—not as reparation but as a kind of radically revelatory compensation. After all, not so long ago we lived in a system where humans were traded as commodities, treated as property. Thus, societies must insist that that is not what is happening here, now. This defensive insistence arises because we have actually never fully left the scene of chattel slavery. Alys Eve Weinbaum (2019) describes this transnational, transhistorical haunting as the surrogacy/slavery nexus in which contemporary biocapitalism inherits and recorporealizes racialized practices of forced reproduction.

If, as Saidiya Hartman says, "Slavery is the ghost in the machine of kinship," it is also the ghost in the machine of all transactions of late capital (quoted in Butler 2002, 15). Slavery haunts surrogacy materially and affectively, producing the terms and limits of its intelligibility. It is for this reason that reproductive labor's marketplace turns to the language of kinship—to family, intimate feeling, and radical reciprocity. Kinship depends on an impossible unconditionality: the false name of family reveals structures of obligation, conditionality, and contract on which surrogacy depends.

Assisting State Reproduction

When introducing the Surrogacy (Regulation) Bill to the Lok Sabha in 2016, Minister of External Affairs Sushma Swaraj decried the degradation of surrogacy from being out of necessity to now being of extravagance. Especially critical of celebrities using surrogates despite already having children, Swaraj insisted surrogacy should not be permitted for unmarried, single parents, those in "live-in relationships," and homosexual couples. Essentially queer (that is, non-"normative"), those surrogacies, Swaraj claimed, went against a national "ethos" (Swaraj 2016). Only Indian citizens, "male and female, legally wedded couples" should be permitted to employ surrogates. Surrogates are also legislated by the bill that Swaraj endorsed. They must be married women who have already sought and received the consent of their husbands and who are "close relatives" to the commissioning couple. The Surrogacy Bill does not just legislate who can employ a surrogate; it also transforms legislative relationships of contract into kinship.

Since the legalization of commercial surrogacy in India in 2002, the parameters of the industry have rapidly dilated and contracted. Until 2013, when the Indian state banned surrogacy for foreign and domestic homosexuals and single people, it was the go-to destination for Euro-American queers looking for surrogates. The draw is unmistakable. It is deliciously shot through with the recognizable imbrication of neoliberalism, pinkwashing, and postcolonial aspiration:[3] surrogacy in India was cheap (on average between $10K and $25K all inclusive, a third of the cost of similar services in America), unregulated, and efficient.[4] Indian surrogates were healthy, docile, and—most importantly—avowedly agential, because the economic value of transnational surrogacy depends intimately on the promise of fair and equitable exchange. Indian women who acted as surrogates had to be seen both by potential commissioning parents and the state as able to fully inhabit the contractual world of liberal subjectivity. Thus, the narrative of women *choosing* to become surrogates emerged, chorused by the state and the burgeoning industry. In it, women financialize their labor within a sector that remunerated far more generously than any other available to them. The "rent-a-womb industry," as it is called, trafficked in the promise that everyone was getting a good deal. Cheap babies, generous wages.

Cracks in this narrative became especially clear when surrogacy clinics began outsourcing the gestational period of surrogacy to Nepal while continuing to perform IVF and implantation procedures domestically. This practice sidestepped the ban on serving queer consumers. Indian surrogacy clinics began to move in a curious dance with a broader national navigation of the question of LGBT rights. In 2009, in the *Naz Foundation v. Govt. of NCT of Delhi*, the Delhi High Court overturned Section 377 of the Indian Penal Code, which banned unnatural offenses, including sodomy. A colonial statute from 1861 modeled on the 1533 Buggery Act, Section 377 made homosexuality a crime in postcolonial India. Although most directly affecting Indian LGBT communities, overturning this statute quietly sanctioned the public life of queer kinship broadly—not least by making India open to overseas LGBT vacations and medical tourism. In 2012 the Ministry of Home Affairs issued guidelines to prevent the "misuse of surrogacy services by foreign nationals," which expressly forbade homosexuals, foreigners, and single people from engaging services of Indian surrogates and clinics (Parliament of India, Rajya Sabha 2017, 9; see also Arathi 2019). By disaggregating foreigners from categories of sexual orientation or marital status, the Home Ministry's announcement effectively barred Indian homosexuals as well as foreigners, both straight and otherwise, from commissioning surrogates.

Six months later, the *Naz Foundation* verdict was overturned by a Supreme Court two-judge bench. The reinstatement of 377 testifies to the unstable and shifting relation of the Indian state to queer rights and to kinds of kin that might therein be made legally recognizable. It would not be until 2018, the same year that the Lok Sabha passed the Surrogacy (Regulation) Bill, that the Indian Supreme Court would finally reverse the 2013 judgment and declare that 377 was unconstitutional, decriminalizing homosexual acts. It remains to be seen how the decriminalization of homosexuality will come to bear on state-mandated technologies of reproduction and kin formation. In India, marriage exists within the purview of personal—that is, religious—law, so overturning 377 clears the way for religiously ordained homosexual unions. Will the homology between family and nation dilate to include homosexual families? Will queerness come to be installed within kinship structure of the state? Parallels between the regulation of commercial surrogacy and homosexuality in India are not mere coincidence: they reveal a continuing negotiation by the Indian state of commercial and intimate relations. As I show in the next section, these relations exemplify neoliberalism's economization of kinship and privatization of labor, despite being cast in the idiom of liberal rights.

The 2013 ban on LGBT surrogacy commissions redistributed the question of goods and labor not just between the global North and South but also within the uneven strictures of postcoloniality. Nepal was positioned as a reproductive catchwater, collecting the runoff of India's now repudiated practices sifted free of already-bare regulations instituted by the original 2002 legalization of surrogacy. A catastrophic earthquake in 2015, which killed 9,000 people and reduced entire portions of Kathmandu to rubble, brought transnational queer surrogacy to the front pages of international news. Israel acted within twenty-four hours of the quake to evacuate 229 Israelis from Nepal, including 29 infants born of Nepali surrogates. *Time* magazine and the *Huffington Post* featured images of gay Israeli couples carrying infant car seats off the plane in Tel Aviv, tearfully thanking the government for saving their children, for rescuing its citizens. Earlier, couples had posed next to a makeshift tent housing the remaining surrogates, which was built on the rubble of a popular clinic. These images drew cries of exploitation. They rudely revealed the transactional nature of commercial surrogacy and made visible the transnational hierarchies of rights, liberties, and protections that underpin surrogacy's conditions of labor.

But in fact, the outcry against exploitative ART practices after the 2015 Nepal earthquake proved India's success as a modern, liberal state. India reinforced why its surrogacy services should continue to be valued—safer, better regulated, *fairer*. This is an argument for market supremacy, not for labor reform. Five years later, in 2018, India's ban on commercial surrogacy—which expanded its ban against surrogacy for queer couples and single people—narrowed the practice of assisted reproduction to only one legal scenario. It did so without any recognition of the labor of the practice and the calculus of its compensation. This is to say that, while claims of exploitation within commercial surrogacy are the putative rationale for the Surrogacy Bill, it openly disavows any interest or investment in the women who perform surrogacy labor. Under the guise of paternalistic care, the Surrogacy Bill limits the scope of the practice for ideological not economic reasons. Rather than regulate the market of the practice, the Indian state has decided to regulate kinship instead.

Keeping It in the Family

The Surrogacy Bill makes it possible for a married heterosexual Indian couple to engage the "assistance" of a close female relative to act as a surrogate. Before the surrogacy can take place, a district medical board must issue certificates of "essentiality" and "eligibility" to the commissioning couple. Essentiality certificates avow the infertility of one or both members of the commissioning couple. They also include an order of parentage and custody for the surrogate child and an insurance policy for the commissioned surrogate for sixteen months postpartum. Eligibility certificates attest that "(i) the couple being Indian citizens and married for at least five years; (ii) between 23 to 50 years old (wife) and 26 to 55 years old (husband); (iii) they do not have any surviving child (biological, adopted, or surrogate); this would not include a child who is mentally or physically challenged or suffers from life threatening disorder or fatal illness; and (iv) other conditions that may be specified by regulations" (Parliament of India Rajya Sabha 2018). Eligibility for assisted reproduction, shorn of contract's reason, is somatically mediated. Commissioning parents must be of an age deemed young enough to raise a child, and their attempts at unassisted reproduction must have failed, either by death or by an ableist imagination of viable life.[5] A commissioned surrogate must also be issued eligibility certificates, verifying first that she is married, has a child of her own, and is between the ages of twenty-five and thirty-five; that she is "a close relative" of the commissioning couple; that she will not be providing her own gametes;

and that she has never before acted as a surrogate. Relational and medical conditions met, surrogacy is then articulated through an idiom of both altruism and necessity. Altruism, as we will see, is the name given by the state for the empty space cleared by banning commercial surrogacy. It is the exchange located outside the market, between kin rather than strangers. Necessity, here, signifies not the intent or labor of the commissioned mother but the object of her labor: the commissioning couple.

For them, unlike those for whom ART is extravagant, this is a necessary outsourcing. What constitutes this need? Moreover, who sanctions the designation of need? That is, what kinds of kinship are the Indian postcolonial state legally and structurally mandating? On its surface, it may appear that this is yet another canonization of the hetero-limited nuclear family. However, a "traditional" kinship form of the subcontinent is in fact being imported into the arena of contemporary finance capital, fully imbued by a nationalist vision of India as Hindu and able-bodied (Bhattacharyya 2006).

The Surrogacy Bill is part of a eugenic state project marketed as a local humanitarian corrective to the ravages of the global market. In its early public relations endeavors, the Indian commercial surrogacy industry turned to mythology and Vedic scripture, referencing examples from the *Mahabharata* of King Dhritarashtra's birth through "Niyogi pratha" (paternal surrogacy) as proof of surrogacy's indigeneity to India. Similarly, the government ban turns to the realm of "native" culture. Sushma Swaraj, a major figure in the Hindu-nationalist Bharatiya Janata Party (BJP), did not need to specify what she meant by the "national ethos" that commercial surrogacy violates. Since independence, postcolonial India has maintained the practice of separating personal law, governed by religious authority, and criminal law, which began under British rule. For example, the Hindu Adoption and Maintenance Act of 1956 specified the legal terms of adoption of children particular to non-Muslim cases, especially as it related to inheritance (Ministry of Law and Justice of India, 1956). Although the terms of the law claim to be secular, they are in name only, for they deploy religious ideology. Moreover, since its rise to power in the national government in 2016, the BJP has enacted across all sectors of life and governance a concerted project of conjoining Indianness and Hinduism. The regulation of reproduction and kinship is a primary vehicle of statecraft. Banu Subramaniam (2019) makes the astonishing link between a variety of biopolitical projects and the rise of Hindu nationalism. By identifying the rise of commercial surrogacy in Gujarat—which has been the hub of the industry—during (now) Indian prime minister Narendra Modi's tenure as chief minister, Subramaniam shows the imbrication of BJP pet projects of neo-liberal finance and Hindu nationalism in nourishing the success of the industry. Modi's vociferous support of private industries such as commercial surrogacy mobilized with it a Hindu nationalist project that has now come to the center of national government.

The Surrogacy Regulation Bill's deployment of kinship is suffused with a particularly Hindu vision of the family. Forms of labor and obligation cohered in the bill are presented as unmediated referents of "Indian" family. This is a part of a broader project of reimagining the modern Indian state as a Hindu one, never more clearly revealed than in its various synecdoches of family as nation. For purposes of tax and inheritance, the 1955 Hindu Marriage Act institutionalized the recognition of the joint family as a "Hindu undivided family." From the moment of marriage, this family constituted "a common ancestor and all of his lineal descendants including their wives and unmarried daughters" (Ministry of Law and Justice 1955). A family, for Indian Hindus (including reform sects such as the Arya and Brahmo Samajs), as well as for Buddhists, Jains, and Sikhs, consists not of nucleated bi-generationality but of a multigenerational and entangled kinship between fathers, sons, and brothers and their children. The law does not mandate family form for Indian Muslims, Christians, or Jews, for whom personal law is still categorized under religious law.

The 1955 law recognized extant structures of kinship in India, in which sons and their families would live together in a single-family property, creating within the family's architecture horizontal and vertical intimacies, dependencies, and obligations. At the head of the joint family sat the karta, quite literally the manager, legally recognized as the most senior male ascendant, who administers family finances and obligations, such as marriage and debt. (The law was changed in 2016 to allow women to ascend to the position.) Affectively, the kinds of relationships that the joint family makes possible might accurately be described as "queer." Proximities demarcated in the nuclear family are more fluid within the joint family, making possible and indeed inviting commitments and intimacies that traverse and often upend the heteronormative frame of kin. In these kinship structures the exchange—whether financially or socially compensated—of reproductive labor, in the form of informal intrafamily adoption, is common because it is inherent to its morphology. But its implicit citation by the 2018 Surrogacy Regulation Bill makes the joint family into a ready source of biological material, unremunerated labor, and affective obligation. Rather than foreclose the question of commerce within the contract created by and for the surrogacy relation, the specter of the joint family reveals kinship to be always already commercialized, mediated by terms of contractual obligation, remittance, and exchange.

Family, we know all too well, is the undoing, not the promise, of equitable relations. By constraining the relation of commissioning couple and surrogate within strictures of "close" family, the Surrogacy Bill displaces common (and justified) critiques of commercial surrogacy's threat of exploitation into the space in which complaints registered are muffled by walls of personal relation. Intimacy and dependence are vexed within familial structures and avenues of redress even more impeded. As much as kinship acts as a buffer from vicissitudes of economic and social precarity, it amplifies and solidifies them into conditions of ongoing vulnerability and debt. To what authority does the commissioned surrogate turn, within this new mandated relational contract, to seek repair, support, or correction? Contract, in its ideal deployment, is designed to limit constrictions and conflicts of intimate relations within exchange.[6] In shifting contractual contact into the sphere of the personal and familial, the Surrogacy Bill radically changes the work that contract can do and the subjects and bodies that it can make.

To be clear, the Surrogacy Bill does not offer terms of contract between commissioning couple and surrogate. The 2002 National Guidelines for the Accreditation, Supervision, and Regulation of ART Clinics in India, which first legalized commercial surrogacy, included a standard consent form and terms of contractual obligation. However, "consent" and "agreement" appear in the Surrogacy Bill only under a clause pertaining to the maintenance of records by surrogacy clinics that have been approved to perform procedures. The commissioned surrogate must give consent when informed of the terms of the procedure and its side effects, but she cannot consent to any other part of the process or agreement. Taking commercial contract off the table has wiped away contractuality more broadly. What the commissioned surrogate now enters into is an agreement to a procedure, not to an exchange relation. Whereas commercial surrogacy forges intimate (though often impersonal and almost always delimited) bonds through contract, in this newly mandated system, intimate (necessarily personal and structurally amorphous) bonds vouchsafe the dispensability of contract. Indeed, in the family imagined by the BJP's Surrogacy Bill, there is an extant management and administrative structure. The karta's patriarchal benevolence makes contracts of the public sphere irrelevant. It is written into the joint family that agreements of dependency and care be administered by this singular figure. To be clear, in no way does the bill guarantee such a mediating figure—even if we were to believe in the fiction of the impartial magnanimity of the father—nor does it offer state paterfamilias in its stead. Rather, it constructs itself around the invisible sign of the father in this markedly Hindu form to marketize familial relations and privatize economic exchange.

Attempts by the Surrogacy Bill to take the "rent-a-womb" industry, which also marketizes intimate relations, and "return" its labor to what it deems the rightful locus—the family—are made possible by the originary imbrication of kinship and commerce. By fleeing into the family, reproduction supposedly escapes exploitation. But it is the family that reveals the necessary conditions of obligation, conditionality, and exchange on which surrogacy depends. Under contract, the exploitation of strangers is hemmed in by the market, the law, and their recognition of surrogacy as commercial transaction. By contrast, the familialization of surrogacy as "gift" domesticizes labor from the realm of the market. Gift stands in for logics of exchange that claim to eschew the financialization of relationality, whereas in contract, each party is an actor ("contractor"). Gift relations shift away from the language of exchange that they depend on. They are fantasized as unidirectional.

This is not new to India and the question of surrogacy. As Melinda Cooper (2017, 21–22) points out, "The nineteenth-century anthropological language of status and contract, for example, served to obscure and sentimentalize the existence of women's unpaid labor in the home at precisely the historical moment when the boundaries between the labor market and the private family were being established. Women were thus relegated to the quasi-sacred space of kinship and the gift relation at a time when they were being actively excluded from the contractual labor market by an alliance of male trade unionists and conservative protectionists."

In the twenty-first century, kinship is resentimentalized as a pseudo-economic force. There is always, especially in altruistic surrogacy agreements, the promise of compensation. But that compensation must come in the form of familial affect and kinship obligation. Within a kin-based surrogacy, dependency, duty, pity, love, guilt, and coercion are deployed. These are the market terms of the family. Indeed, they are the terms necessary for the coproduction, within the family, of a child who, as Viviana Zelizer (1981, 2) reminds us, is understood as "priceless." In *commercial surrogacy*, strangers enter into temporally bound relations of obligation and liability to one another, and the market is positioned as a mediating force between the parties. Intimate bonds, limited to the time and body of gestation, are forged through the contract. By contrast, *altruistic surrogacy* is mediated through generosity and gratitude. In altruistic surrogacy, the intimate bonds that make labor possible are bonds that are imagined to be ongoing, pinned to the transgenerational time of kinship.

Making Strangers of Family/Family of Strangers

"Do not grow to desire (aase) the baby," Indrani, a surrogate employed in Gujarat, tells ethnographer Sharmila Rudrappa (2015). She explains: "In my mind I have no feelings, madam. For my own children I struggle hard enough. Why would I need more children in my life? Loving children is a burden" (Rudrappa 2015, 103). Indrani expresses a sentiment remarkably common in ethnographic and documentary accounts of commercial surrogacy. Surrogates affectively distance themselves from the pregnancy for which they are being compensated: they *care* for their own children, they do this work for them, so that they might have a better life (see Vora 2015; Rudrappa 2015; Pande 2009, 2010, 2016). They counter the common anxiety that surrogates might care too much or the implication that inherent in the value of commercial surrogacy in India is the promise that the surrogate does a kind of affective labor inextricable from bodily labor. Fundamentally, this antisentimental surrogacy upends the romantic premise and promise of affective compensation for the labors of surrogacy, that something like maternal love subsidizes the financial terms of exchange. At the same time, it reveals an underlying market worry about the potential failure of a surrogate to perform adequate affective labor during her somatic labor (see Sheldon 2016). If, as many scholars have argued, market terms designate the "good surrogate" as willing and able to provide the emotional labor of care, attachment, longing, and commitment, then Indrani's claim that love is a burden reveals starkly the calculus underpinning both commercial surrogacy and altruistic surrogacy.[7]

Here is the paradox: the myriad labors involved in gestational surrogacy and the purported capacity to perform those labors make some surrogates more desirable than others, yet these desires cannot be recognized under terms of market-driven contract. This means wanting at once better and worse laborers, cheaper and more expensive services. That is the market. But here, outside that market looking in, the fear that the commissioned surrogate does not feel intense emotional investment (proof of being a "good" worker) in the object of her labor is a not a bad thing. That affective alienation at the limits of contract usefully warns against the sentimentalization of value. Why must we go in search of attachment to shore up the making of kinship? Indrani insists not only that she does not feel maternal desire for the child she gestates in the commercial surrogacy but also implies that even loving her own children comes at a cost. *Loving children is a burden.* There is value in not wanting to connect, in not imagining the creation of new, lasting affective bonds for both commissioned surrogate and commissioning parents. For Indrani, that value is quantifiable; it lacks the weight of the burden of love. Returning to the discourse of necessity and extravagance cited by Sushma Swaraj in her press conference on the Surrogacy Bill, we might then ask: Who is able to want a child—no, *need* a child—without feeling it as a burden? Is this desire a sign of necessity or of the luxuries of affective expansiveness made possible by economic prosperity?

The postulate that we should not be able to simply buy babies is permitted by way of the vociferous articulation that there are some labors for which we cannot be paid. Affect cannot be mandated within contract; it is supplement without sign. So when the Indian state moves to ban commercial surrogacy and install in its place the single exception of altruistic surrogacy, it removes contract, removes compensation, leaves only love and only burden.

Altruism thus imagined is an intimate act, one that is negotiated through extant kinship structures: the commissioned surrogate must be a close relative—ideally no more distant than first cousin—to one of the commissioning couple. The making of kinship through ART is the remaking of kinship through agreements of labor, time, and soma. Altruistic surrogacy, the act in which both parties agree there will be no monetary exchange, here suggests that the surrogate receives compensation of an affective register mediated by the form of the family.

Commonly figured in terms of the gift, altruistic surrogacy departs from the classical conception of altruism as that which does not engage or require social relations. After Marcel Mauss (2002), we are primed to recognize that gift exchange produces the expectation of reciprocity. Far from disinterested, gifts make demands. Within kinship-confined altruistic labor, what terms of reciprocity are demanded? I want to suggest here that by attempting to remove surrogacy from the purview of the market—to both protect the commercial surrogate who is now simply a potentially reproductive woman and to preserve the form of the family espoused by a modern Hindu nationalist state—the Indian government has actually revealed how very queer kinship already is and how very financialized its obligations, entanglements, and exploitations have always been. Kinship is a market form, the private sphere of the family shot through with the economics of dependency and exchange.

When commercial surrogacy is banned, the commissioned surrogate is no longer surrogate: she is cousin, sister, or aunt. But can she remain in this relation *while* she is surrogate? Can she return to this relation? Moreover, how would we know of the perhaps inexorable and unbearable changes to the relations between kin effected by an agreement to make between them new relations? *We cannot know.* The name of the family elides other names created under its sign, the vanishing act by which cousin/sister/aunt is made and unmade, named and unnamed surrogate/womb. Commercial surrogacy has given rise to a staggeringly vast canon of memoirs, documentary films, ethnographies, and narrative fiction, an archive of representation that provides a vocabulary of labor, desire, attachment, and their failings. By contrast, the privatization of surrogacy into the family form refuses public figuration.[8] The publicness of the market for commercial surrogacy compels the profusion of discourse around it. But the value of altruistic surrogacy as a practice is the commodification of privacy and intimacy. Altruistic surrogacy contained within the biological family limits critical terms by which we might understand it, leaving us with the inherited affective clichés of dependency, loyalty, guilt, love, and obligation. Elizabeth Freeman (2007, 298) offers a capacious vision of kinship as the "set of representational and practical strategies for accommodating all the possible ways one human being's body can be vulnerable and hence dependent upon that of another, and for mobilizing all the possible resources one body has for taking care of another." For a woman who, in agreeing to participate in altruistic surrogacy, offers her body and its resources for the reproductive desires of her kin, representational strategies by which she is apprehended within that relation and outside of it falter. Vulnerability and generosity, honeytraps of altruistic reason within existing kinship structures, can also be fraught devices of exploitation and elision.

Of course, we might say in utopian singsong, the transformation of kinship made possible by the generosity of an altruistic act is productive; it generates more than just biological matter and human embryos—it makes family anew. And indeed, by reinforcing the rhizomatic intimacies of communal kinship as articulated within the joint family, this rekinning through labor expands the definition of family. But even if we are to believe that the commissioned surrogate agrees to her labor out of unequivocal altruism and that her financial and affective conditions of possibility are equal to or greater than those of the commissioning couple, we must face a fundamental reappraisal of labor value within familial structures. If, as is likely the case, the commissioned surrogate enters into the agreement out of her own necessity, not just that of the commissioning parents' need for procreation, then the radical reorientation of kinship's economics threatens to further exclude, minoritize, or perhaps disappear her entirely. Kinship, Hortense Spillers (1987) reminds us, is far from a stable condition. Under conditions of chattel slavery, slaves were unkinned, ungendered, unnamed. As she writes, "Could we say, then, that the feeling of kinship is not inevitable? That it describes a relationship that appears 'natural,' but must be 'cultivated' under actual material conditions?" (75). Kin relations are made and unmade within the material conditions of possibility created by the state, by capital, by the hemming of the market. The feeling of kinship, within the commercial and altruistic terms of contemporary surrogacy, is clearly not inevitable.

Just as full-throated critiques of commercial surrogacy pinpoint the impossibility of equity within terms of exchange, we must acknowledge that market impossibility is distilled, not dilated, when moved into the sole purview of the family. The commissioned surrogate who was once kin is now the person to whose generosity the commissioning parents are indebted. Jacques Derrida (1992, 35–36), describing "the madness of economic reason" that governs the gift, tells us that the fact of the gift must be forgotten as soon as it is given, that even the memory of the gift destroys it. The cost of the gift is the necessity—and impossibility—of wishing to forget it. When the gift is that of reproduction, of and within the family, we must desire to forget both the preexisting and future relations of kinship and debt.

Altruism, that promise of worthwhile sacrifice, frames the labor of surrogacy as moral. Like Oprah's ecstatic daisy-chain of feminist care—"Women helping women!"—which, as with her book club and holiday must-buy lists, primes a consumer public for the good and value of transnational surrogacy, the Indian state's efforts to privatize its labor depend on it being a good without a cost. Nothing is without cost. And nothing, especially not kinship, is outside the productive and destructive meter of the market. Altruistic surrogacy must seek to destroy the family in order to fulfill its promise. In this context we might recall Marcel Mauss (2002, 46) on the gift's death drive: "It is not even a question of giving and returning but of destroying so as not even to appear to desire repayment." When surrogacy disguised as altruism returns to the family, which is always already financialized, the destructive force of the gift turns itself to the thing it seeks to make. Kinship is undone at precisely the site of its making.

Notes

1 Sophie Lewis (2019) has argued vehemently for a recognition of all reproductive labor as work, which would allow for a radical valuation of surrogacy. Although the intensity of her argument is unique, its ethos of broadening the scope of reproductive labor and its conception is echoed in the work of Camille Robcis (2013), Nancy Scheper-Hughes (2001), Penelope Deutscher (2017), and Anne Phillips (2013).

2 There is a wealth of extensive and exceptional ethnographic scholarship on gestational surrogacy in India to which this essay is deeply indebted. See, in particular, Rudrappa (2015), Pande (2014), Deomampo (2015), DasGupta and Dasgupta (2014), and Majumdar (2017).

3 Pinkwashing, as has been theorized by Jasbir Puar, Maya Mikdashi, and Sarah Schulman, describes the institutional and "soft" production of Israel as a sign of modernity and tolerance exemplified by apparently pro-queer policies in order to justify and elide its ongoing occupation and genocide of Palestine. Although India is not commonly cited alongside Israel, its techniques of self-representation as modern, liberal, and secular as a screen for its ongoing violent military occupation of Kashmir and growing Hindu nationalism clearly takes several chapters from Israel's playbook. With the overturning of Section 377, we will likely see the apparatuses of pinkwashing resurge in India. See Puar (2007, 2013), Puar and Mikdashi (2012), Schulman (2011), and Schulman and Chávez (2019).

4 Clinics like Pandey's Akanksha Infertility Clinic offer "packaged" services in which all costs of the surrogacy—compensation for the commissioned surrogate, her medical care, her room and board, IVF services, prenatal and postnatal care—are included. This is designed for the transnational market, assuming that international consumers are unable and unwilling to coordinate various parts of the surrogacy themselves. Moreover, the clinic produces itself as a kind of paternalistic structure for both the surrogates and the commissioning parents: promising to oversee the care and health of the process as well as to manage all affective relations through the scripted narrative of equitable exchange and disinterested attention.

5 This eugenicist bent is sharply argued in Pande (2016).

6   On contract theory and consent, see Patricia Williams (1988, 1991), Charles
    Fried (1981), Randy Barnett (1986), and Eric A. Posner (1997).
7   Here Arlie Hochschild's (2012) work on affective labor and "emotional cap-
    italism" is particularly useful. See also Carolin Schurr and Elisabeth Militz
    (2018).
8   For examples of this vast and uneven genre, see Gita Aravamudan (2014),
    Kishwar Desai (2014), Falguni Kothari (2019), Amulya Malladi (2017), Joanne
    Ramos (2019), Meera Syal (2016), Fiona Whyte and Malone Seán (2017), Hans
    Hirschi (2014), and Orran George and David Booher (2016).

06 Beyond Family

Kinship's Past, Queer World Making, and the Question of Governance

In *Unapologetic: A Black, Queer, and Feminist Mandate for Radical Movements,* Charlene A. Carruthers (2018) indicates the importance for social justice movements to ask the questions "Who are my people? What do we want? What are we building?" In exploring these questions, she insists, "Governing is not synonymous with becoming part of the governments we live under—or duplicating them." She indicates, instead, that "making collective decisions about how our lives are lived is governance. It's in that space that we can live out the project of collective liberation" (Carruthers 2018, 108–10). However, governance here need not mean the apparatuses of the nation-state. What, though, could governance mean if not merely a version of statist institutions and infrastructures? The figure of "kinship" points toward such possibilities, to the potential for nonheteropatriarchal formations of belonging, decision making, and resource distribution. However, such a conceptual (re)orientation entails freeing the notion of kinship from its definitional fusion with "family," a mistranslation that genealogically can be traced to nineteenth-century proto-anthropological engagements with modes of Indigenous peoplehood. In such discourse, Native social forms and networks appear as failed family, a confusion of the private with public/political functions marked by their "fictive" extension of proper/natural terms of nuclear homemaking.

Nonnative queer engagements with the notion of kinship have tended to preserve this implicit logic, understanding queer world making as either a refusal of kinship's attachments or as alternative sets of family-like arrangements. Instead, how might we understand the critique of the force and institutionalized matrices of heteronormativity as opening onto other configurations of sociality that do not take "family" as a significant organizing structure?

First, we need to consider by what means we know that the relations, dynamics, or formations we're talking about are "kinship." As David Schneider (1984, 6) suggests of anthropological efforts to distinguish the principles at play in non-Euro-American social contexts, in which kinship supposedly provides the basis for social cohesion and organization but in ways disjunct from the nuclear family, anthropologists make "a complex series of implicit assumptions about the 'idiom of kinship' which, because they are unstated, are not open to easy review or evaluation." He further asks: "If each society had a different social convention for establishing a kinship relationship . . . by what logic were these all considered to be kinship relations since each constituted a different relationship?" (108). He suggests that the "genealogical grid" provides the ground for understanding other modes of relation as "kinship." However, the genealogical grid is not so much a way of figuring "real or putative biological bonds or their culturally defined equivalents" as a naturalization of nuclear family homemaking by de facto casting it as the necessary unit/unity through which human reproduction occurs (62). In other words, the issue is how the architecture of liberal political economy—in its constitution of a private sphere understood as qualitatively distinct from and outside the sphere of proper governance—provides the frame of reference for the modes of relation named as "kinship."

Attending genealogically (pardon the pun) to how kinship comes to be a means of talking about kinds of relationships and social formations draws attention to the ways the concept functions as a racializing and imperial placeholder. It translates formations of collective governance, placemaking, decision making, and resource distribution into the terms of the liberal private sphere as a (distended, perverse, pathological) version of nuclear homemaking. As can be seen by turning back to the work of Lewis Henry Morgan, whose writings in the latter half of the nineteenth century launched the anthropological discourse of kinship around which the uses noted above largely continue to orbit in unacknowledged and politically constraining ways, invocations of kinship largely remain haunted and shaped by this privatizing imaginary, even when they seek to contest liberal norms and envision alternatives.[1] Queer intellectual and activist citations of kinship tend to carve out spaces of exception to this ideology of *enfamilyment* without necessarily challenging the broader infrastructure of liberal governance. If the concept of kinship tends to pinion nonliberal social formations to heteropatriarchal notions of "the family" in ways that cast such formations as other-than-"political," can the invocation of kinship also mark the potential for modes of collective life and governance that do not follow liberal principles and are unintelligible, or cast as racialized aberrations, within them? Indigenous intellectuals' deployments of the concept of kinship have worked not simply to expand the scope of its reference (away from "family"-like modes of affect and intimacy) but to break down the distinction between scales that characterize liberal notions of politics. Such Indigenous analyses refigure kinship in ways that shift the social imaginaries at play in dominant and most oppositional invocations of it, challenging the concept's depoliticizing, privatizing, insulating, and exceptionalizing tendencies in ways that open toward models of radical relational governance.

Distending the Family

Through his writings over the course of the late nineteenth century, particularly *Ancient Society* ([1877] 1977), Morgan develops a model for explaining the presence of various permutations of what he characterizes as "marriage" and "family" among peoples around the world. He situates such differences within a teleology of progressive becoming that eventuates in the interdependent emergence of private property holding, the nuclear family, and the state. It is difficult to overstate the influence of Morgan's work in shaping intellectual and popular conceptions of "kinship" over the past 150 years. In addition to providing an important way of historicizing what kinship has meant as it has moved through intellectual and administrative circuits, Morgan's work offers an illuminating allegory through which to describe certain entanglements within liberal thought and political economy that have been significant from the nineteenth century onward, albeit in shifting ways. More than positioning the nuclear family as the self-evident frame through which to define kinship, Morgan's texts illustrate how the characterization of varied kinds of sociopolitical relations as *kinship* depoliticizes them. Even while showing how formations he refers to as based in kinship enact practices of what he describes as governance, he presents such practices and philosophies of collective belonging, decision making, resource distribution, placemaking, and diplomacy as distended versions of "home" and "family," necessarily distinct from the sphere of political sovereignty. The liberal private sphere serves as the horizon and frame of reference through which "kinship" gains meaning, even as the term/concept seems like it expansively incorporates a wide range of social configurations that qualitatively differ from those normatively enacted by/under the liberal state. In Morgan's analysis, all social formations can be figured within a distinction between "personal" and "political" modes of organization, in which those that do not fit Euro-American bourgeois homemaking can be slotted into the former category. Doing so specifically presents them as failing (yet) to be *political* in ways that allow them, when engaged within liberal ideologies and governance, to be treated in racializing ways as aberrant and/or dangerous anachronisms, distensions, and deformations of the private sphere.

Morgan presents his observations with regard to non-European peoples, particularly Indigenous peoples whose lands are claimed by the United States, as a window on earlier periods in what would become Euro-American modernity. In the preface to *Ancient Society*, he indicates that "the history and experience of the American Indian tribes represent, more or less nearly, the history and experience of our own remote ancestors when in corresponding conditions" (Morgan [1877] 1977, vii). The forms of life at play in "American Indian tribes" thus gain meaning by being understood as earlier versions of the forms that structure the Euro-American present. This "conjectural history" takes shape around the model of the bourgeois household, which by the late nineteenth century already had become dominant in the United States. In a rather stark instance of this approach, Morgan asserts that "modern society reposes upon the monogamian family. The whole previous experience and progress of mankind culminated and crystalized in this pre-eminent institution" (512). Not only has all of human history been building toward heteropatriarchal, couple-centered homemaking, but that mode of family actually functions as the definitional core of "modern society." Reciprocally, this unit—in which intimacy, romance, childbearing, child rearing, household formation, subsistence, placemaking, and interpersonal care are fused—acts as the background, as the frame of reference, through which to interpret all other social formations. Monogamous, privatized couplehood conditions the emergence of all other social formations onto the scene of Morgan's analysis by providing the principal, if at times implicit, way of interpreting the dynamics and significance of the various modes of relation that come to be characterized as kinship.

More than temporally displacing Native peoples to the properly superseded past of mankind, this set of intellectual procedures treats "family"
as itself a transhistorical and transcultural signifier through which to engage what might otherwise be understood as a wide range of kinds of social
arrangements that lack much resemblance to one another. In drawing on
family and marriage as conceptual constants, Morgan de facto presents the
nuclear family unit as a neutral means through which to explain, catego-
rize, and compare all other arrangements of housing, reproduction, collective belonging, and nonliberal systems of governance. He suggests, "With
respect to the family, the stages of its growth are embodied in systems of
consanguinity and affinity, and in usages relating to marriage, by means of
which collectively, the family can be definitely traced through several successive forms" (Morgan [1877] 1977, 5). At various points he provides a tax-
onomy of stages of human evolution (levels of "savagery" and "barbarism"
before culminating in civilization) in which the relations of sexual intimacy,
procreation, allocation of children among groups, forms of housing, and
relation between those prior dynamics and processes of collective decision
making and resource distribution are wildly disparate (9–12). Yet they all
can be narrated "with respect to the family," taking "the family" as an inherent unit of knowledge making and an unquestionably relevant framework
for social order. Morgan's discussion of how those supposedly natural relations are elaborated and extended in early stages of human development
(still present among non-European peoples) indicates that liberal notions
of privatization provide the framework in which the narrative of biological necessity takes shape. He distinguishes between two means of defining
one's "kindred," *classificatory* and *descriptive*, which are the "ultimate forms"
and are "fundamentally distinct": "Under the first, consanguinei are never
described, but are classified into categories, irrespective of their nearness
or remoteness in degree to *Ego*; and the same term of relationship is applied to all the persons in the same category," while "in the second case
consanguinei are described either by the primary terms of relationship or
a combination of these terms, thus making the relationship of each person specific" (403–4). Thus, "the primary terms" (descriptive) are those that
correctly indicate relations of reproduction (such as using the term *father*
only for one's genitor and *mother* only for one's genetrix), whereas classificatory terms stretch descriptive terms to encompass a class of persons that
goes beyond the term's "primary" referent (referring to one's genitor and
his biological brothers all as "father" or one's genetrix and her biological
sisters as "mother," for example).[2] If descriptive and classificatory systems

are "fundamentally" disparate, and these two forms "yield nearly the exact line of demarkation between the barbarous and civilized nations" (407), how do they both belong to the categories of "family" and "marriage"? How can they be understood as versions of the same thing? Morgan suggests that the descriptive form actually underlies all forms, such that the genealogical grid centered on a given individual ("Ego") and radiating outward, but oriented lineally up and down, provides the basis for understanding "kindred" (or kinship) in all modes.

Morgan's text further illustrates how the grounding of kinship in the nuclear family abets a racializing and colonial imaginary in which nonliberal modes of governance constitute a deformation of the private sphere that is antithetical to the proper operation of the liberal state. In laying out the logic of the genealogical grid and of the definition of *kindred* via consanguineous connection with *ego*, Morgan notes that "a brief reference to our own system of consanguinity will bring into notice the principles which underlie all systems" (Morgan [1877] 1977, 404). He indicates that what he presents as the core of civilized society can provide a set of "principles" through which to apprehend the other social systems (and stages) he chronicles. Earlier, in discussing the "monogamian family," he states that "it was founded upon the marriage of one man with one woman, with an exclusive cohabitation; the latter constituting the essential element of the institution. It is pre-eminently the family of civilized society, and was therefore essentially modern. This form of the family also created an independent system of consanguinity" (28). Later, he adds that this monogamous unit "assured the paternity of children and the legitimacy of heirs" in ways that "fell back upon the bare facts of consanguinity" (401). Defined as a married couple who have their own household, the prototypical form of the family takes shape around the legal dynamics of nineteenth-century marriage, bourgeois property holding, and generational transmission of privatized inheritance, such that "consanguinity" as a concept depends on this model of nuclear homemaking, insulation, and ownership. The nuclear unit's status as "independent" (28), then, has less to do with its supposedly necessary role in procreation than with its legal and spatial distinction from other such units, enclosed as they all are within their own private spheres contradistinguished from the broader collective dynamics of the public/political realm. Even when Morgan is talking about social configurations in which what he terms "the family" takes on what he characterizes as "governmental" functions, he still describes those expressions of family/consanguinity/kindred as "domestic institutions," including among the "barbarous" and "savage" segments of "mankind." He also refers to "the marriage relation" as fundamentally "personal" in character (4–5, 466). Since consanguineous relations definitionally are contained in the realm of the "domestic" or the "personal," the term *kin* and its permutations index extended formations of family in which relatedness bleeds out beyond the domestic lineality that defines its proper descriptive boundaries.[3]

The crystallization of the monogamian family as the fruit of "successive stages" of human evolution pairs with the emergence of "political society" as the basis for defining the achievement of civilization. The latter is "founded upon territory and upon property, and may be distinguished as a state (*civitas*). The township or ward, circumscribed by metes and bounds, with the property it contains, is the basis or unit of the latter, and political society is the result." Unlike "a gentile society" (one based on "gens," or kinship groups) in which "relations were purely personal" (Morgan [1877] 1977, 6, 61), the state has a public character divorced from "personal" relations. It is organized around the extension of afamilial modes of jurisdiction over a clearly delimited territory, such that all persons living within that area are subject to its authority irrespective of any "domestic" connections among them. States are organized around "territorial" relations, not "personal" ones, and nonstatist modes of governance ultimately depend on kindred/kinship as the infrastructure for social order in ways that remain tethered to or tainted by familial association. Nonstatist modes of governance deform the domestic into a quasi-public by failing to appreciate/understand both the proper limits of familial affiliation and the necessity for a distinction between such private/personal networks and matters of (the) state.

Yet given that Morgan does describe the territoriality of kinship-based modes of governance (for examples, see Morgan [1877] 1977, 103, 114), the distinction he makes between "tribe" and "nation" seems to falter (104). This apparent paradox underlines the ways that Morgan's invocation of territory envisions a particular kind of geography, one ordered around private property. He asserts that "governments and laws are instituted with primary reference to its creation, protection and enjoyment," earlier arguing that the "dominance" of the pursuit of private property "marks the commencement of civilization" and "led mankind to overcome the obstacles" that had delayed the "establish[ment of] political society" (512, 6). In order for governance over a territory to count as impersonal, then, it must be shaped by and in the interest of the division of the territory into privately held units, which are not enmeshed in extended networks of affiliation (which, themselves, must be understood as deviant distensions of "the family"). *Political* forms of governance arise in the existence of a disjunction between the institutions of governance and the atomized assemblage of property holders whose rights in their privatized territory the state exists to protect. Prior or other forms of *kinship* threaten to rupture the modes of familial household individuation that lie at the core of private property holding while also creating bloated units that disrupt the nested, impersonal hierarchies and geographies of "political" order—the structure of state jurisdiction.

Morgan's work suggests the ways that kinship appears as a comparative way of talking about supposedly familially based modes of governance only against the background of liberal political economy. In addition, this reading points to how modes of governance that differ in their operative principles, internal infrastructural relations, and scalar dynamics from those of the liberal state, especially when they appear within the claimed jurisdiction of such a state, can be discounted as expressions of a not-(yet-)political kinship network or, even worse, as themselves expressions of wrong forms of home and family. The emergence of the nuclear family "marks that peculiar epoch in human progress when the individuality of the person began to rise above the gens, in which it had previously been merged, craving an independent life, and a wider field of individual action," and Morgan ([1877] 1977, 475, 469) earlier notes "the more stable such a family would become, and the more its individuality would increase." The "individuality of the person" arises from and remains contingent on the "individuality" of the family as an institution. Such enfamilyment serves as the crucible for producing kinds of individual personhood consistent with civilized norms and proper political subjectivity. The use of kinship to characterize nonliberal modes of sociality largely reinforces these ideological dynamics of enfamilyment, particularly in the racializing depiction of nonconformity to those norms as expressive of potentially dangerous modes of deviancy (at the level of the person and the population to which that person belongs). The concept of kinship, then, enables nonliberal dynamics of social organization and governance to be translated into liberal terms as a deformation of "the family."

Tracing that process of translation and depoliticization opens possibilities for tracking the ways that the failure to conform to normative narratives of enfamilyment provides a basis for racializing attributions of failed personhood, social menace, and political delinquency to nonwhite populations.[4] Their supposed inability to have proper domesticities can be presented as bespeaking immanent and irremediable tendencies toward criminality, backwardness/savagery, and/or unassimilable alienness (for examples, see Barker 2011; Cacho 2012; Cohen 2010; Rifkin 2011; Shah 2012). A kinship imaginary may be understood as crucial to ideologies of liberalism in (1) normalizing the distinction between the familial and the political in ways that fuse nuclear family homemaking and privatized property holding to each other as the basis for governance while (2) allowing what might otherwise be understood as alternative modes of governance to be cast as alien, backward, and/or criminal (mis)understandings of personal/domestic life—collective inclinations that express forms of racial incapacity that disqualify members of such populations from being proper national subjects and that require remediating state intervention. The kinship concept (when de facto referentially pinioned to "family") helps enact and secure a biopolitics of enfamilyment that normalizes whiteness as the basis for privatized property rights, positioning a racially coded ideal of domestic life as necessary for maintaining the scalar structure and subjectivities (public and private) of the liberal state.

Zones of Queerness

Queerness often is narrated as beyond kinship, as lying outside of the enclosures of dominant conceptions of home and family. Intellectual gestures of this kind speak to the ways same-sex desire historically has been cast as antithetical to heteronormative domesticity and morality while also contesting more recent efforts to seek what often has been characterized as homonormative inclusion within liberal institutions and social forms (see Duggan 2004; Eng 2010; Ferguson 2019; Manalansan 2005; Puar 2007; Reddy 2011). As against the pursuit of the rights to bourgeois homemaking, many intellectuals and activists have insisted on the ways queerness does and should stand outside the privatizing formations of, in Elizabeth Povinelli's (2006) terms, the "intimate event" of liberal enfamilyment. Such efforts can disown normative formations of intimacy, couplehood, and privacy for which "kinship" sometimes provides an encompassing name. However, there also are numerous queer efforts to gesture toward modes and spaces of relation whose coordinates do not match those of bourgeois domesticity: kinds of alternative worlds, principles, and practices for which "kinship" sometimes also serves as the index. In this way, nonnative queer conceptual, cultural, and political work might be understood as harboring a deep ambivalence toward the concept of kinship. This paradoxical doubleness can be seen as a function of the kinship imaginary that I've been describing, in which kinship registers nonliberal social and political formations but translates them into liberal geographies and ideologies of privatization as distended (and racialized) kinds of family. Queer analysis, then, often reiterates the problems of that conceptual oscillation or translation by similarly positioning the forms of world making it seeks to highlight as something of an exception—of *difference*—within liberal geographies of enfamilyment rather than suggesting the need for ways of theorizing, recognizing, and enacting nonliberal modes of governance.

Work in queer studies often gestures toward a space for that which does not conform to the demands and principles of heteronormative privatization—something like a *zone*, even if one whose precise location or boundaries remain unspecified. Heteronormativity itself creates kinds of spaces from which queerness is barred or in which queerness appears as a kind of aberrant, disorienting intrusion. In their much-cited "Sex in Public," for example, Lauren Berlant and Michael Warner (1998, 547) argue for the need to foreground "queer zones and other worlds estranged from heterosexual culture" that support modes of sexual and intimate relation that do not mimic the terms of liberal couplehood and family formation that organize so much of public and political discourse in the United States. Such forms and spaces of queer engagement and desire cannot be constrained within a conception of "community," which itself tends to be "imagined through scenes of intimacy, coupling, and kinship; a historical relation to futurity is restricted to generational narrative and reproduction" (554). The refusal of kinship operates in the service of remapping the terrain of intimacy such that it need not definitionally be located within or tend toward the couple-form or the bourgeois household.[5] Similarly, Sara Ahmed (2006, 77, 81, 92) discusses how sexuality comes to be "oriented," particularly in relation to the reproduction of "the father's line," and she suggests, "The [family] table in its very function as a kinship object might enable forms of gathering that direct us in specific ways or that make some things possible and not others," such that "the queer couple in straight space hence look as if they are 'slanting' or are oblique." Heterosexuality implicitly orders the spaces through which people move as well as how they do so, and the generational unfolding of familial relation (characterized as "kinship") helps produce a lived geography of what I have called enfamilyment, in which participation in hetero-nuclear family households constitutes not just a basis for social belonging but for mapping the terrain through which liberal subjects move.

By contrast, queerness can name a particular sort of space/place that enables modes of relation that do not conform to the dictates of enfamilyment. In understanding queerness as necessarily sutured "to the concept of ephemera," José Esteban Muñoz (2009, 65, 72, 35) argues that "queerness is illegible and therefore lost in relation to the straight minds' mapping of space," and he earlier suggests the need to "carve out a space for actual, living sexual citizenship." Queerness emerges in noninstitutionalized, or underinstitutionalized, ways that temporarily convert spaces into sites for enacting dynamics of desire, intimacy, collective belonging, and interpersonal connection that are both "defiantly public" and provide "glimpses into "an ensemble of social actors performing a queer world" (49). In a similar vein, recognizing the ways that liberal ideologies of enfamilyment construe Black subjects as deviant regardless of object choice, L. H. Stallings (2015, 141) highlights modes of what she terms "erotic maroonage" that provide for some an alternative to dominant conceptions of marriage: "Rather than all-out rebellion against domestication—that is, marriage rooted in monogamy—we get temporary flight from the institution or a group of fugitives banding together to create independent nonmonogamous communities, even within the institution of marriage." The imagination of something like a space of queer world making apart from the constrictions of heteronormative domesticity implicitly territorializes queerness as a particular sort of site. However, that de facto localization tends to leave the structures and dynamics of enfamilyment themselves undisturbed, in the sense that queerness is envisioned as occupying an elsewhere distinct from "straight space." This way of talking about alternatives to heteropatriarchal formations of home and family seems to replicate the dynamics at play in anthropological discourses of kinship, in that dominant processes of enfamilyment serve as the background against which liberal political economy takes shape and against which queer deviations can be marked as such.

However, queer intellectual work also often aims to recast normative configurations of homemaking, to envision how queerness might occupy the space of kinship in order to argue for alternatives to bourgeois domesticity. Juana María Rodríguez (2014, 37) suggests that "the mainstream LGBT movement attempts to secure individual rights through the valorization of normative kinship" by accepting "the logic of neoliberalism." She argues instead for the importance of attending to "multigenerational extended families who cohabit because of economic need, cultural conventions, or their own desires; families whose social and sexual networks extend beyond one couple or one household; 'unstable' households that are in a state of flux with people entering and exiting as space, money, and need dictate; or families that are denied the ability to live together due to immigration policies, economic need, or practices of institutionalization" (36–37). In a similar vein, David L. Eng (2010, 25, 57) insists that "we need to ask how a constitutive violence of forgetting resides at the heart of queer liberalism's legal victory, its (re)inhabiting of conventional structures of family and kinship," and he suggests that "refocusing progressive efforts on household diversity, rather than organizing solely for same-sex marriage, could generate a broad vision of social justice that resonates on many fronts." They both suggest the potential for championing modes of what they characterize as kinship that would be more responsive to forms of desire not centered on conjugal couplehood as well as configurations of intimacy, care, and interpersonal relation that do not conform to the nuclear model. In this way, kinship as family and household formation (as modes of domesticity) marks both that which queerness must critique and evade and that which it must engage and champion. Queerness names what exists beyond the bounds of kinship but also ways of inhabiting the space, forms, and/or feelings of kinship differently.

I want to underline the implicitly minoritizing and exceptionalizing work that kinship does in these queer analyses, situating nonnuclear modes and matrices of relation within a liberal structural and scalar imaginary. As with Morgan, these various permutations of relation all can be understood *as kinship* by virtue of being personal/domestic: they take shape against the de facto background of the nuclear family as the descriptive model, defined as *personal* relations and spaces in contrast to *political* dynamics and logics of governance based on depersonalized spheres of jurisdiction (territory). Queer efforts to expand the possibilities for acknowledging *kinship* (including in terms of forms of state recognition), then, do not undo the heteronormative principles at play in liberal political economy because, as I have been arguing, the concept of kinship itself largely reaffirms the "descriptive" centrality of nuclear family homemaking as the frame of reference in which other social configurations appear as non-"political" deviations— preserving the sense of a space apart that does, or fails to do, the subject-making work of enfamilyment. Kinship constellates with *home* and *family* to index zones of privatized intimacy, desire, care, and interdependence distinct from public processes of political decision making. This invocation of the kinship imaginary seeks to relativize what can constitute legally recognized and protected forms of privacy in ways that also can be understood as aiming to open up the hetero-genealogical presumptions at play in the definition and transmission of property (in Ahmed's terms quoted earlier, the integrity of "the father's line"). Put another way, nonnative queer invocations of kinship as an alternative frame through which to displace nuclear homemaking tend to reiterate the territorializations at play in liberal political economy—as in nineteenth-century formulations of the kinship concept, discussed earlier.

What drops out, though, is the question of governance. I mean less what the government can do with regard to issues and formations otherwise coded as private/personal/domestic than how relations and modes of social organization understood in liberal terms as private/personal/domestic can provide the basis for governance, in ways that do not have to fit within the jurisdictional scale structure of the liberal state. Governance involves collective efforts to develop ways of shaping, in Carruthers's (2018) terms quoted at the beginning of the essay, "how our lives are lived" that may or may not involve engagement with the existing institutional networks and protocols of the state and that certainly do not need to take the normative, jurisdictional, and procedural principles of state policy as the basis for "making decisions." The emphasis on the need to develop and to attend to existing processes of governance (even when not currently self-characterized in those terms)—understanding challenges to existing political and economic formations as involving such work—displaces the propensity within nonnative queer engagements with kinship to envision zones of difference carved out of liberal social mappings: either as queer spaces distinct from those of kinship or nonnormative reconfigurations of relationships conceived of as kinship. Such a shift would also potentially bracket enfamilyment and its racializing dynamics by refusing the de facto distinction between a private sphere and a political one, a distinction that allows for the putatively distended and dysfunctional workings of the former to be understood as expressive of deviant tendencies that bespeak a population's racial character. Taking up the ways collective networks of relation might be envisioned as *governance* moves beyond the forms of ideological containment and the liberal scalar structure at play in the kinship imaginary. This reconceptualization of the political infrastructures constituted by networks of care, and the attendant displacement of liberal domesticity, is theorized more fully in Indigenous deployments of kinship, to which I will now turn.

I've been talking about the ways that a kinship imaginary, as it emerges in proto-anthropological discourse in the late nineteenth century and operates as a way of framing social/cultural difference in the twentieth and twenty-first centuries, presents social formations in terms of a "descriptive" model of nuclear homemaking. This interpretive prism normalizes liberal geographies of governance, ideologies of property, and racializing figurations of enfamilyment. I've further suggested that work within queer studies that has sought to set aside normative arrangements of home and family tends to get caught within the logics and binds of that imaginary. However, Indigenous intellectuals have taken up the concept of kinship in ways that refuse and refunction this dynamic. They do so by explicitly articulating how the kinds of attachments and belonging that have been labeled as kinship operate as part of matrices of governance, thus setting aside the de facto definitional fusion of kinship to family. Native intellectuals' ways of inhabiting the kinship concept highlight webs of ongoing relationality, responsibility, and accountability that animate all engagements—with other persons, other peoples, and nonhuman entities, including lands and waters. Within this framing there is no separate domain of governance operating at a qualitative remove from the principles, ethics, and relationships of quotidian interdependence, no institutional matrix that has its own operative principles at odds with but putatively meant to defend an apolitical or prepolitical zone of privatized, insular, propertied intimacy—a zone that could not exist as such absent state law and policy but that is cast as merely being recognized, rather than actively constituted, policed, and disciplined by state action. From the perspective of this understanding of governance, there is neither the narration of racialized aberrance based on improper enfamilyment nor a carving out of queer exceptions within what largely remain geographies of privatization.

Native theorizations of kinship help illustrate the connection between felt experiences of wrong enfamilyment and histories of racializing intervention by the state that have worked to demean, discipline, and foreclose alternatives to settler political economy. If kinship designates deviations from the liberal family, such deviations can themselves be experienced as personal failure, perversion, and pathology. Kim TallBear (2018, 151) observes, "I was suffocating all my life under the weight of the aspirational ideal of the middle-class nuclear family, including (hetero)normative coupledom with its compulsory biological reproduction." Despite living in and amid nonnuclear arrangements, TallBear describes how she came to view those arrangements of "home" and "family" as expressive of an inability to achieve the ideal of health and well-being with which she and the people around her had been taught to identify despite that ideal's alienness to the actual circumstances in which they live. This personal sense of wrongness emanates directly from the imposition of "a system of compulsory settler sexuality and family that continues building a nation upon Indigenous genocide," one that aims to "free up land for settlement" by *whitening* "red people" (152, 147). TallBear shows how quotidian Indigenous modes of connection can come to be experienced by Native people as a racialized incapacity to attain proper enfamilyment.

In this way, kinship indexes how the jurisdictional imperatives of the state come to be felt as a hierarchical difference among kinds of privatized families/domesticities. The need to clear land for white settlement and to break up Indigenous modes of placemaking and governance is lived in personal and intimate ways as the insufficiency of Native social networks, as the need to understand them in relation to the "middle-class nuclear family." The routinization and normalization of that process of comparison *is* the work of the kinship concept in the everyday operation of settler colonialism as well as the liberal political economy through which it functions. TallBear observes, "Prior to colonization, the fundamental social unit of my people was the extended kin group, including plural marriage. The Dakota word for extended family is *tiospaye*," later adding that "despite colonial violence against our kin systems, we are in everyday practice still quite adept at extended family."[6] Thus, when TallBear asserts that "I grew up in a very pro-kinship world," the referent here for *kinship* is not simply a larger or differently configured version of liberal notions of homemaking but a sociopolitical matrix in which politics and family are not contradistinguished domains (148, 150, 152). Her account testifies to the ongoing colonial work of remaking Native people(s) as racialized subjects and the continued presence of dynamics of decision making, resource distribution, placemaking, and collective belonging that contest such liberal subjectification and that enact alternative principles and practices of governance. Following TallBear's lead, other instances of enforced nuclearization and attributions of racialized failure and incapacity can be interpreted as indicating not so much the need for a more expansive conception of kinship as the importance of understanding the very practices marked as "failure" as themselves expressive of networks of belonging and governance that contest liberal ideologies and imaginaries. In this way, kinship as (failed) family is intellectually remade as kinship as the matrix of Indigenous governance (jettisoning the nuclear family as the paradigmatic core).

The question of how intimate experiences of (wrong) enfamilyment are shaped by the racializing frames of state policy opens onto the dynamics of scale. How are domestic units defined through their location within the encompassing geography(ies) of state jurisdiction(s)? How does that infrastructural imaginary provide the background for delimiting particular networks of relation as *home* and *family* while casting matrices of relation that defy or exceed those boundaries as a deformation of the domestic? Within liberal ideologies, private space remains organized around units of social reproduction—the family—that also are units of property holding. Personhood arises from maturation and participation in such a unit, and governance consists of the exertion of authority over a particular territorial expanse in which such units are situated while itself remaining distinct and detached from such units—following impersonal principles that nonetheless exist to protect those personal spaces and the norms that shape them. Absent that nested structure of governance, though, the domestic makes no sense as a way of thinking about a kind of unit. Conversely, a scalar and infrastructural imaginary animated by continuity, rather than disjunction and privatization, offers a very different picture of the dynamics and aims of governance. Addressing the logics and politics of scale within dominant US mappings of social life, Mishuana Goeman (2017, 101) argues for the importance of being able to think "conduits of connection rather than impermeable entities," which she further describes as a sense of "scale based on connection."

In *Speaking of Indians*, Ella Deloria ([1944] 1998) explores the implications of such a rescaled vision by reformulating the topos of kinship. A Yankton intellectual who studied with Franz Boas, Deloria takes up the terms of anthropological discourse (though notably in a largely non-Boasian idiom) to highlight how within Dakota thought the kinds of collective processes that are characterized as the stuff of politics within liberalism cannot be differentiated from the realm of the familial.[7] Early in her discussion of "A Scheme of Life That Worked," Deloria notes that, prior to direct US intervention into intratribal social organization in the late nineteenth century, "Kinship was the all-important matter. Its demands and dictates for all phases of social life were relentless and exact," adding, "By kinship all Dakota people were held together in a great relationship that was theoretically all-inclusive and co-extensive with the Dakota domain" (24). The text offers no explicit definition of *kinship* as such, drawing on the term's accrued meanings while often figuring it in ways that have little to do with genealogical units of any sort. As a "great relationship" holding together "all Dakota people," it provides the principles through which collectivity, peoplehood, itself is defined and lived. Moreover, the territory encompassed within Dakota peoplehood cannot be distinguished from the contours and character of that "all-inclusive" relationship. There is no jurisdictional mapping that exceeds and encloses the "phases of social life" to which "kinship" here gestures.[8] This notion of kinship marks processes of interaction and enmeshment; as Daniel Heath Justice (2008, 150) argues, "Kinship is best thought of as a verb rather than a noun, because kinship, in most Indigenous contexts, is something that's *done* more than something that simply *is*." In Deloria's framing, the philosophies and practices that constitute such doing transect the liberal distinction between the public and private, enacting a scalar imaginary that moves from the individual (as responsible social actor) outward but that does not posit a break in which a different set of principles, actors, and institutions—*political* ones—take over in order to help actualize a kind of relation and space—the personal/private/ domestic—that is envisioned as qualitatively distinct from the workings of governance. Deloria ([1944] 1998, 31–32) indicates that "kinship held everybody in a fast net of interpersonal responsibility," and she soon thereafter observes, "that was practically all the government there was." If "kinship" indexes forms of "interpersonal" engagement, those patterns of behavior and conceptions of interdependent vulnerability and accountability provide the materials for continually generating a broader "net" that itself is the matrix of "relationship" that defines Dakota belonging and placemaking. Governance is the workings of that net in action, at all scales and in the movements among them—within a dwelling, among persons and dwellings in the tiospaye, relations among tiospayes, and so on.

This scalar imaginary envisions a social infrastructure in which the political arises out of and is embedded within embodied experience, itself understood as inherently relational. If in liberal ideologies public personhood and political subjectivity depend on proper enfamilyment, an insulated space and set of affects that ostensibly train individuals to take up impersonal principles and relations in order to protect norms of privatization, kinship in Indigenous intellectual work defies such segmentation. Offering an account of Michi Saagiig Nishnaabeg self-determination that resonates with Deloria's discussion of kinship as an encompassing relationship and mode of living, Leanne Simpson (2017, 112, 192) argues that "within Nishnaabeg thought, every body is a political order and every body houses individual self-determination," and she later underlines the importance of attending to "the generative and emergent qualities of living in our bodies as political orders."[9] To describe the Indigenous "body" as a "political order" means understanding everyday forms of lived sensation, feelings, and connections with other physical and noncorporeal entities as themselves enactments of governance. Persons are not atomized units (or ones who emerge from families that themselves are discrete units) who live within a polity that encompasses them and to which they belong in a serialized way by institutionalized criteria, such as genealogical inheritance. Instead, personhood involves complex and shifting reciprocities and responsibilities with other beings, and those relationships both constitute one as a person and position the body as a site from which the connections that constitute political life—the collective being and becoming of the polity—emanate. In this vein, Simpson observes, "Nishnaabeg life didn't rely on institutionality to hold the structure of life. We relied upon process that created networked relationship," and through such processes of networked relation, "governance was *made* every day" (23). As in Deloria's discussion of Dakota kinship, a nested jurisdictional logic of scale is replaced by a series of overlapping yet nonequivalent commitments of varied scope (in terms of persons/beings involved and geographic reach).

The body bears political orders because it is always enmeshed in ongoing matrices of relation with a range of persons, groups, and nonhuman entities/collectivities through which lived personhood cannot be differentiated from participation in the politics of governance. As Melanie Yazzie (2017) argues, attending to Indigenous "practices of making kin" can "encourage people to imagine collective forms of belonging and accountability that do not reproduce liberal ideas about citizenship and nationalism like those that give shape to U.S. settler nationalism." In this way, reconceptualizing governance as overlapping and intersecting networks of embodied responsibility seeks to orient away from the institutionalities and scale structure of the state as the de facto background (for collective decision making but also for remediation of problems); to open pathways for envisioning redistributions and alternative coalescences of affects, resources, and placemaking; and to offer normative frames for political life—for processes of governance—not dependent on ideologies and geographies of property.

Liberalism normatively territorializes the individual within the family (what I have termed enfamilyment), and articulations of "kinship" tend to enlarge that space while holding constant the scale structure of "political" institutions and their jurisdictional authority. However, ideologies of property, which, as Morgan's account suggests, can be understood as grounding ideas of home/family, require that familial households operate as discrete units. A similar logic shapes the levels of political scale: they enclose discrete units and are themselves discrete units enclosed within the level above them. This scalar imaginary is atomizing and hierarchical (what we might call the straight line of jurisdiction, echoing Ahmed's [2006, 66] figuration of heteropatriarchal inheritance), allowing for little lateral connection among units. Or such lateral relation itself appears as anomalous and potentially disruptive of both the insular discreteness of units and units' subordinating integration through the exertion of authority at the next level up. If kinship potentially provides a way of recognizing a wide range of social configurations, it also remakes them as a version of family, indexed to nuclear homemaking as (savage and/or perverse, even if sometimes "liberatory") deviations. Nonnative queer efforts to grapple with kinship have tended to run into this imperial and racializing process of translation. These queer critiques of liberalism, capitalism, and property get blunted by the difficulty of not de facto reinstalling liberal imaginaries as the background against which queerness (whatever its contours and character) gains meaning as deviation or exception. Kinship does a good deal of work in this regard: it dislocates intimacy, desire, and social reproduction from the scene and sites of governance/politics in ways that direct queer energies toward disowning the domestic (as the space of normative constriction) or distending/reforming it, rather than seeking to dismantle that distinction between public and private that legitimizes property holding, privatization, and the scale structure of jurisdiction. What is needed is an undoing of family itself, not just for some (as an exception of one form or another) but for all. Turning to the question of governance broadly stated, as Carruthers (2018) suggests, thus requires a revisiting of the kinship imaginary and the ways it orients horizons of critique and sociopolitical transformation.

Indigenous intellectuals inhabit and deploy the concept of kinship in ways that reorient it, helping highlight the often implicitly privatizing work the concept does within liberal political imaginaries. By foregrounding questions of governance and the inadequacy of family as a way of characterizing the networks of interdependence, responsibility, and accountability they address, these accounts theorize nonliberal sociopolitical dynamics and formations. In these accounts, kinship comes to name an alternative way of envisioning governance in which enfamilyment is not the racializing means of (pre)qualifying for personhood and political subjectivity. Rather than seeking to fit within liberal mappings (of personhood, identity, enfamilyment, jurisdiction), this reimagination of governance promotes an attention to existing and possible practices of collectivity and the lived and malleable connections among them. Doing so foregrounds the question of how those forms of belonging and interdependence function as *political* processes (rather than segmenting them off as familial or cultural). How does the United States already contain within itself political orders whose existence is not recognized as such (Indigenous and otherwise)? How do we understand those formations and modes of life that legally and administratively are cast as excessive, deviant, pathological, and criminal as, instead, lived political orders? How does doing so separate the question of governance from that of citizenship and the apparatuses of the liberal state? Indigenous appropriations of the kinship concept mobilize it toward registering the presence and tracing the operation of nonliberal modes of governance that neither segment off a privatized domesticity (however configured) nor remake such modes as cultural difference across a relativist divide (existing in an elsewhere/elsewhen separate from the liberal state). In this way, Native articulations of kinship offer intellectual avenues through which to highlight both the violence of ideologies of enfamilyment and the possibilities for acknowledging nonliberal social forms as governance.

Notes

1   On Morgan's biography and influence across multiple kinds of discourses and institutions, see Ben-Zvi (2007), Deloria (1999), Fortes ([1969] 2006), Simpson (2014), and Trautmann (1987).

2   In a draft of his earlier book *Systems of Consanguinity and Affinity of the Human Family* (1871), Morgan uses *natural* and *artificial* to designate this difference, later substituting *descriptive* and *classificatory*. See Trautmann (1987, 115–47).

3   Morgan ([1877] 1977, 62, 64, 85) defines the *gens* as "a body of consanguinei descended from the same common ancestor, distinguished by a gentile name, and bound together by affinities of blood," and this unit was the principal form of social organization among Native peoples in what is now the United States, often referred to as "tribe and clan," which are "equivalent" to gens. Though addressing the gens as a "unit of a social and governmental system," Morgan continually uses terms such as *consanguinei*, *natural*, and *organic* to refer to it, which imply an expansion from a reproductive core.

4   This analysis takes up and extends David L. Eng's (2010, 47) critique of "queer

liberalism," in which he argues that "intimacy" can be understood "as a racialized property right—one predicated on a long U.S. history of racial subordination and the legal protection of white privilege—[that] now serves to constitute normative gay and lesbian U.S. citizen-subjects as possessive individuals."

5 For questions about what "zones" of queer life can be inhabited by women, people of color, and disabled people, see Treva Ellison (2016), Roderick Ferguson (2019), Christina B. Hanhardt (2013), Alison Kafer (2013), Juana María Rodríguez (2014), and L. H. Stallings (2015).

6 On the tiospaye as a sociopolitical formation, see also Deloria ([1944] 1998), DeMallie (1994), Pexa (2019), and Rifkin (2011).

7 On Deloria, see Cotera (2008), Gardner (2000), and Rifkin (2011).

8 On the complexities of Native nations' exertions of jurisdiction, see Clint Carroll (2015), Jean Dennison (2012), Theresa McCarthy (2016), and Shiri Pasternak (2019).

9 On Indigenous bodies as political orders, see Simpson (2016).

_____

07 Ecstatic Kinship and Trans Interiority in Jackie Kay's *Trumpet*

With so many representations of Black trans people foregrounding violence, the cultural imaginary around trans of color life is saturated with notions of woundedness. In this context, this essay asks: how can a reorientation toward ecstasy rather than injury shift our understanding of Black trans life? What might an emphasis on pleasure make freshly legible about trans of color relationality? And how might Black trans belonging shed a different perspective on the relationship between gender and kinship? To answer these questions, I develop a trans hermeneutic that resists a fetishizing overemphasis on the trans body. Instead, I argue for a mode of reading Black trans texts that hones in on the spirit and soul. By shifting the gaze away from pornotropic violence, which has been reiterated so often in images of Black kinship disruption, this hermeneutic enacts a decolonial trans politics. Through a "trans-interior" reading of Jackie Kay's (1998) *Trumpet*, I move my analytic lens away from woundedness of the Black ungendered subject and toward the decolonial concept of what I call ecstatic kinship. This is not to say that examinations of the wound from which resistance emerges are not important; rather, my argument gestures toward an alternative way to understand Joss's Blackness and transness through decolonial forms of relational ecstasy. Ecstatic kinship discovers the intersections and interconnections of gendered embodiment, trans interiority, and Black diasporic belonging.

Trumpet sketches the afterlife of Joss Moody, a Black Scottish jazz musician whose trans identity is revealed after his death. Most of *Trumpet* is narrated through the points of view of cis characters, who are surveilling the protagonist. The novel thus invites the reader to gaze upon Joss's body and thereby inhabit a colonial gaze that fetishizes and disciplines Black trans bodies. Yet a trans-interior hermeneutic makes available an alternative orientation to the text, one that is less focused on the perspectives on cis characters and more attuned to the quotidian experiences of diasporic ecstasy that are co-constitutive of the protagonist's transness. As I demonstrate, *Trumpet*'s ephemeral moments of ecstatic kinship exceed the visible corporeality of the racialized trans body. These moments do not emerge transparently in the novel but rather linger under the surface constantly, bringing our attention to their opaque presence. Reading for ecstatic kinship in these moments thus orients us toward the expansiveness of the trans interior.

"Looking Elsewhere"

Many popular contemporary representations of trans people of color often hypervisibilize the body, asking viewers to gaze upon or imagine trans people's bodily specificity. Moreover, the prevalence of the medical archive in trans studies that focuses on physical "transitions" erases Black and brown trans people because of the racial violence of the Western medical industry.[1] Instead of analyzing the oft-fetishized bodily and social transitions and transformations undertaken by trans people of color, I seek to "look elsewhere" for Black trans life.[2] What kinds of "elsewheres" evade or refuse the cis gaze of coloniality that lingers on the Black trans exterior? Which trans-of-color lived experiences or realms are outside the reach of the colonial gaze, which is upheld not only by the medical-industrial complex but also by recent liberal transgender visibility politics? I explore these questions by developing a trans-interior hermeneutic that refuses an emphasis on the visual, the exterior, and the real in trans studies. Instead, I look to the interior, toward the internal affective workings of the spirit, namely ecstasy and relationality. My hermeneutic seeks to move beyond the ruptured and sutured skin, and beneath the surface, which so easily becomes a site of racial surveillance or a fetish of the cis gaze of coloniality.

This hermeneutic orientation toward the interior evades the readerly romance with physical and visible specificity that is so often present in realist representations of transgender characters. The cis gaze of coloniality is upheld not only by the racializing and un/gendering eye of the racial capitalist state but also by the ways in which cultural productions invite readers to visually consume Black and brown trans bodies.[3] The mainstreaming of transgender visibility projects in the past decade has constructed a transnormative figure who is often imagined as white, Western, upwardly mobile, and cosmopolitan, hence ontologically transforming its others into criminal and less-than-human.[4] As Western events such as Trans Day of Remembrance get globalized, trans visibility projects capitalize on trans death and grief to feed imperialist, anti-Black, and homonationalist impulses.[5]

My "trans-interior" hermeneutic critiques the readerly surveillance and hypervisibility of Black and brown transgender characters that pervades trans cultural representations, often inviting the reader/audience to dissect and "know" the bodily "truth" of these characters. I use "trans" not only as an identity but also as an analytic and hermeneutic to bring attention to trans experiences not only in the material plane but also in the affective and discursive planes. This trans-interior hermeneutic is based on the premise that critical agency resides in both the reader and the text. Such a reading practice can be applied by the reader to novels that show us glimpses of transcendence within the real to explore the significance of ephemeral affective moments that move outside the limits of the visible and the corporeal. In the second half of this essay I perform a trans-interior reading of *Trumpet* to move *beyond* or *trans* what we or the characters in the novel know and toward the opacity of the trans protagonist's rich inner life.

Because I am apprehensive of a return to essence or inner core in conversations about trans identity, it is worth noting that my move toward interiority maintains the antiessentialist stances of queer theory. There is no biological core that determines the interior; rather, the interior is always informed by the experiences of the body and flesh. Queer theory's attempt to use performativity as a way to depart from the biological essence, and queer-of-color critique's use of performance to highlight embodiment over the abstract, have cultivated groundbreaking theoretical and cultural shifts in conceptualizations of queer life. However, my hermeneutic offers a departure from essentialist *as well as* performative understandings of gender: informed by the theories of the spirit and the body, the interior strives to remain opaque to the external gaze, hence guarded from performative effects.

Although queer and trans are not distinct projects,[6] I nevertheless intentionally use *trans* instead of *queer* as a verb for a number for reasons.

First, queer studies has often co-opted trans embodiment to theorize a radical queer politic while simultaneously erasing the lived experience of trans people (Namaste 1996, 184). For this reason I use trans as a way to intervene in the assumed whiteness of queer studies by referring to what Marquis Bey (2017) calls the transness of Blackness. Recognizing the shared urgencies and genealogies of queer-of-color and trans-of-color critique, I echo Kai M. Green's (2016, 67) speculative argument that "trans* is the queer. Trans* is the colored."

Most important, the etymology of *trans* points to the movement and migrations present in the histories of racialized diasporic formations. The etymology of *trans* is rooted in the Latin *trans*, meaning "across," "on the other side," or "beyond." The prefix *trans* signifies moving from one conceptual or geographical side of the border/boundary to the other. *Trans* as movement captures the migrations, displacements, captivities, and fugitivities that are in perpetual flux in the Black diaspora. Therefore, *trans* can function as a hermeneutic to read for the transness that is always already present in the diaspora. The prefix *trans* in *transatlantic* and *transnational* already does the work of gesturing toward gendered and nongendered forms of transing as well. Although queer diaspora scholars have shown how the diaspora queers the nation, the centrality of movement to the prefix *trans* interweaves diaspora and transnational kinship ties that are constantly *on the move*, concepts that queerness does not easily conjure. A hermeneutic that apprehends the "beyondness" of *trans* thus enables a move away from the medicalized body and toward the rich interior spirit while also keeping in mind the material histories of forced migrations and fugitivities.

The diaspora exemplifies a relational community in which one is always in movement with others, so movement operates as the bridge between trans becoming and the Black diaspora. As Bey (2019, 34) states, "Kinship begotten in the fugitivity of Blackness' coalitional drive" creates a form of companionship in which one is "with a whole bunch of other folks who synesthetically see without light, our co-dwellers on the dark side who move, always, with furtive fugitive movements—movements of thought, movements of gait, movements of flesh, movements of subjectivity." In the kinship community that Bey sketches, people are connected "without light," suggesting a decolonial way of seeing that does not depend on normative visibility. Even in the dark, Bey's kinfolk are always moving, in embodiment as well as in interiority. An examination of interiority reveals not only the transness present in Bey's description but also the rhizomatic flux of movements in Black trans diasporic texts, where protagonists are transing/

moving/shifting genders as well as subjectivities, feelings, and realities. Therefore, sustained multiple movements are essential both to transness *and* to kinship.

Where Is the Ecstasy?

Moving "beyond" the materiality of the violated body and toward the interior entails an exploration of the affective life of transness. I explore transness through the affective politics of ecstasy primarily because ecstasy, or feeling *transly*, can subvert the liberal fetish of "representing" the Black trans body through pornotropic reiterations of violence.[7] This orientation toward affect and feeling also stems from a Black feminist genealogy, particularly June Jordan's ever-important question during her Howard University address: "Where is the love?" (quoted in Nash 2013, 2). This invocation asks us to center love over violence in Black feminist political work because as Jennifer Nash (2013, 18–19) astutely argues, "Black feminist love-politics crafts a political community that eschews the wounded subject that lies at the heart of identity politics." Although diasporic love certainly guides my understanding of kinship, I ask: "Where is the ecstasy?" A trans-interior hermeneutic hones in on fleeting moments of ecstatic interiority and chooses to linger and loiter in their transience, to spend time and share affective space with such ephemeral instances of transcendental joy and love, and to truly invest in the capacity of such moments to theorize Black trans life. In doing so, such a hermeneutic reveals new ways of understanding diasporic trans becoming that undercut the anti-trans surveillance pervading cultural representations of trans-of-color bodies.

This theoretical turn to ecstasy (and other "positive affects") in queer-of-color critique and Black studies is not entirely new. In her exploration of pornography, Nash asks us to shift away from protectionist frameworks that privilege violence to ones that recognize unnerving pleasures. Nash uses ecstasy specifically in the context of sex to mark the fraught nature of "uncomfortable enjoyment *in* embodied racialization." For Aliyyah Abdur-Rahman (2018, 345), however, ecstasy "exceeds pleasure and sex" and "connotes a queer of color beyond that is simultaneously atemporal and communal" because "it resists the logics of teleological progression by opening an immediate space of relational joy for black and brown people." My approach to trans ecstasy recognizes the "communal joy" that is beyond sex and sexualization, and proposes ecstasy as a decolonial way of reading.

My trans hermeneutic is distinct from the antinormativity inherent in many critical queer reading practices. Even though my use of the affective hermeneutics of ecstasy is rooted in a genealogy of queer reading practices that critique the centrality of a hermeneutics of suspicion in literary studies—from Eve Sedgwick's (1997) reparative reading practices to José Esteban Muñoz's (1999) disidentifications—my trans hermeneutic is not oppositional. A trans-interior hermeneutic privileges a *decolonial* politic that strives to imagine transness *outside* of coloniality or in friction with coloniality while also remaining cognizant of postcolonial critiques of the impossibility of an absolute escape from coloniality.

The affective realm of quotidian life provides a way to understand this decolonial relationship because it is not only encapsulated by injury or resistance. Kevin Quashie (2012) argues for the importance of examining Black interiority over resistance as a way to affirm and recognize the importance of quotidian Black life outside of protest.[8] Drawing on Quashie's decolonial premise, I center the ecstasy of diasporic kinship as a way to theorize transness because, as an affect, ecstasy helps us speculate about the imaginative potential of gendered relationality.

The spatial metaphorics of transness bring to mind the rhizomatic movements of the diaspora. The etymology of the word *ecstasy* is rooted in the Greek word *ekstasis*, combining *ek* ("beyond"), and *stasis* ("standing still"). Therefore, ecstatic experiences move the spirit or soul beyond this realm while the body remains still. The spatial metaphorics of "beyondness" in ecstasy are also resonant of the spatial transing implied by the *trans* prefix. The stillness of the body showcases how ecstasy is an interior affective experience, but *ek* also reveals how ecstasy constitutes a movement "beyond" or "out of this world." According to Stallings (2011, 50), ecstasy entails "stepping outside of oneself to know that self." So if Fanon's ([1952] 2008, 110) third-person gaze or Du Bois's ([1903] 2008) double consciousness stems from living in a white supremacist surveillant culture, then ecstasy does the same "stepping out" but for different reasons. The act of "stepping out" in an ecstatic experience is not a response to the external white gaze; rather, it stems from the personal need to find freedom within. Therefore, ecstasy becomes the medium to *trans* in and for diasporic kinship.

How can we eschew the centralization of what Fred Moten (2003, 18), drawing on Nathaniel Mackey, describes as "wounded kinship" and instead look toward a transcendent politic of ecstatic kinship that delineates freedom outside the confines of Western ontology? At the end of her famous essay on the ungendering of Black flesh under enslavement, Hortense Spillers (1987, 80) warns against "joining the ranks of gendered femaleness" and urges her readers to assume "insurgent ground." C. Riley Snorton (2017) suggests that this insurgent ground is always already trans. A trans-interior hermeneutic, I suggest, offers one way to occupy such a trans insurgent ground. This insurgent ground allows for an alternative narrative of trans desire and being. Instead of medicalized dysphoria informing one's trans identity, rhizomatic diasporic kinship ties lead to a desire to constantly *become* the figure that one is in relation with.

Kinship, as a guiding concept and theme, is central to Black diaspora studies as well as queer studies.[9] In queer studies the concepts of fictive and chosen kinship have also critiqued the homonormative liberal movements that seek assimilation into the capitalist heterosexual family structure.[10] Although (white) queer kinship theories have focused strongly on critiques and alternatives to the heterosexual couple, Black diaspora studies and postcolonial studies have often emphasized intergenerational ties in explorations of fictive kinship.[11] Because I am deeply affected by Keguro Macharia's (2019) critiques of a "genealogical imperative" in studies of the Black diaspora and by his notion of frottage as an alternative to this genealogical imperative, I have tried to keep my definition of kinship in this essay as speculative and shifting as possible, and have endeavored to refuse a reification of rigid rootedness in a *certain* genealogy. Trans ecstatic kinship always takes more routes than it does roots.

My emphasis on ecstasy and transcendence eschews the prevalence of family ties in favor of imagined kinship relations that can affectively transport one across and through space, hence embodying the *dia* ("across") of the word *diaspora*. At times, I use *diaspora* and *kinship* interchangeably to highlight the interwoven nature of Black diasporic histories that exceed borders and Black kinship structures that are excluded from the state's notion of the family. As I show in the next section, it is diaspora aesthetics, after all, that allow *Trumpet*'s protagonist to have access to speculative/speculated kinship, gendered improvisations, and self-determination, as well as heightened feeling and pleasure.

A Black Scottish rewriting of the life of Billy Tipton, *Trumpet* takes place in the wake of famous jazz trumpeter Joss Moody's premature death. *Trumpet* opens with Joss's wife, Millie, who is grieving over losing her husband as she is harassed by journalists after the forced public revelation of Joss's trans identity. Slowly the reader learns that Joss was not "out" as a trans person to anyone except Millie; even their son, Colman, lived a traditional life in a seemingly normative household, never knowing the full truth about his father's lived experiences. Joss's forced outing after his death by doctors and administrators leads to a journalistic fetishization of his life, and his public memory shifts away from his musical genius and quotidian family life and toward his gender "deception." Whereas the novel focuses mostly on the violence done to Joss's body by the many cis characters, it also shows transient glimpses of deep loving familial connection between Joss and his father, John Moore, and later between Joss and his son, Colman, all recounted in the wake of Joss's passing.

Reading the novel through a trans-interior hermeneutic reveals the theoretical and aesthetic importance of the brief, nonrealist moments of ecstasy that rupture the novel's form. A trans-interior hermeneutic reorients Joss's identity from one that is centered on injury to one that is perpetually transformed and transforming through ecstasy. Although the novel easily lends itself to an analysis of queer kinship and trans necropolitics, on the surface it is not about ecstasy at all. Rather, the narrations of Joss's life fill the reader with extreme discomfort as we realize how much of Joss's own voice is robbed by other characters. One can read the description of Joss's lived experiences as an ethical authorial move by Jackie Kay as she distances her own voice from the voice of a trans character. While Kay's personal experiences of adoption as a mixed Black Scottish person do seem to inform the novel's politics, I separate the art from the artist to show how the author, in an ethical refusal to speak on behalf of Joss in most of the novel, is choosing to not fully "grasp" or "know" the gendered experiences of her protagonist but rather to only gesture toward his trans diasporic ecstasy. In this case the nontrans author seems to celebrate opacity as she sketches the interiority of a trans character by rupturing the novel only with ephemeral moments of Joss's speculative meditations.

Most literary scholars who have examined *Trumpet* have written about its gender politics while ignoring the importance of race in the text.[12] These readings overlook the co-constitution of Blackness and transness. By contrast, Matt Richardson (2012, 2013) centers *both* race and gender, taking into account historical ungenderings of Blackness under enslavement. Richardson (2013, 108) focuses on Kay's adoption of African American literary aesthetics, particularly her references to jazz. This understanding of the relationality of different histories in the diaspora not only reconfigures larger conceptions of kinship but also points to the relevance of historical, racialized ungendering in Joss's and Colman's lives.

Different kinds of anti-trans surveillance take place in our reading experience of this novel. The journalist Sophie Stones strips Joss's life bare so she can write a sensationalist book about trans identity; Doctor Krishnamurty practices the surveillance inherent in the Western medical industry as she examines Joss's body; the undertaker physically probes Joss's genitals in an act that feels viscerally sexually violent. The novel explicitly critiques these forms of state-based surveillance and their violence. However, the surveillance that I am writing against is the readerly surveillance that is invited by Millie's remembrances of Joss's revelation of his transness, a kind of reading experience that makes us complicit in sexually stripping Joss.

The elaborate and detailed descriptions of Joss undressing for Millie invite the reader to also surveil Joss and ascertain the "truth" of his bodily specificity, even as these scenes are written through the point of view of his partner. Here I am actively choosing not to quote such parts of the text to avoid reproducing the nonconsensual, and at times fetishizing, stripping of the Black trans body. As Saidiya Hartman (1997, 3) contends, a reiteration of scenes of subjection re-creates that violence through the act of description by making us "voyeurs fascinated with and repelled by exhibitions of terror and sufferance." Although it is important to differentiate the discursive violence in *Trumpet* from the horrific material bodily and spiritual violence undergone by Aunt Hester in Hartman's examination, I adopt Hartman's ethic of refusing citations of violence even if the purpose of that citation is critique. The repetitive reiteration of the undoing of Joss's bandages as Millie remembers how he undressed and dressed brings the reader into uncomfortable proximity with Joss's body, asking us at times to also strip Joss's body even as we are asked to critique the objectifying gazes of cis and white characters.

Because the "Music" chapter and the concluding letter are the only parts of the novel where we hear Joss's own voice, Kay simultaneously reproduces, critiques, and undermines anti-trans surveillance while also providing us with a narrative of transness that lies outside Western models of "transitions." She stresses that the process of gendered becoming is deeply interconnected with and co-constitutive of African diasporic kinship ties. Joss did not have direct material contact with his father during his years as a musician; rather, jazz allows him to feel ecstatic oneness with his father and other imagined ancestral figures. The nonrealist, fabulationist, and dream-like musical moments in *Trumpet* reenvision Black diasporic transness through ecstasy rather than through Western and white epistemologies of gender deviance.

To exist ecstatically is to exist decolonially: to be *outside* the socially constructed gendered and raced self, to be stripped to one's core but still be impenetrable to the external gaze. Described through an omniscient, lyrical spirit/narrator, the "Music" chapter outlines Joss's spirit's abstract movements as he plays his trumpet: "When he gets down, and he doesn't always get down deep enough, he loses his sex, his race, his memory. He strips himself bare, takes everything off, till he's barely human" (Kay 1998, 131). In the rest of the novel, other people undress Joss. Here the music allows him to "strip himself bare" in a way that does not render him observable and knowable to the external gaze but rather brings him closer to his inner core "till he's barely human." Barely human, Joss refuses what Sylvia Wynter calls the Western epistemological Human (or Man2) (cited in McKittrick 2015, 24–38). The ecstasy of unbecoming in this instance is not about resistance or successful protest of an anti-Black world; rather, it is about *transcending* that anti-Black world. This eschewing of the imperative to assimilate into the Western Human in order to gain subjectivity is a decolonial move that resists the urge to be defined by the colonizer-colonized binary. Therefore, a trans-interior hermeneutic enables us to see ecstasy as a move not outside of sociality but outside the murderous colonial epistemologies that proscribe Black trans life into social death.

The decolonial orientation of this chapter also lies in its refusal of mimetic representation. Although most of *Trumpet* is written predominantly in a realist mode, its jazz aesthetic disrupts that realism by bringing forth an experience that can be felt by the reader but not fully understood. Joss exists as a sonic body demanding to be "heard, felt and given the attention of listening," not looked at (Henriques 2011, 2). Unburdening Black trans art from the expectation of realist verisimilitude, a trans-interior hermeneutic *feels* beyond the visible in order to fully value the wholeness of a character like Joss. Violence and injury cannot be ignored while examining the necropolitics of the novel as a whole. But the instances of Joss playing his trumpet allow him to embrace his full self without our fixating on the disaster of his premature death.

Thus, *Trumpet* offers glimpses of José Esteban Muñoz's (2009) queer utopia through ecstatic experience. As music strips him bare and he gallops through different memories, Joss is able to step out of chrononormativity.[13] Muñoz conceptualizes ecstasy as a "stepping out of time and place, leaving the here and now of straight time for a then and there that might be queer futurity" (185). Yet the here and now *and* the then and there do not take into account the necropolitical violence done to Black trans people such as Joss, for whom a future is often lived after or outside of death. Having died because of the presumed transphobia and racism of the medical industry, Joss does not have a "then and there."

For Joss, ecstasy is less about looking beyond the horizon and more about losing the self outside of time while also embodying a multiplicity of selves in an imaginative and spiritual act of breathing into his instrument. A need to always look to the future also ignores or diminishes the utopic and ecstatic work that occurs inside memory and imagination; as he plays his horn, Joss stands out of time, connects with his diaspora, and *builds* a whole interior world emptied of coloniality. Jazz bassist William Parker claims that free music is about "emptying oneself and being" (quoted in Such 1993, 131). *Trumpet* echoes this idea of ecstasy as emptying. It demonstrates that the spirit's ecstasy is not about a futuristic wholeness but fully and freely becoming nothing in order to become everything.

Trans/cending into Nothingness

The ecstasy of Joss's trumpet embodies Audre Lorde's (1978) notion of the erotic.[14] It allows Joss to connect with his most inner self, to go deep and down:

> There is music in his blood . . . he feels himself going down. . . . He can go all the way to the bottomless ground. There's the sensation of falling without ever stopping. Each time is like dying. . . .
>
> It is painful. But there is nothing like that pain. That pain is the sweetest, most beautiful pain in the world. Better than sex. Soar or shuffle along, wing or glide, trudge or gallop, kicking out, mugging heavy, light, licking, breaking, screw-balling. Out of this world . . . he can't stop himself changing. Running changes. Changes running. He is changing all the time. It all falls off—bandages, braces, cufflinks, watches, hair grease, suits, buttons,

ties. He is himself again, years ago, skipping along the railway line with a long cord his mother had made into a rope. In a red dress. It is liberating. To be a girl. To be a man.

The music is in his blood. His cells. But the odd bit is that down at the bottom, the blood doesn't matter after all. . . .

His story is blowing the wind. He lets it rip. His story is blowing in the wind. He lets it rip. He tears himself apart. He explodes. Then he brings himself back. Slowly, slowly, piecing himself together. (Kay 1998, 134–35)

Read aloud, the prose has the rhythm of a jazz song, making the reader almost breathless with the sentence breaks as we too are called to "soar and shuffle along" with Joss. The pain that Joss describes is akin to ecstasy not only because of the pleasure in it, a pleasure that's "better than sex," but also because it *moves* his spirit—both emotionally and literally—"out of this world" resonating with the *ek* of ekstasis. Even as he stands still, Joss's inhabitation of a realm "otherwise" or "beyond" results in a transcendental musical experience that moves beyond the constraints of the material world into a reality where he can shed his social self and be one with his trumpet. Here, ecstatic oneness suggests how the notion of transness can be expanded to include not only freedom/pleasure for trans characters but also a musical experience of "beyondness" for the reader. The ecstatic movements of "gliding," "soaring," or "galloping" spatially *trans* Joss's external reality; his movement beyond or *trans* his full self lets him lose his full humanness; once he is outside himself, his spirit is unreachable, unseen, and illegible to the external eye, even as he shares his ecstatic musical experience with his audience. Such trans(cendence) locates Joss simultaneously *outside* and *within* the public.

The jazz aesthetic is particularly important to *Trumpet* because jazz exemplifies the spirit of personal reinvention and fantasy. The aesthetics of this passage also reflects the choice that one has within improvisation, deciding based on what *feels* right, which tune or beat to take on. Joss can "soar *or* shuffle along, wing *or* glide, trudge *or* gallop" based on the affective and ecstatic decisions he makes during the process of playing his trumpet. The exact movements of the song and his body are not predecided; it is during the transcendental moment that he has the freedom to choose a musical route that ultimately takes him on a particular speculative diasporic path. The image of Joss exploding and then piecing himself together brings forth the creative rearrangement that he undertakes with all his parts. Even though he explodes, he has the same bits and pieces that he can rearrange to recreate his self, that can shift and change and gallop between his various memories of being a little girl, of being a man, of being in a red dress, and of being in suits and ties as he blows on his horn.

Moreover, the repetition of change, changing, and running also connotes the improvisational aspect of jazz. The "changes" represent a constant fluidity not only of the gendered body but also of the spirit and the music, and "running" encapsulates the pace of the movement of these changes; as the song picks up, Joss's changes "run" faster. The idea of change, moving, and reinvention comes up time and again in the novel not only in regards to gender but also in relation to kinship; in fact, it is reinvention as a concept which demonstrates that, in Black diaspora, one cannot separate gender from kinship.

Here, movement—encapsulated by performance, spirituality, and transcendence—is essential both to transness *and* to Black kinship, in interconnected and similar ways. When Millie first meets Joss, she wonders if he has "practiced" his physical movements because he moves so much like certain other figures; we learn later that the idea of practice, copying, imitating, and reinvention *is* in fact a part of Joss's gendered and musical genealogy. Later in the novel, Colman remembers Joss's teachings about jazz: "all jazzmen are fantasies of themselves, reinventing the Counts and Dukes and Armstrongs, imitating them" (Kay 1998, 190). It is a larger diasporic kinship that teaches Joss how to perform and move his masculinity through imitation and improvisation. As a practice, jazz allows for the continuous production of the body's meaning, operating as an epistemology that acts as a force behind the reinvention of identities that are fixed under the white cis gaze (Richardson 2013). Therefore, jazz is not only a tool for creating varied and creative diasporic lineages but is also a "site of gender ambivalence and dislocation" that can serve as "a guiding metaphor regarding rethinking Blackness" (Richardson 2013, 132–33).

Trumpet speculates a larger diasporic connection than the limited ancestral history of migration from Africa to Scotland that is available to Joss. As Matt Richardson has shown, the novel insists on the relevance of the history of the transatlantic slave trade to Scottish Black trans life. Therefore, I read Joss's narrative through Spillers's (1987) and Snorton's (2017) notions of violent ungendering to show that interiority is the "insurgent ground" that, in its opacity, can refigure ungendered flesh with subjectivity and life. As Orlando Patterson (2018), Spillers, and Snorton show, one's subjectivation as human depends on kinship ties defined by normative binary genders; as enslaved people were ungendered, they were robbed of familial ties as well. *Trumpet* foregrounds this history by showing the co-constitution of Black diasporic kinship and creative transness.

For example, in his letter to Colman, Joss describes John Moore as "disembodied" because when he reached Scotland, his body was "broken up in the fog" (Kay 1998, 128). Joss's masculinity is thus an act of healing the ancestral traumatic memory of the forced ungendering and disembodiment suffered by his father. He "becomes" a "full" man to heal the ancestral spirit of his father. The repetition of music being "in his blood" highlights the importance as well as the privilege granted to fabulated bloodlines. Multiple times, Colman remembers Joss saying that literal biological lineages do not matter; after all, Colman is adopted. Yet the reiteration of blood suggests a form of corporeal connection between Joss and Colman, and between him and the music, that I read as diasporic. Though not tied to biological lineage or patrilineal bloodline, the blood connects Joss in a corporeal way to his ancestors, which include both his father, John Moore, and his larger diasporic kin. I read the "blood" here as trans-bodily connections that open space for a rearrangement of the self based on ancestral affective connections. To create blood ties in a chosen transatlantic family, Joss bleeds music out of his attachment with his father, who connects Joss with the larger Black diaspora. For Joss, John Moore *is* the diaspora. Indeed, he describes his father's story with a fabulatory multiplicity that encompasses the many stories of the African diaspora. Hence, the music *is* his blood, not because John was his biological father but because John was the bridge that connects Joss to the Black diaspora, providing him access to a kinship structure far more creative and far less restricting than the patrilineal bloodline.

Part of the creativity of this kinship structure lies in Joss's active fabulation of his own bloodline and his demand that Colman, too, creatively *imagine* his bloodline rather than seek essentialist truths about his family. Remembering his father's meditations on blood and family, Colman says, "My father always told me he and I were related in the way it mattered. . . . He said you make your own bloodline, Colman. Make it up and trace it back. Design your own family tree—what's the matter with you? Haven't you got an imagination?" (Kay 1998, 58). The notion of "making it up," designing," and using "imagination" to create one's family tree echoes Tavia Nyong'o's (2018, 5–6) theorization of Afro-fabulation. Through mythmaking, Afro-fabulation challenges an anti-Black world by showing glimpses of other imaginative ways of being and doing. In a world that essentializes gender and race, Joss "makes up" his kinship in order to gain power. Kay sketches a family portrait that may share the facade of assimilation into heteronormative multicultural liberal citizenship, upheld through the interracial nuclear family. Yet through ecstatic kinship, Kay offers a creative and decolonial stance toward bloodlines.

Through fabulation and antirealist speculation, Joss tactically appropriates the violent fungibility of Blackness to forge relations between those historically othered from humanness:

> Look, Colman, he said. Look, Colman, I could tell you a story about my father. I could say he came off a boat one day in the nineteen hundreds, say a winter day. All the way from the "dark continent" on a cold winter day, a boat that stopped at Greenock. . . . Or I could say my father was a black American who left America because of segregation. . . . Or I could say my father was a soldier or a sailor who was sent here by his army or his navy. Or I could say father was from an island in the Caribbean whose name I don't know because my mother couldn't remember it. Or never bothered to ask. And any of these stories might be true, Colman. (Kay 1998, 58–59)

Joss does not assimilate to Enlightenment individuality. Instead, he strategically co-opts and transforms the anti-Black conflation of different histories of people with African descent to comment on the *possibilities* that arise from a diasporic framework. The repetition of *or*, similar to the usage of *or* in the "Music" chapter, highlights the choices that he has given himself. Just as he can improvise the next tune on his horn, Joss can improvise the next narrative of his father's arrival in Scotland.

The ending of *Trumpet* points toward a larger decolonial orientation toward the diaspora. Millie walks toward an unnamed figure who moves exactly like "his father," suggesting that "he" could either be Colman or Joss. Most scholars have read this person as Colman.[15] However, I argue that the intentional unnaming of this figure meditates on the reincarnation of gendered familial/diasporic spirits as they copy, fabulate, perform, and reinvent the meaning of masculinity. Kay refuses to distinguish Colman and Joss at the end of the novel. In doing so she highlights their multiplicity in the diaspora over their individuality. This is a decolonial move to imagine oneness outside the dictates of Western ontology.

The collapsing of individuality into nothingness when Joss blows his horn also brings to mind Fred Moten's (2013) notion of nothingness, of being outside or beyond humanistic ontology. Instead of imagining Joss's personhood as a *response* to anti-trans surveillance or Western trans identity, however, his being and becoming aspire to exist outside the confines of colonial/modern ontology. In a decolonial (rather than anticolonial) world, the collapsing of different individuals is less a theft of uniqueness than a comment on the relationality of different modes of being, whether these modes are gendered or not. Similar to the unnaming of Colman/Joss at the end, or the multiple possibilities of John Moore's history, we see Joss literally transform into nothingness as he plays his trumpet and gallops all over the diaspora. As he blows his horn, he becomes "bigger not only spatially, but also temporally" (Freeman 2007, 299), and he experiences expansive diasporic space and time, along with an expansive sense of multiple genders: "So when he takes off he is the whole century galloping to its close. The wide moors. The big mouth. Scotland. Africa. Slavery. Freedom. He is a girl. A man" (Kay 1998, 136).

As Joss transes space and time, it is not his unique body that is made fungible by the white gaze but rather the ecstasy of jazz and diasporic relations that shatters his whole self in a moment of transcendental and "out of body" jouissance. This ecstasy is a form of acute belonging with a larger kin. As Joss individually becomes nothing, his kin becomes more and more real. He is able to feel a whole century, to touch the wild moors, to "hold out a hand across time and touch the dead or those not born yet, to offer oneself beyond one's own time" (Freeman 2007, 299).

Describing his metamorphosis into nothingness, the narrator claims that all of Joss's self collapses—his idiosyncrasies, his personality, his ego, his sexuality, even, finally, his memory: "All of it falls away like layers of skin unwrapping. He wraps himself with his trumpet. Down at the bottom, face to face with the fact that he is nobody. The more he can be nobody the more he can play the horn. Playing the horn is not about being somebody coming from something. It is about being nobody coming from nothing. The horn ruthlessly strips him bare till he ends up with no body, no past, nothing" (Kay 1998, 134–35).

There is freedom in being *nothing*, in being a nonself, in being and becoming in a manner that is completely opaque to the realism of the rest of the novel. According to Amaryah Shaye, "To become black is to refuse being made a something—to be and become nothing." This is "not because nothing is an absence or a lack of life, but precisely because nothing is the abundance and multiplicity out of which life is formed" (quoted in Bey 2017, 275). This notion of emergence and possibility is seen during Joss's experience of playing the trumpet, where he is able to elude not only the gaze of a white cis world but also the limitations of trans-ing only into a binary gender. The reader assumes Joss's identity as a man based only on Millie's narratives. Because Joss does seem to identify as a binary trans man in his external public life, his interiority is often read as static, through Western-colonial frameworks of transgender identity. Here I want to warn against the false binary between an ecstatic trans movement and a static binary trans identity. In showing Joss's ecstatic moments, I am not disregarding Joss's binary trans identity but rather simply expanding and deconstructing modern conceptualizations of binary (and nonbinary) trans experiences. It is not one's static trans *self-identification* that reflects a Western production of binary gender, but rather the surveillant cis gaze that violently freezes trans experiences into stasis that perpetuates coloniality. However, even within his binary trans identity, we see that Joss's positionality in the Black diaspora allows his interiority to be much richer, more creative, and more conducive to limitless possibilities than his external life. My reading of Joss's expansive transness shows that ecstatic kinship and binary trans identity are not mutually exclusive: we can look for ecstatic modes of trans relationality within normative binary trans identity as well. Because trans life, when informed by and intersecting with experiences of migration, movement, and racialization, is always already more capacious and relational than Western-colonial cultural and medical narratives of gender allow, Joss bounces between genders, between selves, between spaces, and between memories until he shatters and begins to embody a constant "state of emergence."[16]

Being nothing is not the same as being body-less; the interior returns flesh to the stature of body. The cis gaze of coloniality renders Joss fleshly, but music transforms him into a spirit who is still alive or who can still remember, fantasize, imagine, improvise, laugh, cry, and feel fully and erotically even in death. Joss's corporeal wholeness is always in the backdrop of his spirit's meditations on his trumpet, an instrument that requires the full skill of a living, *breathing* body. Joss's spiritual nothingness is tied to his spirit, but his trumpet maintains the significance of his body, reminding us of the relation between ecstasy and embodiment. Ecstasy of the spirit is the bridge between the violence of being rendered/perceived as flesh and the fulfillment of being a full breathing body. Despite its music sounding *in death*, the trumpet demonstrates the importance of breath, life, and the body.

As a wind instrument, the trumpet requires circular breathing and a deep sensing of the body with the spirit. Therefore, his trumpet brings Joss closer to life and living. Even though the novel does not explicitly name Joss's breathing as central to his musical ecstatic experiences, the reader knows that Joss is breathing circularly and deeply as he steps out of time and space. The breath that forms Joss's musical performance intervenes in the way that breath is rendered precarious for Black trans people. From Fanon's ([1952] 2008) claim that we revolt because we can no longer breathe to Eric Garner's utterances of "I can't breathe," breath is central to social and material life and death. After all, breath is the condition for life; the body functions because of breath. To refocus attention on breath, as *Trumpet* asks us to, restates the sacredness of the body. Yet breath and breathing are invisible; Joss's audience can *hear* and *feel* his breath but cannot *see* it. The impossibility of the external gaze to contain, mark, and represent breath keeps the body as well as the interior opaque.

The Opacity of Black Trans Interiority

Although colonial/modern representations of racialized gender often turn readers into ethnographic voyeurs, a trans-interior hermeneutic embraces the "unknowable" in Black trans interiority. During Joss's moments of ecstatic ancestral connection the reader does not have full access to his inner world. "Against this reductive transparency," upheld by the rest of the novel, "a force of opacity is at work" in the "Music" chapter (Glissant 1997).[17] His interior rhythms are at the forefront of such experiences, but his trans spirit and embodiment are always in flux, refusing any kind of capture, refusing compulsory visibility. The cis gaze of coloniality pervading the rest of the novel, the eye of gender administration, and the invasive probes of the medical practitioners can touch Joss's body but cannot reach his elusive and opaque interiority. Joss's musical ecstatic experience lies beyond the reach of the surveillance state and, at times, even beyond the reach of the surveillant reader. Reading *Trumpet* through a fabulationary and speculative trans-interior hermeneutic demands that we too resist an urge to fully *know* Joss's gendered self. The opacity of Joss's ancestral ecstasy personifies a fugitive and self-preserving politic that protects Joss's spirit, even as his body is violated.

A nonsurveillant reading embraces the impossibility of knowing Joss's visible truth and rather *feels* his shifting movements of self, gender, memories, and fabulations with him. Part of Joss's ecstasy in the experience of stripping himself bare during his jazz performances is to become opaque. Fumi Okiji (2018, 82–83) argues that the aesthetics of blues and jazz are "really the amplification of this (right to) opacity" because "their indecipherability holds us analysts at arm's length, and at the very same time, they wrap themselves around those who approach without prejudice." Therefore, the reader cannot fully *understand* what is happening, which also reminds us that despite all the musings and remembrances of Joss through the perspectives of other characters, they can never grasp Joss's interiority. As Okiji suggests, we can only hope to be affectively "wrapped" in it. This is the powerful work of trans-interiority: Joss shape-shifts into the opaque space of nothingness and emerges multiply from within it, blowing rhythms of infinite possibilities.

The ecstasy of jazz in *Trumpet* is but one example of aesthetic opacity. What if we looked for opacity in representations of Black trans identity, not to "know" or "understand" transness but rather to be affectively wrapped up in its movements? The only way to conceptualize Black trans interiority is to feel its opacity, its withholding, and its refusal to be known.

Through *Trumpet* I have demonstrated how trans-interior hermeneutics refocus attention on Black trans interiority by pausing, lingering, and loitering in the ephemeral cadences of Joss's dreamlike and musical consciousness. Trans-interior hermeneutics can be applied to many other postcolonial or Black diaspora texts as well, even texts that have no explicit trans themes and are otherwise not read for their imagining of transness. Take, for example, the classic postcolonial novel *GraceLand* by Chris Abani (2004), when a character's spirit rises up and shape-shifts into a predator to kill the soldier who is demolishing his home. How can this momentary rupture of the realist form theorize trans desire through revenge fantasies? Or Edwidge Danticat's *Breath, Eyes, Memory* (1994), when the protagonist asks to be metamorphosed from a woman to a butterfly as a way to escape trauma: how would our understanding of trans survival shift if we took seriously such dreams of trans-animalizing? Or Nuruddin Farah's *Maps* (1986), when a character desires to become a part of his mother, only to wake up menstruating the mother's blood: how does such intense bodily connection collapse the difference between son and mother to reveal how affective attachment conditions trans desires? Such ephemeral and opaque moments of spiritual or affective bodily transformation imagine an ecstatic way of being and becoming and offer powerful moments for decolonial trans reading.

What if we theorized transness through the affective moments that empty racialized people's bodies of colonial ontological meanings, giving them a right to opacity? What if we lingered in these moments—not to know the "how" of trans becoming but to *feel with* expansive forms of trans becoming that escape definition? An attunement to trans interiority allows affective relation with such fugitive and speculative moments. It is in these fugitive flashes of interiority that we can retheorize transness not as a medicalized dysphoria or gender deviance but as the rhizomatic movement of gender, speculation, memory, and affect cutting through time and space. And it is in this hold of diasporic relationality that trans(gender) desires—or desires to trans—manifest as strategic moments of moving "beyond" the violence of the material and toward the ecstasy of the opaque.

Notes

1   Jules Gill-Peterson (2018) has demonstrated how trans studies' reliance on the medical archive has erased and distorted trans of color life.
2   Here I extend the invocation of Ellison et al. (2017, 166) to create alternate archives for Black trans life.
3   On the state surveillance of trans people, see Toby Beauchamp's *Going Stealth: Transgender Politics and US Surveillance Practices* (2019).
4   For critiques of transnormativity, see Aren Aizura (2018) and Jasbir Puar (2017).
5   See, for example, C. Riley Snorton and Jin Haritaworn (2013). Also see *Trap Door: Trans Cultural Production and the Politics of Visibility* (Gossett, Stanley, and Burton 2017), which provides a critique of recent trans visibility projects.
6   For more on the relationship between queer and trans, see Jian Neo Chen and micha cárdenas (2019, 472).
7   My understanding of the pornotrope here is indebted to the work of Hortense Spillers (1987) and Saidiya Hartman (1997).
8   According to Quashie, a hyperfocus on Black resistance ignores the everyday rich humanness of Black life; therefore, Quashie asks us to meditate upon Black "quiet" rather than simply exploring protest in Black literature, moments that at times recenter whiteness even while (or through) critiquing it.
9   From Alexander Crummell's (1969, 46) claim that races are akin to families to the multitudes of critiques of the Moynihan Report's pathologization of the Black family, Black studies has analyzed diasporic kinship and family structures, questioning the inherent whiteness of the "good" nuclear family.
10 Scholars such as Cathy Cohen (1997) and David Eng (2001) have demonstrated how the heterosexual "good" family is always imagined as white and how racial othering queers families of color.
11 See, for example, Caryl Phillips's classic historical novel *Crossing the River* (1993), which sketches the Black diaspora through multiple intergenerational stories that are tied back to a metaphorical "father" figure who connotes the nation.

12 See, for example, Alice Walker (2007), Ceri Davies (2006), Tracy Hargreaves (2003), Mandy Koolen (2010), and Jack Halberstam (2000). Some of these scholars peripherally mention Joss's Blackness and diasporic history, but they do not closely engage with how his gender is racialized. Important exceptions are Matt Richardson (2012, 2013) and Gigi Adair (2019), who examine how diaspora and race co-constitute gender.

13 Elizabeth Freeman (2010, 3) describes chrononormativity as "the use of time to organize individual human bodies toward maximum productivity" as a way to sustain heteropatriachy.

14 According to Lorde (1978), the erotic is a source of power that dwells in a spiritual plane and can be accessed by recognizing one's unrecognized feelings.

15 For example, Matt Richardson (2012, 2013) reads this figure as Colman in order to understand Colman's final reconciliation with his own and his father's masculinity.

16 This is a reference to Homi Bhabha's argument that "a state of emergency is also a state of emergence" (Bhabha 1986, xxiii, quoted in Snorton 2017).

17 In *Poetics of Relation*, Glissant (1997) argues against the reductive transparency of Western epistemology and instead outlines the importance of opacity in the poetics of the Caribbean.

08 Marielle, Presente

The Present and Presence in
Marielle Franco Protests

"How do we deal with the pain of being thrown into a future
that looks as bleak as our darkened past?" asks Petra Costa in her recent
documentary, *The Edge of Democracy* (2019). Costa's question defines the
current political sentiment in the country of Brazil. A quick Google search
for Brazil illustrates the matter: the reader is confronted with articles,
news, and videos orchestrated around words such as *somber, hopeless*, and
menacing to define its democratic future. Such a vision of national politics is especially present in queer activism as ultra-right president Jair
Bolsonaro has turned the enforcement of sexual and gender normativity
into one of his higher commitments. Among other measures, Bolsonaro
has revived gay-cure law projects and eliminated the committees of gender
and diversity. Furthermore, Bolsonaro's bellicose patriotism sets the stage
for homophobic attitudes to become politically justifiable by arguing that
left-wing agendas employ perverse homosexual practices. In his speeches
it becomes explicit that the achievement of national development depends
on countering left-wing thought, understood as perversely sexual.

In a context of increasing difficulty for queer activism and knowledge
to enter a national dialogue, and alongside injury as the only horizon available to queer identities and expressions in the country, this chapter asks:
how can we forge modes of queer belonging in the future of Brazil? Queer
belonging, as an enduring form of sociability that acknowledges interdependency and vulnerability (Butler 2002; Freeman 2007), informs what

belonging nationally might mean—given Bolsonaro's desire to obliterate queer political participation and queer life—and could alternatively become. Belonging is intimately linked to kinship insofar as both describe and decide "who is connected to whom" (Freeman 2007, 298), hence shedding light on "fundamental forms of human dependency" (Butler 2002, 15). This chapter challenges Costa's vision of what is to come by bringing a future of belonging into being in the style of José Esteban Muñoz's (2009, 97) utopian performative: "a moment when the here and the now is transcended by a *then* and a *there* that could be and indeed should be."

The central mission of this essay is to analyze Brazil's queer activism after the murder of Rio de Janeiro's councilwoman and human rights activist Marielle Franco. The case reflects wider discussions and developments in activism and queer academia concerning the imagination and enactment of new forms of belonging—both explicitly political collectivities and modes of affinities and caretaking traditionally associated with privatized families—that combat right-wing currents arising globally. On March 14, 2018, Marielle,[1] a Black, queer, single-mother activist who denounced state brutality against racialized and queer populations in Rio de Janeiro, was executed alongside her driver, Anderson Gomes, by the Brazilian police militia.[2] The militia is composed of current and former military police officers who organize clandestinely. To the present day, remarkably slow investigations into her case have given no answers about who ordered the militia to kill Marielle and Anderson. At the same time, the speed at which violence has been enacted on bodies such as hers has only increased under Bolsonaro's presidency, galvanizing a homophobic imaginary through a correlation of identity and ideology. Since Marielle's passing, activism around her figure relied on evoking lives that cannot be regained through the collective call for Marielle's presence when her name is mentioned—"Marielle, presente"— an extended practice that takes place across Latin America. I analyze this practice alongside the crafting of street plaques with her name to, in literal terms, remap the cityscape. Finally, I examine the temporality of belonging in Brazil through Marielle's widow, Monica Benicio, and her counting of the days since the murder on online platforms in relation to the militant chant "luto é verbo" (grief is a verb).

I argue that protests against Marielle's killing forge new modes of belonging in the future through the creative and collective uses of tradition and the distortion of common perceptions of time. But Marielle's case does not only offer alternative visions of the future. Navigating through the literature on temporality makes it explicit to and by whom the future has been queered: mostly white and anglophone academia. Queer scholars working at the intersection of queer latinoamericanidad and temporality such as José Esteban Muñoz (2009) and Juana María Rodríguez (2014) have reminded us continuously that our positionality affects the way we come to understand, reproduce, and challenge communities that seek to exclude nonwhite histories from reimagining the future. Although these articulations of latinoamericanidad are valuable and careful, queer Brazilians occupy a space of estrangement in relation to them where often the words employed do not suffice to translate such experiences. Without a doubt, the estrangement toward what for Brazilians is called latinoamericanidade is important, for it incites creativity in identifying familiarities. At the same time, however, the sense of intimacy among some queer Latinx scholars through language may well do the opposite for others under the same category. Brazil's lack of familiarity with the queer Latinx model opens the question of other languages and experiences that fall through the cracks of who else may be the odd cousin of the latinoamericanos. Taking into consideration Silviano Santiago's ([1971] 2002) writings on the space in between of Latin American discourse, which evidences multiple pedagogies and affective encounters embedded in Latinx connections with dominant frameworks, this essay also asks what we can learn if we place Brazilian experiences at the center of queer temporal studies centrally concerned with affinity, belonging, and interdependency.

I will propose in the following pages that the activism around Marielle Franco's life and memory contests naturalized constructions of tradition and the future in the country, which are based on the gendered roles and heterosexual reproduction that constitute normative familialism. Through mixing pieces of literature that seldom speak to one another, I hope not only to make Brazil imaginable in queer studies but also to create new kinships between the country's politics and the field of study. To emphasize, this is not to place Brazil in opposition to Latinx identities but to make explicit the importance of individual histories in their own contexts to create affinities without homogenizing experiences. In this context, I argue that Marielle Franco manifestations not only create modalities of belonging where they resignify perceptions of time to visualize a future but also that, in doing so, they craft a space of affinity with queer temporal studies and queer Latinx pedagogies. Through embodying anachronisms, overlapping national narratives, and using disciplinary techniques to recast a future, the protests against the killing of Marielle Franco provide a different set of alignments that open space for alternative horizons for queer sociability, belonging, and politics—including kinship but not reducible to it—that are representative of broader social and political dynamics in queer Latin America.

Unfamiliar Affinities

At the very furthest edge of stereotypes that pertain to Brazilians and their kinship and alliance practices is anthropophagy, or cannibalism, which early colonizers claimed was a characteristic of the Indigenous cultures in what became Brazil. Yet following Silviano Santiago, I also want to claim cannibalism as a queer form of kinship that creates new modes of affinity; I propose that this optic alleviates the narrow vision of the future for queers in the country. I aim to outline a process where "eating," rather than only "reproducing," the other moves toward a form of queer belonging through difference that does not conflate experiences under one sign. That this is relevant as a celebration of diversity that erases difference is implicit in the national discourse of the future through the employment of mestiça-gem (or mestizaje). Alternatively, the suggested approach offers a different model of kinship and belonging for bodies to ally and depend on one another through time that does not require the dominant familialism as mediator. In Marielle Franco protests, addressed in the following sections, cannibalism appears as a reproductive form of queer social life where the future becomes imaginable through interdependency.

In his classic text "Latin American Discourse: The Space In-Between," Santiago describes the affective dynamics of the Latin American writer within cultural production dominated by the West: "The Latin American writer plays with the signs of another writer and of another work. The words of the other present themselves as objects that fascinate his eyes, his fingers, and the writing of the second text becomes partially the story of a sensual experience with foreign signs" ([1971] 2002, 34). Troubling the dichotomy between source and influence, Santiago locates the Latin American discourse in the space in between, which influences and transforms dominant culture through differentiated repetition, forming an affective and erotic link to text: "Somewhere between sacrifice and playfulness, prison and transgression, submission to the code and aggression, obedience and rebellion, assimilation and expression—there, in this apparently empty space, its temple and its clandestinity, is where the anthropophagous ritual of Latin American discourse is constructed" (38). In other words, in the process of cannibalizing influences the Latin American writer's touch alters the form and function of the source material, creating textual kinships.

Anthropophagy is part of a broader history of decolonial endeavors in the country's twentieth-century poetics. The term describes Brazil's absorption of cultures to produce its own. This process is evidenced in Brazil's native Tupi people's early notion that one takes in the forces of the enemy by consuming them (Kosick 2019, 128). Brazilian modernists brought attention to the significance of cannibalism as a metaphor for the country's aesthetics by recalling the story of the first bishop in Brazil, readily eaten upon his arrival.[3] Charles Perrone (1996, 11) notes that the modernists made explicit that Brazilian cultural production did not copy or derive from the Europeans but rather came to life as "a critical assimilation of foreign (or even nonliterary) information and experiences for reelaboration in local terms." Susan Quinlan (2002, 212) identifies in this scenario an overarching contradiction particular to the Brazilian culture, that of the search for a well-defined brasilidade ("Brazilian-ness") in the country's cultural cannibalism. In Santiago's writings, cannibalism appears not against but as an intrinsic part of brasilidade: "The Latin American writer . . . lives between the assimilation of the original model, that is, between the love and respect for that which is already written, and the need to produce a new text that confronts and sometimes negates that original" (Santiago [1971] 2002, 35). The space of exchange described by Santiago provokes the dissolution of nationhood and cultural absorption, continuously reinventing these practices through reifying them. As such, the tensions created by consuming practices, words, and products of dominant cultures eliminate a preoccupation of being "ahead," "before," or "against" the Latin American author's work and their own culture.

Queer sensibilities arise from the Brazilian anthropophagous approach once we consider José Esteban Muñoz's (1999, 11) reminder that when queers of color disidentify with normative models of identity and strategically use dominant culture by "working on and against" it, they create the possibility of alternative positions and spaces of belonging. Disidentification, for Muñoz, is form of navigating homogenizing culture that disrupts assimilation and total opposition. Similar to Santiago's writings, the performances by queers of color that Muñoz analyzes "allow for the possibility of counterpublics—communities and relational chains of resistance that contest the dominant public sphere" (146). Disidentification, akin to Santiago's description of the Latin American writer's space of production, guides Latinx scholars toward a descriptive model for critical thought that builds up, advances, and converses with earlier works and dominant frameworks without falling into logic of learning as a linear progress (Dinshaw 1999, 23).

In this way, queer *and* Brazilian *and* Latinx projects are able to coexist through an articulation of differences that does not seek to posit one against the other or hide one under the symbol of the other. In fact, the affective exchange produced by cultural anthropophagy might be a queer form of belonging alternative to those currently offered by the majority of Latinx exchanges with queer theory, whose participation is reduced to demanding a position within the field. On the contrary, queer Latinx encounters—through cannibalistic interventions—result in new and nonlinear affective coalitions. This form of belonging that emerges from cannibalistic incorporations is one that privileges a plurivocal and plurivectorial contact with dominant material in order to imagine and produce alternative realities for queer and racialized communities. Berenice Bento's (2017) writings exemplify this alternative form of belonging for and by Brazilian queer studies as she cannibalizes the "queer" and cuir in her call for the transviad@. According to the Michaelis Dictionary, *transviado* means "that which has taken the wrong turn." But the words also come to indicate "trans" and "viado" ("fag" or "queer"). Another interpretation that emerges from Bento's writings is that of "transar": "fucking" and "interweaving" with the queer to birth a Brazilian approach to the field (Machado 2018, 371). These methods of forging relations counter reproductive and other heteronormative models of kinship. The transviad@ model also captures Santiago's vision of the eroticism toward the text brought about by the Latin American author. As the fascination runs through their fingers, the individual writer turns themselves into the social, for their touch "fucks," and fucks with, a broader history of what has been written under the emblem of "queer." The move against, toward, and through the queer, made available by means of its apprehension and shaping by the Brazilian writer, triggers transnational affinities and erotic encounters. National cultural production does not take the position of lateness and backwardness, "catching up" with queer studies, but instead exchanges with and advances both fields as they come into contact. My approach thus builds on theories of queerness and affect (Muñoz 1999, 2009; Ngai 2005; Love 2007; Berlant 2011a) that meditate on the psychosocial aspects of queer life and politics, and it expands them by considering the politics of anthropophagous affect in Latinx queer interventions.

Anthropophagy might also be an alternative queer imagining of kinship nationally, for in Brazil kinship operates in a heteronormative form through the link between mestiçagem and the future. Brasilidade is conjured up by the discourse of mestiçagem (or mestizaje) in the country. This is because in Brazil, questions of nationality have been framed around an approach to race and sexuality drawn from the work of Gilberto Freyre, which upholds a single symbolic national ethnicity, the mestiço. In this paradigm, what anthropologist Roberto DaMatta (1981, 58–85) has identified as the "fábula das três raças" (fable of the three races), Brazilians come to understand themselves as equally mixed by Native American, African, and European populations in terms of race and especially culture (Fry 2005, 215; Eakin 2017, 2). The creation of a mestiçagem as a defining characteristic of Brazilian national identity was forged by Freyre's ([1933] 1946) *Casa Grande e Senzala*, translated to English in 1945 as *The Masters and the Slaves*. A growing academic and professional body sought the maintenance of Eurocentric perspectives (Green 1999, 59), so mestiçagem attempted to optimistically unify Brazil while sustaining racial, class, and gender differences (Mota 1977, 53–74; Gonzalez [1988] 2020, 43–45). Concurrent interpretations of the thesis appeared across Latin America following their specific contexts. In Cuba, José Marti called for "nuestra América mestiza" (our mestizo America), whereas José Vasconcelos (1925) understood the Mexican identity as the "raza cósmica" (cosmic race) (Eakin 2017, 64). Such contributions were able to at once celebrate new forms of hybridity and do away with questions of legal status, political participation, and economic privileges. These concepts, already tacitly authoritarian, became another tool for subsequent political discourse, for leaders could claim a status of "racial democracy" in the country. When differences are made invisible under the umbrella of mestiçagem, individuals cannot speak of their unevenly distributed chances in Brazil and unequally felt experiences as Brazilians.

Gloria Anzaldúa's (1987) reclaiming of the mestiza as a resident of a "third space" and her recuperation and recodification of the border align with this project. Mestizaje, for Anzaldúa, is the disorganization and remaking of boundaries of the social and territorial, including sexual experiences that fall outside the dominant mestiço/mestizo parameter. Yet the term's current employment still shares a close association with what Anzaldúa diametrically opposes—that is, a narrative based on creating a symbolically diverse nation via heterosexual reproduction. Examples of the heterosexual mestiço kinship model are found in the rapid acceleration in institutional violence against queers of color in Brazil and a continuous framing of left-wing parties as supportive of "perverse" homosexual practices,[4] which solidifies the overarching vision of a bleak future for queer individuals in media and social life. All the while, the language of racial democracy and diversity remains in place. Heterosexual mestiço kinship is also evident in the privileging of homonormative experiences and white-centered gay rights in the past decades (De la Dehesa 2010, 115–45). Exemplary of how the Brazilian future is more and more disassociated from queer affections is the increasing popularity of Fernando Holiday, a rightwing São Paulo city councilman. Holiday, a gay Black man who co-runs the Free Brazil Movement (MBL), an association founded on anti–Worker's Party sentiments in 2014, gained recognition when affirming in 2018 that, out of respect for the Catholic Church, he did not have sexual relations. Holiday became a major figure in national right-wing politics and epitomizes how the inclusion of queers of color in the national dialogue is predicated on nonsexual homosexuality.

Juana María Rodríguez (2014, 36–37) suggests that the current legibility of familial structure predicated on a broader sustenance of whiteness forecloses other forms of belonging for queers and offers no space for racialized experiences. As queer scholars have noted, notions of reproduction are not, nor should be, reserved to (white) heterosexuality (Muñoz 2009; Franklin 2013; Golombok 2015). Following Jafari S. Allen (2009) and Sara Ahmed (2004), Rodríguez (2014) declares that queer investigations must comprehend how kinship is structured and organized to stay open to different modes of doing queer: "When we refuse to participate in discourses that perpetuate family life and lifelong monogamous commitment as the epitome of emotional maturity and affective value, when we speak of the losses and crises that love and family also entail, we challenge structures of differential value based on heteronormative investments in national reproduction" (53). Similarly, I offer a queer view of belonging through cultural cannibalism, or the appropriation of dominant discourses, that does not oppose reproduction but that does not interpret it as the only available design for kinship.

Insofar as notions of the future are entwined in heteronormativity (Edelman 2004; Halberstam 2005; Love 2007; Muñoz 2009; Freeman 2010; Berlant 2011a), as well as in mestiçagem (Stepan 1991; Eakin 2017), Brazil's mestiço nationality becomes tightly linked to its sexual landscape. These emancipatory promises of inclusion are wedded to narratives of the future, progress, and tradition (Schwarz 1992; Dussel 1995; Martín-Barbero [1987] 1997; Chauí 2000, 2011; Mignolo 2000; De la Dehesa 2010; Eakin 2017) that have proven to be insufficient to provide a future for queers in the country. Bolsonaro's call to build the country by means of homophobia, alongside racism, xenophobia, and colonial practices, demonstrates how queers inhabit a limited space in his vision of the future. Therefore, queer cannibalism is part of a broader endeavor to counter global movements toward the Right, extending the reach of this research beyond Brazil to provoke unfamiliar affinities in other contexts.

The theoretical changes brought about by the space of Latin American discourse must be carefully understood in order not to be conflated with Brazil's broader history of apprehension of terms such as *difference* and *diversity*. In the scholarship I have cited, it is apparent that the Latin American author does not seek homogenization through difference but rather that the affect produced by authors working at the intersection of these fields aims to create bonds for radical futures and interventions. That is, these authors treat the appropriation of cultures through and for difference, not against it. Taking into consideration the Brazilian national construction, I offer a vision of affective coalitions that do not fall into the myth of racial democracy. As I have shown, the affective bonds generated by Latinx cultural production in Brazil trouble the "diverse" political body through difference instead of reifying it. In the following pages the preoccupation with the Brazilian mestiço nationality and sexuality becomes central for understanding how protests demanding justice for Marielle Franco challenge such a perspective. The activism surrounding Marielle blurs the lines separating the self and the collective, offering new affective links that radically imagine the future through seemingly calcified understandings of tradition and kinship.

Presences within the Present

Amy Kaminsky (1993, 24–25) writes that the Latin American tradition of roll-calling those who have passed unjustly, and collectively responding to the same call through uttering "Presente," is "at once embodied and represented, individual and historical." The chant is part of a broader history throughout Latin American demonstrations to seek justice and honor the life of individuals and groups, although its origin remains unknown. Tracing examples of the chant reveals its plurality in content and location: the practice extends from the 1992 Mexico City demonstration on the five-hundred-year anniversary of Indigenous resistance in the country, followed by the chant "Se ve, se siente, el Indio está presente" (If one sees, if one senses, the Indian is present), to its use at the funeral of the Chilean poet and politician Pablo Neruda in 1973. Likewise, the chant "Marielle, presente," became a crucial tool to express public unrest and the urgency of her case, leading millions to the streets across Brazil. Following Adriana Cavarero's (2005, 173) argument that the "the uniqueness that makes itself heard as a voice" is predicated on the individual's communication with others, Judith Butler (2015, 77) notes that the "body does not act alone when it acts politically." The condition for and actualization of one's space of appearance, or vocality, are not individual action but the space between bodies that "both binds and differentiates" the participants (77). Repetitively responding in the name of Marielle, Neruda, or a community that shares similar struggles, the protests apprehend the logic of the self and shape it toward the interdependent collective, reconfiguring the borders that limit the individual. Extending beyond oneself through the chanting, in a context that emerges across Latin America, I argue, disorganizes the body politic, leading to an articulation of future forms of collective participation. Although the form and function of the chant resonate with a larger variety of demonstrations, the practice queers activist kinship across Latin America. As I will show, queer spaces of belonging materialize through the chant that cannibalizes the past into the present.

"Presente," the affirmation of one's presence used in schools and legislative bodies to monitor and discipline participation, requires one to affirm their individuality according to the name called in contrast to the group. The familiarity with the call for the councilwoman's presence, in turn, allowed the movement to take more complex dimensions: through the continuous practice of a stranger mentioning the name Marielle, followed by the collective statement of her presence, the protesters break away from the common perspective of manifestations as singular events in time and space. To the contrary, they make evident that Marielle's figure, at the intersection of the axes of race, class, gender, and sexuality, is a plurivectorial and plurivocal concern that extends beyond the time of the crisis into everyday life. By turning the evoking of Marielle's life and memory into a performance of discipline that can be enacted at any time, in any space, depending only on those who share the will to bring forth her life and memory, the protesters clarify that one's future is intrinsically tied to the future of another. Butler (2015, 65) argues that the body is "less an entity than a living set of relations" whose "acting is always conditioned acting." Following this premise, the assemblage of bodies that depend on one another to seek an alternative reality reveals that "dependency . . . and . . . dependability are necessary in order to live and to live well" because for one "to lead a good life, it will be a life lived with others, a life that is no life without those others" (218). The individuals at Marielle demonstrations formulate a space of belonging based on a familiarity located precisely at the enactment of unfamiliar voices in unfamiliar spaces. The affinities formed through not knowing and responding for those who are not themselves disfigure the dominant logic of roll calling and confirm the ethical principle of interdependency in order to visualize alternative modes of belonging. In the space in between of presence and absence, the diffuse and multicentered calling consumes the disciplinary practice and rearranges the norms produced by it. In the process the calling, instead of increasing individualization, formulates new affective coalitions through unfamiliarity and a shared interdependency crucial to what kinship means.

In complicating the logic of individual and collective, absence and presence, the movement offers another reading of Santiago's "entre-lugar." Although most analyses understand it as "third" space, in the example of the protests it becomes more productive to think of the space as an in-between zone of affective cultural exchange. "[The entre-lugar] is a place," Quinlan (2002, 212) writes, "that speaks to the infinite ability to change and to know the other and, through the process of change, to manipulate the power structure that effects the politics of who we are in relation to ourselves and others." That is, the new links and affects among participants that emerge from the protests do not live in service of Marielle's presence or absence but reside at the interplay of both. These considerations are crucial when reflecting on mestiçagem. In the context of a country whose broad understanding of nationality has been closely associated with an excuse to do away with internal disputes of race and sexuality, it is important to stress that responding in the name of Marielle Franco does not conform to a logic that those in the streets are equal and share the same hardships: "To act in concert does not mean to act in conformity" (Butler 2015, 157). Those evoking Marielle, I argue, cannibalize the past into the present to recast the colonial and racist traditions present in Brazilian national identity. Through this historical incorporation of the symbol of Marielle, a new form of belonging emerges, grounded in difference and, opposing nationalism's emphasis on rugged individualism and affirming Butler's model of kinship as interdependency, in the need for one another.

As such, "Presente" turns into an incorporation of Marielle into the body politic, extending and reinventing the interpretation of mestiçagem in the style of Anzaldúa's mestiza. However, this reshaping of the body politic is brought about not by a cultural cannibalism but by a historical one instead.

FIGURE 8.1 "Marielle lives. Militarization: not in our name."
Photo: Annelize Tozetto.

It is a form of anthropophagy that incorporates the past into the present to evidence a queer-of-color future that is not merely wounded, against what current perspectives on Brazil suggest. As a consequence of the chant, the protests confuse the lines between the present moment and historical time. The events extend into a continuous practice through the use of the past. A sign that appeared during the manifestations that contributes to such a perspective read "militarização: não em nosso nome," which translates to "militarization: not in our name" (figure 8.1). The sign makes explicit the refusal to share a future that aligns with a history of right-wing military dictatorship in the country, as Bolsonaro followers continuously demand its return. By allocating their voices and names to summon Marielle's presence in the present, activists craft a new mode of participation and belonging in the future, one that can exist only by means of collective force. Finally, the sign suggests an alternative future where these names need not to be invoked to combat new forms of fascism. The protesters apprehend the past and present of ultra-right Brazil to create a new visualization of the future. As the shared affinities take place through troubling presence and absence, past and present, discipline and incompliancy, they recast the role of Marielle as a historical emblem into an "everyday" instantiated creatively and unexpectedly. Such an approach to roll calling undoes the idea of crisis as a single event, for it gains relevance through its continual practice. By doing so, the action brings attention to the fact that the present, as well as the quotidian embedded in it, yields potential for change. Under these circumstances everyday life is energized with possibilities based on unfamiliar encounters, voices, and spaces, which allow the future to be radically reimagined through difference. As an alternative to normative familialistic reproduction, this process forges a way out of the present configuration of kinship and asks us to visualize a different form of relating to and affecting one another.

This everydayness of Marielle's possible presence turns our attention to Lauren Berlant's concept of the impasse. Instead of following queer antisocial approaches that apprehend the figure of the homosexual as the embodiment of social negation, materialized through anal sex for Bersani (1987) and the inability to reproduce to a child-driven future for Edelman (2004), Berlant (2011a, 24) reenergizes the idea of negativity or negation to locate modes of survival within the quotidian, even if this survival predicates harm to the subject itself. Relevant here is Berlant's concept of the impasse, "a stretch of time in which one moves around with a sense that the world is at once intensely present and enigmatic, such that the activity of living demands both a wandering absorptive awareness and a hypervigilance that collects material that might help to clarify things" (4). In short, Berlant describes how the ongoing pressures of everyday life come to take the shape of the impasse, a moment that might require us to find new ways to think about the world so that other possibilities might arise. Marielle Franco protesters, through the continuous roll calling of her name to evoke her presence, deny "moving on" to the next subject, suspending the individual self in ways that resonate with progressive models of kinship as interdependency, collective being, and the streaming of time in the shape of the impasse. Crafting a "thick moment of ongoingness" (200), they *move Marielle with* new demands for justice to expose that becoming aware of oneself makes no sense outside the context of plural and different identities, sometimes familiar to one another, sometimes connecting through these short-lived encounters, with all responding to one name while in the same space. The speech act moves with Marielle as it is "inserted in a citational chain"; that is, "the social plurality designated and produced by the utterance cannot all assemble in the same place to speak at the same time, so it is both spatially and temporally extended phenomenon" (Butler 2015, 176). The disorientation provoked by the protests to locate a defining space, time, and initiating call to represent the movement destabilizes and crafts a new quotidian, a quotidian that is not predicated on the impossibility of a future for queer sociability but one that requires us to search for new modalities of belonging and new forms of kinship precisely through unfamiliar affinities.

The crafting of Marielle Franco street plaques epitomizes such disorientations. Each sign includes Marielle's name, a summary of her life and cause, and the address of where the assassination took place. The network of politically active cultural producers named Chama ("The Flame") popularized the design through an online platform that made it available for print. On the same website, they also created a map that recognizes these signs across the world based on an online form where one can register their respective locations. Although many have been taken down by government officials or broken by Bolsonaro supporters such as federal deputy Daniel Silveira, who destroyed the sign placed at the Rio de Janeiro City Council where Marielle once worked, more continue to appear. These protests eschew the consumption of her memory for personal self-enhancement, and instead openly deal in spatial and temporal instruments of her memory: through the street plaques, activists extend and reduplicate the space for articulation of the Black, queer, militant body, in contrast to that of the rights-bearing liberal subject that has marked Brazilian political discourse. In turn, the artificial quality of the street plaques exposes the mechanisms available for Brazilians to articulate pain, memory, and loss within the context of cultural production. By remapping the city with Marielle's name, protesters cannibalize spaces through recovery and reconstitution of the dominant hold over the present by histories of power, control, and containment embedded in the names of mostly male military figures and elites after whom many of Brazil's streets are named.

Actions such as these disorganize the body politic, for Marielle comes to represent the opposite of a difference-blind country, but they also actualize a space for the councilwoman to exist outside the boundaries of the possible. As such, they open a window on the question of what other mechanisms for cultural expression may become available through shared bonds such as the chanting of "Presente." Centering Marielle's experiences in the mapping of cities across the country, these activists produce what Muñoz (2009, 97) calls "blueprints of a world not quite here, a horizon of possibility, not a fixed schema." This map of the future, and the modality of hope that emerges through redesigning the cityscape, are actions in which enacting Marielle's memory becomes a world-making investment, reorienting queer scholarship and activism toward Latin American experiences to provide a "perception of past and future affective worlds" (27).

The connections and continuities formed through the investment with the unfamiliar take different proportions when considering the work of mourning on the internet. This section pays attention to how Monica Benicio, Marielle Franco's widow, uses her Twitter account to count the days since the councilwoman's passing. Every day, Monica repeats the central question of her wife's case: who mandated Marielle's death? Like the chants, the continuous call for answers, or response to her name, appears as a form of invocation because "the speech act, however punctual, is nevertheless inserted in a citational chain" where "the temporal conditions for making the speech act precede and exceed the momentary occasion of its enunciation" (Butler 2015, 176). It is through these "performative enactments" (176) that Marielle's conditions for living are made visible. Followers routinely share the same preoccupation and spread Monica's message across the platform and to others, interweaving the pressing subject with ones that emerge as time passes. All the while, the insistence on answers—even after two years without Marielle—highlights the slow pace of justice in Brazil, which affects the bodies brutally removed from a future as well as those required to experience the remains of the everyday. As a "performatively induced" practice, an ending to the counting takes shape as both undesirable and unattainable (177). Thus, the persistent call for justice not only confronts the ongoingness of violence in the present for queer and racialized identities but also reveals the radical potential of mourning as a collective practice that can forge affective bonds among strangers. The division of the present and the future is sutured by multiple rhythms involved in Marielle's case. Through rapid online exchanges and debates, protesters apprehend the slow pace of justice in the country to perform the opposite.

Monica's writings, shared daily through the touches on the screen and mousepads across the internet, speaks to Elizabeth Freeman's (2010, 120) suggestion that writing history can be embodied and erotic, deemphasizing queer theory's attachment to loss and trauma. Connecting different subjects within the platform by proximity, and overlapping the tweet with texts of personal authorship, the process of sharing Monica's counting allows an understanding of the bodily pleasures of being in time to participate in the debate and of feeling time by witnessing the slowness of justice, beyond suffering. This is not to imply that there is a kind of relief emerging from Marielle's death but that relief and joy can also emerge from the contact of strangers and unfamiliar voices with one's grief. Here, "relief" reaches beyond the momentary alleviation of distress. The online exchanges also *throw into relief* the enduring sense of loss that permeates the lives of those whose Bolsonaro's ruling threatens. At the same time, they *make a relief*, or what Muñoz would call a blueprint, "for minoritarian counterpublic spheres" (Muñoz 1999, 5), "staging a new political formation in the present" (200). As such, Monica's mourning becomes a shared, but not equal, experience. A popular phrase from Marielle Franco protests that describes such a feeling is "luto é verbo," where *luto* means both "I fight" and "grief" to form the statement "grief is a verb." The singular inflection of the verb takes shape as the collective process of grieving, where the work of mourning extends to, and energizes, the possibility of demanding justice in the country. The sentence, in the context of the tweets, expresses how we can and have accessed the political language of fatality and incurability that is not predicated on a mournful moving on of the present along with the phobic politics it carries, but instead as a living insistence on alternative futures. *Luto* as both grief and verb not only sustains this movement through the implication that it is a constant fight, but it also requires a revaluation of how grief has been commonly understood. The expression may also provide different readings in the context of academia. As the different individuals who engage with Monica's words open a dialogue with current events alongside the mourning of Marielle, they include her memory and struggle while living in the continuing losses of Black and queer lives in our phobic quotidian. But they also turn the call for justice into a practice that must exist routinely in all events. "Within these terms," Freeman (2010, 120) contends, "we might imagine ourselves haunted by bliss and not just trauma; residues of positive affect . . . might be available for queer counter- (or para-) historiographies."

However, death and mourning are not forgotten or put aside. Much to the contrary, nothing is abandoned along the way as mourning is wedded to the work of life itself (Butler 1997, 134; Baraitser 2017, 92, 109). For instance, Luciane Rocha (2012) informs us that grief has been the moving force of Black mothers whose children were the victims of homicide in Rio de Janeiro. Jaime Alves (2018, 1) complements such a perspective, illustrating how "suffering, hopelessness and political resistance" are intrinsic to the experience of Blackness in the "anti-Black city" of São Paulo. Considering Brazil's political discourse, which displaces race from its dialogue while submitting Black individuals to harsher police treatment, leading to shocking numbers of executions (such Marielle's) of the country's population each year, grief can bring new affects into play, but it cannot be displaced from the palpable loss and trauma to which Black communities are subjected in the country. Moving away from a binary reading of affect as either positive or negative that has permeated queer writings on melancholia, where "only negative affects clear a path for becoming both queer and critical" (Bradway 2017, 151), the examples above evidence how grief can be comprehended as both intractable *and* a course of direction toward new affects and affinities that feel like kinship. Taking this into consideration, it is possible to create a framework where we do not let go of the brutality of Brazil's colonial past and present that seeks to exterminate Black bodies and Blackness in all of its forms but instead use it as a moving force to imagine and enact new futures.

In contrast to the slowness of justice and the ongoing need to the call for justice in Marielle's execution is the speed at which people share and engage with Monica Benicio's tweets within the time span of one day. The following day, carrying with it one more tweet, stressing yet another number, leads off both the same and a different demand for answers. Yet those who come in contact with the counting of the days continue to react to the call. In this way, the twenty-four-hour life span of the tweet gains meaning only in the context of a broader period where multiple shares and connections have taken place. Insofar as the fast pace of tweets and the slowness of justice feed off each other, the online participation confuses a dominant understanding of collective mourning as a linear and singular act equally felt and experienced.[5] Although the counting of the days seems to follow the logic of linear time, the demands of the present that come to interact with the events of the past, alongside the persistence yet unreachability of the future, go against such a logic. That is to say, moving forward requires moving with alternative forms and rhythms that offer something more than the phobic time of the "now" that is allocated to queer and racialized bodies. This, in turn, informs how the temporality of justice and the law differ from each other, for the underlying force of the protests lies in the fact that obtaining an answer to the question of who ordered the execution would not undo, alleviate, or end the ongoing accumulation of injustice in the country.

These online practices, embedded in a larger work of activism regarding Marielle Franco, disrupt the present as a heteronormative temporal order and the future as out of reach of queer and racialized identities. They insist on queer life, history, and narrative. What some have called the "Marielle effect" illustrates how the enactment of her life has become a moving force for the participation and election of more Black and queer women in Brazilian politics. In addition, the call for Marielle's presence has extended to other victims living at the intersection of experiences, such as Matheusa Passarelli, a twenty-one-year-old Black, queer, and trans student murdered on April 29, 2018, in Rio de Janeiro. As time passes, names such as Matheusa's have been made visible as the chants invoke their presence alongside Marielle's. At large, these examples make evident the move from Marielle's death toward a broader queer-of-color collectivity in Brazilian politics and activism. They do so through challenging individual pain and the pace of justice, revealing that one cannot be dissociated from the other as long as grief is suspended from language as a quality and is given shape as an action. In turn, "Luto é verbo," brought about with the emerging affinities and bonds created among strangers through Monica's counting, enriches activism with different readings of what the work of mourning can do. As Butler (2002, 40) expresses, "The life of sexuality, kinship, and community that becomes unthinkable . . . constitutes the lost horizon of radical sexual politics, and we find our way 'politically' in the wake of the ungrievable." Feeling connected to unseen or unrelated others through grief places mourning within kinship relations. Insofar as "kinship consists of relationships renewed, and their very renewal is what is relational at all" (Freeman 2007, 308), the politically regenerative effect of mourning in these calls for justice activated by a connection among strangers troubles normative kinship. The particularities of the case and its developments also craft a dialogue with other activist conversations around what mourning as political work can accomplish.

Conclusion

In this essay I have engaged with what is deemed impossible within a horizon of injustice and sorrow, unintelligible within political configurations of time, and unavailable within scholarship. As the Marielle Franco protests illustrate, what has been rendered impossible still yields the potential to break apart the constraint of the horizons that limit queer identities and expressions in political discourse. However, this project does not craft a naively optimistic view of Brazilian politics. Instead, it explores the potentials for breaks and tears in the past that might open up the possibility of resistance within the horizon of widespread violence toward queer and racialized lives. I have suggested that Marielle Franco protests, in their different uses of time, draw up blueprints for less exclusionary futures. The roll calling, Marielle street plaques, and Monica Benicio's counting are examples of grief as action. They arise in the context of short-lived encounters that establish communities in difference; they work against techniques of homogenization enacted by national politics that dictate the pace and space of mourning. Even when picturing a future seems an impossible task, these examples show that there is still the potential for queer designs for affection and affinity, and so alternative forms of kinship, within the present.

Activism pertaining to Marielle evidences the ways in which individuals, groups, and communities craft for themselves conditions of belonging to Brazilian culture and politics, even when the country's discourse disavows them. Through reimagining disciplinary techniques and common understandings of time, these activisms apprehend and give new shape to the ways in which visions of the future circulate through the country. These particular acts, emerging at the interstices of the organized time of political discourse, also counter the current agenda of inclusion in the country that reinforces heteronormativity as the only horizon of national belonging. Furthermore, they incite transnational affinities grounded on a familiarity with the creative work that invoking one's presence does. This is a type of difference that revisits and reshapes dominant uses of time and space instead of reifying whiteness and heterosexuality under the sign of diversity. In this sense, this project and the activist practices described in this essay stand in relation to each other, for both insist on a life beyond survival that, during times of explicit phobias enacted at all levels, seems absurd or almost impossible to materialize.

Notes

1   This chapter employs Marielle Franco's first name to acknowledge and echo the manifestations in her name. Using "Franco" instead of "Marielle" would decontextualize the movement and activists' efforts in keeping her presence alive. This stance develops throughout the chapter as it stresses the importance of strangers' familiarity with Marielle's name. I also refer to the driver, Anderson Gomes, and Marielle's widow, Monica Benicio, in the same fashion to recognize their positions in the movement.

2   Although the preoccupation with obtaining answers extends to Anderson Gomes, this essay acknowledges its limitation in not addressing his role in subsequent activism in Brazil. A proper analysis of Anderson's role in the case requires careful attention to issues of Black masculinity in the country, which would greatly contribute to the topic and current activism.

3 For more on Brazilian anthropophagy, see Oswald de Andrade's ([1928] 2017) *Manifesto Antropófago*.
4 A famous example that emerged from Brazil's 2018 presidential elections, which helped in Bolsonaro's presidency, was the dissemination of the fake news that Brazil's Worker's Party, his biggest opponent, aimed to distribute *mamadeiras de piroca* (penis baby bottles) in public schools.
5 It is important to note that online interventions are valuable and necessary to express solidarity, for some bodies must also preserve themselves from immediate harm at demonstrations, but they also present limits in contrast to the embodied activism of the protests. For as long as bodies need to become evident and present to counter the national logic that seeks to hide the plurality of experiences under the emblem of a mestiço nationality, seizing the space of the streets matters.

Part III   Kinship in the Negative

09 Akinship

This brings us to the discovery, in its latent form, of *a characteristic
which appears in all forms of slavery* and is its very essence: *the
social incapacity of the slave to reproduce socially*—that is, the slave's
juridical inability to become "kin."

CLAUDE MEILLASSOUX, *THE ANTHROPOLOGY OF SLAVERY: THE WOMB
OF IRON AND GOLD* (1991)

Tyrone Garner died of complications related to meningitis in
2006, eight years after his arrest in John Lawrence's Houston apartment.
His brother Darrell, unable to afford the costs for his funeral, solicited the
aid of attorneys at the Lambda Legal Defense and Education Fund—the
same gay rights organization that fought on Garner's and Lawrence's behalf in the 2003 case that challenged their arrest for "homosexual conduct."
Garner's body awaited burial in cold storage at a Houston morgue. Thirty-
seven days after his death, the Lambda Fund had managed to collect only
$225 in donations from its supporter base. Darrell relinquished his broth-
er's body to the county for cremation and narrowed his public request:
$430, just enough to run an obituary in the newspaper and to purchase
a metal urn for Tyrone's ashes, the cheapest alternative to the plastic bag
that the crematorium issues for free. This amount, too, was never reached
(Carpenter 2012, 280). Garner never received a funeral. An inoperative hy-
perlink to the website set up to raise funds for his burial is his only memorial.[1] Gay rights activist Terrance Heath (2006) reflects on this course of
events: "It's hard not to see this as Garner being forgotten at best, and at
worst discarded with no more thought than one would give to tossing out
a used condom."

Three years before his unceremonious death, the 2003 ruling in *Lawrence v. Texas* declared anti-sodomy laws unconstitutional. According to the majority opinion of the court, sexual acts that fulfilled a trio of conditions—that parties are legally adult, consenting, and carry out their sexual acts in private—were constitutionally protected by the right to liberty guaranteed under the due process clause of the Fourteenth Amendment. This case became a flash point in the gay rights movement, a stepping-stone on the path toward (a then not-yet-inevitable) "marriage equality," and a serious bone of contention in queer studies. David Eng (2010) critiques the decriminalization of sodomy and the new accoutrements of "queer liberalism" as gains exchanged in a Faustian pact for the racialization of intimacy, a union that Jasbir Puar (2007) contends was made possible by a historical realignment between the politics of sexuality and neoliberal governmentality. Nothing highlighted the racial limits of privacy more brightly than the events that directly precipitated *Lawrence v. Texas*. Police entered Lawrence's apartment in 1998 not because they suspected foul sexual play but in response to an initial report that a Black man—Garner—was "going crazy with a gun" (Carpenter 2012, xi).

According to the queer critique of the broader political logic of *Lawrence*, any potentially radical reimagining of the social forms of kinship, particularly those that do not revolve around a nuclear couple or that unfold outside the tidy confines of domesticity, was sacrificed by the mainstream gay rights movement at the altar of rights, recognition, and respectability. This critique rings truer today, after the legalization of same-sex marriage, than it did in *Lawrence*'s immediate wake. Indeed, according to this zero-sum calculus, the criminalization of Blackness and poverty goes hand in hand with the privatization of gay kinship, confirming Garner's role as a "used condom," discarded after the copulation of gay rights and state power.

But this critique is also incomplete. Indeed, Garner's deprivation of a proper burial—the denial of the funeral rites that distinguish human from animal or slave (Chanter 2011)—strikes me as a more profound fact than his exclusion from the realm of privacy and the ritual renewal of social life. Reckoning with *Lawrence* demands a language capable of understanding the implications of this exposed corpse, but what we know of Garner's biography makes a critique of kinship appear only remotely relevant. Indeed, his "kinship" seems indistinguishable from a permanent state of emergency. The youngest of ten children, Garner lived and died in poverty. He slept on the couches of friends and family for several weeks or months at a time. If he led a private sexual life, he enjoyed none of its immunities, as we will see. He worked odd jobs, never rented an apartment, did not own a car, and was frequently arrested during his life, at least for the thirty-nine years it lasted. In what way might this existence be queer or fugitive? Is kinship an appropriate category of analysis? Is it relevant only negatively, to the degree that Garner's symbolic and material position remains unintelligible to kinship?

As I argue in this essay, kinship is in fact an indispensable category for analyzing *Lawrence*, but it remains meaningless if it does not incorporate what the extant queer critiques of kinship lack: a theory of the mode of racial production, from slavery to policing. In what follows I make policing the crux of an analysis of the politics of kinship. The existing scholarship on *Lawrence*, and queer kinship theory more generally, is quite capable of critiquing the racial politics that animate the regulation of social life, but it never satisfactorily attends to this mode of racial production. Nor, for that matter, do these critiques have a theory of the production of kinship and its relationship to the mode of racial production at hand. The model developed in this essay addresses these absences by situating racial production as the structural cause of kinship. If the production of Blackness triggers the construction of kinship or, as I will argue, if modern kinship is constituted as a defense against the social metastasis of slavery, then it follows that Blackness is not a logically possible object or system of kinship.

I offer *akinship* as the paradoxical term to describe the social impossibility of Black kinship. This concept indexes simultaneously the history of modern kinship, the internal coherence of its structure, and the impetus of its transformations. Garner's encounter with the police provides a privileged instance for grasping the necessary and contingent relationship between kinship and policing as a form of racial production. The introduction of the concept of akinship consequently shoulders my second intervention, which centers on anthropological theories of kinship. Instead of circumventing the structuralist account of the production of kinship, I channel it back into the structuralist analysis that courses through both the historiography of slavery and the Black feminist critique of kinship.

In suggesting that "slavery is the ghost in the machine of kinship" (as cited in Butler 2002, 15), Saidiya Hartman generates a point of departure for describing the hiatus between Garner and *Lawrence*, and in a larger sense the suspended relation between the production of Blackness and the production of kinship. Hartman's metaphor has been widely cited, but its interpretations have mainly scratched the surface of its signification. This essay begins with a brief genealogy of this metaphor to decrypt its logic. The incommensurability between its terms—the spectral and the machinic—creates a topology in which a queer theory of kinship becomes both new and necessary. Read from the vantage of racial slavery's sexual mode of reproduction, the political significance of kinship is both relativized in one direction and seriously broadened in another. I consequently engage the foundations of the queer and feminist critiques of kinship in order to pluralize their terms of intervention into anthropology, the field that first formalized kinship as an object of study in the late nineteenth century.

My digression into the anthropology of kinship mainly reworks the reception of Claude Lévi-Strauss (1969), whose notorious idea that the "exchange of women" constitutes the sine qua non of kinship has been widely panned. I contend that his critics mistake this notion for a description (or normative ideology) of marriage in contemporary society (see Robcis 2013). They are off significantly enough to warrant reopening the inquiry into this controversial concept. The "matrimonial dialogue of men" (Lévi-Strauss 1969, 496) has always described the work that the elementary structures of kinship perform in "premodern" social systems. By contrast, modern kinship—the complex structures of exchange that have also been "exported" by the West over the course of global colonialism—emerges only after the sexual traffic in women has been suppressed. Reviving Lévi-Strauss's notion of the exchange of women therefore not only reintroduces a sorely needed theory of the production of the social link but permits us to radically rehistoricize the displacement of kinship after the advent of racial production.

I will explain why and how the premodern exchange of women was suppressed and speculate about the structures that took its place. Briefly put, the structural contradictions of the exchange of women result in what I will describe as a crisis in the accumulation of non-Black women. Capitalism twice displaces this crisis—first through the accumulation of slaves and then through the accumulation of force in modern police power. These economies are contiguous. The conditions of police violence that give rise to the possibility of the *Lawrence v. Texas* decision are for this reason not extraneous to the question of kinship nor its mitigating circumstance but its benighted heart.

After the exchange of women failed, kinship ceased to constitute the fundamental activity of culture; commodity exchange took its place. I conclude that the contradictions that previously plagued the complex structures of kinship were thereby transferred to (and transformed by) capitalism. It is my wager that racial slavery acted as both the vanishing mediator and irreducible remainder of this transition from the exchange of women to capitalism. What "remains" of this transition, what I call akinship, presents the structural irresolution or ontological crisis of kinship. It is shorthand for the fact that racial production is a contingent but necessary cause of kinship formation.

"The Ghost in the Machine of Kinship"

Hartman's cryptogram makes its in-print debut twice. The first is as a citation of personal correspondence in one of Judith Butler's most direct statements on the subject, "Is Kinship Always Already Heterosexual?" (2002). "Slavery is the ghost in the machine of kinship" (15) refers, for Butler, to the double bind in which African American families are caught, subject simultaneously to the delegitimization, pathologization, and normalizing pressures of the regulatory state. Butler argues that the legal dispossession of kin relations—racial slavery's hallmark and enduring stigma—is reproduced in contemporary legal and cultural regimes that fatally misrecognize actual formations of Black kinship as either dysfunctional or nonexistent.

The second time that Hartman's cryptogram appears, it serves as the thematic gyroscope for her critical memoir, *Lose Your Mother* (2007). "Slaves were the ghosts in the machine of kinship," writes Hartman in slightly altered prose, insofar as slaves' relations of affiliation and descent—the ties of family and the rights of patrimony—were usurped ab initio by the master's claims to property (194). Race "set the slave apart from man and citizen and sentenced her to an interminable servitude" (73). The "mark of property," continues Hartman, "provides the emblem of kinship in the wake of defacement" (80). If the commodification of Blackness (and/or the Blackness of the commodity) defaces kinship, "Black kinship" names a more radical contradiction in terms. Kinship and Black kinship lack a common denominator. "Black" ultimately does not describe a category of kinship but its negation, whether understood as the absolute usurpation of the relations of kinship by the relations of property (Sharpe 2016b) or as "an enforced state of breach" wrought by subjection to the wanton violence of nonslaves, "where 'kinship' loses meaning" (Spillers 2003, 218). Our challenge lies in thinking the relation between slavery and kinship in a way that does not collapse their terms.

Hartman's construction is not unprecedented. The "ghost in the machine" is an expression closely associated with Gilbert Ryle and a tradition of anti-Cartesian philosophy. Ryle's 1949 monograph *The Concept of Mind* is an extended critique of mind-body dualism, in which Ryle lambastes the "dogma of the Ghost in the Machine" as a long-running (if not *the* long-running) "category-mistake" of Western thought. "Descartes' myth" (Ryle [1949] 2002, 11–15) supposedly mistakes the mental faculty for a mysterious and independent interiority that controls, or works upon, the actions of the machine/body. Ryle argues instead that universal laws explain phenomenal action, including those of the mind, which are "just spectral machines" of another order (20). If Hartman is appropriating Ryle's pejorative expression, she neither endorses nor repudiates his caricature of modern philosophy but rescues the notion of an irreconcilable difference from philosophical disrepute. In other words, the distance that separates the ghost from the machine cannot boil down to a difference within the same (if unequal) law of kinship, or to machines of different orders. Claiming an equivalence in the cultural and material conditions of Black life "now" and "then" will likewise not suffice.

The sexual reproduction of slavery forms a nexus between the materiality of kinship and the ghostly immateriality of slavery. Hartman (2007, 194) illustrates this figural nonrelation through an African proverb: "Only the penis touched the child of a slave woman, since the mother passed no birthright that she could transfer to her child." Because women traded as slaves had no social standing, their children would "belong entirely to the genealogy of the father" (194). Disinheritance is here an inheritance that paradoxically undoes its medium—the genealogy of the mother—in the very act of matrilineal transmission. Birth becomes a strangely material act that transcends itself into an immaterial cause: the disinheritance of the mother. In the US context, the children of the slave mother are additionally excluded from the genealogy of the father, only to be included by default in the "lineage" of the commodity; the Black mother is both the ghost of slavery and the figure possessed, the medium for a touching between penis and child from which she is subtracted as a material agent. If her unintelligibility as a woman and mother threatens to plunge this touching between father and child into the illicit zone of rape and incest, his criminality is also masked by the spectacle of her obliteration. Excluded from kinship but confined within it, the slave mother animates the production of surplus value. We are dealing here with a haunting turned on its head: the machine torments the specter.

The "ghost in the machine" does not represent a type of kinship, whether clandestine or denied, as much as it illustrates the problematic wedding of capital and slavery, the foreclosure of which vouchsafes the inner limits of the structure of kinship. But what precisely is the "machine of kinship," and how does slavery fuel its internal combustion? To make further progress on these categories, we must turn to the queer intervention into anthropology to understand the political stakes of the critique of kinship.

The Accumulation of Women

Kinship became an object for feminist inquiry when it needed a stronger analysis of the oppression of women. Feminist anthropology specifically sought to supplement a Marxist framework of exploitation that inadequately accounted for gender difference, if it did not assume it outright as an uncomplicated fact of nature. The feminist critique of kinship had to make an analytical distinction between human culture in its structure (i.e., its terms of necessity) and culture's historical permutations (i.e., its range of possibilities). It was critical for feminist anthropology to have an account of both to avoid casting patriarchy as a fait accompli, a transhistorical fact equivalent to culture. It also needed an account of the historical structure of kinship to ensure that a political program for women's liberation could describe the historical possibility of its objective.

In her influential interventions into psychoanalysis and structural anthropology, Gayle Rubin (1975, 198) reconceptualized kinship as the "social machinery" that converts sexed bodies (and biological sexuality) into gendered relations, a process that produces and distributes symbolic positions, rights, and claims. Whereas the Marxist "woman question" ends somewhere around the problem of the reproduction of male labor, Rubin's critique of the political economy of sex rethinks gender and sexuality as products of an autonomous mode of production. Like value, women are made. In the process, Rubin reassigns the "traffic in women" from an act at the origin of culture, a claim that she credits to Lévi-Strauss, to a widespread but unnecessary effect of culture, a "product of the specific social relations [of gender] that organize it" (168). Sexual traffic is "shorthand" for the fact that the "social relations of a kinship system specify that men have certain rights [of exchange] in their female kin, and that women do not have the same rights either to themselves or to their male kin" (177). This theory of the sex/gender system historicizes gender difference and describes a form of patriarchy beyond the division of labor: "Kinship is organization, and organization gives power" (174).

Organization *gives* power but is not equivalent to it, just as kinship is not the only or even the principal form of social organization in Western societies. Indeed, Rubin (1975) makes a point to clarify the restricted historical jurisdiction of her object. If the sex-gender system once organized societies, it now "only organizes and reproduces itself" (199). Society organizes kinship, not the other way around. Kinship, stripped of its fundamental social, economic, and political function, is a holdover from premodern society. It survives now as a pure, self-positing power, one that can—and, for the liberation of women, must—be eliminated to defeat the compulsory heterosexuality and gender binarism that Rubin says the incest taboo prescribes (180). What principle or structure organizes society once kinship is displaced from this role? This is unclear from Rubin's account, and for that reason we do not have a clear picture of the minimal difference that separates the radical anarchy of sex and the historical tyranny of gender identification. Without an account of the structural limits that organize society that is irreducible to gendered relations of power, without a distinction between the necessity and possibilities of society, human culture can only be imagined as either an entirely voluntarist affair (i.e., "if we change our behavior, we change the world") or as indistinguishable from the dispossession of women.

Beginning with *Gender Trouble* ([1990] 2007), Butler alters the terms of this debate. A queer critique of kinship—and of feminist anthropology—must "reject the postulation of an ideal sexuality prior to the incest taboo"—that is, Rubin's romance of a body before the historical tyranny of gender identification—and simultaneously must "refuse to accept the structuralist premise of the cultural permanence of that taboo" (102). Butler's solution is as neat as it is effective, preserving the universality of the incest taboo but emptying it of any necessary content. This prohibition "exists in every aspect of the social form" and "operates somewhere in every social form" (103). The object of taboo is entirely variable. Whatever set of sexual relations is barred in a particular historical conjuncture, that barring always "produces a variety of substitute desires and identities that are in no sense constrained in advance" (103). These desires and identities, and the reproduction of the material conditions of life in which those desires and identities circulate, can hypostasize into any number of social configurations. But heterosexuality, a specific configuration of gender or family, and/or any forms of power that institutionalize these identities, desires, and relations are not inherent to kinship.

From this perspective, the incest taboo lies somewhere between the universal and particular, straddling history and structure. This makes Butler, of all things, a structuralist par excellence, suggesting an underdeveloped rapport between structuralism and queer theory. After all, Lévi-Strauss (1969, 12) positions the incest taboo as the "threshold of culture," the constitutive leap whereby "nature transcends itself" (25) into a total structure of social relations defined by the principle of reciprocal gift exchange. The whole point of the incest taboo is not to repress or limit the number and variety of social formations but to compel the social itself—to quite simply prohibit any type of existence that is *not* social. Lévi-Strauss consequently advises his readers "to ignore the difference between the prohibition of incest and exogamy: . . . their formal characteristics are in effect identical" (51). Butler's minor but pivotal correction to Lévi-Strauss's account conclusively shatters any necessary correspondence between the incest taboo and heterosexual exogamy.

Despite claiming that a distinction between the symbolic and the social is both unwarranted and unnecessary, Butler's structuralism posits a form of prohibition that cannot be reduced to a social and historical convention. Where else but in a concept of the symbolic could this law be universal without constituting a fact of nature? Taboo "works precisely through proliferating through displacement the very crime that it bars"; it "delineates lines of kinship that harbor incest as their ownmost [sic] possibility, establishing 'aberration' at the heart of the norm" (Butler 2000, 67). Taboo does not erase incest but universalizes its desire, making all forms of kinship possible (i.e., not incestuous) *and* impossible (i.e., incestuous), always destabilized by its inner negation. The queer critique of kinship relies on this idea of a universal failure. Only by establishing the aberration that haunts all types of kinship can queer critique "normalize" (in the sense of de-pathologize) forms of kinship that lie outside the regulatory ideal of the heteronuclear model.

Thanks to this universal prohibition, kinship exists everywhere in one shape or another, with gender always alongside it. In fact, Butler largely remolds the theory of kinship into an extension of her theory of bodies and gender.[2] As a provisional identity, as a practice both enabled and constrained by the relations of kinship that it also constantly remakes, gender is likewise universal in its limitless differences. The performance of gender is a practice of kinship. The burden of human subjectivity lies in this inevitability, that any existence outside the gender/kinship system is precluded from the get-go by the incest prohibition. Butler is very clear about this: "The very formation of subjects, the very formation of persons, presupposes gender in a certain way. . . . Performativity has to do with repetition, very often with the repetition of oppressive and painful gender norms to force them to resignify. This is not freedom, but a question of how to work the trap that one is inevitably in" (Butler 1992).

What is the status of the "exchange of women" after this revision? For her part, Rubin (1975, 176) suggests that the traffic in women is not limited to premodern society but has become "more pronounced and commercialized in more 'civilized' societies," although she provides few convincing examples. Drawing on her ethnography of kinship in Melanesia, the feminist anthropologist Marilyn Strathern (1984) also faults the structuralist account for reifying "woman" as a "thing-gift" that mystifies inequality in social transactions, a fact that seems to preserve the notion of exchange as good for thinking the institution of marriage in Western contemporary culture, albeit with an importance attenuated with respect to more-determinative economic and political systems. Butler, an avid reader of both theorists, is less interested in recycling the notion of the "exchange of women," reading it as too much of an ideological expression of power to be reset as a legitimate description of it. In *Antigone's Claim* (2000) she effectively replaces Lévi-Strauss's illustration with a reading of the myth of Antigone to figure the adversarial relation between queer kinship and the state. But the corresponding deferment of a theory of exchange—and the type of negation that would set the economy of kinship in motion—leads Butler to relinquish an account of the specific mode of the production of gender that Rubin is after (gender being now "presupposed" in subject formation). A theory of exchange and the mode of production that it underwrites is vital for explaining the mechanism that institutes a social system.

Now, these accounts contrast sharply with the explanation that Lévi-Strauss (1969) provides for the emergence of modern kinship, which he strongly insists occurs through the *dissolution* of the exchange of women. The "complex" and "generalized" form of sexual traffic that emerges afterward is therefore qualitatively distinct from the "simple" (i.e., elementary) structures that occupy most of Lévi-Strauss's attention, demanding a different if related analysis (474). In a generalized or continuous system of exchange (which is said to operate in traditional Indian and Chinese society), marriage partners are not exchanged between clans in a one-to-one fashion; rather, patriarchs give wives and sisters away to another family without immediate remuneration of a woman in kind. The surrender of a direct gain in exchange is incentivized by the expectation of an interest-added return later in the form of a wife of higher social standing. Kinship in a generalized system is effectively conducted "on credit." Debt, speculation, and risk are thereby introduced throughout the whole exchange. Profit, not reciprocity, becomes its governing principle. Every marriage becomes a long-term wager, but the system as a whole realizes newly unbounded profits as the circle of potential partners expands outward and the cycles of exchange multiply.

With the financial speculation on women comes inequality between men and, paradoxically, *within* the "value" attributed to each woman between her use value and exchange value. The surplus that each woman could potentially yield in an exchange becomes calculated into her cultural price, leading men to fetishistically hoard women as wealth. This "result[s] in the accumulation of women at some stage in the cycle" (Lévi-Strauss 1969, 266). Polygamy is one cultural expression of this tendency. Women in polygamous societies shed their status as gifts or signs and in many ways become formally identical to the commodity. Women are both exchanged and accumulated. Yet the inequality between men that is exacerbated by each ensuing round of accumulation contradicts the conditions of equality that a generalized system presupposes and on which its reproduction relies. Each patriarchal family must originally be equal to all others, and exchange proceeds only insofar as the "last" transaction hypothetically equals the value of the "first" betrothal: "Generalized exchange leads almost unavoidably to anisogamy, i.e. to marriage between spouses of different status," which "must therefore lead to its downfall" (266).

Lévi-Strauss (1969, 477) speculates that European societies averted the crisis of the accumulation of women through an ingenious mechanism, the "assertion of female rights," which abolishes generalized exchange. What emerges approximates the Western system we know today. For Lévi-Strauss, modern marriage includes the freedom to choose one's partner, gender equality in marriage vows, emancipation from relatives, and the individualization of the marriage contract (477). Once women gain these equal "rights of exchange" in themselves (through a combination of structural tendencies and their own political organizing), they become formally equal partners in kinship. In losing their status as symbolic currency (i.e., "reciprocal gifts"), women also cease to serve as the object transacted to constitute the basis of society. Gender equality (in the loose sense of the term denoted here) therefore demotes kinship to a nonessential if still significant sphere of social activity. We arrive now back at the same question on which the queer critique of kinship ends, if from a new standpoint. What economy organizes society once kinship loses that function and is content to only "organize itself"?

The Accumulation of Slaves

It would hardly abuse poetic license to figure capital as an emergent property of the generalized exchange of women. Replacing "women" with "capital" in Lévi-Strauss's description gives us a striking if rudimentary portrait of financial crisis. If this is not just a metaphor, capitalism appears to both begin in the exchange of women and fully emerge after women are decommodified (McKinnon 2001). It combines the problem and solution to the contradictions inherent in the generalized exchange of women, merging the main characteristics of both: the depersonalized commodity, the individualization of economic contracts, abstract gender equality, and so on. This transition is as miraculous a leap as the one that the incest taboo effects from nature to culture. Lévi-Strauss (1969, 475) likens the enfranchisement of women to a "deus ex machina" that rescues the stalled economy of kinship and "gives the necessary push for a new impetus." But this achievement is no cause for celebration, considering that capital plays the part of the deus ex machina that replaces kinship as the organizing principle of society, which downgrades the function of marriage before the new exchange of commodities (Damon 1980). If this mediation gives way to the crises of capital accumulation, it is necessary to consider how this transition does not become possible until racial slavery effects a crucial separation between personhood and property as autonomous social orders.

Hartman (2007, 73), as noted above, describes race as the device that "set the slave apart from man." Let us venture that "free man" is able to realize the abstract gender equality that discontinues the accumulation of women only through men's and women's concrete relations to slavery, through their equal difference or distinction from chattel property. The nature of exchange and accumulation undergo a dramatic transformation as a result. At least two main differences set the generalized system of kinship apart from the mode of the production of slavery that succeeds it. First, women under precapitalist forms of kinship could be transacted only in kind, for other women. "The notion of equivalence of individuals with goods is not relevant to domestic [i.e., precapitalist] societies," writes Claude Meillassoux (1991, 13) in his anthropology of West African slavery. Second, each woman could be transacted only once, not regifted to a third party or recirculated in additional rounds of exchange (63). Racial slaves, on the contrary, are regulated by neither of these norms, thus representing the first fully convertible species of property. Between the matrimonial and commercial circuits of exchange, there is a qualitative change in nature. The superimposition of racial slavery on the generalized exchange of women mediates the leap between gift and commodity, between premodern kinship and modern capital.

The separation and distinction between woman and commodity, and, critically, the new modes of intercourse between these "spheres" of production—that is, the manner in which the family, now as an economic unit, becomes integrated into the capitalist mode of production "outside" itself—transfers the contradictions that plague the generalized exchange of kinship into the sexual economy of slavery.

Jennifer Morgan (2004) tracks this separation between woman and commodity in her analysis of the role of the female slave in the early modern family, offering a snapshot of the practical enfranchisement that would have immobilized the accumulation of (white) women. Seventeenth-century tax and probate court records from the English colonies reveal that non-Black women commonly inherited slaves from their husbands, which they would use, sell, or bequeath to their own children. The paradigmatic slave was female, owing to the fact that her reproductive capacities introduced the dimension of speculation into the exchange system (i.e., the surplus of her future "issue" over and above her labor time). Men and women frequently divided single female slaves among more than one legatee based on her calculated capacity to "multiply." Once the Black body came to signify a value over and above itself, the exchange and accumulation of slaves became a historical possibility. The gender parity achieved here is in any event a perverse one, consisting in the shared capacity of free men and women to act equally as givers and receivers of slaves. In this reading, slavery is neither wholly capitalist nor an extension of kinship, but a function of their mutual separation and conjunction.

The law that defines and guarantees the reproduction of slave status we now generally refer to as *partus sequitur ventrem*, meaning that the status of the child "follows the womb" or, more literally, "offspring follows the belly" (Morgan 2018). Legal practitioners appended this Latinate expression to the 1662 Virginia statute that first codified the matrilineal transmission of slave status, which conspicuously departs from the patrilineage that predominates in patriarchal societies. Yet more consequential than the gendered coding of the mode of transmission is the statute's logic of racialization. In declaring that "all children borne in this country shall be held bond or free only according to the condition of the mother" (Hening 1823, 170), the law rests the future of slavery on the extension of the present "condition of the mother," for which it provides no explanation. The obliteration of the present condition of the mother from legal contemplation guarantees the status of her future children. Her bondage, and that of the hypothetical "primal mother" of the entire line of racial descent, is the nonposited presupposition crucial to the law's obscure rationality. Her obliteration ensures that the nature of slavery remains unqualified, just that and nothing more: slaves beget slaves.

Slave owners were ultimately seeking clarity about the legal status of their chattel property, but the seemingly simple contrivance of *partus sequitur ventrem*, and the broader logic of racial production it metonymized, also threw the foundations of kinship into crisis. Whereas the law of kinship depends on defining discrete symbolic positions that determine the scope and limits of social intercourse, the law of slavery negates the slave's symbolic position, tout court. Because this precludes any form of affiliation to the slave, the incest taboo is powerless to govern her. *Partus sequitur ventrem* thus supersedes the entire dialectic of compliance and violation, norm and exception, kin and incest. To the law, the slave is incest incarnate, an ontological transgression. She subverts kinship and dethrones its function as the universal organizing principle of society.

But the law of slavery also resolves the crisis it creates by defining the slave exclusively in terms of property, transforming the limit of kinship into a unique species of biologically self-reproducing commodity. As a commodity, the slave does not subvert the incest taboo but enters the wider circuit of commodity exchange that incorporates the practices of kinship—and the private family—into the universal structure of capital. We thus reach the conclusion that the law of slavery is not just antithetical to kinship but is a *second-order law of kinship*: the law that negates the law of kinship.

If race set slave apart from man, race just as importantly set man apart from commodity, preserving the minimal distance between kinship and the logic of universal equivalence that capital aspires to erase. By revoking the incest taboo in the slave, *partus sequitur ventrem* defines the deconstruction between person and property as a racial inheritance, erecting a racial firewall between capital and kinship. The racialization of slavery, in other words, halts the generalization of equivalence and the universalization of value inherent in the social form of the commodity at the threshold of modern kinship, preventing what would have otherwise become a moral crisis, the accumulation of non-Black women.

Partus sequitur ventrem in this way acts as both an instrument of bondage (i.e., the racialization of slavery) and an instrument of emancipation (i.e., the decommodification of man), an ambidexterity that interestingly also characterizes its career before becoming the governing principle of colonial slavery. Under English civil law, *partus sequitur ventrem* originally acted as a protective clause that prevented slavery from becoming a heritable property. It specifically neutralized the patrilineal transmission of status when children were at risk of being "infected with the Leprosie of his fathers [*sic*] bondage" (Swinburne 1590, cited in Morris 1996, 44). By introducing a legal exception to the traditional patrilineage, this original variation of *partus sequitur ventrem* ensured that male heirs would inherit the freeborn status of their mother, "notwithstanding the bondage of the father." Yet this principle held only in cases of lawful matrimony. For children born out of wedlock, the civil law recognized no father at all. The "bastard" in question consequently inherited from his mother a rather different form of infamy. He was liberated from having "a" father, only to be incorporated into a hyperextended family, a pariah community. The medieval euphemisms for "bastard" describe this cursed offspring as both *filius nullius* and *filius vulgi*: the "son of no man" and the "son of every man" (43).

Racial slavery renders the difference between lawful and unlawful matrimony inconsequential, just as it blends these previously separate civil and common law conventions into an unprecedented technology of domination. When bastardy becomes race, slavery endows Blackness with the status of being *child of no man* and the *child of every man*. The first status denotes an absolute alienation, the latter an unlimited intimacy. As the structural incarnation of incest, slaves themselves are sexually prohibited, suspending the question of any sexual relation; all sex is instead transformed into a meaningless confusion between the licit and the illicit. The minimal distance between the incest taboo and the formations of kinship disappears as the slave becomes a "near relative" to every person and to no one at all.

Akinship is therefore readable as both *akin*-ship ("akin" or related to all kinship formations) and *a* kinship (not kinship). Akin to all, the slave is not kin. Near relatives to all, she is near relatives to none.

Slavery is essential to the structure and historical formation of modern kinship. It is the deus ex machina that founds it and the impetus that reproduces it. If slavery is modern kinship's origin and condition of possibility, akinship (i.e., Black kinship) constitutes its essence and condition of impossibility. This antagonism is the "ghost in the machine of kinship," but at this stage we can ignore the difference between slavery and Black kinship: their formal characteristics are in effect identical. They both refer (from different vantages) to a "queer kinship" between all possible formations of kinship that are *not* Black—just as they point to the Black aberration at the heart of each social organization. This conclusion opens a new problematic. If actually existing Black life is intensely disciplined, pathologized, punished, and policed, as the *Lawrence* case makes clear, the logic of akinship is strangely homologous to the logic of policing. The ghost of kinship has a double. *Blackness comprises a spectral mixture of incest and kinship in the exact same ratio that policing comprises an unnatural combination of law-making and law-preserving violence.* To work out the connections within this strange homology, I will turn now to a closer examination of the function of policing in the extenuating circumstances surrounding *Lawrence v. Texas.*

Police Power, or, the Ghost in the Machine of *Lawrence*

On September 17, 1998, John Lawrence and Tyrone Garner were arrested for "deviate sexual intercourse" (Texas Penal Code §21.06). Houston police claim they caught the pair red-handed, although it was neither news of the crime nor pure happenstance that brought officers to the premises with their guns drawn. The plaintiffs' mutual acquaintance, Robert Eubanks, drunk and jealous that Garner, his on-again-off-again boyfriend, was supposedly flirting with Lawrence, initially dispatched the police in a jealous rage, calling 911 to report a "black male going crazy with a gun" (Carpenter 2012, 73). Historically, sodomy statutes were rarely enforced. Most gathered dust in state lawbooks for the majority of their tenure, fulfilling their purpose as an inert sign of condemnation. The reason they were not enforced is stated bluntly in the amicus brief filed by the American Civil Liberties Union (2002, 20) on behalf of the *Lawrence* plaintiffs: "People do not report the sexual activities of their neighbors and acquaintances and have not done so for a very long time." This case was no exception. *Lawrence* presents the peculiar case of a law undone by its own application.

Long before the rights of privacy and same-sex intimacy became matters for criminal investigation, the specter of the "armed" and "crazy" Black male initiates the intervention of the police. Modern police power, in Walter Benjamin's (1978, 287) description, "intervene[s] 'for security reasons' in countless cases where no clear legal situation exists." It creates legal situations but neither responds to nor resolves them. The police do not essentially patrol borders, enforce regulatory norms, or serve a sovereignty beyond themselves but exist to dispose of public threats. Because police power is authorized to respond with absolute freedom to any threat to the public welfare, it cannot be legally limited in its powers, including in its power to invade the private domain (Wagner 2009).

Embodying the public welfare and opposing the breakdown of the social order into pure relations of force, the police seize the capacity to collapse the difference between the two—the political and social orders—as their fundamental prerogative. The essential act of policing is therefore the destruction of the difference between the political and the social; its power is the capacity to make existence equal to violence. Blackness is both the product of this act of policing and the incarnation of the threat to the public welfare. Kinship is impossible amid the deployment of police, or, put another way, akinship is the form of kinship that is destroyed at the moment of its production.

Through these contractions—between the political order and the social order, and between the public welfare and the police itself—the power of the police accumulates indefinitely. Operating outside a legal framework, the police have no ethical limits. "Crisis" is an inappropriate concept to describe this accumulation of force, for police power is always insufficient with respect to its gratuitous object, having no sovereign or normative aims beyond those of the accumulation and expansion of its own power (Martinot and Sexton 2003).

Underlining the simultaneously productive and destructive capacities of the police, Lawrence and Garner testified in subsequent interviews that they were not having sex when the police stormed Lawrence's apartment—nor, in fact, did they have any sexual relations before or after their arrest. According to their respective accounts, they were either fifteen feet apart when the police barged through the door or in separate rooms entirely. "Actual" sodomy was in all likelihood a convenient fiction that the lawyers for the Lambda Legal Defense Fund were happy to endorse to advance the legal case against "homosexual conduct" laws. Interviews with police officers at the scene tell a fantastically different story. One could not recall if the sex he barged in on was oral or anal, certain only that "Lawrence was the dominant, insertive partner" (Carpenter 2012, 68). Another officer remembered a sickening "anal odor" in the air: "the whole apartment smelled of gay" (78). A third claimed that both plaintiffs continued to have sex "well in excess of a minute" after officers burst into the room, ceasing only after the police pried their bodies apart (69). Amid shouted orders to desist, neither plaintiff was supposedly startled. Lawrence is said to have remained expressionless, staring blankly at the officer, whereas Garner mustered only a muted "Oh!"

We can conclude that Tyrone Garner fails to cohere into a governable subject even *after* this orgy of fantasy quiesces and the subsequent legal situation (i.e., criminal homosexual conduct) emerges. After his imagined danger to the public welfare dissipates, after the social separates back out from the political through the decampment of police power, the intoxicating nature of Garner's imagined queer ecstasy renders him unreflective to interpellation and incapable of responding to authority. The epistemology of the state, its technologies of calculation and documentation, only retroactively organizes the phantasmagoric elements of the police imagination—the sights, sounds, and smells of Black sodomy—into a legal situation. The images conjured by the police are the ones that the law then arranges into the production of legal power, a relation between the imaginary and the symbolic that forms what Sora Han (2012, 81) calls the dreamwork of the law: "the aporetic relationship between the written and imaginative domains of the legal text."

If Blackness threatens the public welfare, triggering the police's essential act of collapsing the social and the political, what position would Garner otherwise inhabit *inside* the social order of kinship, in the wake of police power? Is Black life assimilable to the public welfare? Put another way, could a law that protects private, consensual adult sex—the very constitutional guarantee achieved by *Lawrence v. Texas*—provide legal relief to Garner in a hypothetical case of domestic abuse?

This conjecture is not as idle as it seems. In addition to reporting him to the police, Eubanks was Garner's boyfriend of eight years (Carpenter 2012, 44). More to the point, he was "prone to calling Garner a 'n——'" when he was drunk or angry" (45, elision mine) and placed a temporary domestic-violence protection order (of dubious veracity) against Garner while *Lawrence* was pending in 2000 (166). Eubanks's affidavit accused Garner of punching him in the eye, beating him with a hose while "using crack and drinking," whipping him with a belt, stabbing him in the finger with a box cutter, burning him with a hot iron, and sexually assaulting him (166). The case was eventually dropped, and both continued living together until Eubanks was murdered in 2000 (a case that remains unsolved). Garner, initially a suspect in the crime, was barred by Eubanks's family from attending his boyfriend's funeral.

"What protection against the turning wheels of the legal system did Garner have on his own?" Marc Spindelman (2013, 1133) asks this question in light of the expanded mandate that *Lawrence* provides the state to criminalize and punish nonconsensual sex. Had Eubanks's accusation of sexual abuse stood, what plausible defense would Garner have had at his disposal? This is not a question about legal strategy but about the extent to which the legal text, through the dreamwork of the law, remains beholden to the imaginary of policing. Before the "domestic violence system's grip," speculates Spindelman, Garner's standing would have been overdetermined:

> The judge hearing the protection order case may have been primed by Eubanks's [domestic violence] affidavit (and, if he saw it, by Garner's own rap sheet), along with the discriminatory social stereotypes involving sexual orientation, gender, class, and race that they triggered, to see Garner as a criminal perpetrator already: the male-dominant aggressor, his class and race marked by the crack he was said to have taken with drink, tormenting his poor, white, older gay lover with fists, hose, belt, box cutter, hot iron, as well as sexually assaulting him, presumably with his black penis. (1133)

In this speculative outcome, Garner and his Black penis cannot be distinguished. This phantom phallus enters a sordid chain of equivalents, an array of sexual weapons or mechanized appendages, less a body that can be harmed than a swarm of organs. His ungendered masculinity is a threat to the public welfare, and all recourse to the battery of signifying schemas in which a "castrated" subject is capable of being represented as injured subsequently loses its coherence. Garner's total self-possession paradoxically obviates the coherence of legal subjectivity. A "Black male going crazy with a Black penis" or, more fractally, a "Black penis going crazy with a Black penis" appears only as an insentient agent of sexual violence.

This excess masculinity has a gendered double. Spindelman (2013) wonders in the same vein whether Garner could obversely claim a state of injury, whether he could present himself as a victim of sexual violence—as a victim of Eubanks's abuse, for instance. For Spindelman, however, Garner's material conditions make "any sex-based injuries that result seem, when not affirmatively wanted, minimal or nonexistent, or anyway tendentious, if not flat out incredible" (1135). The legal legibility of Garner's sexual injury

> assumes the law would help a gay gender nonconformist, a feminine homosexual, or more precisely, a black, feminine homosexual, who is already so far from the norms of straight, white masculinity that it might be hard to perceive any harm—like the loss of manhood, autonomy, or dignity through sexual violation—for the legal system to repair. It is also worth asking: What would it mean—what would the legal system be understood to be producing—if it repaired a loss like that? (1136)

In Spindelman's second scenario, Garner's demasculinizing masculinity as a hypothetical defendant turns into a defeminizing femininity as a hypothetical plaintiff. If the former makes his publicly threatening nature a foregone conclusion, the latter outright precludes his claim to a stake in the public welfare. With a body so violated that additional injury is inconceivable by the law, or conceivable only as his own desire, Garner gains the imaginary invulnerability of a ghost who, already dead, cannot suffer any redressable injuries. Where the law recognizes no injury and nothing to redress, the police do not recognize a body to defend.

Not only must it be destroyed for the social life of kinship to emerge, but a ghostly Black kinship haunts the machine of kinship as the negation of gender. All kinship, in other words, emerges out of the negation of the indeterminate negation of Black gender.

If the gendered practices of social reproduction flower only in the wake of the police power's decampment, then Black kinship conversely exists only in that zone of indistinction between the social and the political, in the throes of police violence. The police amount here to a mode of racial production that creates akinship but also a force that preserves Blackness in the interstices of the social—*as* the cancellation of gender. This is the ultimately irresolvable paradox that akinship presents: each formation of kinship exists only in a repetition of the obliteration of the negation of Black gender. Akinship therefore signifies a perverse form of "kinship," a structural affiliation *between* all forms of kinship and police power.

Akinship

Hartman's cryptogram is most readily interpreted as a statement on the warped temporality of anti-Blackness, which would read the ghost as the trace of history, or slavery as "both the past and a living present" (Trouillot 1995, 147). Although this interpretation is far from simple, its historical angle licenses us to sketch at least a preliminary line of correspondence between the kinships that policing makes possible and impossible, on the one hand, and a structural process—"de-sexualization"—that the Marxist anthropologist Claude Meillassoux (1991) conceives as a defining moment in the slave mode of production, on the other. Desexualization does a better job than concepts such as "pathologization" to explain Garner's position because it is integrated into a theory of the relationship between the respective modes of slave production and kin/gender production. Hortense Spillers has advanced the most systematic translation and revision of Meillassoux's concept, and its part in theorizing slavery as the "anti-thesis of kinship" in precolonial West Africa, into the American grammar of *ungendering* that this chapter has used to triangulate Garner's structural position in the dreamwork of the law. For Spillers (2003, 74), Meillassoux's work "becomes useful as a point of contemplation" to the extent that transatlantic contact metastasizes and mutates rather than replaces the African mode of the production of slavery. I will carry Spillers's homology forward to conclude on the role of policing in the production of akinship.

Desexualization describes the outcome of two processes in the capture and institutionalization of slaves in precapitalist West Africa. For Meillassoux (1991), desocialization—the total alienation of a person from the kinship relations of their birth—is accompanied by the process of depersonalization—the institutional foreclosure of slaves' capacity to produce new social ties in the society in which they are inserted. This second process transforms the kinless alien into a slave "beyond social death [who is] seen as *not-born*" (107). This two-step exclusion desexualizes, meaning that slaves are not held to the prerogatives and cultural conventions of femininity and masculinity. This is because the only role of the slave in a slave society is submission to a mode of material production undifferentiated by the sexual division of labor.

To be clear, it was not the case that differences between male and female slaves were not recognized or that the so-called sexes were press-ganged in equal proportions into all types of work (they were not), but that the "sexual distribution of tasks" in a slave society was not limited by the conventions of the predominant gender ideology (Meillassoux 1991, 111). Gender was not regulated among slaves because slaves were not governed as gendered subjects. The institutionalization of slavery sought only to insert slaves into a free society in a socially sustainable manner.

Yet it is precisely at this point that gender began to be regulated *in free society*. As Meillassoux (1991, 102) writes, "Societies which had not conceived and elaborated conservative notions to define the social norms of reproduction *were obliged to do so when confronted with slavery in order to distinguish their own members from slaves*. Kinship was strengthened, developed and refined in opposition to non-kin" (emphasis mine). Slavery compels the defensive invention of conservative notions of kinship. It functions as the anti-thesis of slavery, a means of distinguishing free society from the unfree persons increasingly inserted in its midst. The refinement and conservation of gender, a coefficient of the practices of kinship, follows as a result, designating a mode in which free society governs itself *as* free. Gender is, in this sense, a codification of slavery, not only, as Butler (1992) contends, a "trap that everyone is inevitably in." If race set slave apart from man, then gender set man apart from slave. This can explain why kinship becomes inhospitable to queerness at various historical junctures, just as it provides us a new vantage for imagining what queerness can or should become.

The "mode of insertion" of slaves into free society forms the very crux of the slaving enterprise, but the retention of slaves *as* slaves could not be achieved without formalizing a minimal link between the slave and free society. This consisted of establishing a "*univocal* institutional link which bound [slaves] to their master," incorporating the slave into free society on the sole basis of their subordinate role in the sphere of production, which includes first and foremost the production of the slave as a being for the master (Meillassoux 1991, 113). This unary link establishes the minimal and necessary difference between slaves and free persons, who by contrast are instituted on the basis of a double link—to both the productive (i.e., labor) and reproductive (i.e., kinship) orders of existence. Absent a secondary line of filiation to the sphere of kinship, the slave was inserted into society both *unsocially* and *politically*. Slaves entered, existed, and died as entities subject purely to the relations of power.

If the formal characteristics of slavery and Black kinship are in effect identical, as we proposed above, then policing functions as the "mode of insertion" of Black kinship into society univocally, solely on the political level. The inexistence of Blackness on the social level perforce indexes a fugitive and imaginary existence—hence akinship, a purely political form of kinship.

What can a purely political form of kinship possibly mean, and what are the implications of this concept for kinship theory? In this essay, akinship conceptualizes the structural identity and discrepancy between Black *social* kinship—which slavery constitutes as universally prohibited—and the compulsion to elaborate *non-Black* social ties. There is a model for this mode of social production in the anthropology of kinship. Recall that the function of the incest taboo, its generative tautology, is not to prescribe any particular expression of family life but to compel the social itself—it quite simply prohibits any type of existence that is *not* social. In a parallel manner the fundamental purpose of akinship is not to repress or limit the variety of social formations in a racialized society, whether heteronormative or queer, traditional or fictive. It is to compel kinship as such—akinship quite simply prohibits any type of existence that is *not non-Black*. If the specter of the impossibility of the social electrifies the incest taboo with its specific "horror," the absolute prohibition against Black kinship is animated by the distinct fear among social subjects of becoming slaves.

Therefore, a purely political form of kinship refers, on the one hand, to a form of kinship that can appear only as an unlimited public threat. But on the other hand, akinship—untethered from the social and undefined by a specific set of sex/gender practices—also refers to a political affiliation founded in the Lacanian real, untethered to the exchanges of the symbolic. A purely political form of kinship would thus constitute something like an ideal *alliance without exchange*. Such a notion of a (political) alliance without (social) exchange, or an anti-social alliance, strikes me as a way of conceiving akinship as a template for political organizing that obeys a different polarity than that of "coalition" or "solidarity," although its precise difference would have to be developed in subsequent work.

For the scholarship on queer kinship, the foregoing holds a more immediate implication. Whereas this essay at no point dismisses heteropatriarchy as a vector in the determination of kinship, it does displace it, theoretically repositioning its function within the modes of accumulation in racial capitalism. In contrast to the regulation of social life, we must foreground the political mechanism that constitutes the social. Heteropatriarchy is undoubtedly a force within this broader frame of reference. But hypothetically, the heterosexual form and normative content of kinship could be eliminated without extinguishing the racial mode of production—slavery and policing—that structures it. Kinship is not necessarily heterosexual, but it is always the absolute repudiation of Black kinship, already a negation of kinship's own ontological crisis. To incorporate this insight, queer theories of kinship will have to redouble their efforts and redistribute their critical focus: between the biopolitical apparatuses that calcify the possibilities of life in a given historical dispensation and the mode of racial production that crystallizes akinship as the very fissure of the social bond.

Notes

1 Tyrone Garner Funeral Fund: www.stephenhyland.com/2006/09/tyrone
_garner_f.html.
2 "Kinship matters for queer theory in a way that Judith Butler reminds us that
'bodies matter': (1) a culture's repetition of particular practices actually *produces* what seem to be the material facts that supposedly *ground* those practices in the first place, and (2) when those repetitions are governed by a norm,
other possibilities are literally unthinkable and impossible" (Freeman 2007,
297).

LEAH CLAIRE ALLEN AND JOHN S. GARRISON

10 Against Friendship

In a 1981 interview with the French magazine *Gai Pied*, Michel Foucault (1996, 309) remarked that what profoundly troubles people about homosexuality is not the sexual acts involved but rather "the formation of new alliances and the tying together of unforeseen lines of force." That interview, titled "Friendship as a Way of Life," is part of a long and ongoing queer tradition of celebrating same-sex friendship as an equitable, reliable, and politically productive alternative to heterosexual family relations. In queer narratives, expulsion from the family home can be a terrible violence for queer people, but such trauma can be counterbalanced by embracing the *chosen family*, which Kath Weston (1997, xv) has shown to catalyze "the kinship potential of other sorts of ties," including "the connecting tissue of friendship."[1] In many contexts *chosen family* is a much-needed liberatory framework that uses "unforeseen" alliances to reimagine social force through friendship. Yet this model of community has also come to have its own normalizing tendencies. In particular, *narratives* of chosen family are often replete with notions of choice and futurity that link fulfillment with relation to others.

Though not always, depictions of queer life that make it into the mainstream (including those produced by queers) often present chosen families as notably intergenerational, multiracial, and gender diverse. Consider, for example, the costume-party scene in the mainstream gay classic *Philadelphia* (1993). The gay, white protagonist and his lover are joined by their straight Black lawyer in a scene that showcases a loving, diverse group of friends who seemingly come from all walks of life and are costumed to emphasize their diversity. Popular conceptions of chosen family in this tradition usually depict queer friendship as offering social and political linkages between unlike individuals through the shared experience of rejection. This scene, and so many others like it, seems to fulfill the promise of a richer form of community and connection available to those who stand outside of the normative family and its emphasis on sameness. A range of queer texts from ensemble TV dramas to contemporary experimental poetry elaborately and lovingly affirm the truism that "friendship means more to gays than it does to straights," plainly stated in *The Joy of Gay Sex* (Silverstein and Picano 2006, 100). And to a certain extent, this truism exists because it is correct: friendship *does* sustain material and emotional life for many queer people.

We do not dismiss the reality of chosen family out of hand. We are not positioning ourselves against queer friendship itself but rather against the normalizing *narrative* of queer friendship as a site of self-actualization through nonfamilial interpersonal ties. Positivistic views of queer friendship—as eliding conflict and replacing the oppressive nuclear family structure with a family only differentiated by "choice"—overlook the more radical potentiality of such relations. The normalizing narrative of chosen family relies on a neoliberal conception of choice, replicates the temporality of the nuclear family, and often emphasizes the diversity of chosen family as part of a perhaps overly optimistic faith in queer friendship's capacity to challenge the defining features of the straight family. As well, we note that mainstream representations of the racial diversity of chosen families often focus on white protagonists, thus instrumentalizing difference in service of whiteness.[2] As a result, when narratives of chosen family center on a white queer protagonist, they often reveal queerness's inability to challenge racial hierarchies.[3] Consequently, we are interested in queer rejections of chosen families in favor of other modes of sociality. This essay sets aside a dominant view of friendship as ameliorative and restorative in order to consider a queerer view of amity. To accept the idealized vision of chosen family as reality is also to ignore the often disappointing and frustrating nature of actual queer community. Such a view overlooks the antinormative potential of difficult, tenuous, casual, and even anonymous friendship. As such, this essay explores representations of other potential forms of alliance.

In this chapter we explore two case studies where the isolated queer resists the fantasy of self-actualization through relation, whether sexual or platonic. In Ocean Vuong's (2016) poem "Someday I'll Love Ocean Vuong," a same-sex bond shatters its own promise of self-acceptance and self-actualization, and in Valerie Solanas's ([1967] 2013) *SCUM Manifesto*, the polemics of alliance across difference ultimately mandate rejection of others. These texts resist heterosexual understandings of futurity by valorizing brief, contingent, and casual social relations. We thereby build upon claims by thinkers such as Lauren Berlant (Berlant and Edelman 2014), Leo Bersani (1987, 2000, 2002), and Lee Edelman (Edelman 2004; Berlant and Edelman 2014), who suggest that sex is the site where the queer (often cisgender, white, and male) subject is undone. We argue that the politics that have become linked with casual or anonymous sex can, and should, be extended to friendship. However, rather than simply extend the "anti-social" turn to a new realm, we more polemically reconceive friendship as achieving a productive isolation that affords queer possibilities for self-realization.

The anti-assimilationist potential of queer autonomy enables expressions of casual friendship that point to a politics of alliance and kinship which relies on disconnection, disaffection, and temporary association. This politics might, in its own way, be the thread that binds queers. It offers the potential for realizing relations that sit comfortably with the simultaneous "alienation and fulfillment" that Jodi Dean (2019, 101–2) has identified at the heart of political "comradeship," an alliance that views failure or separation as "nothing to fear." Queer people should valorize the fleeting, asynchronous, contextual forms of contact that are often reserved for queer sex and expand them into additional spheres of sociality. Although our title might evocatively suggest that we are against all friendship always, we are not advancing a politics of individuality, nor do we see singularity as the only alternative to friendship. Instead, we offer a polemical alternative to the prescriptive, optimistic narratives of chosen family, reconceptualizing what we seek from friendship as well as where we might find it.

A Brief History of Queer Friendship

Friendship—as an affective relation, as a form of alliance, as a way of life— has a central place in a genealogy of thinking that celebrates same-sex relations over heterosexual bonds. At an early point in the Western canon, Aristotle's ([c. 350 BCE] 1998) *Nicomachean Ethics* praises male friendship, based in profound forms of likeness, as the highest of all relations. The ancient thinker considered a true friend to be an alter idem: "another self" or one just like oneself. For Aristotle this likeness leads to bonds that are closer knit than those between married couples. In a famous example of Aristotle's influence, Michel de Montaigne's ([1580] 1897, 10) sixteenth-century essay "On Friendship" describes perfect amity as available only to two men, who are capable of having their "minds . . . intermix and confound themselves one in the other, with so universal a commixture, that they wear out, and can no more find the seam that has conjoined them together."[4] For Montaigne as for the ancients, same-sex relations were central to both self-care and self-improvement.[5]

The same-sex friendships valorized in this long-running strand of thought not only benefit the individuals involved but also link productively to futurity. Plato's *Symposium* invokes the heroic friends Achilles and Patroclus as a case study in order to explain the link between love and immortality. Plato argues that same-sex pairs are superior to opposite-sex pairs given that they realize "far surer friendship, since the children [prudence and virtue] of their union are fairer and more deathless" (Plato [c. 385–370 BCE] 2009, 209d). And whereas Lee Edelman (2004, 113) argues that queer desire is often characterized as a "child-aversive, future-negating force," Plato lionizes queer relations as productive in ways outside of normative sexual reproduction: they generate new knowledge or engage in acts that express new levels of virtue. Instantiating this long line of thinking, Valerie Rohy (2012, 106) suggests that the "cultural system of relationships, institutions, values, and rituals" in the queer community renders visible a "fecundity" with equivalencies to "the event of conception." Such formulations emphasize that queer relationships, including friendships, might rethink those rubrics typically used to posit the superiority of heterosexual relations. We advocate going even one step further in order to delineate forms of queer friendship divorced from the terms by which heterosexual relations are valued. In many ways we extrapolate from Michael Warner's (1999, 116) claim that "where there are patterns [in kinds of relationships in the queer community], we learn them from other queers, not from our parents or schools or the state"; we specifically extend his suggestion that "queers have an astonishing range of intimacies."

Although friendship (specifically, male friendship) has long been celebrated as a private alliance between two people, it has also been seen as having direct relations to the political aims of the state. For example, Achilles and Patroclus are key to the success of the Greek campaign against the Trojans, even if they fantasize at one point that they might decimate Troy on their own. Yet the intimate nature of friendship can position it as antithetical to the larger aims of the nation. Consider E. M. Forster's (1951, 68–69) famous quip: "If I had to choose between betraying my country and betraying my friend I hope I should have the guts to betray my country." Despite its potential to exclude the larger interests of the state or even just the large social group not part of the close-knit dyad, friendship offers a binding relationship with political potential. Reflecting on Aristotle's model of amity, Giorgio Agamben (2009, 36) writes that "friends do not share some*thing* (birth, law, place, taste): they are shared by the experience of friendship. Friendship is the con-division that precedes every division, since what has to be shared is the very fact of existence, life itself. And it is this sharing without an object, this original con-senting, that constitutes the political." Agamben showcases the role of consent that grounds idealized models of friendship and underscores that this freedom to choose, modeled through friendship, defines the political. Like Jacques Derrida, Agamben is wary of the phallocentrism that links male same-sex friendship to the larger systems of patriarchy.[6] However, he still sees friendship's political potential as relying on its long-celebrated qualities of mutuality and durability (26–27).

Friendship has also had a central place in discourse about modern queer social relations and political alliances. Social movements often use the language of chosen family and/or grow out of friend groups. Interviewing lesbians involved in ACT UP, for instance, Ann Cvetkovich (2003, 173–74) observes how "friendship compensates for the unpleasant aspects of activism," such as sharing a jail cell or mourning the death of a fellow activist. Yet as Cvetkovich shows, friendships are also a "volatile source" of power because of their tendency toward exclusivity (174). Of course, structural divisions of race, class, and sexuality underpin all claims to sameness, as was frequently noted by women of color during feminism's second wave. For example, the Combahee River Collective's (1982) statement indicts white feminist claims to shared experience on the basis of gender. Likewise, Audre Lorde's now-famous 1979 speech about racism within the feminist "sisterhood" was later published in a collection evocatively titled *Sister Outsider* (1984). Lorde's speech appeared alongside an open letter to Mary Daly in which Lorde wrote, "for then beyond sisterhood is still racism" (70). The mobilization of "sisterhood" in feminism's second wave was most often an attempt by white feminists to minimize the existence and importance of racial difference.

During the HIV/AIDS epidemic, the political promise of friendship as chosen family became urgent for queers yet was still complicated by underlying social differences. Queers understood and spoke about friendship and chosen family as a necessity for actual survival in a moment of crisis and, in the process, attempted to embrace forms of social difference. For instance, Tom Roach (2012, 41) argues that the unique promises of friendship help us understand the deep bonds between people living with HIV and their volunteer caregivers; their "relation of shared estrangement" fosters social and political linkages between unlike individuals. Individuals need others for a limited period of time, and their bond need not depend on likeness. Although they may not come to know one another on an intimate level, these individuals nonetheless develop a powerful closeness that is mutually beneficial.

Such queer understandings of friendship open up political alternatives to the brotherhood lionized by ancient and early modern treatises on friendship as well as to the often false or limited sisterhood advocated by forms of feminism that use only gender as the basis of alliance. Yet many queer valuations of friendship still reinforce qualities of sameness that erase differences in race, gender, and class; they do so in the form of a shared goal and in the ostensibly shared quality of being "different."[7] Friendship continues to be understood as an alliance that can satisfy queer needs for family, love, and survival. We can hear this range of expectations in *Lesbian Friendship: For Ourselves and for Each Other*, a 1996 anthology on the role of friendship in lesbians' lives. The editors write that "when we asked for submissions for that anthology about lesbian friendships, we wanted to make friendships more visible. Women wrote about extraordinary friendships, about the politics of friendship, and about lesbian community. Several examined the fluidity of movement from friends to lovers and back to friends, or else the places in between the boundaries between friends and lovers. Many authors described friendship across difference, between African American and White lesbians, between lesbians and heterosexual women, between lesbians and heterosexual men. Often, lesbians described their friends as 'family'" (Weinstock and Rothblum 2018, 2).

What emerges from these few examples is not just a rosy distinction between friendship and other forms of sociality. Instead, we hear the promise of queer friendship as something other than the friendship available to straight people. It is supposed to unlock a barrier to achieving diversity in relations, sexual congress, and community.

A Brief Critique of Queer Friendship

Queers have long relied on kinship as a meaningful site of self-actualization outside of the toxic, hierarchical nuclear family. *Chosen family* ostensibly provides the positive support and care denied the queer child in their family of origin and allows for stronger, better bonds between individuals. An immense amount of queer energy has gone into the maintenance of the platitude "Friends are the family you choose." John Preston (1995, 8) captures this sentiment nicely: "Perhaps because we have so often been separated from the automatic kinship of our blood families, gay men seem to approach friendships with a certain self-conscious determination." The notion of developing significant nonfamilial bonds has been the silver lining for many queer people rejected from family or mainstream culture. Not only is a chosen family preferable to a family of origin, but the ability to choose and maintain authentic, meaningful bonds is often described as precisely what makes queer people different from straight people.

The notion of *chosen family* has offered a life-affirming alternative to familial rejection. Yet we ought to be suspicious of the fact that the juxtaposition between the constrained, limiting family of origin and the expansive queer kinship network relies simply on *choice*, that most neoliberal of concepts. How is it that simply *choosing* to participate in a familial dynamic can render its most hierarchical structures benign? Why are the patterns and dynamics of blood relations (e.g., leather daddies, house mothers in drag cultures) acceptable, or even desirable, when they have been "freely chosen"? Capturing the notion that friendship represents a volitional and seemingly individuated form of kinship, Karen Lindsey (1994, 469) remarks that "while there are social formulae for commitments to both family and lovers, there aren't any for commitments to friends."

Chosen family also reinforces the pernicious notion of the queer as consumer, choosing family members like products. Queers are unbound from heterosexual norms because we can try on different people as parents or even have a surplus of queer familial relations. Why do we accept this normative model of choice? Why have we resoundingly critiqued the "family" portion of *chosen family* but left the equally complex notion of choice mostly intact in this formulation? Freedom of choice is a cornerstone of the very Western democratic individualism that queer kinship supposedly subverts. For example, just because one willingly chooses one's daddy does not mean that the hierarchical, conflict-laden, inequitable distribution of power and resources inherent in the father-child role will fall away. Or if we embrace such familial inequalities by eroticizing them, we simply affirm the value of choice in and of itself (interestingly coupled with consent in BDSM communities, in that consent represents the freely chosen).

Might our investment in social construction overly affirm the importance of our supposedly free, rational choices? As Kath Weston argues in the present volume, the "voluntarism" inherent in queer understandings of chosen family and queer kinship structures has even been complicit with the rise of gay and lesbian marriage and parenthood as socially sanctioned forms of queer family making at the expense of other, more radical links that might valorize nonmonogamy or nondyadic romantic relationships. Indeed, the present understanding of chosen family ironically affirms the importance of the family of origin by measuring friend connections in terms of their resemblance to the relations accepted by law and state. As Kadji Amin (2017, 109) points out, practices such as BDSM daddy play can be lent "a certain gravitas" or even rehabilitated by "combining the queer historical emotions of exile and longing with the empowering new ideal of freely elected and creatively constructed families." We echo Amin's question: "Why is it that identifying a relational form as 'queer kinship' implicitly dignifies it, redeems it, and invests it with pathos?" Of course, one answer to this question is that we consistently conceptualize queer friendship according to the lines, dynamics, and structures of the nuclear family. As Weston ([1991] 1997) points out, dilating on the model of the nuclear family can overlook the value of more subversive interpersonal relations, such as artistic collaborations or companion relations with nonhumans. In turn, these relations have the potential to undermine the primacy of the family of origin.

Anonymous Friendship

Queers have known for a while now that the self-shattering inherent in the sexual encounter might yield new forms of community. In queer thought and practice, anonymous sex is celebrated as offering new forms of intimacy and higher forms of pleasure than parity-based relations, such as those imagined in the loving-couple form. The seminal (so to speak) image of the self-shattering encounter has been male sexual cruising, iconically depicted by figures such as Jean Genet or David Wojnarowicz in the shadows of parked cars or abandoned warehouses along the docks. Leo Bersani's (1987) oft-quoted notion that the rectum is a grave is positive in nature: anonymous anal sex between men allows participants to give up the confines and limits of the normative masculine self and achieve higher forms of subjectivity. The promise of "nameless, identity-free contact" inherent in "sexual sociability" seems antithetical to the tenets of friendship valorized in the chosen family model of queer kinship and to broader understandings of friendship itself (Bersani 2002, 11). By definition, friendship relies on recognition, intimacy, and endurance. But might there be queer possibilities in friendships that fail or do not even try to endure? What happens when we conceptualize friendship as a relation marked by unachievability or what José Esteban Muñoz (2009, 1) calls the "not quite here yet"? Rather than awaiting the future arrival of sustainable friendship, we value friendship's failure to deliver connections and communities.

Within queer studies it is axiomatic that sex does not lead to a successful, fulfilling human relation. This promise is a fantasy. Lauren Berlant and Lee Edelman (2014, 2) draw on Jacques Lacan to argue that sex is inseparable from "the encounter with what exceeds and undoes the subject's fantasmatic sovereignty." We often imagine that friendship might bolster that so-called sovereignty because it affirms the subject's existence in relation to others. Yet it is a mistake to imagine that friendship can deliver what sex cannot. Friendship's promise of a successful, fulfilling human relationship might be just as imagined as sex's claim to be a path to wholeness.

Positivistic views of queer friendship have hidden the radical potential of reconceptualizing friendship along the lines of what we term *anonymous friendship*. Indeed, friendship has a queerer and more antinormative potential: it can challenge idealized, prescriptive notions of family and subjectivity rather than replicate them with the thin veneer of choice on top. Valorizing anonymous friendship revises the existing vision of queer friendship by embracing brief, non-future-oriented forms of nonsexual contact, the kinds that the socially anxious among us increasingly avoid. Recognizing these fleeting forms of social contact helps us understand ourselves, not just our sexuality, "as an improvisational possibility within a field of constraints" (Butler 2004, 15). Is it friendship when two strangers nod at each other on the street? When we wave at someone and then realize we've mistaken them for someone else? When someone replies to a wrong-number text? When a smile (or an eye roll) moves through a crowd watching the same scene? Interactions without any expectation of futurity whatsoever can teach us that friendship might be desirable precisely because it is not achievable. We should avoid evaluating friendship on the basis of its capacity to deliver authentic, mutual relations to others for as long as possible. Instead, we suggest revaluing the figure of the isolated queer to reframe the difficult, destructive, and painful queer friendships most of us have experienced; perhaps these are not failures but rather opportunities to expand the definition of what constitutes a successful encounter with amity.

This revised queer vision disaggregates friendships from valuations of whether they are necessarily egalitarian, harmonious, and enduring. Such accounts, we suggest, are a neoliberal fantasy of friendship subtended by qualities often imaginatively associated with marriage. Rather than taking the family as the origin point—the point to resist—yet still transferring its logics into the social group, anonymous friendship repositions the past as a point in the future. We find compelling examples of this queer temporality in poetry, inspired by Kara Keeling's (2019, xii) description of poetry as "a way of entering the unknown and carrying back the impossible; it is productive of ideas or knowledges that were incomprehensible and unacceptable before their distillation as such via poetry." For example, Ocean Vuong (2016) conceptualizes the past as part of the future in his poem "Someday I'll Love Ocean Vuong":

> Here's the house with childhood
> whittled down to a single red tripwire.
> Don't worry. Just call it *horizon*
> & you'll never reach it.
> (lines 12–15)

The lines break from normative genealogies of the future and the past. Subtitled "After Frank O'Hara / After Roger Reeves," the poem rethinks heteronormative lines of relation that are based on blood. Vuong recalls O'Hara's use of "some day I'll love Frank O'Hara" in the poem "Katy" and Reeves's poem title "Someday I'll Love Roger Reeves." These shared formulations across texts and eras highlight not only the poets' shared interest in productive forms of self-love but also how poets have long used the terms of familial or romantic relations to figure their ties to previous generations of writers.[8]

Vuong's (2016) poem is nonteleological, resisting the chrononormativity associated with the logics of the heteronormative family.[9] The notion that opens the poem, "The end of the road is so far ahead / it is already behind us" (lines 2–3), both echoes and complicates Muñoz's (2009, 1, 113) notion of queerness as "not yet here" and "always in the horizon." Vuong (2016) imagines another possibility that simultaneously defers the need for linear progression in the encounter while settling on a queer now.[10] Indeed, the use of the deictic *here* and the present tense in the interpersonal encounter at the center of the poem underscore the focus on the *nowness* of the scene:

> Here's the man
> whose arms are wide enough to gather

your leaving. & here the moment,
just after the lights go out, when you can still see
the faint torch between his legs.
(lines 17–21)

We recognize that the scene is charged with the valences of the erotic, including a dark room and a "torch between his legs" as an unsubtle metaphor for a penis. At the same time, the man's embrace is a site of separation, as the arms "gather / your leaving." The man's embrace constitutes a departure; the encounter with the anonymous partner's body engenders a nonexhaustive coalescing of the self that can happen repeatedly through encounters with the same or different partners. In fact, the torch/penis becomes irrelevant as it is used to generate direction, self-knowledge, and an even more cohesive self as "you use it again & again / to find your own hands" (lines 22–23). This anonymous encounter, rather than being self-shattering, allows the subject to find wholeness in their individuality.

The poem frames a relation to the self that is, paradoxically, fractured and bound together; the present self and the future self are separate entities with a loving relationship to each other: "Ocean. Ocean— / get up" (lines 28–29). In the doubled direct address, a single person imagines themselves in a loving relation with another version of themselves. The lines are a form of apostrophe but more specifically prosopopoeia, a rhetorical device where the absent addressee is capable of hearing. The term derives from the ancient Greek roots *prósopon* ("face" or "person") and *poiéin* ("to make").[11] Prosopopoeia's origins point to the way that relations link to self-fashioning. Yet Vuong's poem adds new dimension to the idea that *askesis* derives from relations to others. Here the friend is not a different person who constitutes the Aristotelian "another self" but rather a forthcoming version of the subject's self.

The future granted by anonymous friendship is neither reproductive nor teleological. It is a space of promise only insofar as it has a halo effect on the present moment:

The most beautiful part of your body
is where it's headed. & remember,
loneliness is still time spent
with the world.
(Vuong 2016, lines 29–32)

Vuong frames loneliness and aloneness as productive forms of relation. The couple formation is not needed to justify the poet's place in the world.

Rather, sociality includes even a solitary relation with one's future or past self. Summer Kim Lee reminds us that Vuong's body, that of a "queer Vietnamese American refugee," is a "space of refuge" (2019, 28, 44). It contains multitudes but does not necessarily need another person to realize that sense of inner community. In addition, those who are not physically present still constitute a community insofar as they act upon the poet:

> Here's
> the room with everyone in it.
> Your dead friends passing
> through you like wind
> through a wind chime.
> (lines 32–36)

These lines would seem to answer the questions that David L. Eng and David Kazanjian (2002, 2) associate with mourning: "As soon as the question 'What is lost?' is posed, it invariably slips into the question 'What remains?'" Eng and Kazanjian accept Freud's conception of melancholia as an experience discrete from mourning but reject his negative characterizations of it because "in melancholia the past remains steadfastly alive in the present" (3–4). Here, loss has a positive effect: the dead friends initiate the wind chime's song. For Vuong, as for Eng and Kazanjian, melancholia represents a way to form community, even with a self who may not desire the presence of others. The egocentric focus in the poem can resurrect friends from the past to form a social *now* in which the poet sings alone.

Anonymous friendship does not rely on the temporality that structures chrononormative friendship on the basis of longevity or the availability of return. As Vuong shows, friendship can be ephemeral yet still impactful. Absence, departure, and aloneness also constitute relationality. In this sense Vuong helps us disaggregate friendship from love, which has implications as profound as disaggregating sex from love. Sara Ahmed (2004, 123) warns against linking politics and love: the exclusion many queers have felt from "the community" underscores how political alliance based on love "reproduces the collective as ideal through producing a particular kind of subject whose allegiance to the ideal makes it an ideal in the first place."[12] Vuong disaggregates the friendship experienced in the *now* of the poem from the love which has been postponed to the temporal space of *someday*. Such a formulation might point to a politics of alliance that excludes love but rather is built on contingent and even coincidental social relations.

In Vuong's poem the anonymous encounter with a stranger—and the encounter with one's future self that it enables—is counterposed to relations of violence. Future-Ocean tells present-day-Ocean, "Don't be afraid, the gunfire / is only the sound of people / trying to live a little longer" (Vuong 2016, lines 26–28). The version of the poem first published in a 2015 issue of *The New Yorker* leaves this fragment here without further commentary. However, the version published in Vuong's 2016 collection adds the phrase "and failing." This afterthought—that people are "trying to live a little longer and failing"—emphasizes the potential friction of interpersonal relations and affirms even more strongly a solitary queer life in the present. We are not necessarily suggesting this vision of aloneness as a more politically valuable replacement for chosen family. However, anonymous friendship calls into question the notion that the "ecstasy towards a future that will go beyond death," which Derrida ([1997] 2006) associates with politicized friendship, necessarily needs another person or must be so dramatically future oriented.[13] We are pointing out that queer-identified subjects might be sustained by brief, finite, and fleeting forms of contact in which our selves are revealed as constantly remade in relation to others.[14]

We see the concept of anonymous friendship as a response to Eileen Joy's suggestion that one of the "tragedies" of gay life is that "we have never really taken up, collectively, Foucault's (1996) call to work on ourselves in order to invent improbable manners of being, new modes and styles of living, polymorphous affective intensities, and new relational virtualities and friendships." The "manners of being" to which Foucault gestures in "Friendship as a Way of Life" need not take the form of previously seen modes of sociality. In fact, *virtuality* is a term that befits the encounter depicted in Vuong's poem as it values fantasy. Casual or anonymous friendships embrace forms of sociality previously considered unimportant or nonexistent and bring them into being as "new modes and styles of living" (Joy 2015, 222).

Friendship without Futurity

How can we valorize fleeting forms of relation when friendship and longevity are so deeply intertwined? What might it look like to separate futurity and intimacy in the realm of friendship? An array of classic gay texts provides innumerable possibilities for disaggregating long-lasting bonds and intimacy via sex, from John Rechy's (1963) *City of Night* to Samuel R. Delany's (1999) *Times Square Red, Times Square Blue*.[15] Yet there has not been enough literary critical attention paid to models of this disaggregation in texts by and about those who are not cisgender gay men. Likewise, there is a dearth of models of casual or anonymous friendship in literary history, queer or otherwise. In paradigmatic queer texts where the protagonist remains isolated from both chosen family and family of origin, such as James Baldwin's ([1956] 2013) *Giovanni's Room*, loneliness is often a torment. In the final paragraph of Baldwin's novel, the protagonist, David, experiences the "dreadful weight of hope" as he tears up an envelope representing the tragedy of his past actions and the impossibility of a viable gay life. He looks back as the pieces of the envelope "dance in the wind, watching the wind carry them away." But his hope for the future is immediately dashed: "yet, as I turn and begin walking toward the waiting people, the wind blows some of them back on me" (169). Devastated, David has no future other than to repeat the excruciating past. Here it is impossible to be both gay and in authentic relation to friends and lovers; the wind will always blow pieces of the past back onto him.

Later queer texts are more optimistic about dislodging marriage and family from their sacrosanct position, but that optimism usually replaces the family of origin with chosen family. For instance, in Leslie Feinberg's ([1993] 2004) *Stone Butch Blues*, the protagonist moves away from the unsympathetic family of origin toward celebrated family-like relations with fellow queer and gender-non-conforming people. Even when chosen family relations are divisive and marked by jealousy or suspicion, the novel endorses queer friendship as a site of self-actualization. In the closing paragraphs of *Stone Butch Blues*, the protagonist, Jess, thinks back to the words of a longtime friend and union brother: "*imagine a world worth living in, a world worth fighting for.*" Reflecting on that invocation, Jess enters a reverie: "I closed my eyes and allowed my hopes to soar. I heard the beating of wings nearby. I opened my eyes. A young man on a nearby rooftop released his pigeons, like dreams, into the dawn" (301). Unlike the scraps of paper blowing backward in *Giovanni's Room*, marking the perpetual return of loneliness and death, the pigeons soar away toward a future of queer solidarity; the scene takes place shortly after Jess participates in a gay demonstration for the first time and is hailed as both "brother" and "sister" by fellow demonstrators. When chosen family offers a future, queer life is worth living.

The notion that chosen family repairs the harms of the family of origin goes deep into the heart of queer literature and life. Audre Lorde's (1982, 93) canonical lesbian text *Zami: A New Spelling of My Name* also offers a vision of friendship and chosen family as a respite from the "family wars" of the difficult, stifling family of origin. In Lorde's biomythography, a long list of platonic friends, roommates, and lovers come into and out of protagonist Audre's life, representing a welcome space away from the ever-present judgment of her mother. At several points in the text, lesbian bars literalize that space, always serving "as an important place for those of us who met and made some brief space for ourselves there. [The bar] had a feeling of family." Audre conflates warmth and the presence of lesbians, noting that being in "convivial surroundings—meaning around other lesbians—was a big treat for most of us" (222). *Zami: A New Spelling of My Name* participates in the long, robust tradition of valorizing not just queer community but also the spaces and places where queers gather. Likewise, Lorde's biomythography ends by embracing the transformative potential of a non-future-oriented sexual relationship. It offers an example of a casual relationship to lesbian sex that is often overlooked when gay-male narratives are taken as paradigmatic of self-shattering cruising. Lorde writes of a sexual encounter: "We had come together like elements erupting into an electric storm, exchanging energy, sharing charge, brief and drenching. Then we parted, passed, reformed, reshaping ourselves the better for the exchange. I never saw Afrekete again, but her print remains upon my life with the resonance and power of an emotional tattoo" (253). Both Feinberg and Lorde supplant the family of origin with long-lasting chosen family and short-term, casual sex. Such narratives are so central to our understanding of queer life that even the anti-social turn in queer theory did not fully articulate the ways in which the concept of the chosen family is structured by the same temporality as the family of origin.

For this reason, we look toward disruptive figures such as Valerie Solanas, who is rarely included in the archive of queer theory, for suggestions on how we might escape normative and normalizing temporalities of friendship. Solanas's body of work includes the nonfiction SCUM Manifesto ([1967] 2013) and the unpublished script for the play *Up Your Ass or, From the Cradle to the Boat or, The Big Suck or, Up from the Slime* (1965).[16] Both works offer a surprisingly prescient commentary on the anti-social turn. In the SCUM *Manifesto*, first self-published in 1967, Solanas argues against not just the patriarchal family or marriage but against sociality in general. Many critics have described her manifesto as genocidal because it advocates for the elimination of men, but Solanas's close readers have also noted her musings on the end of humanity itself. At first, her manifesto outlines why "civic-minded, responsible, thrill-seeking females" should "overthrow the government, eliminate the money system, institute complete automation and destroy the male sex" (Solanas [1967] 2013, 24). Near the end of the tract, however, Solanas goes further and asks: "Why produce even females? Why should there be future generations? What is their purpose? When aging and death are eliminated, why continue to reproduce? Why should we care what happens when we're dead? Why should we care that there is no younger generation to succeed us?" (62). Solanas's resistance to an unquestioned faith in the value of future generations is remarkable. At its core the manifesto argues that patriarchy infects not just institutions, such as government and economy, but also goes so deep into humanity itself that we might as well cease reproducing.

The SCUM Manifesto articulates a nuanced response to Tim Dean's (2006, 828) polemic that "queer theory and politics need a vigorously argued antisocial thesis, in order to grasp how beyond the normative coordinates of selfhood lies an orgy of connection that no regime can regulate." Solanas does not describe those unregulated connections. Rather, she asks how far beyond normative selfhood we can go. Ultimately, she contends that radical aloneness and the end of human reproduction lie beyond our understanding of selfhood, which is deeply contingent on others. As such, we might as well enjoy the present: "SCUM is impatient," she says. "SCUM is not consoled by the thought that future generations will thrive; SCUM wants to grab some thrilling living for itself" (Solanas [1967] 2013, 62). This "thrilling living" looks like what Muñoz (2009, 49) describes as "a future in the present," a "notion of utopia in the service of subaltern politics." However, Solanas's utopia is oriented toward death. SCUM operates through "systematically fucking up the system, selectively destroying property, and murder," and it recruits by engaging in "fucking-up, looting, couple-busting, destroying, and killing" (Solanas [1967] 2013, 65, 69). For Solanas, the best future for men is one in which they do not "kick or struggle or raise a distressing fuss, but will just sit back, relax, enjoy the show and ride the waves to their demise" (75). Solanas's impatient, present-oriented "thrilling living" is in the *now* of her manifesto. She posits a utopian society where men, money, and work have vanished, but she is unconcerned about future generations of women who might inhabit it.

By escaping the temporality of reproduction, Solanas develops a theory of relationality that does not depend on mutuality *or* futurity but rather can be anonymous and firmly located in the "future in the present" (Muñoz 2009, 49). According to Solanas ([1967] 2013), "A true community consists of individuals—not mere species members, not couples—respecting each others [sic] individuality and privacy, at the same time interacting with each other mentally and emotionally—free spirits in free relation to each other." The legal and social commitments of the family are a barrier to individual autonomy, but, crucially, so are the commitments of chosen family: "Traditionalists say the basic unit of 'society' is the family; 'hippies' say the tribe; no one says the individual" (39). Solanas wants total autonomy; whatever sociality she might desire can emerge only when all individual women are freed from obligation to one another, familial or chosen. Solanas redefines love "as not dependency or sex, but friendship," and says that love "requires complete economic as well as personal freedom, leisure time, and the opportunity to engage in intensely absorbing, emotionally satisfying activities, which, when shared with those you respect, lead to deep friendship" (48, 49). This is not the autonomy of the neoliberal individual; it absolutely requires the destruction of both capitalism and patriarchy.

Because the utopian, autonomous, and post-work society Solanas imagines is always in the future, the manifesto endlessly defers real friendship. As such, we might see Solanas as an example of aloneness as a way of life. Her life story bears out this perspective: as Breanne Fahs (2014) documents, Solanas spent most of her life alone, an outsider wherever she went. Near the end of her life, Solanas was so far removed from her family of origin that they only knew she was still alive when her cousin spotted a letter she had written to *High Times* magazine in response to a reader's query about whether she had died (Fahs 2014, 324). She was so alone and friendless that when she did die, no one knew she had passed away until her body was found, "covered with maggots," in the decrepit hotel room in which she had been living (328, quoting the police report). We could read Solanas's life story as a deliberate decision to turn away from all family forms and also as a recognition of the impossibility of self-actualizing individual friendship under patriarchy and capitalism. Under such conditions, aloneness is the only recourse. Sex provides no respite. It is "the refuge of the mindless" (Solanas [1967] 2013, 53). Indeed, Solanas idealizes "those females least embedded in the male 'Culture,' . . . these females are cool and relatively cerebral and skirting asexuality" (53–54). In many ways, SCUM women ironically embody Bersani's (2002, 11) vision of cruising as affording sociality outside the couple form because "the pleasure of sociability is the pleasure of existing, of concretely existing, at the abstract level of pure being." Yet Solanas focuses on what comes *after* cruising: SCUM women have seen "the fucking scene, the dyke scene—they've covered the whole waterfront, been under every dock and pier—the peter pier, the pussy pier . . . you've got to go through a lot of sex to get to anti-sex" (Solanas [1967] 2013, 54). Anticipating queer theory, Solanas recognizes that sex cannot provide wholeness.

Because nothing can provide human connection—not sex, not the family of origin, not chosen family—Solanas offers a model of radical aloneness that dovetails with Foucault's (1996, 309) vision of "the formation of new alliances and the tying together of unforeseen lines of force," just, notably, in the singular.

Solanas's play *Up Your Ass* takes up the project of dramatizing new alliances unencumbered by futurity. The play's protagonist, Bongi Perez, prowls the streets of a US city looking for women to proposition and men to buy her dinner in exchange for sex. Bongi moves among characters who slip in and out of the play almost at random. Bongi has sex, debates, and altercations with strangers, always getting the better of everyone with her quick wit. Near the end of the play, Bongi meets a new character whom she quickly converts to her autonomous lifestyle. After a brief conversation with Bongi, the woman unceremoniously murders and quickly buries her five- or six-year-old son. As the play ends, Bongi and the woman walk away from the dead boy together, both catcalling a woman on the street, seeking a connection they know will either be thwarted or, if it actually occurs, brief.

The play deifies Bongi and shows the superiority of her casual way of life. Bongi's fleeting, random connections are what define her as happily out of step with a poisonous society. She maintains only the shortest casual friendships with those she does not even know by name. Her singular resistance to family and futurity is politically productive precisely because it represents an alternative already being lived in the present. Solanas's commitment to aloneness in her writing and her life offers a glimpse of the truly antinormative potential of queer forms of alliance. At times, Solanas may seem to embody the figure of the lonely queer. Yet she reclaims the individual as potentially politically efficacious on her own; her singular existence suggests that another way to organize the family, time, and the social is not only possible but already exists. Solanas enacts a model of association that values a life lived apart and connections felt temporarily and sporadically.

Against Queer Friendship

In "Sociality and Sexuality," Bersani (2000) takes up Foucault's hypothesis about the potentiality of "unforeseen" relationships. As Bersani remarks, "Nothing, it would seem, is more difficult than to conceive, to elaborate, and to put into practice 'new relational modes'" (641). Our critique of chosen family and our vision of alternative modes for queer friendship have shown just how difficult this project can be. Yet through our case studies we have pursued two alternatives, anonymous friendship and queer autonomy, that build on the anti-social thesis and take it in new directions. Vuong and Solanas point toward a political and self-sustaining conception of alliance divorced from the fantasies of sameness, mutuality, and optimistic futurity. As such, they suggest new models for narratives about ourselves that might participate in decentering the white, cisgender gay male subject in queer theory; might further denaturalize the tenets that undergird normative family relations; and/or might attenuate queer reliance on "choice" as a main mechanism for subverting the nuclear family.

It may be tempting to read the work of Vuong and Solanas as records of miserable loneliness. The figures of the *spinster*, the *confirmed bachelor*, and the *lonely queer* haunt our readings of their work. These pejoratives have long been used to exclude queer people from normative sociality and, in turn, the cultural imaginary in which alliances take place. Of course, alliances have long been formed between and among these figures, especially as these figurations were often simply perceptions of queer people from the outside. Yet what if we take to heart Avery Gordon's (2006, xvi) claim that "haunting, unlike trauma, is distinctive for producing a something-to-be-done"? What if the fear of existing alone or ending up alone has precluded a full consideration of the queer uses of aloneness? We must note that Vuong and Solanas seem quite content in the isolation they describe. As such, in the midst of all of our highly valued friendships and allied communities, might we pause for a moment and consider validating the isolated queer, trying on such a role for ourselves, and imagining a politics of casual or anonymous friendship?

Notes

1   Despite the emphasis on choice in the term *chosen family*, Weston (1997, xv) also points out that such families are not necessarily "*freely* chosen families [because] color, access to money, and social connections leave some people more constrained than others."

2   The 2019 Showtime series *Work in Progress* and the 2020 Channel 4 series *Feel Good* are both relevant here: both shows focus on white, butch lesbians and include a racially and economically diverse supporting cast whose lives are explored only in relation to the protagonists.

3 An additional popular media example is the film *Stonewall* (2015), which places its protagonist in the center of a welcoming group of friends and of queer history. The narrative follows Danny, an imagined white, cisgender gay man, as he leaves small-town Indiana and immediately establishes a group of racially diverse friends of many genders in New York City. The film suggests that Danny instigated the first Stonewall riot, with the obvious political consequences of downplaying the roles of Sylvia Rivera, Marsha P. Johnson, Stormé DeLarverie, and many other queer and trans people of color in the events of June 28, 1969.

4 We have modernized the spelling here from the essay's first publication in English during the early modern period.

5 Foucault (1988) has traced how friendship was central to the practice of *askesis*, or the art of self-improvement, in classical antiquity.

6 Derrida ([1997] 2006, 202) warns of the long-reaching aftereffects of Aristotle's positioning of "fraternity" and "political fraternization" as "natural." Instead, he calls for "questioning and analyzing [fraternity] in its range and with its political risks (nationalism, ethnocentrism, androcentrism, phallocentrism, etc.)."

7 The "future orientation" of many queer and activist friendships is often shadowed by an urgent sense of limited time. As Eve Sedgwick (2003, 149) reminds us, threats of racist or homophobic violence, as well as lack of access to healthcare, often foreshorten the lives of those on the margins and thus make friendships within these communities "more intensely motivated."

8 For an incisive study of this practice, see Stephen Guy-Bray (2006), *Loving in Verse: Poetic Influence as Erotic*.

9 Elizabeth Freeman (2010, 3) defines chrononormativity as "the use of time to organize individual human bodies toward maximum efficiency."

10 The poem escapes what Muñoz (2009, 1) describes as the "prisonhouse" of the "here and now" and mines what Carolyn Dinshaw (2012, 4) envisions as "the possibility of a fuller, denser, more crowded *now* that all sorts of theorists tell us is extant but that often eludes our temporal grasp."

11 We wish to thank Dustin Dixon for his assistance with this translation.

12 Ahmed offers an additional caution against love-based alliances: often, hate groups strategically reposition themselves as love groups as they cohere membership around love of the race or the family.

13 Derrida ([1997] 2006, 104) locates the politics of friendship in forms of collectivity and democracy as yet unforeseen.

14 For a resonant approach, see Lauren Berlant (2011b, 687), "A Properly Political Concept of Love: Three Approaches in Ten Pages."

15 The consistent recurrence of this theme in specifically gay-male novels, and literary critical attention to those novels, perhaps bolsters the seeming solidity of the link between self-shattering sexual encounters and cisgender gay men.

16 According to Solanas's biographer Breanne Fahs (2014), very few copies of this unpublished manuscript exist. Desireé Rowe (2013) has written about the inaccessibility of the play in an article titled "The (Dis)appearance of *Up Your Ass*: Valerie Solanas as Abject Revolutionary." The play takes a central role in Andrea Long Chu's (2019) recent controversial polemic *Females* but has otherwise received little scholarly attention. Like Rowe, in 2014 Sara Warner and Mary Jo Watts (2014, 84) described obstacles in accessing the text as a partial reason for the text's obscurity. In this chapter we summarize rather than quote directly from the text because we have not viewed an original copy of the unpublished script.

11 Kidless Lit
Childlessness and Minor Kinship Forms

What does it mean *not* to reproduce? As philosopher Christine Overall points out in *Why Have Children?* (2012, 2), this question is often posed to child*less* people but almost never to the child*full*, a term whose awkwardness belies its refusal to be taken as anything but natural. Overall ultimately offers a justification for *having children* and thus reverses the burden placed on the childless for not doing so. Yet that reversal maintains a popular dichotomy that might be reducible to the following algorithm. Biological reproduction: you're either for it or against it. If you're for it, you get to inhabit that particularly reviled state called normativity (always already hetero, even when homo). If you're against it, popular-media panic ensues. Take the title of Lauren Sandler's (2013) *Time* magazine article: "The Childfree Life: When Having It All Means Not Having Children." Here the "all" signals an especially overreaching attachment to capitalist accumulation, and the childless feature as narcissistic material accumulators. Indeed, the dominant narratives about childlessness revolve around panic and demand: the ranks of the childless are growing at an alarming rate, particularly in North America, which occasions denunciations of the childless, responsible for nothing less than the extinction of the species and the decline of civilization as we know it. The following examples collectively limn the anxiety that underwrites childlessness while also presuming that the childless have no meaningful relationships to children.

Exhibit A: Unbirthdays

Let's start with numbers. News outlets across North America have been sounding the alarm about declining birthrates in Canada and the United States. The *Time* magazine issue cited above reports that between 2007 and 2011 alone, the birthrate in the United States declined by 9 percent. It is well known that North American birthrates have been declining for decades and that immigration is the key driver of population increases. In an analysis of the Statistics Canada data, a *National Post* opinion piece points out that couples who do not have children now outnumber those that do: "44.5% of couples are 'without children' compared to 39.2% with children" (O'Connor 2012). In 2020 Canadian news media continue to trot out these statistics, yearning for a pre-1970s birthrate of 2.1 children per woman.[1] Similarly in the United States, a *New York Times* story (Tugend 2016) suggests that "according to census figures, more women in the United States are childless than at any other time since the government began keeping track in 1976. Nearly half of women—47.6 percent—between the ages of 15 and 44 did not have children in 2014, up from 46.5 percent in 2012. And 15.3 percent of women ages 40 to 44 are childless." Nor did 2020 reports in the *Times* change much either, as headlines warned readers "Don't Expect a Quarantine Baby Boom" and then rehearsed the decades-long decline in American birthrates (Yuhas 2020). It must be pointed out that nonwhite populations show the slowest rates of decline, which is hardly surprising as a form of resistance to violence perpetrated against Black, brown, and Indigenous communities, but even these numbers are relative: birthrates show declines across all population groups. Data from the United Nations show that global birthrates have declined steeply for decades—all despite the fact that the world's overall population continues to increase steadily and that population increase itself has become a threat to planetary sustainability. Indeed, more and more young adults are choosing not to have children out of concern for the Earth's overpopulation.[2]

Exhibit B: "The Age of Reproduction"?

What do we do in the face of such seemingly damning statistics? One answer seems to be to double down on reproduction. Sarah Franklin (2013b) goes so far as to declare ours to be "the age of reproduction," insisting that scholars attend to the "reproductive turn in social thought." This turn is marked by "the reproductive paradox": namely, that reproduction has been both central to and insufficiently theorized within the social sciences and the natural sciences. As Franklin sees it, this "reproductive turn" specifically concerns the making of babies and intensification of technological advances for supporting reproductive logic. The result is a contradictory relationship to reproduction that foregrounds its naturalness while also critiquing and disavowing that very naturalization. Sociologists have also expanded their ways of conceptualizing the scales of reproduction: Shellee Colen's (1986) concept of "stratified reproduction" names how kinship is structured according to hierarchies of race, sex, and class in global economies; Michelle Murphy's (2017b) idea of "distributed reproduction" describes the infrastructures beyond bodies that support and/or diminish life; and Adele E. Clarke's (1998) attention to "disciplining reproduction" reveals how reproduction has become rationalized (rationed and controlled) over time. Despite the relative decline in global birth*rates*, reproduction as a concept would seem to be taking center stage, affirming the otherwise seemingly divergent positions of Marxist feminist social reproduction theorists and critics of queer repro-futurists (such as Lee Edelman [2004]), alike. If this focus on reproduction is not so much new as it is resurgent, this begs the question: what else does *not* reproducing itself produce, alongside the reproduction of reproduction itself?

Exhibit C: Doomed to Be Dumb

One thing produced by childlessness is, apparently, a decline in our collective intelligence. In "Intelligence and Childlessness," Satoshi Kanazawa (2014) argues that more intelligent people are choosing to remain childless early in their "reproductive careers" but that single women are more likely to remain childless by the end of this "career" span. As Kanazawa claims, "Because women have a greater impact on the average intelligence of future generations, the dysgenic fertility among women is predicted to lead to a decline in the average intelligence of the population in advanced industrial nations" (157). If professional and presumably intelligent and well-educated women elect not to have children, they are not, in turn, passing on their intelligence to the next generation. In effect, we are all getting dumber, generationally speaking. These educated women, with their refusals to be baby makers, can in turn be blamed for the decline in general intelligence and education. And it is the feminists, by implication, with their successful lobbying for birth control and abortion rights, who have imperiled our collective intelligence.

Anxiety is perhaps always a shape-shifting phenomenon, and these exhibits collectively gesture outward to the range of social, personal, and infrastructural concerns that childlessness raises: class resentments, differential access to reproductive technologies, the missing child care and educational supports that secure the promises of feminism and make women's careers possible. The list of such concerns is a long one. However, what these exhibits do not provide are stories of the world-making, kin-generating forces of childlessness. To counter this thin statistical imaginary, we need the robust narrative lifeworlds that literature can offer us under the umbrella of *kidless lit*.

Kidless Lit

Kidless lit illuminates the narrative and affective life of childlessness beyond the dominant popular understandings of an anxiety-ridden present. A seemingly nascent genre, kidless lit has a much longer history and more expansive features than presentist narratives of panic and decline would suggest—particularly if we refuse to characterize childlessness as the absence or rejection of relationality to children. Through kidless lit, I rethink child relationality in terms of experiments in kinship centered on what it might mean to relate to *other people's children*. Whether we imagine the childless as figures of capitalist conversion narratives (Scrooge or Daddy Warbucks), as care workers and teachers (Jo March), or as the central weavers of elaborate kinship structures (Gordon, Maria, and all the other adult characters on *Sesame Street*), the fictionally childfree, rather than eschewing relationship to children entirely, frequently find themselves transformed by relationships to children who are not their own. These relationships, in turn, transform the scale of capacity for kinship in the social worlds they inhabit. Kidless lit expands the repertoire of officially sanctioned modes of stranger sociability, exploring not just what reproduction reproduces, socially, but also what it refracts, what exists adjacent to it, and what models of ex loco parentis might look like—models for *not* taking the place of parents, even for refusing the place of parents, for existing in adjacent relationship to parents. Kidless lit offers models for developing relationships with children with whom you cultivate a nonparental duty of care.

Kidless lit's experiments in kinship take place in the shadow of the paradox that the conditions of declining birthrates are also the conditions of increasing global population as well as gaping income inequality. Those same conditions also create the expansion of caretaking labor specifically organized around caring for other people's children.[3] If most care for children by strangers takes the form of ersatz or substitute parenthood, these texts ask this: what other models of cross-generational relationships might exist that exceed this relational structure? How do we tell those stories, to whom, and how? Who gets to reproduce, and who elects not to? What does it mean to relate to children where parenthood and its attendant modes of care are not the default options?

My aforementioned exhibits suggest that discussions of childlessness tend to create division instead of producing solidarities. The childless and the childfull exist, rhetorically, on opposing sides, leaving the sphere of social reproduction, ironically enough, fully intact. By contrast, I suggest that there is a productive site of minor kinmaking to be explored in the missing middle ground of social refraction: a space adjacent to social reproduction, where childless people find unusual kinship with children, where child figures can be read nonparentally or as detached from the family form, and where solidarities might be established in the wake of failed kinship norms. The childless and the unfamilied alike create spaces of imagination that are adjacent to both biological and social reproduction. This driving force of imagination and desire can be observed in the gap between social reproduction and social refraction. Taste and desire can be understood as interrupting both identification and social reproduction just as easily as they can be seen as affirming sameness across generations. Having had parents does not mean you want to be one. Having been a child doesn't mean you want to have one. Even if one can learn to long for difference or to cultivate aesthetic judgment, those longings can refract rather than reproduce familial norms. Indeed, taste and desire can be seen as drivers of productive estrangement from normative kinship, generating surprising solutions to status-quo social forms that sanction some modes of belonging at the expense of others.

Indeed, the panic around childlessness is not just about biological reproduction but about social reproduction as well: the reproduction of dominance in the form of whiteness, of settler colonialism, of capitalism, and of cultural monogamy. For this reason, my work is inspired by Michelle Murphy's (2017a) concept of "alterlife": the condition of life recomposed by the molecular productions of capitalism but also enmeshed within ancestral relations imbricated in the horizons of the future.[4] She develops this concept further in later work to provide a decolonial alternative to the racist concept of population; alterlife, Murphy (2018, 116) argues, is "a project aimed at summoning new forms of humanity" that does not reproduce the violence of the past. These new forms of kinship must move beyond the nuclear family, which is a key technology for settler colonialism, and to embrace poly-kin networks, as Kim TallBear (2018) insists in her contribution to *Making Kin Not Population* (Clarke and Haraway 2018, a volume that also includes Murphy's work). Kidless lit enables us to read kinship, social relations, and social responsibility beyond the containments of population and the nuclear family—to expand lived and figural forms of "alterlife."

One way it does so is by revisiting our phobias and complacencies about both stranger danger and benign statehood. Children's stories remain saturated with fears of wicked stepmothers, abusive foster parents, and child abusers lurking around every corner.[5] Meanwhile, our infrastructural models for caring for other people's children are steeped in legacies of colonialist and capitalist violence. Kidless lit might thus be a site for elaborating an ethic of care for *children as strangers*. These texts refuse to yield to phobic scenes of violence that saturate stories about adult-child relations. Instead, kidless lit reorients our understanding of adult-child relations by asking how these relations might be intelligible outside the nuclear family and any other context that presumes the de facto relation of adult to child is either in loco parentis or, by contrast, criminal.

The Childless Write Back

In the face of the alarm about declining births, the demand to reproduce, and the metrification of population more generally, the childless have begun to write back. From the pages of the *New York Times* and *Time* magazine to periodical articles by Rebecca Solnit and essay collections such as Megan Daum's (2015) *Selfish, Shallow, and Self-Absorbed*, reactions to the meaning of childlessness have taken center stage in popular discourse. Statistical childlessness has found narrative realization in a host of testimonials, primarily creative nonfiction essays, all telling us what it's like not to reproduce. Examples include Solnit's (2015) *Harper's Magazine* essay "The Mother of All Questions" (and later a book by the same title), Sheila Heti's *Motherhood* (2018), Kate Bolick's *Spinster: Making a Life of One's Own* (2015), and Vivian Gornick's *The Odd Woman and the City* (2015). Most of these texts have been penned by women—women who, despite being childless, nonetheless talk about children in their lives. Their relations to children are sometimes emotional, sometimes familial-adjacent (nieces, nephews, niblings), sometimes matters of labor (day care) or of structure (stepparents). But a relation to other people's children for the childless just as often includes a political commitment to paying taxes that are down payments on future lifeworlds, or establishing solidarities with activists whose work involves liberating children from abusive domestic or state-sanctioned circumstances.

Collectively, these authors highlight how compulsory maternity is wielded against women's intellectual aspirations and careers. In "The Mother of All Questions," Solnit recalls being grilled on the matter in an interview: "Instead of talking about the products of my mind, [a British man insisted] we should talk about the fruit of my loins, or the lack thereof."[6] Childlessness was pitted against her writing because of the questioner's incredulity at Solnit's suggestion that books might matter more to women than babies. Such is the predicament of many women writers: reduced to their status as childbearers, whether they are childless or childfull. But Solnit's ambivalence about having children is just as interesting as her critique of compulsory maternity: "I'm not dogmatic about not having kids. I might have had them under other circumstances and been fine—as I am now." Despite the pressure to account for their seeming rejection of childbearing, childless women often imagine childfullness as a path not taken.

A similar absence of antipathy to biological reproduction can traced throughout Daum's *Selfish, Shallow, and Self-Absorbed*. As Daum points out in the introduction, people who opt out of parenthood don't necessarily hate kids: "Many of us devote quite a lot of energy to enriching the lives of other people's children. . . . Statistically, we are more likely to give back to our communities than people who are encumbered with small children—not just because we have time but because 'giving back' often includes returning the kids to their parents at the end of the day" (2). Laura Kipnis's (2015) essay in Daum's volume offers a refreshing refusal of the naturalization of maternal instincts through an account of her sideways relationships to young people. Nestled within Kipnis's jeremiad against the mawkishness that naturalizes "maternal instincts" are multiple examples of her intimacies with other people's children (taking nieces and nephews to movies and using fast-talking, witty repartee with them). To ensure that her point is clear, she declares: "Let no one say that I don't love kids!" (32–33). Almost all of the other writers in the volume likewise at some point reference their relationship to various children, even though their primary focus tends to be on matters of compulsory maternity, public policy, reproductive rights, kinship relations beyond the nuclear family, and feminist theories of science. Indeed, children feature regularly in the volume as nieces, nephews, stepchildren, and even anonymous abstractions in whose name taxes must be paid for the social good.

Attending to other people's children in texts like these requires us to read differently, for both children and adults function as supporting characters for each other, characters who exceed the plots of nuclear family-hood. Minor characters in novels are often childless persons, persons whose stories also include relationships with age-defined minors. In a protagonist-oriented style of reading organized around the happy endings of couplehood, these real and figural minors can easily be overlooked. The pitting of procreation against childlessness becomes an overriding narrative structure that shields minor kinships from view even when they are crucial to the plot.

Social Refraction and Minor Kinship: Reading and Relating to Other People's Children

Such minor kinship forms raise a host of questions: What might it mean to read for these minor figures who are both drivers of plot and adjacent to the plot? How might we imagine social obligations to children as significant minors without assuming them to be property of families or wards of the state (essentially fungible)? How can we apprehend children as both material beings—in need of bodily and emotional care—but also as abstract figures in whose name taxes must be paid and day cares run? How can we resist reifying both the child and the childless into a kinship that looks like familial intimacy as usual? Can the relation of the childless to children exist adjacent to other kinds of familial or care relations without absorbing that stranger-child into familial frameworks and, in turn, reproducing dominant family forms or state-sanctioned care relations (such as that of teacher-student or doctor-patient)? All of these questions about the form of relation that the childless might have to other people's children requires an attention to what exists to the side of both biological and social reproduction without being purely in opposition to it.

Just as Kathryn Bond Stockton (2009) argues for a model of queer childhood as sideways growth, we might also imagine models of sideways relationality. *Social refraction* might be a good companion term to name sideways relations that are lateral to *social reproduction*: the by-products of socially reproductive forces that are not themselves biologically reproductive and that have the potential to interrupt social reproduction. Socially refractive kinship names what exists alongside social reproduction and displaces the metaphoric backdrop of biologism and replication that the horizon of reproduction suggests. Social refraction demands an attention to the relationships of childless people to children and a focus on the web of relations that looks beyond the reproduction of the family. These relations might disarticulate the figural child from its capture by the reproductive futurism that Lee Edelman (2004) diagnosed in his treatise on the limits and sexual normativities of social reproduction.

Social refraction builds on, yet is distinct from, recent calls by Marxist feminists to disarticulate biological reproduction from the family form altogether. In *Full Surrogacy Now*, for example, Sophie Lewis (2019) calls for a refusal of the family form and a recognition and redistribution of the labor of social reproduction beyond the feminized maternal sphere. Lewis seeks "a world beyond propertarian kinship and work alienation" (44). She states that "we need ways of counteracting the exclusivity and supremacy of 'biological' parents in children's lives; experiments in communizing family-support infrastructures; lifestyles that discourage competitiveness and multiply nongenetic investments in the well-being of generations" (130). "Full surrogacy" universalizes the labor of child raising to create solidarities of gestation with "cleaners, nannies, butlers, assistants, cooks, and sexual assistants," whose work "is figured as dirtied by commerce, in contrast to the supposedly 'free' or 'natural' love-acts of an angelic white bourgeois femininity it in fact makes possible" (56). Madeline Lane-McKinley and Marija Cetinic (2015) make a similar argument about kinship in "Theses on Postpartum." "Radical kinship," they insist, "begins with the expansion of parental responsibilities, the un-imagining of the child as property, and the de-naturalizing of the mother as labourer. In radical kinship, the child experiences love and support from a community that undermines the property relations of the family. In collectivizing this project of loving a child, practices of radical kinship attempt to work out of models of 'self-sacrifice' and improvise strategies for communal-care." The authors proceed to advocate for "radically challeng[ing]" the distinction between mothers and non-mothers, just as Lewis challenges the distinction between the familial and the nonfamilial. These authors share the bold claim that the family itself is a problem for both children and kinship, arguing instead for communal lifeworlds.

My insistence on the specific relation to "other people's children" is less radical than full surrogacy. It runs the risk of accepting the structural condition of children's being "owned" by some people over others. Yet an acknowledgment of the distinct relations of parents to children does not have to trade on (or to trade in) the specific forms of parent labor that continue to exist under the conditions of social belonging today. Arguments for full surrogacy tend to seek a sameness of relationality to children in order to dissolve the family and make more radical kin of everyone. But in doing so, they efface the different responsibilities and relationalities that exist with children. Not everyone has or even wants the kind of parenting responsibilities that would attend the collapse of the mother and nonmother. Not all states of childlessness are chosen, but the ones that are deserve consideration in their own right for the forms of relationship to children that they might engender. Indeed, to collapse the distinctions among modes of child relationality would leap over the undertheorized relations of social refraction between adults and children who are functional strangers to each other.

Although the critique of social reproduction has long been a staple of Marxist thought, especially Marxist feminist thought, interest in the term *nonreproduction* within these conversations is relatively recent. Chantal Jaquet's (2014) *Les transclasses ou la non-reproduction*, which is as yet unavailable in English translation, argues that nonreproduction is an affective state defined by a gap where the social order sidesteps reproduction per se. "Les transclasses" are the result of social reproduction that has in some way failed to reproduce class itself or that creates distances from the putative scene of the tastes and desires of others. For Jaquet, nonreproduction is not the opposite of reproduction: "Every non-reproduction is in some sense a reproduction by other means." As one commentator on the text puts it, "Reproduction is an imitation of the immediate tastes and desires of one's family and class, [whereas] non-reproduction, or what Jaquet calls transclass, often involves an imitation at a distance of the tastes and desires of others, a teacher, a friend from a different class, or the mediated images of a different life" (Unemployed Negativity 2015). Jaquet's concept of the *transclass* echoes Judith Butler's notion of performativity, except in terms of tastes and desires rather than identity and identification.[7] In focusing on the figural and abstract field in which both tastes and desires come to be articulated, Jaquet considers reproduction and nonreproduction less as opposites than cognates, as social and conceptual kin. Her work effectively foregrounds a field of social refraction in which the literal and figural operate together to distort both capitalism's dominant structures of belonging and identity's scenes of identification. This spatial account of class serves not just to spotlight spaces adjacent to conventional family forms and commodity relations but also to imagine the comparatively distanced necessity of forging relations to other people's children.

Jaquet's insights about distant class or category relations are useful for understanding the conditions of possibility for the psychic dimensions of kinship produced under such conditions of distance, such as the relation to other people's children. Over, without being against, the prevailing demand that childhood makes on the concept of reproduction (where childbearing embodies reproduction), nonreproduction opens up alternative social relations with the child. These social relations inform the inner life of subjectivity without reproducing the universalizing form of the family. Such investigations are central to José Esteban Muñoz's (1999) concept of disidentification, a process that "scrambles and reconstructs the encoded message of a cultural text" and that "exposes the encoded message's universalizing and exclusionary machinations" (31). The effect is "cracking open the code of the majority" and using it as "raw material for representing a disempowered politics or positionality that has been rendered unthinkable by the dominant culture" (31). Muñoz's process of scrambling the coded messages of a text at the psychic level spotlights the conditions for nonsocially reproductive *trans classes* and opens up the possibility for theorizing the tastes of children at a distance from their parents' reproductions of taste and desires. Such relations exceed the norms of social and biological reproduction without refusing them entirely, and without completely torpedoing the specificity of parent-child relations.

Imagining relations to "other people's children" with the goal of "making kin not population" requires drawing on the insights of queer theory and critical race theory into sociability. Queer theory understands stranger sociability as central to the project of world making. Public sex is often positioned as the apex of queer stranger sociability. Yet Michael Warner (2000), for example, characterizes world making broadly: "The idea is that the activity we undertake with each other, in a kind of agonistic performance in which what we become depends on the perspectives and interactions of others, brings into being the space of our world, which is then the background against which we understand ourselves and our belonging." Kinship with children can be a potential site of stranger sociability that is performatively agonistic to the dominant modes of white settler monogamy. As TallBear (2018) notes, the relational forms of Indigenous kinmaking exceed the technology of the settler colonial nuclear family by having an elaborate system of aunties and responsible adults. Stranger sociability, in other words, converges with Indigenous nonmonogamy, and Indigenous modes of kinmaking put pressure on queer theory's claims about stranger sociability as a specifically modern form.

Critical race theory shifts our thinking about kinship from agonistic performativity to the question of repair, given the structural violence that Murphy and others have identified as the legacy of population management. A reparative approach to kinship might therefore open up inquiry into the minor forms of kinship with children and with the idea of children, including failed or spoiled relationships in one's own childhood. As Elizabeth Freeman observes, one way to think about kin is to suggest that "kin are people who have hurt each other in ways that feel irreparable, and yet have found their way to some kind of repair" (Elizabeth Freeman, email message to author, October 15, 2019). Although Freeman is referring here more to interpersonal than structural harm, this definition of kinship might offer a path to conceiving reparation in a broader sense. Making kin with other people's children requires not just agonistic performativity but also a reparative practice that deals with what Deborah Britzman (1998) calls the "difficult knowledge": the ways in which the subject is implicated a scene of social trauma that creates internal conflicts and psychic defenses at the scene of knowing that complicate learning when subjects encounter the unbearable stories of others. In attending to these scenes of nonreproduction encrypted within compulsory forms of both biological and social reproduction, we begin to see ourselves implicated in the violences that inform population reproduction.

Minor Kinship Forms: Social Refractions and Estrangements

What might it mean to use kidless lit as a prompt for theorizing a socially refractive relationship to childhood? The domain of the childless used to be the fantasy domain of queers and other social outcasts: that perverse, lonely, often suicidal and barren crowd who could pluck the cloud out of every silver lining any novel might offer them. In "Tales of the Avunculate," the late great Eve Kosofsky Sedgwick (1993) rails against what she calls the "demeaning" effects of the "heterosexist hygiene of childrearing" (63). What she called an "avunculosuppressive" (62) family structure is modeled by and organized around how a child can desire. (It also organizes how adults relate to children more generally.) For Sedgwick the constant question (can the family be saved?) is a compulsion. Rather than reject or retrench the nuclear family form, she turns to the avunculate: "Forget the name of the Father. Think about your uncles and aunts" (59). The uncles and aunts in question, like the legion of stepparents, foster parents, and others, exist in the socially refractive space of nonparenthood—or at least to the side of parenthood in the usual sense. This refractive space is often occupied by pretenders, substitutes, and unbelongers.

To be clear, the space of adjacency to the family is not always a progressive space. It has also been occupied by colonizers, sexists, abusers, and other violently dominant figures. Not all minor kinship forms, in other words, interrupt the violent, often anti-social features of reproduction. The space of adjacency is not inherently subversive or radical. But it has potential: in addition to naming elusive and sometimes diminished social relations that exist alongside familial and reproductive ones (not necessarily in contrast to them), the relation to other people's children is also the space for an active set of political choices or refusals, and indeed a series of actions (not just inactions): the web of thought and agency that goes not only into being childless but also into interrupting reproduction without displacing it—and of engaging ethically from the perspective of childlessness while respecting the relative sovereignty of the child. In these ways, kidless lit allows us to understand *social refraction* as a productive scene of ethical dilemma.

In classic Foucauldian fashion, the narratives of childlessness and nonreproduction discussed thus far should be read less in terms of refusing or repressing forms of child relationality but in generating alternatives to it. For example, Daum (2015) and Kipnis (2015) both describe the social value of relating to "other people's children." They also describe nonreproductive ways of living that exceed the stigmas of capitalist accumulation or the logic of missing out. Such conventions of kidless lit have a much longer and varied narrative history, particularly in literary fictional texts. Most literature for children, for instance, is actually kidless lit. (It's a pretty rare book for a young person that features the scandal of children having children.) Other genres of nonreproduction might include realist stories about old maids and bachelors, radical theoretical critiques of capitalism, and science fiction futures—sometimes all of these together. Such genres show how kidless lit narrates minor kinships with children that refract the social in ways that do not reproduce the familial form.

The Ones Who Don't Walk Away from Omelas

Ursula K. Le Guin's ([1973] 1975) very short story, "The Ones Who Walk Away from Omelas," opens with a seemingly utopian scene: the city of Omelas, preparing for the Festival of Summers, with its children. The narrator insists that Omelas's citizens are "not simple folk," (253) "not less complex than us," "not naïve and happy children—though their children were, in fact, happy" (254). Their complex happiness owes itself to the fact that, seated in a basement beneath one of the city's beautiful public buildings, in their own excrement, is a child—a child whose existence is the condition of possibility for that happiness: "It could be a boy or a girl. It looks about six, but actually is nearly ten. It is feeble-minded. Perhaps it was born defective, or perhaps it has become imbecile through fear, malnutrition, and neglect. It picks its nose and occasionally fumbles vaguely with its toes or genitals" (256–57).

At some point every person in the city is either exposed to or told about this nameless child, so "they all know it is there" (257). And no one is permitted to do a thing about it: "If the child were brought up into the sunlight out of that vile place, if it were cleaned and fed and comforted, that would be a good thing, indeed; but if it were done, in that day and hour all the prosperity and beauty and delight of Omelas would wither and be destroyed. Those are the terms. . . . The terms are strict and absolute; there may not even be a kind word spoken to the child" (258).

Much is made of the moment at which other children are exposed to this child. They "go home in tears, or in a tearless rage" (258)—although a few of them never go home at all. These are the ones who walk away from Omelas. And each one goes alone—leaving their home and refusing the contract that underwrites the city itself in the interests of that child, who is also a stranger.

The scene is a chilling reminder of our social implication in the suffering of other people's children—that, in fact, this nameless and abandoned child's debased state is the condition of possibility for the society itself. This is the point that Elizabeth Povinelli (2011) makes when she argues that Le Guin's story "rejects th[e] ethics of liberal empathy": "The ethical imperative is to know that your own good life is already in her broom closet, and as a result, either you must create a new organization of enfleshment by compromising on the goods to which you have grown accustomed (and grown accustomed to thinking of as 'yours' including the health of your body) or admit that the current organization of enfleshment is more important to you than her suffering" (4). Inverting the logic of empathy, Povinelli suggests that refusing to accept the conditions of the world—a world that has put the child in the basement to begin with—refusing these conditions through "the 'not this'" of walking away amounts to a moment of sheer potentiality. Another society becomes possible. The story's title, after all, focalizes the act of the ones who see and then walk away. And to be sure, the ones who walk away from Omelas engage in a relationship of social nonreproduction that is made possible by this child. They eschew family bonds and citizenship; they do not attempt to possess the dispossessed child or make her their own; they neither sentimentalize nor name the child. The act of walking away is political. Doing so arguably is not a less significant alignment with the spoiled child than that of the child-loving adults the leavers leave behind. The ones who walk away become nonreproductive subjects in an act of affiliation with the nonreproductive subject: that spoiled child who dwells in Omelas's basement.

Is there not potentiality, however, for the ones who see the abandoned, seemingly orphaned child yet stay, living with that knowledge but without knowing that child intimately? Indeed, is there not potentiality for the child herself who escapes both the abandonment to the basement and the basement itself? It is worth considering these alternative potentialities, each of which invites a broader consideration of what it might mean to develop readings of relations to other people's children. The first is a story of the child as figure or concept but a figure unceded to the logic of reproductive futurism. Such an approach makes the case for reclaiming the figure of child for the logic of social *non*reproduction. The second is the story of the child as character untethered from the logic of the nuclear family, a prominent figure in the pages of children's literature, even if the genre's frames of reference, fantasy, and reception tend, paradoxically enough, to be the very scene of the nuclear family itself.

Consider the latter first. In the world of children's literature the unfamilied child is a very storied child. How different is the Omelas child from, say, Harry Potter, shoved in a cupboard beneath the stairs of his abusive relatives' home? Or the Little Match Girl? Le Guin doesn't write the stories of those children, but versions of such stories persist, full of both potentiality and constraint, particularly in contrast to normative racial, class, and family plots. There is much to be said about the pluck of fictionally abandoned children and their creativity in the face of living with risk. The world of children's literature is a world populated by childless protagonists who find themselves aligned in minor kinship forms with manifold strangers.

Consider the orphaned or isolated child as a standard feature of children's literature, with a revolving cast of characters who swoop in to help. For every Dorothy, a Lion, a Tin Man, and a Scarecrow. For every Harry Potter, a Dumbledore, a McGonagall, a Sirius, and a Snape. For every Baudelaire orphan, a Quigley. For every Alice, a set of strangers who befuddle and challenge her without really exposing her to danger. The scenes of childless-child stranger relationality in these texts are robust, even as the overall whiteness of children's literature foregrounds the extent to which it is whiteness itself that needs rescue, companionship, and solidarity. What if our canonical narratives of sentimental estrangement expanded beyond white children and were not tidied up at the end through repatriation to conventional family forms?

No less significant to the scene of the orphaned or estranged child is the figure of the often childless stepparent. In fairy tales like "Snow White and the Seven Dwarves" and "Cinderella," the stepparent is almost always a counterfeit parent, a poor substitute who is out to get the child. Children's literature features an archive of characters who exist ex loco parentis, but not so anonymously and *not* in the place of the parent, as a kind of *trans class* that builds worlds at a distance from the tastes and desires of the adults who otherwise populate their shared plots. Both parentless children and childless subjects, whether they are children or adults, can be read nonparentally to the extent that they figure relationality beyond the strictures of the nuclear family unit. Without overriding the significance and labor of parenthood altogether, kidless lit reads adults beyond their roles as substitute parents alone.

But even for those who stay, the only option is not liberal empathy. One need not collapse into identification with the child or incorporate the child into one's direct care to heed the call to have a political relation to that child as symbolic subject. Beyond attending to the narrative handcuffs that govern the stories we tell about adults and children, kidless lit expands the possibilities for conceiving of the relation of the childless to children. These texts demand new attention to the figural, abstract, or anonymous child. The nameless neglected child can mobilize a politics and a political imaginary that need not be about repatriating that child as family property. No less for those who stay than for those who go, that child becomes a political abstraction, a figure or a concept that mobilizes actions that are not acts of care for her but that exist adjacent to her.

The child-as-figure has been most trenchantly theorized by Lee Edelman (2004). Edelman takes aim at the reproductive logic of the social by counterposing two figures and their attendant logics: the figure of the child, who "alone embodies the citizen as an ideal, entitled to claim full rights to its future share in the nation's good, though always at the cost of limiting the rights 'real' citizens are allowed" (11), and the figure of the *sinthomosexual*, "who comes to figure the bar to every realization of futurity, the resistance, internal to the social, to every social structure or form" (4). In one sense Edelman is a theorist of childlessness. "Queerness," he argues in one of the most frequently cited passages of his book, "names the side of those *not* 'fighting for the children,' the side outside the consensus by which all politics confirms the absolute value of reproductive futurism" (3). Even in opposing the logic of reproductive futurism and the child who embodies it, is queerness not actually defined, for Edelman, precisely in its (refused) relationship to the child? In attempting to resist the logic of reproduction, we see how fully reliant that logic is on its seeming opposite: the child and the queer, reproduction and nonreproduction are more entangled or positioned alongside each other than they seem at first. Little wonder, then, that one of the pressure points against Edelman became arguments about the ways in which real historical children might complicate his claims, as critics sought the places in his writing where the figural and the real seemed to collapse into each other. In one of the milder variations of this critique, Nina Power (2009, 5) observes, blithely, that "Edelman sometimes slips from the figural to the literal."

But what if we were not to cede the figure of the Child to the future or to the version of conservative social politics in whose name Edelman observes it is wielded? In other words, might the figural Child be mobilized to different ends? After all, the childless might have multiple relations to such a figural child: the child is not only a real material child for progressive causes. The Child might be an abstraction (for voting, public spending, and so forth). The Child might be read as a public good in whose name actions could be taken (as in Omelas) without persons necessarily entering into material relations of care with actual children. Conceptual children— symbolic, abstract, figural, and often nameless children—expand life chances for real, historical children. They might further arguments in contexts that have to do not with children themselves but with the complexities of the political and economic systems we occupy.

A Child Is Being Beaten

This essay has so far outlined the challenges of relating to other people's children that arise because of panicked narratives about childlessness and the narrative constraints that govern both adult strangers and stranger-children. It has argued that kidless lit and reading for other people's children discover socially refracted (rather than socially reproduced) models of stranger sociability across generations. There is a psychic limit to this process. A major obstacle to our care of "other people's children" is our own psychic life. The limits of reading, the limits of narrative, the difficult knowledge of overcoming the sedimentations of violent histories all might be well understood through Sigmund Freud's (1919) "A Child Is Being Beaten.'"

The central fantasy under discussion in this essay, Freud tells us, is a common one. The child and the beater are both anonymous. It is "*a child*," and the analysand claims to know no more about it: "The child being beaten is never the one producing the phantasy, but," he eventually discloses, "is invariably another child" (184). Moreover, Freud very quickly observes that "the phantasy," at this stage, "has feelings of pleasure attached to it. . . . At the climax of the imaginary situation," he says, "there is almost invariably a masturbatory satisfaction" (179). Only in the next stage of the fantasy does the analysand realize that the pleasure has given way to guilt via repression and really the anonymous child is the analysand herself. The identity of the person doing the beating is only later established as the "father"—who, of course, becomes a symbolic father. Understanding the scene through the mechanism of displacement thus dispenses with the initially anonymous child—"a child"—in the service of understanding that the indefinite child has been the subject himself all along.

But is it not possible to hold on to Freud's insights about the subject while also allowing the possibility that there has, in fact, been another child, a stranger or an indefinite child? After all, the fantasy begins as a story about the subject's solidarity with an unknown child. It is the very idea of the child as stranger (whether the child is real or not) that is the starting point for the analysis, which progresses something like this: "A child is being beaten" (184); "My father loves only me and not the other child, for he is beating it" (185); "My father is beating the child whom I hate" (185); and "I am probably looking on" (186). The subject needs the concept of the stranger-child, as does Freud. This phase of the fantasy gratifies the child's jealousy and pleasure: "My father does not love this other child, he loves only me" (187). The very idea of loving an other child, someone else's child, must be eliminated from this fantasy sequence in order to make clear that the child being beaten really is the subject in question. But the concept of that "other child" is necessary both to the subject and the analyst. The "other child" is the condition of possibility for the process, the analytic starting point. The conclusion Freud draws is that the adult has repressed the fact that "I am being beaten by my father" (185). This insight becomes available to the adult only through the analysis, when they can recognize that guilt has replaced the earlier feeling of pleasure, even as both continue to coexist in the unconscious. But this insight is not diminished by the possibility that the "other child" may still actually exist, even if they are a screen for the analysand's own displacements. Indeed, the emotional complexity of the scene can really be understood only if the analyst and the analysand both take seriously the idea of there being an other child.

There is, after all, great pleasure in diagnosing the misfortune of the child who is being beaten as well as great repugnance at the fact that the child is being beaten. What Freud calls the "excited feeling" is thus of "mixed character" (180): combining the pleasures, simultaneously, of satisfaction, repugnance, and intolerance. If the fantasy begins with a scene of schadenfreude—pleasure in the recognition that "a child is being beaten"—it would seem to end with one of *fremdscham* (the German word for stranger shame, a structure of identification with a stranger, across difference, and often in embarrassment). The analysand's admission of an identification with the child facilitates the recognition that one *is* the child being beaten but that the figure of the stranger is nonetheless necessary for that moment of self-recognition. Freud doesn't use the word *fremdscham* (a neologism coined later), but for Freud the scene of a child being beaten is ultimately a case study in the life cycle of masochistic fantasy, defined both by pleasure *and* guilt: guilt in the pleasure, guilt in the fact that the child has done something that has led to the beating. The child and the "I" are in this together. While Freud would think of this symbolic father as the patriarchal superego, for our purposes, we might think of this symbolic father as a *political* superego—for the conditions of the child's being are not merely familial, not only gendered.

Freud's work thus demonstrates the necessity of imagining "other people's children" to the conditions of possibility for recognizing not just one's own formation but also one's implication in and responsibility for the world around oneself. If "a child is being beaten" in our narrative, figural, and material lives, how might we manage our pleasures and embarrassments, our projections and our identifications, our sanctimonies and our guilt? In the move from "A child is being beaten" to "I am being beaten," a potential space of solidarity opens up, the space of social refraction, the space of refiguration, and possibility of a trans class through the figure of the "other child." The space can be available to us, I think, only if we can position ourselves at some distance from the saturations of reading children, adults, and strangers as usual. If the child and I are in this together, perhaps we begin to see a shared implication in the face of political error. Ultimately, a recognition that the child who is being beaten in a scene of social injustice does not just implicate an individual speaker. It implicates us all in the shared political and affective structures in which we live: the child-full and the childless, the intimates and the strangers, the others and ourselves. For that child—the one in the basement, the one being beaten—is us. But not only us in the singular. If the ranks of the childless are growing just as the global population is and just as the planet is confronting its apocalypse, it will take a solidarity of strangers of across generations—as well as an understanding of the strangeness of kinship—to make a difference. Kidless lit may provide us with some models of solidarity as well as identification for living under conditions in which we all are being beaten, and not always by our parents.

Notes

An amazing amount of support has made this essay possible. Thanks go first to Tyler Bradway and Beth Freeman, editors extraordinaire and dream readers, who have made this essay immeasurably better, attending to details large and small with great generosity. I am also indebted to the anonymous reviewers of the manuscript, who offered crucial feedback, and to Meredith Snyder, who provided essential polish at the end stages. The Social Sciences Research Council of Canada made this project possible, while my daily writing comrades (Judy Davidson, Catherine Kellogg, Natalie Loveless, Susanne Luhmann, Jerine Pegg, and Sheena Wilson) kept me attached to the habit of doing my own work. Finally, I am grateful to Susanne Luhmann, who reads and sustains me with unwavering grace through it all.

1   See, for example, stories complicating optimism about a post-COVID-19 baby boom: "Painful Truth: No Baby Boom Coming Out of Coronavirus Quarantines" (2020). Note as well the continued tone of measured panic in stories such as Gibson (2019).

2   The group Birth Strike (2019), for instance, was founded in Britain precisely as an activist strategy against population increase by refusing biological

reproduction. United Nations Department of Economic and Social Affairs (2017) statistics report that global population will continue to rise, to an estimated 11.2 billion by 2100, despite the global decline in fertility. For a compelling study of rates of population increase and decline, see Alison Bashford (2014). Also of interest is Gretchen Livingston's (2015) "Childlessness."

3 See Endnotes Collective (2013).

4 Murphy (2017a) first defines *alterlife* in "Alterlife and Decolonial Chemical Relations": "Alterlife names life already altered, which is also life open to alteration. It indexes collectivities of life recomposed by the molecular productions of capitalism in our own pasts and the pasts of our ancestors, as well as into the future. . . . Alterlife is a figuration of chemical exposures that attempts to be as much about figuring life and responsibilities beyond the individualized body as it is about acknowledging extensive chemical relations" (497).

5 As Kadji Amin's (2017) *Disturbing Attachments* has made clear, our idealizations of queer history have sought to purify our historical understandings of queer history's pederasts. The very need for that purification affirms the extent to which queers are still haunted by fears that they prey on other people's children, as evidenced through historical anxieties about the North American Man-Boy Love Association. For more on the ways panic about the erotics governs childhood innocence, see James Kincaid's (1998) *Erotic Innocence: The Culture of Child-Molesting*.

6 Solnit has since published a book by the same title, but these quotations first appeared in the article version cited here.

7 Kevin Floyd's (2009, 15–16) *The Reification of Desire* likewise sought to bring Marxian theory and queer theory into conversation with each other by focusing less on totalizing gestures and more on the internal "social differentiations" within the field of capitalism.

12 Till Death Do Us Kin

Sworn Kinship and Queer Martyrdom in Chinese Anti-imperial Struggles

Shocking news, truly sad, reached my ears.

We mourn you. When will they wrap your corpse for return?

You cannot close your eyes. On whom are you depending to voice your complaints?

If you had foresight, you should have regretted coming here.

Now you will be forever sad and forever resentful.

Thinking of the village, one can only futilely face the Terrace for Gazing Homeward.

Before you could fulfill your lofty goals, you were buried beneath clay and earth.

I know that even death could not destroy your ambition.

POEM 112, ANGEL ISLAND DETENTION BARRACKS

(LAI, LIM, AND YUNG 2014, 140)

Among hundreds of Chinese poems carved onto the wooden walls of the detention barracks on Angel Island in the heart of the San Francisco Bay, Poem 112 mourns an irrecuperable loss that is exceptionally tragic. Like tens of thousands of Chinese being detained indefinitely on the island after the passage of the Chinese Exclusion Act of 1882, the unnamed author found himself locked up with his fellow countrymen, far away from his own blood kin and homeland. Lamenting the death of one of his co-detainees, the author evokes imageries of the underworld, where the dead stand on the Terrace for Gazing Homeward to see their hometown, but without the possibility of an actual return. Having no kin within reach, even the body of the deceased faced an uncertain fate at the hands of US immigration officials. With his eyes unclosed, the deceased lacked a qualified advocate who could seek justice on his behalf—whether in front of a US judge or the emperor of the Daoist underworld.[1]

The poem is a vivid reminder of the precarious conditions facing those who cannot depend their survival on blood or normative kinship. Cut off from one's village and kin network, the Chinese diasporic subject lives a life teeming with death. For him the detention station resembles the terrace in Hell, for it serves the same purgatory function that torments the detained while foreclosing their futurity. Nonetheless, the last line of the poem seems to offer a glimpse of hope, for the author believes that "even death could not destroy your ambition." If death marks not the end of one's existence but a continuation of one's life in a new form, there could be grounds for relational possibilities that transcend the limitations of life. Even if blood kinship may hold a monopoly over the realm of life, queer kinship can still emerge from the ruins of death worlds.

For instance, "till death do us part,"[2] the end of a commonly used Christian marital vow proclaiming a couple's lifelong fidelity to each other, implies a dissolution of the marital covenant upon death. If normative kinship relies on "life" as a key anchorage point, queer kinship might need to turn to "death" in search for a logic of resistance that defies life's hegemony. The theme of death has become central to queer studies: driven by homophobic and transphobic sentiments, murders, suicides, and slow deaths have become a literal part of the queer condition, intersecting with and bolstering anti-Black and necropolitical realities (see Stanley 2011; Berlant 2007). The unjust deaths of marginalized others demand a theory of kinship that continues to signify beyond death, even if it calls for a refashioning of kinship's violence. To this end I turn to a non-Western kinship model—the sworn kinship tradition in China and the Chinese diaspora, during the late imperial era, which was plagued by colonial, imperial, and biopolitical powers. Focusing on the blood oaths and collective deaths intrinsic to these sworn affinities, I argue that rituals of death and rebirth performatively position sworn brothers and sisters in a queer paradigm of kinship, one that binds them in perpetuity through a set of strict discipline techniques. Linking this model of sworn kinship to rebellions and revolutions in Chinese history, I then explain how it could be effectively mobilized for countering symbolic and physical violence. Marked through a sovereign ban as *bare life*, members of sworn kinship engage in a form of queer martyrdom and sacrifice that opens up radical possibilities for relating to others beyond life's reach.

The Queerness of Chinese Sworn Brotherhoods

In contemporary China the idea of unrelated men becoming sworn brothers largely remains a celebrated part of the Chinese cultural and nationalist imagination. Despite homoerotic and incendiary undertones that must be repudiated, the brotherhood tradition offers a timeless blueprint for a phantasmatic Chinese masculinity that is heroic, loyal, and securely heterosexual. This sworn tradition, with ancient roots, happens to be a central theme in at least two of the "Four Classic Novels" canonized and promoted by the Chinese party-state after the Cultural Revolution (1966–76), during a time when decimated cultural treasures of "Old China" had to be mined to rebuild China's national identity in an increasingly neoliberal world. In their popularized forms, sworn brotherhoods have been depicted and performed repeatedly in highly successful historical TV dramas and video games based on these classic novels. Lately, even an explicitly gay male couple from a Boys' Love novel were strangely transformed into members of a "socialist brotherhood" as the book was adapted to a TV series under state censorship (Li 2020).

Given how easily the brotherhood tradition can be co-opted in service to state agendas, one must look beyond the present distortions into the rich history of the tradition to evaluate its queer, subversive potentials. Far from being an innocuous form of sociality compatible with a purportedly harmonious police state, sworn brotherhoods tended to proliferate during times of deep social unrest and crisis, often immanent in rebellions and revolutions that resulted in mass deaths and destruction between different dynasties. As early as Eastern Zhou (770 to 256 BCE), for example, elite men from multiple lineages used blood covenants to secure alliances as they struggled for dominance after the centralized Zhou court broke down (Lewis 1990, 43). These covenantal bonds between men of different surnames carried various functions and meanings throughout Chinese history, practiced by both elites and commoners. The Qing era in particular (1644–1912) turned out to be a fertile ground for sworn affinities in their nonelite yet popularized forms. Toward the middle to late nineteenth century, the Qing empire had sunk into an unprecedented crisis, with Western powers vying for colonial control over Chinese ports, trade policies, and territories. Domestic rebellions ensued, motivated in part by the Qing's inability to fend off the Western encroachment.[3] Under these unique historical conditions, brotherhood activities concentrated along the Chinese southern coastlines—the farthest regions from the Qing imperial reach that also had the closest encounter with colonial fleets.

This historical link to oppressive imperial and colonial powers renders sworn brotherhoods an intriguing phenomenon, a dialectic in which an alternative kinship structure became a site of resistance to the forces that were once conducive to its own emergence. A closer examination of how a break with normative kinship translates into revolutionary possibilities is thus warranted. David Ownby (1996, 2), in his pioneering study of Chinese brotherhoods and secret societies during early and mid-Qing China (mid-1600s to mid-1800s), argues that these secretive Chinese associations were "informal, popular institutions, created by marginalized men seeking mutual protection and mutual aid in a dangerous and competitive society." Unlike their Western counterparts, in which bourgeois elites formed the bulk of membership (see Bullock 2011), Chinese sworn brotherhoods in the late imperial period were predominantly formed by and for the most marginalized men, who had no proper place in the elite Confucian kinship structure. The brotherhoods' origins have been debated among scholars, some favoring the "Ming Restoration" thesis, which holds that they originally aimed to resist Qing Manchu rule and restore the previous Ming Dynasty, whereas later works have found increasing evidence that these societies were formed for mutual aid, primarily in response to a changing and challenging socioeconomic environment, but could be mobilized for anti-Qing resistance (Murray and Qin 1994, 13).

If these mutual-aid associations were devoid of a clear Ming restorationist agenda in their origins, then why would an all-powerful Qing government, at the height of its sovereign power, fear them so much that they deemed active suppression necessary? Because written materials about these societies were produced only after such threats had materialized, a historical approach to answering these questions could be limited by the biases of Qing officials charged with documenting them. What if, rather than a deep-seated anti-Qing agenda, it was the very nonnormative kinship forms in these brotherhoods that animated the state's anxiety, given that the state's very claim to political legitimacy rested on a sex-gender system that helped facilitate a biopolitical management of its population? As an ethnic minority, the Manchus could not legitimize their rule over Han Chinese without adopting Confucianism, whose political philosophy rested on a hierarchical social order in which the proper functioning of the family was crucial for maintaining political stability. As political crisis deepened in late Qing, kinship and gender relations became even more scrutinized and regulated. For instance, women's fidelity to their husbands took on intensified salience during these times as male authors further expanded the literature on "exemplary women" (Bossler 2015, 9). In its not-yet-pathologized form, male homosexuality became a government concern not because of male-male relations per se but because of its potential to disrupt proper social hierarchies (Sommer 1997). In short, any deviation from Confucian kinship norms observed in the populations could be a cause for concern, for such promiscuous deviation might destabilize the constructed fantasy of a Chinese empire as eternally Confucian.

Indeed, even before the state's active suppression of brotherhood societies, Qing officials had found the sworn brothers' kin relations to be what we now might call queer. For example, Jin Qiguang, a magistrate in Taiwan immediately following the establishment of Qing rule on the island in the mid-1680s, describes the family lives of brotherhood members as promiscuous and morally dangerous: "If A and B join together in a brotherhood, then A's mother is B's mother, B's elder sister is A's elder sister, A's wife becomes elder aunt, B's wife becomes younger aunt. . . . The dwellings of peddlers and tenant farmers [i.e., those likely to be attracted to such brotherhoods] lack the levels and refinements necessary to keep inner divided from outer, and in such circumstances [brotherhood members, including women] will circulate through one another's houses as if they were true flesh and blood" (quoted in Ownby 1996, 48). He then goes on to express his fear that over time, fornications between members of these dwellings would become inevitable and that consequently these brotherhoods would destroy families and obscure bloodlines, leading to poverty and banditry. The reference to the dwellings of association members points to the anxiety emanating from the lack of clear inner/outer spatial distinction that divides people into recognizable households and social hierarchies. The official also regarded this queer living arrangement as conducive to promiscuous desires and criminal acts offensive to Confucian morality.

Such suspicions of promiscuity and lawlessness were likely magnified by the geopolitical significance of the imperial frontiers in southeastern coastal regions and Taiwan as the last territories to be incorporated into Qing rule. To stamp out the last stronghold of pro-Ming resistance, the Qing officials even depopulated the entire coastal regions and forced people to move inland. This created fertile conditions for local leaders to forge alternative lineages for mutual protection in the midst of social turmoil during the Ming-Qing transition (1618–83) (Murray and Qin 1994, 10). Depopulation disrupted local lineages based on more traditional kinship ties and obscured property relations, which made resettlement afterward especially challenging. Local lineages found themselves in need of people with different surnames to engage in feuds, or *xiedou*, in order to reclaim lands and ensure their survival.[4] It is within this particular social milieu that many brotherhood societies emerged.

Thus, the "queer" dwellings observed by the Qing official were not isolated inventions or innocuous local customs but rather by-products of a tumultuous social chaos that the Qing rulers were complicit in engendering. Coupled with a harsh natural environment, increasing absentee landlordism under Qing rule exacerbated the problems of overpopulation, land scarcity, and a declining man-land ratio in the region, forcing many of the dispossessed to earn their living far away from home (Murray and Qin 1994, 6–7). Taiwan became a popular destination for many single men, who formed the bulk of the frontier settlement. The resulting male-dominated communities in Taiwan soon drew attention from Qing officials obsessed with protecting Confucian family values. Notably, Lan Dingyuan, an influential Qing scholar-official interested in regulating women's conduct and maintaining the Confucian family order, attributed the chaos and rebellions on the island to an asymmetrical gender ratio. He suggested to the Qing emperor that to bring order to Taiwan, family migration should be actively preferred over the migration of single men. In 1732 the Qing government finally sanctioned family migration to Taiwan, likely influenced by broader concerns over single men, who had been regarded as threats to the Confucian order even in the more developed regions of China (Lo 2015, 48–50). This trope of labeling single men and their brotherhood societies as serious threats even followed their later migration to Chinese diasporic communities around the world.

Interestingly, the Qing official's comments on brotherhood dwellings mirror those of nineteenth-century US officials visiting the Chinese diasporic enclave in San Francisco during the last years of the Qing Dynasty. In *Contagious Divides*, Nayan Shah (2001) coined the term *queer domesticity* to describe nonnormative kinship forms in Chinatown preceding and during the period of Chinese exclusion (1882–1943).[5] Even in the decades prior to the Exclusion Act, Chinese communities in San Francisco and other American cities experienced anti-Chinese sentiments and expulsion attempts at the hands of white vigilantes. Chinatown became a site where the "Chinese race" was constructed as filthy, immoral, unsanitary residents living in cramped spaces, and the "idea of Chinatown as a self-contained and alien society" in turn justified rounds of policing, statistical surveys, and investigations for corroborating racial classification (Shah 2001, 18).

At the center of such knowledge production was the question of Chinese domesticity. An 1854 investigation of Chinese residential spaces imagined Chinese boarding houses as the "filthiest places imaginable" after noticing that in some of the Chinese boarding houses, "hundreds of Chinamen are crowded together," making the air quality insupportable. Travelogue writer Walter Raymond even compared the living conditions of the boarding houses to the "horrors of a catacomb, packed with the living, disease-breeding flesh, slowly drifting into their graves" (Shah 2001, 22–32). These descriptions present the Chinese boarding house as a necropolitical "death-world" in which Chinese bachelors slowly wasted away their lives.

Within Chinatown, the *huiguans* (companies/meeting halls) that underlay mutual aid and governance in turn-of-the-century Chinatown bore strong resemblance to their historical predecessors, brotherhood associations in China proper. For the migrants the American West could be regarded as another frontier, full of dangers manifested in anti-Chinese hostility and uncertainty in a foreign land. Offering much-needed protection and mutual assistance in this environment, these huiguans served as a refuge from and a site of resistance to the biopolitical racism in the United States, just as earlier brotherhoods had helped mobilize resistance to Qing rule. The active efforts by both American and Qing officials to study and erase nonnormative kinship forms in brotherhood communities reflect the mechanism of biopolitics that "make live or let die" (Foucault 2003), as some forms of life or subset of populations are weeded out to protect the health of the social body. Similarly, in the Straits Settlements in Malay (1826–1946), British colonial officials decided to deviate from the typical British "divide and rule" colonial governmentality when dealing with local Chinese brotherhoods when they passed the Suppression of Dangerous Societies Act of 1890 (DeBernardi 2004, 74). The Chinese difference was regarded as too unbridgeable, and secret societies as too autonomous, to be governable, justifying active suppression and criminalization of brotherhood activities. Thus, the transnational nature of Chinese brotherhoods has allowed them to take shape in political systems that had varying degrees of modernization, bureaucratization, and biopoliticization. But underlying the anxiety of all three cases is the way that nonnormative kinship relations were represented as sites of danger, mystery, and plague-like characteristics threatening other populations deemed more worthy and desirable.

Blood Oaths and Collective Death

As a sovereign with the absolute power to kill, but taking on increasingly biopolitical characteristics, between 1650 and 1812 the Qing state had written into its penal code targeted punishments for those who dared to join brotherhoods. The punishments tended to be harsh and extreme, ranging from 100 blows of heavy bamboo and exile to a distance of 3,000 li (more than 1,000 miles) to immediate decapitation upon arrest, depending on the particularity of an offense. During early Qing, those who joined simple brotherhoods with fewer than 20 members bearing different surnames received 100 lashes for being presumptively guilty of violating kinship norms, but those who swore a blood oath faced imminent execution. Among the substatutes later introduced, one stood out as particularly reflective of the Confucian state's concern over kinship heterodoxy: immediate or deferred strangulation of the leaders of brotherhoods that invested leadership in a young person, thereby proving guilty of subverting Confucian age hierarchy. Oddly, Qing rulers seemed to worry about how well Confucian hierarchy was observed in a kinship system that they had already deemed heterodox and illegal, as if a parodic play of kinship constituted a double transgression of Confucian norms. But overall, brotherhoods that practiced blood oaths received the harshest punishments. Their heterodoxy was self-evident and could not be tolerated, whether or not they posed serious threats to Qing rule (Ownby 1996, 148–54).

The blood oaths for which harshest punishments were warranted deserve a closer analysis. As a covenant-making practice that had forged alliances among kings, tribes, family units, and outlaws for thousands of years, oath taking culminating in a blood sacrifice had been popularized by the late imperial era (1368–1911) in literary texts such as *Romance of the Three Kingdoms* and *Outlaws of the Marsh*—two novels later canonized in the "Four Classics." But despite the tradition's status in popular imaginations, ruling dynasties often feared its subversive potential. When blood oaths were used for the purpose of forging covenants among equals, they contradicted the hierarchical Confucian tradition of patriliny.

Having surveyed and analyzed various iterations of blood oaths, David Ownby (1996) is intrigued by the fact that blood oaths were used even in simple brotherhoods engaged in seemingly innocuous mutual-aid activities. It seemed unnecessarily risky, for the use of blood sacrifices would "imbue their organizations and activities with a powerfully dangerous symbolism that the Qing state could not ignore." He suggests that one way to understand this choice is to recognize how perilous life was at the margins of society. Given that "mutual aid" sometimes took criminal and predatory forms, including looting and murders, "the blood oath bound these young men to each other in the face of potential risk, and perhaps also made them seem more fearsome to outside groups" (41). Understood as such, blood oaths convey a fearless criminality that defies the sovereignty of the Qing state through both embodied and symbolic strategies. To extend the sacrificial logic underlying Ownby's account of blood oaths, I build upon Giorgio Agamben's (1995) insights on sovereignty and biopolitics to argue that the blood oaths of Chinese brotherhoods symbolize a ritualized death of *unsacrificible* individual life in marginality and serve as a rite of rebirth into a realm of *bare life* imbued with collective sovereign potentiality. Blood oaths then sustain the covenant through a violently and performatively enacted regime of rules that seeks to enforce the original oath with costly consequences and sacrifices.

Many brotherhood societies borrowed from the widely known Peach Garden Oath sworn by three legendary heroes depicted in *Romance of Three Kingdoms*. In this fourteenth-century historical novel, three men from dispossessed backgrounds meet for the purpose of rescuing the Eastern Han Dynasty (AD 25–280), which was threatened and divided by eunuchs, warlords, and peasant rebellions (a historical particularity different from the time of the novel's writing). They decide to become sworn brothers the very next day at a local peach garden, and after preparing the sacrifices and burning incense, the three recite the oath as follows: "We Liu Bei, Guan Yu, and Zhang Fei—though of different surnames, swear to become brothers, and promise mutual help in the midst of difficulties and dangers with a single mind; to serve the country and save the people; we ask not the same day of birth, but seek to die together on the same day; may Heaven—the all-ruling, and Earth—the all-producing, witness our heart; and if we betray our *yi* (chivalry, righteousness) and forget our *en* (affection, mutual-indebtedness), let Heaven and men smite us!"[6]

Their oath resignifies the relationships among the three friends who were just strangers a day ago, as well as their collective identity and obligations. "With a single mind" suggests that they are no longer discrete individuals seeking self-interests and self-preservation but a collectivity united in a desire to die "on the same day" fighting for the same cause. The fact that they were born into different lineages in separate years is regarded as a hindrance to their desire for brotherhood. To overcome the limitations posed by their births, the sworn brothers invoke their desire for a collective death—an extremely unlikely future outcome unless the brothers manage to remain faithful and face every battle as one throughout their lives. The brothers do not end up dying on the same day, but their oath brings them under a death-driven kinship paradigm that performatively solidifies their brotherly bonds whenever their loyalty to each other is tested and their lives are at stake in dangerous situations. In other words, just as the subversion of gender norms requires a parodic play on gender that exploits the immanent incoherency of laws governing the heterosexual matrix (Butler 1990), the subversion of kinship norms requires an arduous performance of kinship that becomes "real" only after the men inhabit the roles of "natural" brothers, who then repeatedly demonstrate that men of different surnames can experience even stronger affections and carry out obligations far more difficult than what brothers of bloodlines could ever achieve under Confucianism.

This is not to necessarily suggest that these three heroes intentionally or agentially perform "drag" on kinship for the sake of subversion, for their sworn brotherhood could just as well result from the "misfiring" of a normative kinship system that failed to assert its coherency when confronted with a plethora of desires for same-sex affinities in people's lived experiences. However, it is important to recognize the near impossibility of establishing an alternative kinship regime from, in lieu of, or in parasitic relationship to a hegemonic system of kinship signification without a parallel system of compulsory or obligatory practice of norms. The invocation of religious authority and the curse at the end of the blood oath detailing what befalls those who violate the terms of their sworn brotherhood serve as means to ensure the obligatory performances under this alternative kinship system, clauses without which the oath could lose its binding power.

In short, the blood oaths of the Chinese sworn brotherhood tradition impose a double, sacrificial bind on the initiates: they must give up an atomized mode of existence, and they must also take up their obligations under a new sovereign regime with its own violent rule-enforcement mechanism. Recall that most initiates wishing to join sworn brotherhoods during the Qing Dynasty lived on the margins of society under necropolitical environments created by a bloodthirsty sovereign, a colonial regime of governmentality, or a "democratic" regime infused with biopower. Having been marked for death or as a plague that threatens the life of the more worthy population, the brotherhood initiate (and the life he takes on after blood oath) closely approximates bare life or the figure of the homo sacer in Giorgio Agamben's (1995) analysis of biopolitics in *Homo Sacer*. For Agamben the homo sacer exists outside of both human and divine laws and is characterized by "the unpunishability of his killing and the ban on his sacrifice" (73). Stripped of legal protections reserved for citizens or subjects on good terms with the sovereign, the homo sacer exists in a state of exception in which both human and divine laws are suspended. The victim is neither protected by human law nor eligible as a sacrifice that would propitiate the divine for the sake of the larger community (Girard 1977).

Paradoxically, however, anyone can kill the homo sacer. This condition of the homo sacer is most clearly evident in the killing of Chinese laborers at the hands of white vigilantes before and during the era of Chinese exclusion in the United States, often with impunity (Lew-Williams 2018). Similarly, under Qing rule, members of sworn brotherhoods could be killed during xiedou while the Qing rulers turned a blind eye and rarely held killers accountable. Ownby (1996, 177–78) explains that the Qing officials considered local lineage leaders (who led feuds) to be part of the Confucian hierarchy, governed by "the rule of men" rather than by "rule of law"; in contrast, brotherhood associations fell outside of Confucian hierarchy and presented "an absence of control" and therefore deserved more active suppression and eradication by Qing rulers or all men alike. Furthermore, if we consider Confucianism to be the state religion, the brotherhoods' falling outside of Confucian hierarchy necessarily excludes them from Qing's version of "divine law." The executions and deaths of sworn brothers could not be considered as legitimate sacrifices to Heaven, nor could beheadings or strangulations of brotherhood members be considered simply as individual cases of state enforcement of the law. Rather than a mere exercise of repressive power, the penal code also wielded biopower aimed at eradicating the fast-spreading *phenomenon* of sworn brothers, or an undesirable way of life, as it targeted this abnormality in China's population, whose exponential growth invited large-scale state intervention during the late imperial era.

Under this nascent biopolitical governmentality, the great majority of brotherhood initiates were already marked for death in a dangerous environment, facing risks of poverty, starvation, and random acts of violence. Thus, to join a brotherhood, even with the knowledge that it was a forbidden practice with extreme punishments, was to embrace the mark of death, to accept the social projection of death onto oneself, and to march toward it in an act of seeming madness—like the queer figure of the sinthomosexual in Lee Edelman's (2004) *No Future*. And if we accept the analysis of the sworn brotherhood tradition as a parallel or alternative regime of kinship performatively engendered, the blood oath ritual resignifies the dispossessed as not only sworn brothers but also members of a sovereign collectivity under a new system of signification governed by an alternative set of kinship rules. In other words, the initiates experience a rebirth in an alternative symbolic realm in which their sacrifices could be made intelligible once again.

This symbolic significance of death and rebirth is noticeable in a firsthand account of a Heaven and Earth Society initiation ceremony that surfaced after an investigation of brotherhood activities by colonial officials following the Penang riots of 1867. According to the report, the initiate went through a ritual act that symbolized death and rebirth—he had to crawl toward a higher table to face an image of a deity, whose protection allowed the initiates to walk through fire and water into safe passage, before officially taking the blood oath, which involved drinking drops of blood from each initiate. To mark this symbolic meaning of rebirth, the initiates were also told to take on a new age determined by counting from the time of their initiation (DeBernardi 2004, 86–87).

To performatively bind initiates to a new symbolic order in perpetuity, the ritual of rebirth must be coupled with enforceable rules and punitive measures that deter betrayal of the brotherhood after this one-time ceremony. According to several Tiandihui documents, these rules and the consequences for violating them were to be recited during each initiation ceremony to cement the blood oath. They include:

1 You must observe the rules (of the society); if you do not, may you die by the bite of a serpent!
2 If a brother die in a foreign country and there is not sufficient money for funeral expenses, whoever does not contribute something to assist, let him die childless!
3 If a brother be disabled in his hands or feet, you must draw out your purse and help him to buy food!
4 A brother must nourish another brother (in time of need); if you have food, you must share it with him; if you do not, may a tiger devour you!
5 After entering, you swear you will not oppress the weak by employ-

ing the strong, nor the poor by means of the rich, nor the few by the many: if you do, may you die by myriads of knives.

6 After entering, you swear, if you are a father, not to reveal the laws of the Brotherhood to your son, if an elder brother, not to tell them to your younger brother, nor to disclose them to your relations or friends: if you do, you may die under the sword.

7 After entering, you swear to regard the parents of a brother as your own father or mother, and if a brother place his wife, or deliver his son into your charge, you will regard them as your own sister-in-law or your own nephew: if you do not, may Heaven destroy you.

8 A member who does not attend a brother's marriage when he has leisure shall receive twelve strokes! (Murray and Qin 1994, 240–43)

Rules 2–4 speak to the mutual-aid obligations that each sworn brother must uphold. One must generously place a brother's needs before one's own, sacrificing self-interest. Rule 5 states an ethical principal that exemplifies the ethos of protecting the least vulnerable, although it is unclear whether this commandment also regulated the brothers' behaviors toward people outside the covenant. The sixth and seventh rules echo the observations of promiscuous kinship relations by the Qing official discussed in an earlier section; juxtaposed, they suggest the brotherhood's ambivalence toward traditional kinship ties. On one hand, sworn brothers must extend and merge their blood ties into one, essentially sharing one another's parents and siblings; on the other hand, they must not disclose the secrets of the society to their blood relatives, lest they die under the sword. Even friends (presumably nonmembers) are excluded from knowing about the brotherhood, suggesting that the idea of friendship had substantively different meanings than that of a sworn brother. Nonetheless, certain provisions, such as rule 8, which requires sworn brothers to be present at each other's weddings, do seem to endorse heteronormativity; some even prohibit fornication and adultery with a brother's wife. Far removed from queer and feminist visions today, the practice of marriage, coupled with observations of prostitution in certain brotherhood communities, suggests that even a transgressive sworn kinship form cannot be entirely immune from more hegemonic paradigms of blood kinship. Patriarchy, the incest taboo, and the traffic in women could have been part of life in brotherhood societies.

Fortunately, there were also sworn sisterhood traditions that might have actively resisted Chinese patriarchy, some of which employed a similar enforcement mechanism to sustain their sworn covenants. Despite also having a rich history and tradition, female sworn affinities have disproportionately fewer available archival materials compared to male same-sex associations. Here I will briefly illustrate two traditions that very much deserve their own extensive scholarly analyses: *handkerchief sisters* and *Jinlan sisters*, both emerging during the Ming Dynasty (1368–1644). Handkerchief sisters were lower-class women serving as courtesans in brothels. Similar to their marginalized male counterparts, these courtesans forged sworn relations for the sake of survival and mutual support in a hostile social milieu. But they were not merely mirror reflections of the sworn-brotherhood tradition, for they employed the symbol of handkerchief, a common daily object, and resignified its affective meaning to express affection and love among sworn sisters—making it a tradition with its own unique symbolic system independent from sworn brotherhoods (Cui 2017, 65).

As for the Jinlan sisters tradition, enforcement of sisterhood oaths and resistance to Chinese patriarchal culture were clearly significant. Many women who joined this sisterhood were also called *Zishu* women, which literally means women who "comb their own hair," indicating that they managed their own affairs, vowing never to marry. A pair of Zishu sisters could enter a Jinlan covenant through a marriage-like ceremony, after which the covenant was supposed to be vigorously enforced. The larger Jinlan sisterhood prohibited any change of heart in sworn sisters: those who betrayed the sisterhood and entered into heterosexual marriage would face harsh penalties, such as group chastisement, being locked into a pig cage, or corporal punishment. Even in the case of forced marriage, the sisterhood would help their coerced sister devise ways to escape the marriage; if an escape wasn't plausible, the sisters would make an extremely tight piece of garment for the sister to wear, designed to resist the groom's sexual advances on the wedding night. If the sister failed to resist and the marriage was consummated, she would be considered a traitor and face punishment. In certain cases, sworn sisters forced into a marriage used physical violence to resist the grooms. Some late Qing sources even recorded instances of the collective, coordinated suicide of Jinlan sisters who were coerced into marriage (Yang 2005, 53).

The logic of sworn affinities is thus not limited to the Chinese brotherhood tradition. Jinlan sisterhood employed a similar mode of mutual aid, oath taking, and coercive enforcement that together forged a formidable force that deterred the encroachment of Chinese patriarchy. Some of these sister dyads clearly resemble modern lesbian relationships, although such coupled relationships were not organized along strict essentialist, identitarian lines, nor did they follow a neoliberal logic of choice. The decision to enter a sisterhood covenant was irreversible, and any form of betrayal was met with punitive measures to ensure the survival of the collectivity, a model of belonging that paradoxically also included collective death. It seems that the more deeply entrenched and violent a dominant kinship system is, the harsher the enforcement mechanism must become in order to sustain an alternative regime of kinship. This explains why punishments for violating sworn covenants were just as extreme if not sometimes harsher than what was written into the Qing penal code against brotherhoods. This mirroring effect suggests an interlocking relationship between hegemony and marginality, patriarchy and sisterhood, or even the sovereign and the homo sacer. A closer examination of this peculiar "kinship" is key to understanding the revolutionary potentiality of sworn affinities.

Violence and Symbolic Terror in Queer Martyrdom

For Agamben (1995), the sovereign occupies the same state of exception as the homo sacer, a paradoxical symmetry that undermines their polarized difference as conventionally understood: "At the two extreme limits of the order, the sovereign and *homo sacer* present two symmetrical figures that have the same structure and are correlative: the sovereign is the one with respect to whom all men are potentially *homines sacri*, and *homo sacer* is the one with respect to whom all men act as sovereigns" (84). This striking symmetry suggests that the sovereign is merely the mirror image of the homo sacer—the latter is a reflection that threatens even as it confirms the former's status as the all-powerful sovereign. To maintain his status as king, the sovereign must constantly deny the sovereignty of homo sacer through a sovereign ban or a biopolitical death camp. The sovereign refuses to recognize the homo sacer's privileged mode of existence outside of both human and divine law: a realm infused with sovereign potentiality. Similarly, despite living a life of utmost abjection, Chinese sworn brothers and sisters devised their own regimes of kinship and law as a survival strategy in banishment. Understood as such, sworn affinities could present an immanent existential threat in the state of exception that they occupy simultaneously with the sovereign. The moment when the sovereign recognizes himself in the mirror image of the homo sacer, or when the homo sacer discovers her own sovereignty, the sovereign/homo sacer binary collapses, opening up possibilities for radical resignifications, reversals, or revolutions. This was also true for sworn kinship, whose success in forging lasting bonds among nonrelated members of the same sex jeopardized normative kinship's monopoly over the natural and the permanent, collapsing the divide between "real" and "fictive" kinship.

One can build a strong historical case that sworn brotherhoods played a significant role in the success of the Xihai Revolution of 1911, which ended the Qing Dynasty as well as thousands of years of dynastic rule in China. Sun Yat-sen, the chief leader of the revolution who also served as the first president of the new Republic of China, raised funds from brotherhood associations in diasporic communities around the world. He also organized various brotherhood societies with the specific aim of ending Qing rule, and he joined forces with other influential grassroots brotherhoods. The Gelaohui (Society of Brothers and Elders), which originated in Sichuan province, made perhaps the greatest contribution (Cai 1984). Responding to Sun's call for revolution, the Gelaohui quickly mobilized local populations to rise up against the local Qing government after a massacre in the capital city, Chengdu, during a peaceful demonstration in September 1911 triggered their uprising (Felsing 1979). Historians of the revolution have noted the Gelaohui's unique, effective contribution to revolutionary efforts: their extensive grassroots network, efficient organization and leadership, as well as bravery in battle made them a formidable force against the best-equipped branch of the Qing army (Shao 1991, 50–51). In light of the analysis of sworn brotherhoods' unique kinship system above, this organization's effectiveness could be attributed to the ethos of collective sacrifice, coupled with a coercive enforcement of brotherhood obligations. If any brotherhood members died during the Chengdu massacre, sworn kinship would compel all sworn brothers to avenge their deaths, charging toward Qing gunfire over the bodies of martyrs.

While there is a clear historical link between sworn brotherhoods and the downfall of the Qing empire, locating the exact moment of sovereign recognition and the collapse of the sovereign/bare life dualism is no easy task. Although many sworn brothers died for the sake of the revolution, very few were able to directly subvert the symbolic divide between the sovereign and the homo sacer through their death. One could be executed as a brotherhood member without ever challenging the executioner's sense of sovereignty. To succeed in queer martyrdom, one must die not as a homo sacer but as a sovereign figure who queers through death. To explore this possibility as it plays out in sworn brotherhood, I turn to the figure of the suicide bomber examined in Jasbir Puar's (2007) *Terrorist Assemblages*. Building on Achille Mbembe's meditation on necropolitics and the Palestinian suicide bomber, Puar recognizes the suicide bomber as a "bio-weapon" that "carries with it the bodies of others" upon detonation, as "death and becoming fuse into one." She then writes that "these bodies, being in the midst of becoming, blur the insides and the outsides, infecting transformation through sensation, echoing knowledge via reverberation and vibration. The echo is a queer temporality—in the relay of affective information between and amid beings, the sequence of reflection, repetition, resound, and return (but with a difference, as in mimicry)—and brings forth waves of the future breaking into the present" (217–18).

For Puar, a queer assemblage is antithetical to an identitarian regime of essentialist self/other distinction. The terrorist bodies, already marked for death under necropolitics, intimately fuse with the bodies of enemies when the bomb goes off, blurring seemingly unbridgeable divides in an act of self-annihilation. Puar recognizes the echo created by the blast as a "queer temporality," one that collapses even the future/present divide. Unlike José Esteban Muñoz's (2009) queer futurity, which always seems to be on the horizon but is never actualized, Puar's queer assemblage offers a much more immediate dose of relief from the oppressive status quo, as the blown-up bodies dis-integrate with their previous social markings while opening up new signifying possibilities. In the midst of reverberation, bodies previously living under the power of death may even briefly achieve an ontological status of being: a privileged position, as some philosophers have argued, that was often categorically denied to the colonized and the dispossessed.[7]

Interestingly, Puar's suicide bomber strongly resonates with a Chinese feminist named Qiu Jin, a revolutionary figure whose story best affords her the title of a queer martyr. As a prominent feminist thinker, Qiu Jin was heavily invested in her mission to save Chinese women from the marginalizing shackles of feudal patriliny in late Qing. After having increasing friction with her husband and suffering under the patriarchal family firsthand, Qiu decided to leave her family and pursue her studies of gender and feminism in Japan, where in the Chinese diaspora community she encountered Chinese brotherhood societies devoted to overthrowing the Qing. She recognized the overlapping goals shared between the anti-Qing revolution and a Chinese feminist revolution as she became centrally involved in these societies' affairs pertaining to the revolution. With no recorded intention to be perceived as biologically male, she even decided to cross-dress in men's clothes while carrying her signature knife, a decision that may have helped her become a member of the brotherhood. In a poem on men's clothes, Qiu appears to denote her life prior to adopting male dress as a "past life" distinct from her "future" (Zhang 2018, 104). This demarcation is similar to a ritualized death and rebirth in many brotherhood initiation ceremonies, but it may also indicate her desire to leave her abject life as a Chinese woman behind and appear as a new self whose very drag-like presence destabilizes gender hierarchy and gender difference. But her queerness goes even further than infiltrating the heart of secretive male-homosocial environments while performing drag. Beyond these male-centric spaces, she also entered Jinlan covenants with her closest friends as sworn sisters who shared similar feminist aspirations. In short, Qiu Jin remarkably traversed both sworn brotherhood and sworn sisterhood traditions, becoming a hinge figure who helped resignify the Xinhai Revolution with a Chinese feminist bent.

Qiu Jin's death was no less remarkable and transgressive than her prominent lived life. While she was leading a preparation for an armed uprising in 1907, her leaked plans led local Qing troops directly to her headquarters, which were camouflaged as an academic institution. Li Zhongyue, the local Qing official charged with leading the troops, had heard of Qiu's widely respected scholarly reputation. As Qiu began to open fire to cover her comrades' escape, Li ordered his soldiers not to return fire on any women, which caused more Qing casualties and allowed some revolutionaries to escape. Still, Qiu did not escape and was captured alive. During questioning, Qiu recognized Li's sincerity in extending sympathy to her, and she decided to share her life story with him. Her confiding in her interrogator reinforced Li's admiration, causing a great moral dilemma for him (Zang 2002, 18–22).

This is a precise moment when the sovereign power recognizes the sovereignty in the mirror image of the homo sacer; meanwhile, the homo sacer, with her double transgression of gender and law, recognizes the helpless vulnerability long concealed under the facade of sovereign omnipotence. The process of displacing the sovereign/bare life binary had thereby begun: Li was no longer simply a tentacle of Qing sovereignty but an abject figure charged with carrying out an execution order against a cherished object of his own admiration. As a proxy of Qing sovereignty, Li had no choice but to order Qiu's beheading in a public square. But the tragedy did not conclude at the moment of Qiu becoming a martyr. Li became severely depressed after Qiu's death, resigned from his post, and committed suicide only sixty-eight days after the execution (Zang 2002, 21). In other words, Qiu Jin's martyrdom carried with it the body of her executioner. Like the suicide bomber theorized by Puar, Qiu Jin collapsed the self/other distinction, opening up a queer temporality conducive to radical resignifications.

The news of Li's suicide caused great public outcry: major newspapers published strongly worded articles denouncing the injustice caused by a corrupt Qing government; some theaters even began performing plays that recounted this tragic double martyrdom (Zang 2002, 21). It is also quite plausible that Qiu's death led to an intensification and proliferation of anti-Qing discourse that helped further delegitimize Qing rule and indirectly contributed to the success of the revolution just several years later. Moreover, the descendants of Li built friendships with Qiu's family, and Li's spirit tablet (used to commemorate the dead) was even placed into the Qiu Jin Memorial long after the revolution (Zhou 2012, 49), cementing a blood-forged kinship between Li and Qiu that intimately and violently binds the two polar extremes of a sovereign order into a terrorizing assemblage.

Conclusion

The story of Qiu Jin powerfully demonstrates the blurred, mirroring relationship between the Qing sovereign and the sworn societies it sought to eradicate. The collapse of the Qing empire coincided with the height of sworn Chinese societies as society leaders leveraged their highly effective kinship networks to fuel anti-Qing uprisings. Returning to the detention barracks holding Chinese migrants on Angel Island, one may find that the bunker beds in the tightly packed same-sex quarters bear a strong resemblance to the "bachelor society" in San Francisco Chinatown. Put differently, the US immigration officials ironically re-created queer domesticity for the Chinese under their watch while justifying anti-Chinese laws using their caricature of Chinese domesticity as un-American. In this modern camp environment, the sovereign and bare life can become indistinguishable in this co-occupied state of exception. As the US officials engaged in a mimicry of queer domesticity, the Chinese were busy forging kinship documents showing blood ties to American citizens, thanks to their mutual-aid networks in the diaspora.[8] Again, queer kinship hijacked the logic of normative kinship to achieve its own survival and status as sovereign.

Often situated in necropolitical death worlds, Chinese sworn kinship could still carve out spaces for survival and resistance against great odds. Far from idealized and peaceful, these sworn traditions carry with them a naked monstrosity: to ensure collective survival and solidarity, these kinship practices must impose their own regimes of violence and coercion on the sworn members, performing a mimicry of sovereign violence. To overcome the symbolic violence of normative kinship, sworn brothers and sisters underwent ritualized deaths and rebirths so that their sworn relations could become intelligible under an alternative kinship paradigm. Life in such kinship systems may never parallel the comfort of a conjugal same-sex couple living in nuclear domesticity; nonetheless, the promise of an unbreakable bond that lasts far beyond death and a collective drive toward a radical futurity may yield their distinct pleasures.

Notes

1   In some popularized Chinese Daoist and Buddhist practices, the dead could receive posthumous justice from officials in underworld bureaucracies. For more on traditional Chinese underworld courts, see Valerie Hansen's *Negotiating Daily Life in Traditional China* (1995).

2   Rites containing "till death do us part" can be found in "The Witnessing and Blessing of a Marriage" (2015).

3   For example, the Boxer Rebellion (1889–1901), organized by secret societies of the peasantry, was primarily directed at foreign powers and Christian communities in China.

4   To engage in xiedou, families of different lineages banded together to forge larger "lineage groups" that fought against other lineage alliances. One could analogize these feuds to elite covenants that fought each other during Eastern Han. For more on Chinese lineage during the late imperial period, see Szonyi (2002).

5   The Chinese Exclusion Act was enacted in 1882 and repealed in 1943, but the Page Act had already banned immigration of Chinese women in 1875.

6   Author's modified translation is based on Guanzhong Luo, *Romance of the Three Kingdoms*, trans. C. H. Brewitt-Taylor (2002), and is cross-referenced with the Chinese original.

7   See Fanon ([1952] 2008), Spillers ([1987] 2003), and Warren (2018). Here I am not suggesting that queer martyrdom offers a unique solution to ontological erasure; rather, it momentarily disrupts the grid of intelligibility through which terms of sovereignty and ontology can be articulated and negotiated in zones of indistinction.

8 A fire following the 1906 San Francisco earthquake destroyed public birth records in City Hall, creating opportunities for Chinese with US legal status to sell and transfer documents of their "sons" back in China. For individual stories of Chinese paper children, see Chin and Chin (2000) and Djao (2003).

KATH WESTON, ELIZABETH FREEMAN,
AND TYLER BRADWAY

————

How Did It Come to This? Talking Kinship with Kath Weston

Tyler Bradway: We would like to start with how you see the trajectory of kinship running through your work. So much of the significance and importance of *Families We Choose* (Weston 1991, rev. 1997) is its thinking about the meaningfulness of kinship structures that are not entirely determined by or bound up with the state. This seems to be an ongoing question for you, one that continues in your work on the War on Terror and biosecurity, where you question whether kinship and politics should be thought together or reframed in radically different terms (Weston 2005, 2013). Then in *Animate Planet* (Weston 2017), you turn to what you call "political ecologies of the precarious," tracing visceral relations of intimacy between bodies and their social and material worlds. Do you still see kinship as a vital term in your work and for thinking politics with or against the state?

Kath Weston: I think it might be helpful for me to start by saying a bit about the context in which I was writing *Families We Choose* (FWC). FWC was the first piece of research I did that focused on kinship. I'm a sociocultural anthropologist by training, and that matters because kinship was always considered something you had to study that was very central to anthropology. In the mid-1980s, when I was doing the field research in the San Francisco Bay Area for FWC, a lot of things were happening that had a bearing on what people would later call queer kinship, perhaps most significantly HIV/AIDS. It was a pivotal moment. At the time, within anthropology, you were studying kinship primarily as something that was a very vital area of inquiry in the past but had become a bit passé. Not too many people were writing about kinship. Job ads for anthropologists seldom mentioned it. FWC worked against that trend. The book became important in the academy in certain ways and in the rest of the world in other ways. I'm always humbled to look around and see that it's still in print, that people are still assigning it in courses, that court briefs cite it, that young folks still occasionally give it to their parents. Within anthropology the book circulated as part of what became known as the new kinship studies (see Peletz 1995). In tandem with work by Janet Carsten (2000, 2004), Sarah Franklin (2007, 2013), Sarah Franklin and Susan McKinnon (2001), Faye Ginsburg and Rayna Rapp (1995), Ellen Lewin (1993, 1998), Leith Mullings and Alaka Wali (2001), Marilyn Strathern (1992a, 1992b, 2005), Sylvia Yanagisako (1985, 2002), and many others, FWC helped revitalize the study of kinship. New kinship studies opened up new areas of inquiry, not just for queer scholarship but with regard to reproductive technologies, power relations, and, of course, what counts as a family in the first place. It's very hard to talk about something like surrogacy, much less "gay marriage," without getting into bodies of law and the rule of law, so you have to confront the state whether you want to or not.

Many of the legal recognitions in place today for queer relationships were aspirational in the 1980s when I did that fieldwork. The chances of achieving gender-neutral marriage rights seemed almost fantastical, even for people who were working to achieve it. Meanwhile, people were pursuing all sorts of creative alliances. They were looking at business law, not just family law, to think about how people could, if they were in a same-sex couple, continue to live in a rent-controlled apartment after one person passed away, for example. And so it was a certain historical moment. I didn't set out to study kinship, actually. I set out to study coming-out narratives. But any decent ethnographer attends to what's going on around them, which always includes things no one can anticipate. In the Bay Area, people had started using the term *families we choose*. That was not my language. It was not an analytic language. It was me as an ethnographer trying to attend to the categories that people themselves brought into play.

You asked about the analytic utility of kinship, whether we should keep framing things in terms of kinship. This is a question that comes around every so often. New kinship studies arose as a "yes" to an earlier genera-tion's "no," building on, but also taking issue with, the legacy of anthropolo-gists like David Schneider (1980, 1984), who were critical, or at least ambiv-alent, about the concept. However one answers questions about the utility of "kinship" today, it's important to remember that this revitalized study of kinship within anthropology opened up new lines of inquiry into all sorts of things that could come under the sign of kinship but might also exceed it. This is the road to someone like Janet Carsten (2000) talking about "cul-tures of relatedness" or Marilyn Strathern (2020) casting new light on the intellectual and social history of "relations." So now, in this moment, peo-ple may decide that this term, *kinship*, serves for some things and doesn't serve so well for other things. But I think even if people set "kinship" aside *for the moment*, it's important not to lose sight of its intellectual lineage, in-cluding the part that queer scholarship on kinship has played in opening up investigations that go way beyond queerness or the field of queer stud-ies as such.

Elizabeth Freeman: I think that's one thing that really animated this volume. There is a long history of queer kinship studies and of kinship studies having been revitalized by queer studies, and also queer studies has recently moved toward thinking queer relationality, where "relationality" was sort of becoming the key term. It's not necessarily a term that does the same kind of work that kinship does. Relationality can be very vague about how structures replicate themselves over time.

Kath Weston: Or don't! Something similar happens if you think about other terms in kinship's associational field, such as *belonging*. In coming-out stories, people often say, "Growing up in my family, somehow I felt that I didn't belong." *Belonging* in that statement is certainly not a syn-onym for kinship, even as it gestures toward an enduring sense of affilia-tion of the sort often attributed to kinship ties. A feeling of not-belonging can coexist, however uneasily, however poignantly, with a claim to having a family.

But there's another way to approach this question of whether kinship, as an analytic concept, still has vitality. As an ethnographer, I look around and I see things going on that there are not easy names for. Or there are names, but not names that reference kinship. Do cases like that offer pro-ductive opportunities to queer kinship? In the US you've got people build-ing what are sometimes called "community hamlets," where they try to move to the same vicinity to support each other cooperatively. They might all live in households that look nuclear or otherwise conventional, but then they're doing things like growing and sharing food in urban space in their yards. They're doing things that many people would consider the job of a household or a family—figuring out how to get food and feed it to one another—but they're doing it in a collective way. If you asked them to fill out a census form, you wouldn't see any of that. There's certainly no legal recognition for it. If something went wrong, people couldn't sue each other and say: "But you told me I can raise eggplants in your yard, and now you're not letting me have them!" These arrangements are flying below the radar of the state for the most part, and they are scarcely being studied. So let's take that as an example. It certainly queers the notion of what's going on in terms of affiliation, belonging, residence, relatedness, kinship, and family in a place like the US. To the degree that a community hamlet gets studied, it tends to be put in a box called environmental studies, or "here's a great eco project." I'm not saying that's bad, but suppose you take something like a community hamlet and you say: if I look at this as queering certain things about what we usually think of as being within a domain called "kinship," does it suggest interesting questions? Can I notice some things I might not otherwise notice? And does that help open a space for activism, for reimagining all the things we need to reimagine in the face of climate change, white supremacy, the rise of fascism, and extreme inequality?

Tyler Bradway: When you describe this method of being open to surprise, but also being interested in the details on the ground, I think about the richness of ethnographic narrative in your work. Your newest work is especially interested in the political work that storytelling can do. Do you see narrative as linked in a particular way to embodiment and affect, as crystallizing certain intimacies that otherwise fall beneath the idioms we currently have to describe relationality?

Kath Weston: This is not something that's unique to my scholarship. If you look at the second generation of work, post-new kinship studies by both younger scholars and people of my cohort with newer projects, you'll see lots of attention to materiality. You get Vanessa Agard-Jones (2012) in "What the Sands Remember" looking to sand, materially and metaphorically, to gain insight into same-sex desire in Martinique. In FWC, I originally explored how the voluntarism of "families we choose" took shape vis-à-vis "blood relations," which culturally signified permanence but no longer seemed so permanent when parents threatened to disown their kids for being queer. My current project looks at the persistence of corporeal analogies in finance, from the circulation of blood/credit (who knew financial systems could have "cardiac arrests"?) to notions of generativity embedded in questions about the proliferation of wealth. You could put my books in a line and say: well, wait a minute, here's FWC and that's kinship, and then she's over here doing *Animate Planet*, that's political ecology, and now she's got a project on the anthropology of finance and the history of science. Those are really different boxes! But for me, flowing through it are blood and other bodily substances, as well as a kind of intimately visceral engagement with the world. If you go back and look at some of my other work— *Render Me, Gender Me* (Weston 1996) or *Traveling Light: On the Road with America's Poor* (Weston 2008)—you'll also see a focus on people trying to read one another across the interface of a body and what happens when these readings conflict. You can have a moment of incredible violence as well as wonder or surprise.

To address the other part of your question about narrative: when I was a kid, I wanted to become a writer. I grew up in a working-class household, raised to be white but also part Gypsy. I was good at writing, and with that talent, against the backdrop of the war in Vietnam, the Black Power movement, La Raza, the Occupation of Alcatraz, came a deep sense of responsibility. People were in the street then as they are now. I thought writing might have something to do with activism; it might be able to make some kind of contribution. I still believe that, but initially I wasn't committed one way or the other to writing fiction or nonfiction, much less documenting things in a social-sciency kind of way. I was trying to find a shelter for writing, a place in the world where I could eat *and* write, hoping that the academy could be that place. I happened to be in graduate school at a moment when the literary and reflexive turns in anthropology were happening. There was enough room within my discipline to be able to incorporate narratives, including one's own, into the text, even as a graduate student. I had the great fortune of working with Renato Rosaldo, Sylvia Yanagisako, and Mary Louise Pratt, who encouraged me.

"Writerly" ethnography required an ear for how people put things and then, increasingly, a refusal to pretend that you yourself did not have a story. This eventually developed into a kind of imperative: OK, I need to locate myself with an "I" in the text because my positionality might be affecting my analysis. But if you read my work, you can see that my "I" is not much concerned with older worries about bias. I have always been much more in the "creativity" camp that says: if you go back and approach an episode in your life with an ethnographic sensibility, it can be valuable. (In *Animate Planet*, I call this an "ethnographic stopgap.") Just as there can be something compelling about having the cadence of James Baldwin or Arturo Islas ringing in your head as you search for the rhythm of your own text.

 Elizabeth Freeman: It also strikes me that in anthropology—and this is probably true of all disciplines in some way or another, but particularly true of anthropology—the encounter itself and the exchange of story produces a bond that's very hard to name. That exchange produces forms of relationality that anthropologists have had to be enormously self-critical about but that can also endure over time. Anthropologists and the communities that they're part of, and the communities that they study, are often grappling for a language for these relations. Kinship can become part of that language. There are occasional gestures in people's work toward "this is my other family." That's a really interesting thing about the discipline to me, that it is based on forms of relationality that both are taking place in and across the cultures as they meet one another. And they're being formed in the scene of encounter.

 Kath Weston: I think what an anthropologist, or any writer, does with a story depends on what kind of questions they're asking, what they're trying to understand. Not all stories in an anthropological text work the same way. You can tell a story to present illustrative evidence, an example of what you're talking about that supports your argument but doesn't bear the weight of an entire argument. Or maybe you want to bring some dry bit of theory to life so people can say, "OK, I see what you mean. I feel you now." I've often done that. But a story can also do much more than that.

 Take, for example, the concept of political ecologies of the precarious, which I introduced in *Animate Planet*. I developed the concept to convey how people can be seduced into participating in their own demise, in the guise of working against it. At that very moment when they think, "I'm trying to make the world a different place, a more survivable place, a more just place," they're getting hooked into practices, habits, ways of imagining that reinforce the very thing they're fighting against. There's a double move there that's very hard to lay out for a reader. Even as an ethnographer, it can be hard to notice that dynamic as it happens. A story can help.

I've always been a bit of a "theory head," but I've tried in many cases to develop what I've called "embedded theory," where I lay things out in a very intentional order, using a selection of vignettes and narrative juxtapositions to help make an otherwise abstract point in a nuanced way. Then I don't have to hit you over the head as a reader and say: OK, today, class, we are going to study a seriously intimidating multisyllabic concept using other equally enigmatic words. The story becomes a way to prepare the theoretical ground. And from it, you can pull on different threads.

Tyler Bradway: Returning to FWC, something that I find especially important are moments where you address gay liberation and feminist critiques that call for abolishing the family. In contrast, your work seems to ask: what is it exactly that we're calling "the family"? You stress nonidealized ways in which families operate in practice, which are not necessarily encapsulated by this particular abstraction.

Kath Weston: Calls to abolish "the family" assume that family exists as some unified form, albeit perhaps with a range of variants. It's important to unpack this notion of a form and also think carefully about the political implications of "families" plural versus "family" singular. FWC is not called *The Family We Choose* or even *Chosen Family*. If you read my work, you'll notice that I don't write about "the family" unless I'm discussing somebody else who does, and there's a reason for that.

I'm not particularly interested in thinking about families in terms of forms or structures. Why is that? If you're queer, it's obviously difficult to rest easy with the continuous invocation of one hegemonic family form that traffics in heterosexuality, whiteness, class "respectability," etc. But if you then go on to counterpose "chosen family" as some *alternative form* of family, it becomes all too easy to map that so-called form back onto a group of people which is imagined as being bounded and readily denominated: LGBTQ+, you know, they must be the ones with the chosen families, right? Whereas if you actually look at how the term *chosen family* has traveled, you see it being picked up now by all sorts of people, not all of them queer-identified, to talk about something they call family. If you start to fetishize family as a form, then this mapping onto groups starts to happen and you miss all the rest of it: a kind of voluntarism that increasingly crosses identity lines in the US when it comes to claiming nonerotic relations as kin.

In North America the gay liberation and feminist movements historically also entertained calls to abolish the family: families are hierarchical—there are age and gender hierarchies inside families—and we don't want that. The thinking was that if we get rid of "the family," then we make inroads against inequality. "Family" conceived as a form becomes an object of critique because "it" is not doing what you expected it to do or because "-isms" have weaponized or monetized it in some way. But the thing is, almost anything can be monetized or weaponized these days, right? Twenty years ago, who would have thought that a company could fill cans with air from the Canadian Rockies and go to a polluted city and sell them? Who would have thought anyone would pay for that? So saying, you know, let's get rid of the family because there's hierarchy associated with it, or it's a conduit for inequitable wealth transfers between generations, or there's domestic violence that happens in families, well, there's violence that happens on the street. That's why everyone's in the street protesting police violence and racism right now. Systemic violence occurs in many locations. So it doesn't necessarily follow that violence is the inevitable by-product of a particular social form. If you don't deal with whatever keeps generating inequalities and violence, they will begin to permeate whatever new arrangements you put in place.

Elizabeth Freeman: I do want to say that the pressure against the family form, and the relationship between that and critiques of neoliberalism, have to do with what would otherwise be commonly held resources, which are contained by the family and travel along some channels and not others. To be very crudely schematic, it becomes sort of like communism versus the family or socialism versus the family, right? So it really has to do with questions of distribution and allocation.

Kath Weston: That's precisely it. I wrote an essay, "Families in Queer States" (Weston 2005), to help make that case. The problem is not that families continue to be meaningful sources of imperfect support, at least for some people. The problem lies with institutions that insist on addressing needs via kinship. Why can you not lay claim to certain resources and privileges unless you can show that you're in a marriage or that you have legally adopted the person you've raised for fifteen years? Rather than blaming an abstraction called "the family" for that, you could instead critique the demand that kinship must mediate access to resources and entitlements. Call it "distributive injustice."

Elizabeth Freeman: Exactly. And you can imagine a world—and I think this is what a lot of queer work has tried to do—where ameliorating that distributed injustice does not evacuate the structures of affinity, affection, interdependence, and care. It's just somehow prying those two things apart. For example, I remember thinking organized religions can go ahead and bless marriages—that's totally fine. Anybody who wants a particular kind of union could go find a religion that says amen to it. We don't need to get the state involved. It's prying apart those mechanisms for the support of human life from structures of recognition and affection that has been central to queer thinking about kinship.

Kath Weston: For all the work that's been done critiquing dualism and oppositions, there's still a shadow framing of individual versus collective, family versus collective, that creeps back in. But look, there's lots of collective organizing in fascist societies, too, and we're fighting to stop new versions of that coming back. So rather than valorizing the collective or disparaging kinship across the board, why not focus on the doing and what emerges in particular circumstances? What I'm trying to understand in my newer work is a time in which bodies and borders are understood to be more permeable, with no sharp line between collective and individual.

Elizabeth Freeman: So what account of queer kinship could we have in this context? What concepts could take hold of a moment marked by this permeability, this breakdown of subject and object? I'm thinking about very shifting forms of micro-sociability or communality that are produced in this moment, like suddenly we have this idea of "podding" with other households under COVID-19. What do we even call that? You said don't fetishize the form, so it's not important what we call the structure. But what do these micro-social practices tell us about kinship?

Kath Weston: What I'm saying is that we have this nineteenth- and twentieth-century language for social theory that continues to frame questions about kinship, including queer kinship. It's a language predicated on a notion of discrete individuals coming together. They're already imagined as composed and separate before they do something "social" or make alliances. Yet we're living in this moment when kids feel that if the internet goes out, or someone takes away their smartphone, they aren't fully themselves. What does *that* mean for making kin? In *Animate Planet* I wrestle with these problems in a material sense by asking what kind of analytic language can begin to grasp the co-constitution of bodies and industrialized environments.

Take a kid who is growing up and starting to think that they are in some sense queer. Their "I" looks bounded and solid, in the old way of imagining it, but they're actually growing up in a social media era where the "I" is being formed in a different way than it was for my generation. The "I" that experiences itself choosing is arguably not the same "I." If I was researching FWC today, I would have to approach things differently. We need to come up with accounts as well as theories that are adequate to this sort of experience and also the different historical conditions in which people are coming of age.

Suppose you have a young person today whose parent finds out they are not resolutely heterosexual and kicks them out of the house. This sounds like a story I could tell you from the nineties or the seventies or the twenties: painfully familiar. But with COVID-19 we also have lockdown stories: an unprecedented situation in which queer kids who began building chosen families before they legally came of age suddenly find themselves locked down 24/7 for an indeterminate amount of time with their parents. How do we write kinship, or whatever we end up wanting to call it, for these times?

Elizabeth Freeman: You've alluded to your newest project, but it would be great to finish with a description of it, in part because I know there are eager readers out there who will want to know what you are working on right now and how your new project takes up these questions.

Kath Weston: I'm working on a project now about body finance. Right there you can see there's some continuity with my earlier work on the gender/race/class politics of embodiment. When people want to understand finance, and finance these days is pretty complicated, it's hard to understand how it works. NAV, ROIC, ABS, CDO: even the acronyms are daunting. There's been a fair amount of work done on the use of corporeal metaphors such as *savings glut* to characterize financial arrangements. I'm interested in how these metaphors are spun into elaborate organic analogies, as when people explain a financial crisis by saying that credit, as the "lifeblood" of the economy, stopped circulating because the financial system just had a heart attack. Finance has become medicalized, in a way that positions central bankers as physicians ministering to critically ill economies. I'm asking second-order questions about these analogies: Why do bodies remain good to think when it comes to finance, what *sort* of bodies are at issue, and what are the implications for policy? In an effort to answer those questions, I'm going back to seventeenth-century Britain, when scientific investigations of how bodies work coincided with a credit revolution that allowed people to reassign newly invented instruments of credit from one person to another. It's a very important chapter in the history of monetization, which is affecting all our lives now.

At the time, you had lots of debates, not only about how bodies work and the sources of prosperity, but also about generation, another kind of kinship question. Where does money come from? Where do babies come from? These are not unrelated questions, actually, to anyone who's thinking sociohistorically. When financiers these days talk about central banks creating money "out of thin air," they are using a language steeped in old scientific theories about spontaneous generation. Leaders end up debating financial policies in terms that draw heavily on corporeality, but they're talking across one another because they have in mind different moments in the history of medicine, with different theories about how to bring bodies back to health and how organisms (read: money or capital) can multiply. I'm hoping to trace the corporeality forward through blockchain, synthetic biology, and synthetic bonds. It's ambitious. I can't really tell you much more than that because it's too early in the project. You know how these things are: they start out being one thing, and by the time you're finished, they're always different.

Tyler Bradway: One of the mainstays for our collection is John D'Emilio's work. We found ourselves going back to his piece ["Capitalism and Gay Identity," D'Emilio 1983] to think about the formation of gay and lesbian identity as emerging through industrial capitalism, wage labor, and the unbinding of subjects from the nuclear family. Are you seeing a sort of different notion of the social body, and of queerness, emerge from this historical trajectory for finance capital, starting in the seventeenth century, as opposed to the one that we've been more familiar with in queer studies?

Kath Weston: I've always loved that D'Emilio piece. At this point in the project the answer to your question can only be "Probably." But what if we shift your question slightly? Sometimes when critics look at what's happened with people who were doing queer studies back in the 1980s, they'll say these people went on to do "other things." Why "other" what they have done? I don't think I could have conceived *Animate Planet* if I hadn't gotten there through queer kinship. Would I have spent so much time contemplating visceral engagement, noticed how eccentrically blood metaphors travel, or been as quick to denaturalize circulation? I always think it would be interesting to go back and look at some of the people who were very active in writing early material in LGBTQ+ studies, not just John D'Emilio but Ed Cohen and many more, and ask: What if we don't think of the other things they went on to do as being "other"? What if we think of their later work as being a segue that was made possible in important ways, in generative ways, by the work on queer kinship and queer communities that preceded it?

Note

This interview was conducted via Zoom on June 30, 2020. It has been edited for length and clarity. The editors are grateful to Kath Weston for her generosity in agreeing to be interviewed and to be part of this volume.

References

Abani, Chris. 2004. *GraceLand*. New York: Farrar, Straus and Giroux.

Abdur-Rahman, Aliyyah I. 2018. "The Black Ecstatic." *GLQ: A Journal of Lesbian and Gay Studies* 24, nos. 2–3: 343–65.

Adair, Gigi. 2019. *Kinship across the Black Atlantic: Writing Diasporic Relations*. Liverpool, UK: Liverpool University Press.

Adams, David Wallace. 1995. *Education for Extinction: American Indians and the Boarding School Experience, 1875–1928*. Lawrence: University of Kansas Press.

Adams, Katherine. 2019. Email correspondence with Brigitte Fielder, October 21 and 23.

Adams, Katherine, Sandra A. Zagarell, and Caroline Gebhard, eds. 2016. "Recovering Alice Dunbar-Nelson for the Twenty-First Century." Special issue, *Legacy: A Journal of American Women Writers* 33, no. 2.

Agamben, Giorgio. 1995. *Homo Sacer: Sovereign Power and Bare Life*. Translated by Daniel Heller-Roazen. Palo Alto, CA: Stanford University Press.

Agamben, Giorgio. 2009. "The Friend." In *What Is an Apparatus and Other Essays*, translated by David Kishik and Stefan Pedatella. Palo Alto, CA: Stanford University Press.

Agard-Jones, Vanessa. 2012. "What the Sands Remember." *GLQ: A Journal of Lesbian and Gay Studies* 18, nos. 2–3: 325–46.

Ahmed, Sara. 2004. *The Cultural Politics of Emotion*. London: Routledge.

Ahmed, Sara. 2006. *Queer Phenomenology: Orientations, Objects, Others*. Durham, NC: Duke University Press.

Aizura, Aren Z. 2018. *Mobile Subjects: Transnational Imaginaries of Gender Reassignment*. Durham, NC: Duke University Press.

Allen, Jafari S. 2009. "For 'the Children': Dancing the Beloved Community." *Souls: A Critical Journal of Black Politics, Culture and Society* 11, no. 3: 311–26.

Alves, Jaime A. 2018. *The Anti-Black City: Police Terror and Black Urban Life in Brazil*. Minneapolis: University of Minnesota Press.

American Civil Liberties Union. 2002. *Brief Amici Curiae of the American Civil Liberties Union and the ACLU of Texas in Support of Petitioner. Lawrence v. Texas* (No. 02-102): 1–30.

Amin, Kadji. 2014. "Temporality." *Transgender Studies Quarterly* 1, nos. 1–2: 219–22.

Amin, Kadji. 2017. *Disturbing Attachments: Genet, Modern Pederasty, and Queer History*. Durham, NC: Duke University Press.

Amin, Kadji, Amber Jamilla Musser, and Roy Perez. 2017. "Queer Form: Aesthetics, Race, and the Violences of the Social." ASAP/Journal 2, no. 2: 227–39.

Ammons, Elizabeth. 1992. *Conflicting Stories: American Women Writers at the Turn into the Twentieth Century*. New York: Oxford University Press.

Anderson, Benedict. 1983. *Imagined Communities: Reflections on the Origin and Spread of Nationalism*. London: Verso.

Andrade, Oswald de. (1928) 2017. "Manifesto Antropófago." In *Manifesto Antropófago e Outros Textos*, organized by Jorge Schwartz and Gênese Andrade, 43–60. São Paulo, Brazil: Penguin Classics Companhia das Letras.

Anzaldúa, Gloria. 1987. *Borderlands/La Frontera: The New Mestiza*. San Francisco: Aunt Lute.

Arathi, P. M. 2019. "Silent Voices: A Critical Analysis of Surrogacy's Legal Journey in India." *Social Change* 49, no. 2: 344–52.

Aravamudan, Gita. 2014. *Baby Makers: A Story of Indian Surrogacy*. Noida, Uttar Pradesh: HarperCollins Publishers India.

Aristotle. (c. 350 BCE) 1998. *The Nicomachean Ethics*. Edited by J. L. Ackrill and J. O. Urmson. Translated by David Ross. Oxford: Oxford University Press.

Bachelard, Gaston. 1958. *The Poetics of Space*. New York: Penguin Classics.

Bahloul, Joëlle. 1996. *The Architecture of Memory: A Jewish-Muslim Household in Colonial Algeria, 1937–1962*. Cambridge: Cambridge University Press.

Bailey, Marlon M. 2013. *Butch Queens Up in Pumps: Gender, Performance, and Ballroom Culture in Detroit*. Ann Arbor: University of Michigan Press.

Baldwin, James. (1956) 2013. *Giovanni's Room*. New York: Vintage.

Barad, Karen. 2007. *Meeting the Universe Halfway: Quantum Physics and the Entanglement of Matter and Meaning*. Durham, NC: Duke University Press.

Baraitser, Lisa. 2017. *Enduring Time*. London: Bloomsbury.

Barker, Joanne. 2011. *Native Acts: Law, Recognition, and Cultural Authenticity*. Durham, NC: Duke University Press.

Barnett, Randy. 1986. "A Consent Theory of Contract." *Columbia Law Review* 86: 269–321.

Bashford, Alison. 2014. *Global Population: History, Geopolitics, and Life on Earth*. New York: Columbia University Press.

Beauchamp, Toby. 2019. *Going Stealth: Transgender Politics and US Surveillance Practices*. Durham, NC: Duke University Press.

Benjamin, Walter. 1978. "Critique of Violence." In *Reflections: Essays, Aphorisms, Autobiographical Writings*, edited by Peter Demetz, translated by Edmund Jephcott, 277–300. New York: Harcourt Brace.

Bennett, Jane. 2010. *Vibrant Matter: A Political Ecology of Things*. Durham, NC: Duke University Press.

Bentley, Nancy. 2002. "Marriage as Treason: Polygamy, the Nation, and the Novel." In *The Futures of American Studies*, edited by Donald E. Pease and Robin Wiegman, 341–70. Durham, NC: Duke University Press.

Bento, Berenice. 2017. *Transviad@s: Gênero, Sexualidade e Direitos Humanos*. Salvador, Brazil: EdUFBA.

Ben-Zvi, Yael. 2007. "Where Did Red Go? Lewis Henry Morgan's Evolutionary Inheritance and U.S. Racial Imagination." *CR: New Centennial Review* 7, no. 2: 201–29.

Berlant, Lauren. 1998. "Intimacy: A Special Issue." *Critical Inquiry* 24, no. 2: 281–88.

Berlant, Lauren. 2007. "Slow Death (Obesity, Sovereignty, Lateral Agency)." *Critical Inquiry* 33, no. 4: 754–80.

Berlant, Lauren. 2011a. *Cruel Optimism*. Durham, NC: Duke University Press.

Berlant, Lauren. 2011b. "A Properly Political Concept of Love: Three Approaches in Ten Pages." *Cultural Anthropology* 26, no. 4 (November): 683–91.

Berlant, Lauren, and Lee Edelman. 2014. *Sex, or the Unbearable*. Durham, NC: Duke University Press.

Berlant, Lauren, and Michael Warner. 1998. "Sex in Public." *Critical Inquiry* 24, no. 2: 548–66.

Bersani, Leo. 1987. "Is the Rectum a Grave?" *October* 43 (Winter): 197–222.

Bersani, Leo. 1995. *Homos*. Cambridge, MA: Harvard University Press.

Bersani, Leo. 2000. "Sociality and Sexuality." *Critical Inquiry* 26, no. 4: 641–56.

Bersani, Leo. 2002. "Sociability and Cruising." *UMBR(a): A Journal of the Unconscious* 1: 9–24.

Bersani, Leo. 2010. *Is the Rectum a Grave? And Other Essays*. Chicago: University of Chicago Press.

Bey, Marquis. 2017. "The Trans*-ness of Blackness, the Blackness of Trans*-ness." *TSQ: Transgender Studies Quarterly* 4, no. 2: 275–95.

Bey, Marquis. 2019. *Them Goon Rules: Fugitive Essays on Radical Black Feminism*. Tucson: University of Arizona Press.

Bhabha, Homi. 1986. "Foreword: Remembering Fanon." In *Frantz Fanon, Black Skin, White Masks*. London: Pluto.

Bhattacharyya, Swasti. 2006. *Magical Progeny, Modern Technology: A Hindu Bioethics of Assisted Reproductive Technology*. Albany: SUNY Press.

Birth Strike. 2019. https://www.facebook.com/BirthStrikeBook.

Bolick, Kate. 2016. *Spinster: Making a Life of One's Own*. New York: Crown.

Borneman, John. 1996. "Until Death Do Us Part: Marriage/Death in Anthropological Discourse." *American Ethnologist* 23, no. 2: 215–35.

Bossler, Beverly, ed. 2015. *Gender and Chinese History: Transformative Encounters*. Seattle: University of Washington Press.

Bourdieu, Pierre. 1977. *Outline of a Theory of Practice*. Cambridge: Cambridge University Press.

Bowles, Nellie. 2018. "Dorm Living for Professionals." *New York Times*, March 4, 2018, B1.

Bradway, Tyler. 2017. *Queer Experimental Literature: The Affective Politics of Bad Reading*. New York: Palgrave Macmillan.

Bradway, Tyler. 2020. "Inchoate Kinship: Psychoanalytic Narrative and the Performance of Queer Belonging in *Are You My Mother?*" In *The Comics of Alison Bechdel: From the Outside In*, edited by Janine Utell, 148–66. Jackson: University of Mississippi Press.

Bradway, Tyler. 2021. "Queer Narrative Theory and the Relationality of Form." *PMLA* 136, no. 5: 711–27.

Braithwaite, William Stanley. 1901. Book Reviews. *Colored American Magazine* 4, no. 1: 73.

Briggs, Laura. 2012. *Somebody's Children: The Politics of Transracial and Transnational Adoption*. Durham, NC: Duke University Press.

Britzman, Deborah. 1998. *Lost Subjects, Contested Objects: Toward a Psychoanalytic Inquiry of Learning*. Albany: SUNY Press.

Brooks, Kristina. 1998. "Alice Dunbar-Nelson's Local Colors of Ethnicity, Class, and Place." *MELUS* 23, no. 2: 3–26.

Bullock, Steven C. 2011. *Revolutionary Brotherhood: Freemasonry and the Transformation of the American Social Order, 1730–1840*. Chapel Hill: University of North Carolina Press.

Bump, Philip. 2018. "What the Legal Process Looks Like for an Immigrant Child Taken Away from His Parents." *Washington Post*, May 27, 2018. https://www.washingtonpost.com/news/politics/wp/2018/05/27/what-the-legal-process-looks-like-for-an-immigrant-child-taken-away-from-his-parents.

Butler, Judith. (1990) 2007. *Gender Trouble: Feminism and the Subversion of Identity*. New York: Routledge.

Butler, Judith. 1992. "The Body You Want: Liz Kotz Interviews Judith Butler." *Artforum* 31, no. 3: 82–89.

Butler, Judith. 1997. *The Psychic Life of Power: Theories in Subjection*. Palo Alto, CA: Stanford University Press.

Butler, Judith. 2000. *Antigone's Claim: Kinship between Life and Death*. New York: Columbia University Press.

Butler, Judith. 2002. "Is Kinship Always Already Heterosexual?" *differences: A Journal of Feminist Cultural Studies* 13, no. 1: 14–44.

Butler, Judith. 2004. *Undoing Gender*. New York: Routledge.

Butler, Judith. 2015. *Notes toward a Performative Theory of Assembly*. Cambridge, MA: Harvard University Press.

Butler, Judith. 2017. "Breaks in the Bond: Reflections on Kinship Trouble." University College of London Houseman Lecture, published as pamphlet. London: University College of London Department of Greek and Latin.

Butler, Octavia. (1979) 2003. *Kindred*. Boston: Beacon.

Cacho, Lisa Marie. 2012. *Social Death: Racialized Rightlessness and the Criminalization of the Unprotected*. New York: NYU Press.

Cai, Shaoqing. 1984. "On the Origin of the Gelaohui." *Modern China* 10, no. 4: 481–508.

Çalışkan, Dilara. 2019. "Queer Postmemory." *European Journal of Women's Studies* 26, no. 3: 261–73. https://doi.org/10.1177/1350506819860164.

Cameron, Sharon. 1992. *Choosing Not Choosing: Dickinson's Fascicles*. Chicago: University of Chicago Press.

Carpenter, Dale. 2012. *Flagrant Conduct: The Story of Lawrence v. Texas*. New York: W. W. Norton.

Carroll, Clint. 2015. *Roots of Our Renewal: Ethnobotany and Cherokee Environmental Governance*. Minneapolis: University of Minnesota Press.

Carruthers, Charlene A. 2018. *Unapologetic: A Black, Queer, and Feminist Mandate for Radical Movements*. Boston: Beacon.

Carsten, Janet, ed. 2000. *Cultures of Relatedness: New Approaches to the Study of Kinship*. Cambridge: Cambridge University Press.

Carsten, Janet. 2001. "Substantivism, Anti-substantivism, and Anti-anti-substantivism." In *Relative Values: Reconfiguring Kinship Studies*, edited by Sarah Franklin and Susan McKinnon, 29–53. Durham, NC: Duke University Press.

Carsten, Janet. 2004. *After Kinship*. Cambridge: Cambridge University Press.

Cavarero, Adriana. 2005. *For More Than One Voice: Toward a Philosophy of Vocal Expression*. Translated by Paul A. Kottman. Palo Alto, CA: Stanford University Press.

Çelik, Belgin. 2012. *80'lerde Lubunya Olmak*. Black Pink Triangle Izmir Association, Turkey.

Chanter, Tina. 2011. *Whose Antigone? The Tragic Marginalization of Slavery*. Albany: SUNY Press.

Chauí, Marilena. 2000. *Brasil: Mito Fundador e Sociedade Autoritária*. São Paulo, Brazil: Fundação Perseu Abramo.

Chauí, Marilena. 2011. *Between Conformity and Resistance: Essays on Politics, Culture, and the State*. Translated by Maite Conde. New York: Palgrave Macmillan.

Chen, Jian Neo, and micha cárdenas. 2019. "Times to Come: Materializing Trans Times." *TSQ: Transgender Studies Quarterly* 6, no. 4: 472–80.

Chin, Tung Pok, and Winifred C. Chin. 2000. *Paper Son: One Man's Story*. Philadelphia: Temple University Press.

Christian, Shawn Anthony. 2016. "'Upon the Young People of Our Race, by Our Own Literature': Alice Dunbar-Nelson's 'Negro Literature for Negro Pupils.'" *Legacy: A Journal of American Women Writers* 33, no. 2: 267–85.

Chu, Andrea Long. 2019. *Females*. New York: Verso.

Clarke, Adele E. 1998. *Disciplining Reproduction: Modernity, American Life Science, and the Problems of Sex*. Berkeley: University of California Press.

Clarke, Adele, and Donna Haraway, eds. 2018. *Making Kin, Not Population: Reconceiving Generations*. Chicago: Prickly Paradigm.

Clastres, Pierre. (1974) 1989. *Society against the State: Essays in Political Anthropology*. Translated by Robert Hurley and Abe Stein. Brooklyn, NY: Zone.

Cohen, Cathy. 1997. "Punks, Bulldaggers, and Welfare Queens: The Radical Potential of Queer Politics?" *GLQ: A Journal of Lesbian and Gay Studies* 3, no. 4: 437–65.

Cohen, Cathy J. 2010. *Democracy Remixed: Black Youth and the Future of American Politics*. New York: Oxford University Press.

Colen, Shellee. 1986. "'With Respect and Feelings': Voices of West Indian Child Care Workers in New York City." In *All American Women: Lines That Divide, Ties That Bind*, edited by Johnnetta B. Cole, 46–70. New York: Free Press.

Collier, Jane Fishburne, and Sylvia Junko Yanagisako, eds. 1987. *Gender and Kinship: Essays Toward a Unified Analysis*. Palo Alto, CA: Stanford University Press.

Combahee River Collective. 1982. "A Black Feminist Statement." In *All the Women Are White, All the Blacks Are Men, but Some of Us Are Brave: Black Women's Studies*, edited by Gloria T. Hull, Patricia Bell Scott, and Barbara Smith, 13–22. New York: Feminist Press.

Cooper, Melinda. 2017. *Family Values: Between Neoliberalism and the New Social Conservatism*. Cambridge, MA: MIT Press.

Cotera, María Eugenia. 2008. *Native Speakers: Ella Deloria, Zora Neale Hurston, Jovita González, and the Poetics of Culture*. Austin: University of Texas Press.

Coviello, Peter. 2019. *Make Yourselves Gods: Mormons and the Unfinished Business of American Secularism*. Chicago: University of Chicago Press.

Crummell, Alexander. 1969. *Africa and America: Addresses and Discourses*. New York: Negro Universities Press.

Cui, Rounan 催若男. 2017. "Shoupa Zimei: Mingqing Jiangnan diqu changji jiebai xisu yanjiu" 手帕姊妹：明清江南地区娼妓结拜习俗研究 [Handkerchief Sisters: The Study of Ming-Qing Sworn Customs between Courtesans in the Jiangnan Region]. *Wenhua Yichan* 文化遗产 [*Cultural Heritage*] 2: 64–70.

Cvetkovich, Ann. 2003. "AIDS Activism and Public Feelings: Documenting ACT UP's Lesbians." In *An Archive of Feelings: Trauma, Sexuality, and Lesbian Public Cultures*, 156–204. Durham, NC: Duke University Press.

DaMatta, Roberto. 1981. *Relativizando: Uma Introdução à Antropologia Social*. Petrópolis, Brazil: Vozes.

Damon, Frederick H. 1980. "The Kula and Generalised Exchange: Considering Some Unconsidered Aspects of the Elementary Structures of Kinship." *Man*, n.s., 15, no. 2: 267–92.

Danticat, Edwidge. 1994. *Breath, Eyes, Memory*. New York: Soho.

DasGupta, Sayantani, and Shamita Das Dasgupta, eds. 2014. *Globalization and Transnational Surrogacy in India: Outsourcing Life*. New York: Lexington.

Daum, Megan, ed. 2015. *Selfish, Shallow, and Self-Absorbed: Sixteen Writers on the Decision Not to Have Kids*. New York: Picador.

Davies, Ceri. 2006. "'The Truth Is a Thorny Issue': Lesbian Denial in Jackie Kay's *Trumpet*." *Journal of International Women's Studies* 7, no. 3: 5–16.

Davis, Julie Hirschfeld. 2018. "Trump Wants to Use Executive Order to End Birthright Citizenship." *New York Times*, October 30, 2018, A18.

De la Dehesa, Rafael. 2010. *Queering the Public Sphere in Mexico and Brazil: Sexual Rights Movement in Emerging Democracies*. Durham, NC: Duke University Press.

Dean, Jodi. 2019. *Comrade: An Essay on Political Belonging*. London: Verso.

Dean, Tim. 2006. "The Antisocial Homosexual." PMLA 121, no. 3: 826–28.

Dean, Tim. 2009. *Unlimited Intimacy: Reflections on the Subculture of Barebacking*. Chicago: University of Chicago Press.

Dean, Tim, Hal Foster, Kaja Silverman, and Leo Bersani. 1997. "A Conversation with Leo Bersani." *October* 82 (Autumn): 3–16.

DeBernardi, Jean. 2004. *Rites of Belonging: Memory, Modernity, and Identity in a Malaysian Chinese Community*. Palo Alto, CA: Stanford University Press.

Deer, Sarah. 2015. *The Beginning and End of Rape: Confronting Sexual Violence in Native America*. Minneapolis: University of Minnesota Press.

Delany, Samuel R. 1999. *Times Square Red, Times Square Blue*. New York: NYU Press.

Deleuze, Gilles, and Felix Guattari. (1980) 1987. *A Thousand Plateaus: Capitalism and Schizophrenia*. Translated and with a foreword by Brian Massumi. Minneapolis: University of Minnesota Press.

Deloria, Ella. (1944) 1998. *Speaking of Indians*. Lincoln: University of Nebraska Press.

Deloria, Philip J. 1999. *Playing Indian*. New Haven, CT: Yale University Press.

DeMallie, Raymond J. 1994. "Kinship and Biology in Sioux Culture." In *North American Indian Anthropology: Essays on Society and Culture*, edited by Raymond J. DeMallie and Alfonso Ortiz, 125–46. Norman: University of Oklahoma Press.

D'Emilio, John. 1983. "Capitalism and Gay Identity." In *Powers of Desire: The Politics of Sexuality*, edited by Ann Snitow, Christine Stansell, and Sharon Thompson, 100–113. New York: Monthly Review Press.

Dennison, Jean. 2012. *Colonial Entanglement: Constituting a Twenty-First Century Osage Nation*. Chapel Hill: University of North Carolina Press.

Deomampo, Daisy. 2015. *Transnational Reproduction: Race, Kinship, and Commercial Surrogacy in India*. New York: NYU Press.

Derrida, Jacques. 1992. *Given Time*. Chicago: University of Chicago Press.

Derrida, Jacques. (1997) 2006. *The Politics of Friendship*. Translated by George Collins. London: Verso.

Desai, Kishwar. 2014. *Origins of Love*. New York: Simon and Schuster.

Deutscher, Penelope. 2017. *Foucault's Futures: A Critique of Reproductive Reason*. New York: Columbia University Press.

Dinshaw, Carolyn. 1999. *Getting Medieval: Sexualities and Communities, Pre- and Postmodern*. Durham, NC: Duke University Press.

Dinshaw, Carolyn. 2012. *How Soon Is Now? Medieval Texts, Amateur Readers, and the Queerness of Time*. Durham, NC: Duke University Press.

Djao, Wei. 2003. *Being Chinese: Voices from the Diaspora*. Tucson: University of Arizona Press.

D'Orsi, Lorenzo. 2019. "Touching History and Making Community: The Memory of the 1980 Turkish Military Coup in the 12 September Museum of Shame." *History and Anthropology* 30, no. 5: 644–67.

Douglas, Mary. 1991. "The Idea of a Home: A Kind of Space." *Social Research* 58, no. 1: 287–307.

Doyle, Jennifer, and David Getsy. 2013. "Queer Formalisms: Jennifer Doyle and David Getsy in Conversation." *Art Journal* 72, no. 4: 58–71.

Driskill, Qwo-Li, Chris Finley, Brian Joseph Gilley, and Scott Lauria Morgensen. 2011. "Introduction." In *Queer Indigenous Studies: Critical Interventions in Theory, Politics, and Literature*, edited by Qwo-Li Driskill, Chris Finley, Brian Joseph Gilley, and Scott Lauria Morgensen, 1–28. Tucson: University of Arizona Press.

Du Bois, William Edward Burghardt. (1903) 2008. *The Souls of Black Folk*. New York: Oxford University Press.

Duggan, Lisa. 2004. *The Twilight of Equality? Neoliberalism, Cultural Politics, and the Attack on Democracy*. Boston: Beacon.

Dunbar-Nelson, Alice. n.d. "The Child Is Father to the Man." Hand-corrected typescript, Alice Dunbar-Nelson Papers, University of Delaware Special Collections.

Dunbar-Nelson, Alice. 1922. "Negro Literature for Negro Pupils." *Southern Workman* 51, no. 2: 59.

Dunbar-Ortiz, Roxanne. 2014. *An Indigenous Peoples' History of the United States*. Boston: Beacon.

Dussel, Enrique. 1995. *The Invention of the Americas: Eclipse of "the Other" and the Myth of Modernity*. New York: Continuum International.

Eakin, Marshall. C. 2017. *Becoming Brazilians: Race and National Identity in Twentieth-Century Brazil*. Cambridge: Cambridge University Press.

Edelman, Lee. 2004. *No Future: Queer Theory and the Death Drive*. Durham, NC: Duke University Press.

The Edge of Democracy. 2019. Directed by Petra Costa. Produced by Busca Vida Films. Distributed by Netflix.

Ellison, Treva. 2016. "The Strangeness of Progress and the Uncertainty of Blackness." In *No Tea, No Shade: New Writings in Black Queer Studies*, edited by E. Patrick Johnson, 323–45. Durham, NC: Duke University Press.

Ellison, Treva, Kai M. Green, Matt Richardson, and C. Riley Snorton. 2017. "We Got Issues: Toward a Black Trans*/Studies." *TSQ: Transgender Studies Quarterly* 4, no. 2: 162–69.

Endnotes Collective. 2013. "The Logic of Gender: On the Separation of Spheres

and the Process of Abjection." *Endnotes* 3 (September). https://endnotes
.org.uk/issues/3/en/endnotes-the-logic-of-gender.

Eng, David L. 2001. *Racial Castration: Managing Masculinity in Asian America*.
Durham, NC: Duke University Press.

Eng, David L. 2010. *The Feeling of Kinship: Queer Liberalism and the Racialization of
Intimacy*. Durham, NC: Duke University Press.

Eng, David L., and Shinhee Han. 2019. *Racial Melancholia, Racial Dissociation: On
the Social and Psychic Lives of Asian Americans*. Durham, NC: Duke University
Press.

Eng, David L., and David Kazanjian. 2002. "Introduction: Mourning Remains."
In *Loss: The Politics of Mourning*, edited by David L. Eng and David Kazanjian,
1–26. Berkeley: University of California Press.

Engels, Friedrich. 1902. *The Origin of the Family, Private Property, and the State*.
Translated by Ernest Untermann. Chicago: Charles H. Kerr.

Erll, Astrid. 2011. "Locating Family in Cultural Memory Studies." *Journal of Comparative Family Studies* 42, no. 3 (May–June): 303–18.

Erll, Astrid. 2014. "Generation in Literary History: Three Constellations of
Generationality, Genealogy, and Memory." *New Literary History* 45, no. 3:
385–409.

Estes, Nick. 2019. "The US Stole Generations of Indigenous Children to Open the
West." *High Country News*, October 14, 2019. https://www.hcn.org/issues
/51.17/indigenous-affairs-the-us-stole-generations-of-indigenous-children
-to-open-the-west.

Everett, Georgia. 2019. "Trump Plans to 'Extract' DNA from Undocumented
Immigrants." *BioNews*, September 2, 2019. https://www.bionews.org.uk
/page_144664.

Fahs, Breanne. 2014. *Valerie Solanas: The Defiant Life of the Woman Who Wrote SCUM
(and Shot Andy Warhol)*. New York: Feminist Press.

Fanon, Frantz. (1952) 2008. *Black Skin, White Masks*. Translated by Richard Philcox. New York: Grove.

Farah, Nuruddin. 1986. *Maps*. London: Pan/Picador.

Feel Good. 2020. Created by Mae Martin and Joe Hampson. Channel 4, All 4, Netflix.

Feinberg, Leslie. (1993) 2004. *Stone Butch Blues: A Novel*. New York: Alyson.

Felsing, Robert H. 1979. "The Heritage of Han: The Gelaohui and the 1911 Revolution in Sichuan." PhD diss., University of Iowa.

Ferguson, Roderick A. 2004. *Aberrations in Black: Toward a Queer of Color Critique*.
Minneapolis: University of Minnesota Press.

Ferguson, Roderick A. 2019. *One-Dimensional Queer*. Medford, MA: Polity.

Fielder, Brigitte. 2020. *Relative Races: Genealogies of Interracial Kinship in
Nineteenth-Century America*. Durham, NC: Duke University Press.

Floyd, Kevin. 2009. *The Reification of Desire: Toward a Queer Marxism*. Minneapolis:
University of Minnesota Press.

Forster, E. M. 1951. "What I Believe." In *Two Cheers for Democracy*. New York: Harcourt, Brace.

Fortes, Meyer. (1969) 2006. *Kinship and the Social Order: The Legacy of Lewis Henry Morgan*. New Brunswick, NJ: Aldine Transaction.

Fortier, Anne-Marie. 2001. "'Coming Home': Queer Migrations and Multiple Evocations of Home. *European Journal of Cultural Studies* 4, no. 4: 405–24.

Fortier, Anne-Marie. 2003. "Making Home: Queer Migrations and Motions of Attachment." In *Uprootings/Regroundings: Questions of Home and Migration*, edited by Sara Ahmed, Claudia Castañeda, Anne-Marie Fortier, and Mimi Sheller, 115–35. Oxford: Berg.

Foucault, Michel. (1981) 1998. "Friendship as a Way of Life." In *Ethics: Subjectivity and Truth*, edited by Paul Rabinow, 135–40. New York: New Press.

Foucault, Michel. 1988. *The History of Sexuality*. Vol. 3, *The Care of the Self*. New York: Vintage.

Foucault, Michel. 1990. *The History of Sexuality*. New York: Vintage.

Foucault, Michel. 1996. "Friendship as a Way of Life." In *Foucault Live: Interviews 1961–1984*, edited by Sylvère Lotringer, translated by Lysa Hochroth and John Johnston. New York: Semiotext(e).

Foucault, Michel. 2003. *Society Must Be Defended: Lectures at the College De France, 1975–76*. New York: Penguin.

Franklin, Sarah. 2007. *Dolly Mixtures: The Remaking of Genealogy*. Durham, NC: Duke University Press.

Franklin, Sarah. 2013a. *Biological Relatives: IVF, Stem Cells, and the Future of Kinship*. Durham, NC: Duke University Press.

Franklin, Sarah. 2013b. "After IVF: the Reproductive Turn in Social Thought." Sarah Franklin Inaugural Lecture at ReproSoc, University of Cambridge, October 30, 2013.

Franklin, Sarah, and Susan McKinnon, eds. 2001. *Relative Values: Reconfiguring Kinship Studies*. Durham, NC: Duke University Press.

Freeman, Elizabeth. 2002. *The Wedding Complex: Forms of Belonging in Modern American Culture*. Durham, NC: Duke University Press.

Freeman, Elizabeth. 2007. "Queer Belongings: Kinship Theory and Queer Theory." In *A Companion to Lesbian, Gay, Bisexual, Transgender, and Queer Studies*, edited by George E. Haggerty and Molly McGarry, 293–314. Malden, MA: Blackwell.

Freeman, Elizabeth. 2010. *Time Binds: Queer Temporalities, Queer Histories*. Durham, NC: Duke University Press.

Freeman, Elizabeth. 2019. *Beside You in Time: Sense-Methods and Queer Sociabilities in the American Nineteenth Century*. Durham, NC: Duke University Press.

Freud, Sigmund. 1919. "'A Child Is Being Beaten': A Contribution to the Study of the Origins of Sexual Perversions." In *The Standard Edition of the Complete Psychological Works of Sigmund Freud*, translated by A. and J. Strachey, 17:179–204. London: Hogarth.

Freyre, Gilberto. (1933) 1946. *The Masters and the Slaves: A Study in the Development of Brazilian Civilization*. Translated by Samuel Putnam. New York: Knopf.

Fried, Charles. 1981. *Contract as Promise: A Theory of Contractual Obligation*. Cambridge, MA: Harvard University Press.

Fry, Peter. 2005. *A Persistência da Raça: Ensaios Antropológicos Sobre o Brasil e a África*. Rio de Janeiro, Brazil: Civilização Brasileira.

Fry, Richard. 2018. "More Adults in the U.S. Now Share Their Living Space, Driven in Part by Parents Living with Their Adult Children." Pew Research Center, January 31, 2018. https://www.pewresearch.org/fact-tank/2018/01/31/more-adults-now-share-their-living-space-driven-in-part-by-parents-living-with-their-adult-children.

Gardner, Susan. 2000. "Speaking of Ella Deloria: Conversations with Joyzelle Gingway Godfrey, 1998–2000, Lower Brule Community College, South Dakota." *American Indian Quarterly* 24, no. 3: 456–81.

Gebhard, Caroline. 2016. "Masculinity, Criminality, and Race: Alice Dunbar-Nelson's Creole Boy Stories." *Legacy: A Journal of American Women Writers* 33, no. 2: 336–60.

Gebhard, Caroline, and Barbara McCaskill. 2016. "Introduction." In *Post-Bellum, Pre-Harlem: African American Literature and Culture, 1877–1919*, edited by Caroline Gebhard and Barbara McCaskill, 1–16. New York: NYU Press.

George, Orran, and David Booher. 2016. *Made in India*. New York: Createspace.

George, Rosemary M. 1996. *The Politics of Home: Postcolonial Relocations and Twentieth-Century Fiction*. Cambridge: Cambridge University Press.

Gibson, John. 2019. "Who's Having Babies—and When—Has Changed Dramatically in Canada." Canadian Broadcasting Corporation, April 25, 2019. https://www.cbc.ca/news/canada/calgary/canada-women-fertility-rates-kneebone-university-study-1.5110369.

Gill-Peterson, Jules. 2018. "Trans of Color Critique before Transsexuality." *TSQ: Transgender Studies Quarterly* 5, no. 4: 606–20.

Ginsberg, Faye, and Rayna Rapp. 1995. *Conceiving the New World Order: The Global Politics of Reproduction*. Berkeley: University of California Press.

Girard, René. 1977. *Violence and the Sacred*. Translated by Patrick Gregory. Baltimore: Johns Hopkins University Press.

Glissant, Édouard. 1997. *Poetics of Relation*. Ann Arbor: University of Michigan Press.

Goeman, Mishuana. 2017. "Ongoing Storms and Struggles: Gendered Violence and Resource Exploitation." In *Critically Sovereign: Indigenous Gender, Sexuality, and Feminist Studies*, edited by Joanne Barker, 99–126. Durham, NC: Duke University Press.

Golombok, Susan. 2015. *Modern Families: Parents and Children in New Family Forms*. Cambridge: Cambridge University Press.

Gonzalez, Lélia. (1988) 2020. "Por um Feminismo Afro-latino-americano." In

Pensamento Feminista Hoje: Perspectivas Decoloniais, organized by Heloisa Buarque de Hollanda, 38–51. Rio de Janeiro, Brazil: Bazar do Tempo.

Google Baby. 2009. Directed by Zippi Brand Frank. Produced by Brandcom Ltd. Distributed by Filmmakers Library.

Gordon, Avery. 2006. *Ghostly Matters: Haunting and the Sociological Imagination*. Minneapolis: University of Minnesota Press.

Gornick, Vivian. 2015. *The Odd Woman and the City: A Memoir*. New York: Farrar, Straus and Giroux.

Gossett, Reina, Eric A. Stanley, and Johanna Burton, eds. 2017. *Trap Door: Trans Cultural Production and the Politics of Visibility*. Cambridge, MA: MIT Press.

Green, James N. 1999. *Beyond Carnival: Male Homosexuality in Twentieth-Century Brazil*. Chicago: University of Chicago Press.

Green, Kai M. 2016. "Troubling the Waters: Mobilizing a Trans* Analytic." In *No Tea, No Shade: New Writing on Black Queer Studies*, edited by E. Patrick Johnson, 65–82. Durham, NC: Duke University Press.

Grosz, Elizabeth. 2017. *The Incorporeal: Ontology, Ethics, and the Limits of Materialism*. New York: Columbia University Press.

Gutman, Herbert. 1976. *The Black Family in Slavery and Freedom, 1750–1925*. New York: Pantheon.

Guy-Bray, Stephen. 2006. *Loving in Verse: Poetic Influence as Erotic*. Toronto: University of Toronto Press.

Halberstam, Jack (Judith). 2000. "Telling Tales: Brandon Teena, Billy Tipton, and Transgender Biography." *a/b: Auto/Biography Studies* 15, no. 1: 62–81.

Halberstam, Jack. 2005. *In a Queer Time and Place: Transgender Bodies, Subcultural Lives*. New York: NYU Press.

Halberstam, Jack. 2007. "Forgetting Family: Queer Alternatives to Oedipal Relations." In *A Companion to Lesbian, Gay, Bisexual, Transgender, and Queer Studies*, edited by George E. Haggerty and Molly McGarry, 315–24. Malden, MA: Blackwell.

Han, Sora Y. 2012. "The Long Shadow of Racial Profiling." *British Journal of American Legal Studies* 1, no. 1: 77–108.

Hanhardt, Christina B. 2013. *Safe Space: Gay Neighborhood History and the Politics of Violence*. Durham, NC: Duke University Press.

Hansen, Valerie. 1995. *Negotiating Daily Life in Traditional China: How Ordinary People Used Contracts, 600–1400*. New Haven, CT: Yale University Press.

Haraway, Donna. 2016. *Staying with the Trouble: Making Kin in the Chthulucene*. Durham, NC: Duke University Press.

Hargreaves, Tracy. 2003. "The Power of the Ordinary Subversive in Jackie Kay's *Trumpet*." *Feminist Review* 74: 2–16.

Hartman, Saidiya V. 1997. *Scenes of Subjection: Terror, Slavery, and Self-Making in Nineteenth-Century America*. New York: Oxford University Press.

Hartman, Saidiya. 2007. *Lose Your Mother: A Journey along the Atlantic Slave Route*. New York: Farrar, Straus and Giroux.

Hartman, Saidiya. 2019. *Wayward Lives, Beautiful Experiments: Intimate Histories of Social Upheaval*. New York: W. W. Norton.

Hayden, Corinne P. 1995. "Gender, Genetics, and Generation: Reformulating Biology in Lesbian Kinship." *Cultural Anthropology* 10, no. 1: 41–63.

Heath, Terrance. 2006. "A Dignified Burial for Tyrone Garner, Lawrence v. Texas Plaintiff." *Daily Kos* (blog), October 18, 2006. http://www.dailykos.com/story /2006/10/18/258680/-A-Dignified-Burial-for-Tyrone-Garner-Lawrence-v -Texas-Plaintiff.

Hening, William Waller. 1823. *The Statutes at Large; Being a Collection of All the Laws of Virginia, from the First Session of the Legislature in the Year 1619*. New York: printed for the author.

Henriques, Julian. 2011. *Sonic Bodies: Reggae Sound Systems, Performance Techniques, and Ways of Knowing*. New York: Bloomsbury.

Heti, Sheila. 2018. *Motherhood: A Novel*. New York: Henry Holt.

Hickman, Jared. 2014. "*The Book of Mormon* as Amerindian Apocalypse." *American Literature* 86, no. 3: 429–61.

Hill, Christina Gish. 2017. *Webs of Kinship: Family in Northern Cheyenne Nationhood*. Norman: University of Oklahoma Press.

Hind, John. 2006. "Hot Bedding: Why the Nation Shares the Same Bed—for Sleep Shifts." *Guardian*, August 5, 2006. https://www.theguardian.com /lifeandstyle/2006/aug/06/homes.

Hirsch, Marianne. 2008. "The Generation of Postmemory." *Poetics Today* 29, no.1 (Spring): 103–28.

Hirsch, Marianne. 2012. *The Generation of Postmemory: Writing and Visual Culture after the Holocaust*. New York: Columbia University Press.

Hirschi, Hans. 2014. *Dads: A Gay Couple's Surrogacy Journey in India*. London: Yaree AB.

Hobson, Brandon. 2018. *Where the Dead Sit Talking*. New York: Soho.

Hochschild, Arlie. 2012. *The Outsourced Self: Intimate Life in Market Times*. New York: Metropolitan.

Holland, Sharon P. 2012. *The Erotic Life of Racism*. Durham, NC: Duke University Press.

Hull, Akasha (Gloria). 1987. *Color, Sex, and Poetry: Three Women Writers of the Harlem Renaissance*. Bloomington: Indiana University Press.

Hurley, Natasha. 2018. *Circulating Queerness: Before the Gay and Lesbian Novel*. Minneapolis: University of Minnesota Press.

ILGA-Europe. 2020. *Annual Review of the Human Rights Situation of Lesbian, Gay, Transgender, Bisexual and Intersex People*. https://ilga-europe.org/annual review/2020.

Jacobs, Margaret D. 2014. *A Generation Removed: The Fostering and Adoption of Indigenous Children in the Postwar World*. Lincoln: University of Nebraska Press.

Jaquet, Chantal. 2014. *Les Transclasses ou la non-reproduction*. Paris: Presses Universitaires de France.

Joy, Eileen. 2015. "Improbable Manners of Being." GLQ: A Journal of Lesbian and Gay Studies 21, nos. 2–3: 221–24.

Justice, Daniel Heath. 2008. "'Go Away, Water!': Kinship Criticism and the Decolonization Imperative." In Reasoning Together: The Native Critics Collective, edited by Craig S. Womack, Daniel Heath Justice, and Christopher B. Teuton, 147–68. Norman: University of Oklahoma Press.

Justice, Daniel Heath. 2018. Why Indigenous Literatures Matter. Waterloo, ON: Wilfrid Laurier University Press.

Kafer, Alison. 2013. Feminist, Queer, Crip. Bloomington: Indiana University Press.

Kaminsky, Amy K. 1993. Reading the Body Politic: Feminist Criticism and Latin American Women Writers. Minneapolis: University of Minnesota Press.

Kanazawa, Satoshi. 2014. "Intelligence and Childlessness." Social Science Research 48: 157–70.

Kay, Jackie. 1998. Trumpet. London: Picador.

Keeling, Kara. 2019. Queer Times, Black Futures. New York: NYU Press.

Kimmerer, Robin Wall. 2013. Braiding Sweetgrass: Indigenous Wisdom, Scientific Knowledge and the Teachings of Plants. Minneapolis: Milkweed.

Kincaid, James. 1998. Erotic Innocence: The Culture of Child-Molesting. Durham, NC: Duke University Press.

Kipnis, Laura. 2015. "Maternal Instincts." In Selfish, Shallow, and Self-Absorbed: Sixteen Writers on the Decision Not to Have Kids, edited by Megan Daum, 31–46. New York: Picador.

Knadler, Stephen P. 1996. "Untragic Mulatto: Charles Chesnutt and the Discourse of Whiteness." American Literary History 8, no. 3: 426–48.

Koolen, Mandy. 2010. "Masculine Trans-formations in Jackie Kay's Trumpet." Atlantis: Critical Studies in Gender, Culture & Social Justice 35, no. 1: 71–80.

Kosick, Rebecca. 2019. "Decolonial Developments: Participatory Politics and Experimental Poetics in Ferreira Gullar's Writing 1957–1975." College Literature 46, no. 1: 127–50.

Kothari, Falguni. 2019. The Object of Your Affections. New York: Graydon House.

Lai, H. Mark, Genny Lim, and Judy Yung. 2014. Island: Poetry and History of Chinese Immigrants on Angel Island, 1910–1940. Seattle: University of Washington Press.

Lane-McKinley, Madeline, and Marija Cetinic. 2015. "Theses on Postpartum." Guts, May 22, 2015. http://gutsmagazine.ca/theses-on-postpartum.

Latour, Bruno. 2005. Reassembling the Social: An Introduction to Actor-Network Theory. Oxford: Oxford University Press.

Lau, Jacob Roberts. 2016. "Between the Times: Trans-Temporality, and Historical Representation." PhD diss., University of California, Los Angeles.

Lee, Summer Kim. 2019. "Staying In: Mitski, Ocean Vuong, and Asian American Asociality." Social Text 138, no. 1: 27–50.

Le Guin, Ursula K. (1973) 1975. "The Ones Who Walk Away from Omelas." In The Wind's Twelve Quarters, 251–59. New York: Bantam Books.

Levine, Caroline. 2015. *Forms: Whole, Rhythm, Hierarchy, Network*. Princeton, NJ: Princeton University Press.

Lévi-Strauss, Claude. 1969. *The Elementary Structures of Kinship*. Edited by Rodney Needham, translated by James Harle Bell and John Richard von Sturmer. Boston: Beacon.

Lewin, Ellen. 1993. *Lesbian Mothers: Accounts of Gender in American Culture*. Ithaca, NY: Cornell University Press.

Lewin, Ellen. 1998. *Recognizing Ourselves: Ceremonies of Lesbian and Gay Commitment*. New York: Columbia University Press.

Lewis, Mark E. 1990. *Sanctioned Violence in Early China*. Albany: SUNY Press.

Lewis, Sophie. 2019. *Full Surrogacy Now: Feminism against Family*. London: Verso.

Lew-Williams, Beth. 2018. *The Chinese Must Go: Violence, Exclusion, and the Making of the Alien in America*. Cambridge, MA: Harvard University Press.

Li, Peter S. 1977. "Fictive Kinship, Conjugal Tie and Kinship Chain among Chinese Immigrants in the United States." *Journal of Comparative Family Studies* 8, no. 1: 47–63.

Li, Xiaomeng. 2020. "Queerbaiting and Queer Excess in Contemporary China: Examining Producer, Viewer, and State Practices around the Guardian Web Series." Paper presented at the annual meeting for the Modern Literature Association, Seattle, Washington, January 11.

Lindsey, Karen. 1994. "Friends as Family: No One Said It Would Be Easy." In *Living with Contradictions: Controversies in Feminist Social Ethics*, edited by Alison M. Jaggar, 467–71. San Francisco: Westview.

Livingston, Gretchen. 2015. "Childlessness." Pew Research Center, May 7, 2015. https://www.pewsocialtrends.org/2015/05/07/childlessness.

Lo, Guotong. 2015. "The Control of Female Energies: Gender and Ethnicity on China's Southeast Coast." In *Gender and Chinese History: Transformative Encounters*, edited by Beverly Bossler, 41–57. Seattle: University of Washington Press.

Lomawaima, K. Tsianina. 1994. *They Called It Prairie Light: The Story of Chilocco Indian School*. Lincoln: University of Nebraska Press.

Lorde, Audre. 1978. "Uses of the Erotic." In *Sister Outsider: Essays and Speeches*, 53–59. Freedom, CA: Crossing.

Lorde, Audre. 1982. *Zami: A New Spelling of My Name*. Trumansburg, NY: Crossing.

Lorde, Audre. 1984. *Sister Outsider: Essays and Speeches*. Trumansburg, NY: Crossing.

Love, Heather. 2007. *Feeling Backward: Loss and the Politics of Queer History*. Cambridge, MA: Harvard University Press.

Love, Heather. 2010. "Close but Not Deep: Literary Ethics and the Descriptive Turn." *New Literary History* 41, no. 2: 371–91.

Luibhéid, Eithne. 2002. *Entry Denied: Controlling Sexuality at the Border*. Minneapolis: University of Minnesota Press.

Luo, Guanzhong. 2002. *Romance of the Three Kingdoms*. Translated by C. H. Brewitt-Taylor. Boston: Tuttle.

Machado, Alisson. 2018. "Bento, Berenice. 2017. *Transviad@s: gênero, sexualidade e direitos humanos*." *Anuário Antropológico* 2: 371–75.

Macharia, Keguro. 2019. *Frottage: Frictions of Intimacy across the Black Diaspora*. New York: NYU Press.

Made in India: A Film about Surrogacy. 2010. Directed by Rebecca Haimowitz and Vaishali Sinha. Produced by Rebecca Haimowitz and Vaishali Sinha. Distributed by Women Make Movies.

Majumdar, Anindita. 2017. *Transnational Commercial Surrogacy and the (Un)Making of Kin in India*. Oxford: Oxford University Press.

Malladi, Amulya. 2017. *House for Happy Mothers*. New York: Lake Union.

Manalansan, Martin F. IV. 2005. "Race, Violence, and Neoliberal Spatial Politics in the Global City." *Social Text* 84–85, nos. 3–4: 141–55.

Manalansan, Martin F. 2019. "Enmeshment: Queer Togetherness and Care." Unpublished manuscript from Global Queer Studies Lecture series, Wesleyan University, April 4, 2019.

Marcus, Sharon, and Stephen Best. 2009. "Surface Reading: An Introduction." *Representations* 108, no. 1: 1–21.

Martín-Barbero, Jesús. (1987) 1997. *Dos Meios às Mediações: Comunicação, Cultura e Hegemonia*. Translated by Ronald Polito and Sérgio Alcides. Rio de Janeiro, Brazil: Editora UFRJ.

Martinot, Steve, and Jared Sexton. 2003. "The Avant-Garde of White Supremacy." *Social Identities* 9, no. 2: 169–81.

Mauss, Marcel. 2002. *The Gift: The Form and Reason for Exchange in Archaic Societies*. Foreword by Mary Douglas, translated by W. D. Halls. London: Routledge.

McCarthy, Theresa. 2016. *In Divided Unity: Haudenosaunee Reclamation at Grand River*. Tucson: University of Arizona Press.

McKinnon, Susan. 2001. "The Economies in Kinship and the Paternity of Culture: Origin Stories in Kinship Theory." In *Relative Values: Reconfiguring Kinship Studies*, edited by Sarah Franklin and Susan McKinnon, 277–301. Durham, NC: Duke University Press.

McKittrick, Katherine, ed. 2015. *Sylvia Wynter: On Being Human as Praxis*. Durham, NC: Duke University Press.

Meillassoux, Claude. 1991. *The Anthropology of Slavery: The Womb of Iron and Gold*. Chicago: University of Chicago Press.

Menke, Pamela Glenn. 2002. "Behind the Veil: Alice Dunbar-Nelson, Creole Color and 'The Goodness of St. Rocque.'" In *Songs of the Reconstructing South: Building Literary Louisiana, 1865–1945*, edited by Suzanne Disheroon-Green and Lisa Abney, 77–88. Westport, CT: Greenwood.

Menon, Madhavi. 2019. "Surrogacy (Regulation) Bill Punishes Women for Being Independent, Mystifies Motherhood as Sacred." *Scroll.in*, August 6, 2019.

https://scroll.in/article/932879/surrogacy-regulation-bill-punishes-women-for-being-independent-mystifies-motherhood-as-sacred.

Mignolo, Walter. 2000. *Local Histories/Global Designs: Coloniality, Subaltern Knowledges, and Border Thinking*. Princeton, NJ: Princeton University Press.

Ministry of Law and Justice of India, Legislative Department. 1955. The Hindu Marriage Act, 1955. Act ID: 195525, enacted May 5.

Ministry of Law and Justice of India, Legislative Department. 1956. The Hindu Adoption and Maintenance Act, 1956. Act ID: 195687, enacted December 12.

Mitchell, Ernest Julius, II. 2010. "'Black Renaissance': A Brief History of the Concept." *Amerikastudien/American Studies* 55, no. 4: 641–65.

Montaigne, Michel de. (1580) 1897. "On Friendship." In *The Essayes of Michael Lord of Montaigne*, translated by John Florio, *The First Booke, Volume 2*, edited by A. R. Waller. London: J.M. Dent.

Montgomery-Anderson, Brad. 2015. *Cherokee Reference Grammar*. Norman: University of Oklahoma Press.

Mooney, James. 1995. *Myths of the Cherokee*. New York: Dover.

Morgan, Jennifer L. 2004. *Laboring Women: Reproduction and Gender in New World Slavery*. Philadelphia: University of Pennsylvania Press.

Morgan, Jennifer L. 2018. "*Partus Sequitur Ventrem*: Law, Race, and Reproduction in Colonial Slavery." *Small Axe* 55, no. 1: 1–17.

Morgan, Lewis Henry. (1877) 1977. *Ancient Society, or Researches in the Lines of Human Progress from Savagery through Barbarism to Civilization*. New York: Gordon.

Morris, Thomas D. 1996. *Southern Slavery and the Law, 1619–1860*. Chapel Hill: University of North Carolina Press.

Mota, Carlos. G. 1977. *Ideologia da Cultura Brasileira (1933–1974)*. São Paulo, Brazil: Editora Ática.

Moten, Fred. 2003. *In the Break: The Aesthetics of the Black Radical Tradition*. Minneapolis: University of Minnesota Press.

Moten, Fred. 2013. "Blackness and Nothingness (Mysticism in the Flesh)." *South Atlantic Quarterly* 112, no. 4: 737–80.

Moynihan, Daniel Patrick. 1965. *The Negro Family: The Case for National Action*. Washington, DC: US Department of Labor Office of Policy Planning and Research.

Mullings, Leith, and Alaka Wali. 2001. *Stress and Resilience: The Social Context of Reproduction in Central Harlem*. New York: Kluwer Academic/Plenum.

Muñoz, José Esteban. 1999. *Disidentifications: Queers of Color and the Performance of Politics*. Minneapolis: University of Minneapolis Press.

Muñoz, José Esteban. 2009. *Cruising Utopia: The Then and There of Queer Futurity*. New York: NYU Press.

Murphy, Michelle. 2017a. "Alterlife and Decolonial Chemical Relations." *Cultural Anthropology* 32, no. 4: 494–503.

Murphy, Michelle. 2017b. "Distributed Reproduction." In *The Economization of Life*, 135–45. Durham, NC: Duke University Press.

Murphy, Michelle. 2018. "Against Population, Towards Alterlife." In *Making Kin Not Population: Reconceiving Generations*, edited by Adele Clarke and Donna Haraway, 101–24. Chicago: Prickly Paradigm.

Murray, Dian H., and Baoqi Qin. 1994. *The Origins of the Tiandihui: The Chinese Triads in Legend and History*. Palo Alto, CA: Stanford University Press.

Musser, Amber Jamilla. 2020. "Sweat." *Social Text Periscope*, April 27. https://social textjournal.org/periscope_article/sweat.

Nagle, Rebecca. 2019. "The Next Battleground." *This Land*, episode 8, July 22. Podcast. https://crooked.com/podcast/this-land-episode-8-the-next -battleground.

Namaste, Viviane. 1996. "'Tragic Misreadings': Queer Theory's Erasure of Transgender Identity." In *Queer Studies: A Lesbian, Gay, Bisexual and Transgender Anthology*, edited by Brett Beemyn and Mickey Eliason, 183–203. New York: NYU Press.

Nash, Jennifer C. 2013. "Practicing Love: Black Feminism, Love-Politics, and Post-Intersectionality." *Meridians* 11, no. 2: 1–24.

Nealon, Christopher. 2001. *Foundlings: Gay and Lesbian Historical Emotion before Stonewall*. Durham, NC: Duke University Press.

Newman, Matthew, and Kathryn Fort. 2017. "Legal Challenges to ICWA: An Analysis of Current Case Law." *American Bar Association Child Law Practice Today* 36, no. 1: 13–15.

Ngai, Sianne. 2005. *Ugly Feelings*. Cambridge, MA: Harvard University Press.

Ngai, Sianne. 2015. *Our Aesthetic Categories: Zany, Cute, Interesting*. Cambridge, MA: Harvard University Press.

Norman, S.J, and Joseph M. Pierce. 2020. "Liminal Tension/Liminal Gifts: SJ Norman in Conversation with Joseph M. Pierce." *Critical Correspondence*, March 20, 2020. https://movementresearch.org/publications/critical -correspondence/sj-norman-in-conversation-with-joseph-m-pierce.

NYC Health. 2020. "Safer Sex and COVID-19." https://www1.nyc.gov/assets/doh /downloads/pdf/imm/covid-sex-guidance.pdf.

Nyong'o, Tavia. 2018. *Afro-fabulations: The Queer Drama of Black Life*. New York: NYU Press.

O'Brien, Brendan. 2016. "Ohio Woman Sues Sperm Bank after Birth of Mixed-Race Baby." *U.S. Legal News*, April 22, 2016. https://www.reuters.com/article /illinois-sperm/ohio-woman-sues-sperm-bank-after-birth-of-mixed-race -baby-idUSL2N17P1OA.

O'Connor, Joe. 2012. "Trend of Couples Not Having Children Just Plain Selfish." *National Post*, September 19, 2012. https://nationalpost.com/opinion /joe-oconnor-selfishness-behind-growing-trend-for-couples-to-not-have -children.

Okiji, Fumi. 2018. *Jazz as Critique: Adorno and Black Expression Revisited*. Palo Alto, CA: Stanford University Press.

Overall, Christine. 2012. *Why Have Children? The Ethical Debate*. Cambridge, MA: MIT Press.

Ownby, David. 1996. *Brotherhoods and Secret Societies in Early and Mid-Qing China: The Formation of a Tradition*. Stanford, CA: Stanford University Press.

"Painful Truth: No Baby Boom Coming Out of Coronavirus Quarantines." 2020. *Today in BC*, April 9, 2020. https://www.todayinbc.com/opinion/painful -truth-no-baby-boom-coming-out-of-coronavirus-quarantines.

Pande, Amrita. 2009. "It May Be Her Eggs but It's My Blood: Surrogates and Everyday Forms of Kinship in India." *Qualitative Sociology* 32, no. 4: 379–97.

Pande, Amrita. 2010. "Commercial Surrogacy in India: Manufacturing a Perfect Mother-Worker." *Signs: Journal of Women in Culture and Society* 35, no. 4: 969–92.

Pande, Amrita. 2014. *Wombs in Labor: Transnational Commercial Surrogacy in India*. New York: Columbia University Press.

Pande, Amrita. 2016. "Global Reproductive Inequalities, Neo-eugenics and Commercial Surrogacy in India." *Current Sociology* 64, no. 2: 244–58.

Paris Is Burning. 1990. Directed by Jennie Livingston. Produced by Academy Entertainment. Distributed by Off-White Productions.

Parliament of India, Rajya Sabha, Department-Related Parliamentary Standing Committee on Health and Family Welfare. 2017. *One Hundred Second Report on the Surrogacy (Regulation) Bill 2016*. New Delhi: Rajya Sabha Secretariat, August.

Parliament of India, Rajya Sabha. 2018. Surrogacy (Regulation) Bill, 2018, Bill No. 257-C of 2016. Passed by Lok Sabha on December 12.

Pasternak, Shiri. 2019. *Grounded Authority: The Algonquins of Barriere Lake against the State*. Minneapolis: University of Minnesota Press.

Patterson, Orlando. 1982. *Slavery and Social Death*. Cambridge, MA: Harvard University Press.

Patterson, Orlando. 2018. *Slavery and Social Death: A Comparative Study, with a New Preface*. Cambridge, MA: Harvard University Press.

Paugh, Katherine. 2017. *Politics of Reproduction: Race, Medicine, and Fertility in the Age of Abolition*. Oxford: Oxford University Press.

Pearce, Ruth. 2018. "Trans Temporalities and Non-Linear Ageing." In *Older Lesbian, Gay, Bisexual and Trans People: Minding the Knowledge Gaps*, edited by Andrew King, Kathryn Almack, Yiu-Tung Suen, and Sue Westwood, 61–74. New York: Routledge.

Peletz, Michael G. 1995. "Kinship Studies in Late Twentieth-Century Anthropology." *Annual Review of Anthropology* 24: 343–72.

Perdue, Theda. 1998. *Cherokee Women: Gender and Culture Change, 1700–1835*. Lincoln: University of Nebraska Press.

Perreau, Bruno. 2012. *Penser L'adoption: La Gouvernance Pastorale du Genre*. Paris: Presses Universitaires de France.

Perrone, Charles. A. 1996. *Seven Faces: Brazilian Poetry since Modernism*. Durham, NC: Duke University Press.

Peterson, Dawn. 2017. *Indians in the Family: Adoption and the Politics of Antebellum Expansion*. Cambridge, MA: Harvard University Press.

Pexa, Christopher. 2019. *Translated Nation: Rewriting the Dakota Oyáte*. Minneapolis: University of Minnesota Press.

Philadelphia. 1993. Directed by Jonathan Demme. Produced by Clinica Estetico and TriStar Pictures. Distributed by TriStar Pictures.

Phillips, Anne. 2013. *Our Bodies, Whose Property?* Princeton, NJ: Princeton University Press.

Phillips, Caryl. 1993. *Crossing the River*. London: Bloomsbury.

Picchi, Aimee. 2016. "Young Adults Living with Their Parents Hits a 75-year High." CBS News, December 21, 2016. https://www.cbsnews.com/news /percentage-of-young-americans-living-with-their-parents-is-40-percent -a-75-year-high.

Piepzna-Samarasinha, Leah Lakshmi. 2018. *Care Work: Dreaming Disability Justice*. Vancouver, BC: Arsenal Pulp.

Pierce, Joseph M. 2015. "In Search of an Authentic Indian: Notes on the Self." *Indian Country Today*, July 28, 2015. https://indiancountrytoday.com/archive /in-search-of-an-authentic-indian-notes-on-the-self-tm5fCGkRpE-ZOIy3 _SVUiA.

Pierce, Joseph M. 2017. "Trace, Blood, and Native Authenticity." *Critical Ethnic Studies* 3, no. 2: 57–76.

Pierce, Joseph M. 2022. "Allotment Speculations: The Emergence of Land Memory." In *Allotment Stories: Indigenous Responses to Settler Colonial Land Privatization*, edited by Daniel Heath Justice and Jean O'Brien, 63–73. Minneapolis: University of Minnesota Press.

Plato. (c. 385–370 BCE) 2009. *The Symposium*. Translated by Robin Waterfield. Oxford: Oxford University Press.

Posner, Eric A. 1997. "Altruism, Status, and Trust in the Law of Gifts and Gratuitous Promises." *Wisconsin Law Review*: 567–609.

Povinelli, Elizabeth. 2002. *The Cunning of Recognition: Indigenous Alterities and the Making of Australian Multiculturalism*. Durham, NC: Duke University Press.

Povinelli, Elizabeth. 2006. *The Empire of Love: Toward a Theory of Intimacy, Genealogy, and Carnality*. Durham, NC: Duke University Press.

Povinelli, Elizabeth. 2011. *Economies of Abandonment: Social Belonging and Endurance in Late Liberalism*. Durham, NC: Duke University Press.

Power, Nina. 2009. "Non-reproductive Futurism: Rancière's Rational Equality against Edelman's Body Apolitic." *Borderlands* 8, no. 2: 1–16. https://research online.rca.ac.uk/id/eprint/1464.

Pratt, Richard Henry. 1892. "The Advantages of Mingling Indians with Whites."

In *Proceedings of the National Conference of Charities and Correction*, edited by Isabel C. Barrows, 45–59. Boston: George H. Ellis.

Preston, John. 1995. Introduction to *Friends and Lovers: Gay Men Write about the Families They Create*, edited by John Preston and Michael Lowenthal, 1–10. New York: Dutton.

Puar, Jasbir K. 2007. *Terrorist Assemblages: Homonationalism in Queer Times*. Durham, NC: Duke University Press.

Puar, Jasbir. 2013. "Rethinking Homonationalism." *International Journal of Middle East Studies* 45, no. 2: 336–39.

Puar, Jasbir K. 2017. *The Right to Maim: Debility, Capacity, Disability*. Durham, NC: Duke University Press.

Puar, Jasbir, and Maya Mikdashi. 2012. "Pinkwatching and Pinkwashing: Interpenetration and Its Discontents." *Jadaliyya*, August 9, 2012. http://www.jadaliyya.com/pages/index/6774/pinkwatching-and-pinkwashing_interpenetration-and-its-Discontents.

Qadeer, I., and Mary John. 2009. "The Business and Ethics of Surrogacy." *Economic and Political Weekly* 44, no. 2: 10–12.

Quashie, Kevin. 2012. *The Sovereignty of Quiet: Beyond Resistance in Black Culture*. New Brunswick, NJ: Rutgers University Press.

Quinlan, Susan. 2002. "Cross-Dressing: Silviano Santiago's Fictional Performances." In *Lusosex: Gender and Sexuality in the Portuguese Speaking World*, edited by Susan Quinlan and Fernando Arenas, 208–32. Minneapolis: University of Minnesota Press.

Ramos, Joanne. 2019. *The Farm: A Novel*. New York: Random House.

Rancière, Jacques. 2004. *The Politics of Aesthetics: The Distribution of the Sensible*. Translated by Gabrielle Rockhill. London: Continuum.

Rechy, John. 1963. *City of Night*. New York: Grove.

Recollet, Karyn. 2018. "Kinstillatory Gathering." *C Magazine* 136. https://cmagazine.com/issues/136.

Recollet, Karyn, and Emily Johnson. 2019. "Kin-dling and Other Radical Relationalities." In "Sovereign Movements: Native Dance and Performance," edited by Rosy Simas and Ahimsa Timoteo Bodhrán, special issue, *Movement Research Performance Journal* 52/53: 18–23.

Reddy, Chandan. 2011. *Freedom with Violence: Race, Sexuality, and the US State*. Durham, NC: Duke University Press.

Reid-Pharr, Robert F. 1999. *Conjugal Union: The Body, the House, and the Black American*. New York: Oxford University Press.

Reid-Pharr, Robert. 2007. *Once You Go Black: Choice, Desire, and the Black American Intellectual*. New York: NYU Press.

Rich, Adrienne. 1980. "Compulsory Heterosexuality and Lesbian Existence." *Signs: Journal of Women in Culture and Society* 5, no. 4: 631–60.

Richardson, Matt. 2012. "'My Father Didn't Have a Dick': Social Death and Jackie Kay's *Trumpet*." *GLQ: A Journal of Lesbian and Gay Studies* 18, nos. 2–3: 361–79.

Richardson, Matt. 2013. "'Make It Up and Trace It Back': Remembering Black Trans Subjectivity in Jackie Kay's *Trumpet*." In *The Queer Limit of Black Memory: Black Lesbian Literature and Irresolution*, 107–35. Columbus: Ohio State University Press.

Rifkin, Mark. 2006. "Romancing Kinship: A Queer Reading of Indian Education and Zitkala-Ša's *American Indian Stories*." GLQ: *A Journal of Lesbian and Gay Studies* 12, no. 1: 27–59.

Rifkin, Mark. 2011. *When Did Indians Become Straight?: Kinship, the History of Sexuality, and Native Sovereignty*. New York: Oxford University Press.

Rifkin, Mark. 2017. *Beyond Settler Time: Temporal Sovereignty and Indigenous Self-Determination*. Durham, NC: Duke University Press.

Roach, Tom. 2012. *Friendship as a Way of Life: Foucault, AIDS, and the Politics of Shared Estrangement*. Albany: SUNY Press.

Robcis, Camille. 2013. *The Law of Kinship: Anthropology, Psychoanalysis, and the Family in France*. Ithaca, NY: Cornell University Press.

Roberts, Dorothy. 1997. *Killing the Black Body: Race, Reproduction, and the Meaning of Liberty*. New York: Vintage.

Roberts, Sam. 2010. "Extended Family Households Are on Rise." *New York Times*, March 19, 2010, A12.

Rocha, Luciane. 2012. "Black Mothers' Experiences of Violence in Rio de Janeiro." *Cultural Dynamics* 24, no. 1: 59–73.

Rodríguez, Juana María. 2014. *Sexual Futures, Queer Gestures, and Other Latina Longings*. New York: NYU Press.

Rodríguez, Richard T. 2009. *Next of Kin: The Family in Chicano/a Politics*. Durham, NC: Duke University Press.

Roebuck, Christopher. 2013. "Tyranny of the Couple, or Anthropology—Kinship—Marriage." Unpublished manuscript on file with the author.

Rohy, Valerie. 2012. "On Homosexual Reproduction." *differences: A Journal of Feminist Cultural Studies* 23, no. 1: 101–30.

Rohy, Valerie. 2017. "Exchanging Hours: A Dialogue on Time." GLQ: *A Journal of Lesbian and Gay Studies* 23, no. 2: 247–68.

Roscoe, Will. 1991. *The Zuni Man-Woman*. Albuquerque: University of New Mexico Press.

Ross, Marlon. 2004. *Manning the Race: Reforming Black Men in the Jim Crow Era*. New York: NYU Press.

Rowe, Desireé. 2013. "The (Dis)appearance of *Up Your Ass*: Valerie Solanas as Abject Revolutionary." *Rethinking History: The Journal of Theory and Practice* 17, no. 1: 74–81.

Rubin, Gayle. 1975. "The Traffic in Women: Notes on the 'Political Economy' of Sex." In *Toward an Anthropology of Women*, edited by Rayna Rapp Reiter, 157–210. New York: Monthly Review Press.

Rubin, Gayle. 1984. "Thinking Sex: Notes for a Radical Theory of the Politics of

Sexuality." In *Pleasure and Danger: Exploring Female Sexuality*, edited by Carole S. Vance, 1–27. Boston: Routledge and Kegan Paul.

Rubin, Gayle. (1994) 2011. "Sexual Traffic: Interview with Gayle Rubin by Judith Butler." In *Deviations: A Gayle Rubin Reader*, 276–309. Durham, NC: Duke University Press.

Rudrappa, Sharmila. 2015. *Discounted Life: The Price of Global Surrogacy in India.* New York: NYU Press.

Ryle, Gilbert. (1949) 2002. *The Concept of Mind.* Chicago: University of Chicago Press.

Sahlins, Marshall. 2013. *What Kinship Is—and Is Not.* Chicago: University of Chicago Press.

Samuels, Ellen, and Elizabeth Freeman. 2021. "Introduction." *Crip Temporalities.* Special issue, *South Atlantic Quarterly* 121: 245–54.

Sandefur, Timothy. 2017/2018. "Suffer the Little Children." *Regulation: The Cato Review of Business and Government* 40, no. 4: 16–20.

Sandler, Lauren. 2013. "The Childfree Life: Where Having It All Means Not Having Children." *Time*, August 12, 2013. https://time.com/241/having-it-all-without-having-children/.

Sanger-Katz, Margaret, and Noah Weiland. 2020. "Trump Administration Erases Transgender Civil Rights Protections in Health Care." *New York Times*, June 12, 2020. https://www.nytimes.com/2020/06/12/us/politics/trump-transgender-rights.html.

Santiago, Silviano. (1971) 2002. *The Space In-Between: Essays on Latin American Culture.* Edited by Ana Lúcia Gazzola, translated by Tom Burns, Ana Lúcia Gazzola, and Gareth Williams. Durham, NC: Duke University Press.

Savcı, Evren. 2018. "Transing Religious Studies: Beyond the Secular/Religious Binary." *Journal of Feminist Studies in Religion* 34, no. 1: 63–68.

Scheper-Hughes, Nancy. 2001. "Bodies for Sale—Whole or in Parts." *Body & Society* 7, nos. 2–3: 1–8.

Schneider, David. 1980. *American Kinship: A Cultural Account.* Chicago: University of Chicago Press.

Schneider, David M. 1984. *A Critique of the Study of Kinship.* Ann Arbor: University of Michigan Press.

Schulman, Sarah. 2011. "Israel and 'Pinkwashing.'" *New York Times*, November 22, 2011. https://www.nytimes.com/2011/11/23/opinion/pinkwashing-and-israels-use-of-gays-as-a-messaging-tool.html.

Schulman, Sarah, and Karma R. Chávez. 2019. "Israel/Palestine and the Queer International," interview from August 28, 2013. In "Palestine on the Air," by Karma R. Chávez. Supplement, *Journal of Civil and Human Rights* 5: 139–57. https://doi.org/10.5406/jcivihumarigh.2019.0139.

Schumaker, Erin. 2020. "How to Form a COVID-19 Social Bubble." *ABC News*, June 20, 2020. https://abcnews.go.com/Health/form-covid-19-social-bubble/story?id=70912495.

Schurr, Carolin, and Elisabeth Militz. 2018. "The Affective Economy of Transnational Surrogacy." *Environment and Planning A: Economy and Space* 50, no. 8: 1626–45.

Schwarz, Roberto. 1992. *Misplaced Ideas: Essays on Brazilian Culture*. Translated by John Gledson. London: Verso.

Schweik, Susan. 2009. *The Ugly Laws: Disability in Public*. New York: NYU Press.

Sedgwick, Eve Kosofsky. 1985. *Between Men: English Literature and Male Homosocial Desire*. New York: Columbia University Press.

Sedgwick, Eve Kosofsky. 1993. *Tendencies*. Durham, NC: Duke University Press.

Sedgwick, Eve Kosofsky. 1997. "Paranoid Reading and Reparative Reading; or, You're So Paranoid, You Probably Think This Introduction Is About You." In *Novel Gazing: Queer Readings in Fiction*, 1–37. Durham, NC: Duke University Press.

Sedgwick, Eve Kosofsky. 2003. *Touching Feeling: Affect, Pedagogy, Performativity*. Durham, NC: Duke University Press.

Seitler, Dana. 2019. *Reading Sideways: The Queer Politics of Art in Modern American Fiction*. New York: Fordham University Press.

Shah, Nayan. 2001. *Contagious Divides: Epidemics and Race in San Francisco's Chinatown*. Berkeley: University of California Press.

Shah, Nayan. 2012. *Stranger Intimacy: Contesting Race, Sexuality, and Law in the North American West*. Berkeley: University of California Press.

Shao, Yong 邵雍. 1991. "Gelaohui yu Xinhai geming" 哥老会与辛亥革命 [Gelaohui and Xinhai Revolution]. Shanghai shifan daxue xuebao 上海师范大学学报 [Shanghai Normal University Journal] 3: 50–55.

Shaputis, Kathleen. 2004. *The Crowded Nest Syndrome: Surviving the Return of Adult Children*. Olympia, WA: Clutter Fairy.

Sharpe, Christina. 2016a. *In the Wake: On Blackness and Being*. Durham, NC: Duke University Press.

Sharpe, Christina. 2016b. "Lose Your Kin." *New Inquiry*, November 16. https://thenewinquiry.com/lose-your-kin.

Sheldon, Rebekkah. 2016. *The Child to Come: Life after the Human Catastrophe*. Minneapolis: University of Minnesota Press.

Silverstein, Charles, and Felice Picano. 2006. *The Joy of Gay Sex*, 3rd ed. New York: William Morrow.

Simpson, Audra. 2014. *Mohawk Interruptus: Political Life across the Borders of Settler States*. Durham, NC: Duke University Press.

Simpson, Audra. 2016. "The State Is a Man: Theresa Spence, Loretta Saunders and the Gender of Settler Sovereignty." *Theory & Event* 19, no. 4. https://muse.jhu.edu/article/633280.

Simpson, Leanne Betasamosake. 2017. *As We Have Always Done: Indigenous Freedom through Radical Resistance*. Minneapolis: University of Minnesota Press.

Snorton, C. Riley. 2017. *Black on Both Sides: A Racial History of Trans Identity*. Minneapolis: University of Minnesota Press.

Snorton, C. Riley, and Jin Haritaworn. 2013. "Trans Necropolitics: A Transnational Reflection on Violence, Death, and the Trans of Color Afterlife." In *The Transgender Studies Reader 2*, edited by Aren Aizura and Susan Stryker, 66–76. New York: Routledge.

Solanas, Valerie. 1965. "Up Your Ass, or, From the Cradle to the Boat, or, The Big Suck or, Up from the Slime." Unpublished theatrical script.

Solanas, Valerie. (1967) 2013. *SCUM Manifesto*. Oakland: AK Press.

Solnit, Rebecca. 2015. "The Mother of All Questions." *Harper's Magazine*, October 2015. https://harpers.org/archive/2015/10/the-mother-of-all -questions.

Solnit, Rebecca. 2017. *The Mother of All Questions*. Chicago: Haymarket Books.

Sommer, Matthew H. 1997. "The Penetrated Male in Late Imperial China." *Modern China* 2: 140–80. https://doi.org/10.1177/009770049702300202.

Spade, Dean. 2020. *Mutual Aid: Building Solidarity during This Crisis (and the Next)*. London: Verso.

Spillers, Hortense. 1987. "Mama's Baby, Papa's Maybe: An American Grammar Book." *Diacritics* 17, no. 2: 64–81.

Spillers, Hortense. (1987) 2003. "Mama's Baby, Papa's Maybe: An American Grammar Book." In *Black, White, and in Color: Essays on American Literature and Culture*, 203–29. Chicago: University of Chicago Press.

Spillers, Hortense. 2003. *Black, White, and in Color: Essays on American Literature and Culture*. Chicago: University of Chicago Press.

Spindelman, Marc. 2013. "Tyrone Garner's *Lawrence v. Texas*." *Michigan Law Review* 111, no. 6: 1111–44.

Stack, Carol. 1983. *All Our Kin: Strategies for Survival in a Black Community*. New York: Basic.

Stallings, L. H. 2011. "'Redemptive Softness': Interiority, Intellect, and Black Women's Ecstasy in Kathleen Collins's *Losing Ground*." *Black Camera: An International Film Journal*, n.s. 2, no. 2: 47–62.

Stallings, L. H. 2015. *Funk the Erotic: Transaesthetics and Black Sexual Cultures*. Urbana: University of Illinois Press.

Stanley, Eric. 2011. "Near Life, Queer Death: Overkill and Ontological Capture." *Social Text* 29, no. 2: 1–19.

Stepan, Nancy Leys. 1991. *The Hour of Eugenics: Race, Gender, and Nation in Latin America*. Ithaca, NY: Cornell University Press.

Stevens, Jacqueline. 1999. *Reproducing the State*. Princeton, NJ: Princeton University Press.

Stockton, Kathryn Bond. 2009. *The Queer Child, or Growing Sideways in the Twentieth Century*. Durham, NC: Duke University Press.

Stonewall. 2015. Directed by Roland Emmerich. Produced by Centropolis Entertainment. Distributed by Roadside Attractions.

Strathern, Marilyn. 1984. "Marriage Exchanges: A Melanesian Comment." *Annual Review of Anthropology* 13: 41–73.

Strathern, Marilyn. 1992. *Reproducing the Future: Essays on Anthropology, Kinship, and the New Reproductive Technologies.* Manchester, UK: Manchester University Press.

Strathern, Marilyn. 2005. *Kinship, Law, and the Unexpected: Relatives Are Always a Surprise.* New York: Cambridge University Press.

Strathern, Marilyn. 2020. *Relations: An Anthropological Account.* Durham, NC: Duke University Press.

Stremlau, Rose. 2011. *Sustaining the Cherokee Family: Kinship and the Allotment of an Indigenous Nation.* Chapel Hill: University of North Carolina Press.

Strychacz, Thomas. 2008. "'You . . . Could Never Be Mistaken': Reading Alice Dunbar-Nelson's Rhetorical Diversions in *The Goodness of St. Rocque and Other Stories*." *Studies in American Fiction* 36, no. 1: 77–94.

Subramaniam, Banu. 2019. *Holy Science: The Biopolitics of Hindu Nationalism.* Seattle: University of Washington Press.

Such, David. 1993. *Avant-Garde Musicians Performing 'Out There'.* Iowa City: University of Iowa Press.

Swaraj, Sushma. 2016. Press conference, August 24. https://www.youtube.com/watch?v=16jWwR2r0DM.

Swinburne, Henry. 1590. *A Briefe Treatise of Testaments and Last Willes.* London: J. Windet.

Syal, Meera. 2016. *The House of Hidden Mothers.* New York: Sarah Crichton Books/Farrar, Straus and Giroux.

Szonyi, Michael. 2002. *Practicing Kinship: Lineage and Descent in Late Imperial China.* Palo Alto, CA: Stanford University Press.

TallBear, Kim. 2013. *Native American DNA: Tribal Belonging and the False Promise of Genetic Science.* Minneapolis: University of Minnesota Press.

TallBear, Kim. 2018. "Making Love and Relations beyond Settler Sex and Family." In *Making Kin, Not Population: Reconceiving Generations*, edited by Adele Clarke and Donna Haraway, 145–64. Chicago: Prickly Paradigm.

Taşçıoğlu, Esen Ezgi. 2015. "'I Lived and Learned': Violence, Survival and Self-Making in Trans Women's Lives in Istanbul, Turkey." *Oñati Socio-Legal Series* 5, no. 6: 1452–70.

Taussig, Michael. 1993. *Mimesis and Alterity: A Particular History of the Senses.* New York: Routledge.

Teuton, Christopher B., ed. 2012. *Cherokee Stories of the Turtle Island Liars' Club.* Chapel Hill: University of North Carolina Press.

Traub, Valerie. 2013. "The New Unhistoricism in Queer Studies." *PMLA* 128, no. 1: 21–39.

Trautmann, Thomas R. 1987. *Lewis Henry Morgan and the Invention of Kinship.* Berkeley: University of California Press.

Troester, Rosalie Riegle. 1984. "Turbulence and Tenderness: Mothers, Daughters, and 'Othermothers' in Paule Marshall's *Brown Girl, Brownstones*." *Sage: A Scholarly Journal on Black Women* 1, no. 2: 13–16.

Trouillot, Michel-Rolph. 1995. *Silencing the Past: Power and the Production of History*. Boston: Beacon.

Tsing, Anna Lowenhaupt, and Sylvia Junko Yanagisako. 1983. "Feminism and Kinship Theory." *Current Anthropology* 24, no. 4: 511–16.

Tuck, Eve, and K. Wayne Yang. 2012. "Decolonization Is Not a Metaphor." *Decolonization: Indigeneity, Education & Society* 1, no. 1: 1–40.

Tugend, Alina. 2016. "Childless Women to Marketers: We Buy Things Too." *New York Times*, July 9, 2016. https://www.nytimes.com/2016/07/10/business /childless-women-to-marketers-we-buy-things-too.html.

Unemployed Negativity. 2015. "The Class Struggles at Home: Chantal Jaquet's *Les Transclasses*." *Unemployed Negativity* (blog), January 2, 2015. https://www .unemployednegativity.com/2015/01/the-class-struggle-at-home-jaquets -le.html.

United Nations Department of Economic and Social Affairs. 2017. "World Population Prospects: The 2017 Revision." June 21. https://www.un.org /development/desa/publications/world-population-prospects-the-2017 -revision.html.

U of T AstroTours. 2017. "AstroTours—Night Skies over Turtle Island: Indigenous Perspectives on the Cosmos." Roundtable discussion with Karyn Recollet, Hilding Neilson, and Frank Dempsey, University of Toronto, November 7. https://youtu.be/DxkFVuqi1Bk.

Vasconcelos, José. 1925. *La raza cósmica: misión de la raza iberoamericana, notas de viajes a la América del Sur*. Barcelona, Spain: Agencia Mundial de Librería.

Viveiros de Castro, Eduardo. 2009. "The Gift and the Given: Three Nano-Essays on Magic and Kinship." In *Kinship and Beyond: The Genealogical Model Revisited*, edited by Sandra Bamford and James Leach, 237–68. New York: Berghahn.

Vizenor, Gerald. 1999. *Manifest Manners: Narratives on Postindian Survivance*. Lincoln: University of Nebraska Press.

Vora, Kalindi. 2015. *Life Support: Biocapital and the New History of Outsourced Labor*. Minneapolis: University of Minnesota Press.

Vuong, Ocean. 2015. "Someday I'll Love Ocean Vuong." *New Yorker*, May 5, 2015, 50–51.

Vuong, Ocean. 2016. "Someday I'll Love Ocean Vuong." In *Night Sky with Exit Wounds*, 82–83. Port Townsend, WA: Copper Canyon.

Wagner, Bryan. 2009. *Disturbing the Peace: Black Culture and the Police Power after Slavery*. Cambridge, MA: Harvard University Press.

Walker, Alice. 2007. "As You Wear: Cross-Dressing and Identity Politics in Jackie Kay's *Trumpet*." *Journal of International Women's Studies* 8, no. 2: 35–43.

Warner, Michael. 1999. *The Trouble with Normal: Sex, Politics, and the Ethics of Queer Life*. New York: Free Press.

Warner, Michael. 2000. Interview by Annamarie Jagose. *Genders* 31. https://

www.colorado.edu/gendersarchive1998-2013/2000/05/01/queer-world
-making-annamarie-jagose-interviews-michael-warne.

Warner, Michael. 2002. "Publics and Counterpublics." *Public Culture* 14, no. 1: 49–90.

Warner, Sara, and Mary Jo Watts. 2014. "Hide and Go Seek: Child's Play as Archival Act in Valerie Solanas's *SCUM Manifesto*." *TDR: The Drama Review* 58, no. 4: 80–93.

Warren, Calvin L. 2018. *Ontological Terror: Blackness, Nihilism, and Emancipation*. Durham, NC: Duke University Press.

Weinbaum, Alys Eve. 2019. *The Afterlife of Reproductive Slavery: Biocapitalism and Black Feminism's Philosophy of History*. Durham, NC: Duke University Press.

Weiner, Joshua J., and Damon Young. 2011. "Introduction: Queer Bonds." *GLQ: A Journal of Lesbian and Gay Studies* 17, nos. 2–3: 223–41.

Weinstock, Jacqueline S., and Esther D. Rothblum. 2018. "Just Friends: The Role of Friendship in Lesbians' Lives." *Journal of Lesbian Studies* 22, no. 1: 1–3.

West, Elizabeth. 2009. "Religion, Race, and Gender in the 'Race-less' Fiction of Alice Dunbar-Nelson." *Black Magnolias Literary Journal* 3, no. 1: 5–19.

Weston, Kath. 1991 (revised 1997). *Families We Choose: Lesbians, Gays, Kinship*. New York: Columbia University Press.

Weston, Kath. 1995. "Get Thee to a Big City: Sexual Imaginary and the Great Gay Migration." *GLQ: A Journal of Lesbian and Gay Studies* 2, no. 3: 253–77.

Weston, Kath. 1996. *Render Me, Gender Me: Lesbians Talk Sex, Class, Color, Nation, Studmuffins*. New York: Columbia University Press.

Weston, Kath. 2001. "Kinship, Controversy, and the Sharing of Substance: The Race/Class Politics of Blood Transfusion." In *Relative Values: Reconfiguring Kinship Studies*, edited by Sarah Franklin and Susan McKinnon, 148–51. Durham, NC: Duke University Press.

Weston, Kath. 2005. "Families in Queer States: The Rule of Law and the Politics of Recognition." *Radical History Review* 93: 122–41.

Weston, Kath. 2008. *Traveling Light: On the Road with America's Poor*. Boston: Beacon.

Weston, Kath. 2013. "Biosecuritization: The Quest for Synthetic Blood and the Taming of Kinship." In *Blood and Kinship: Matter for Metaphor from Ancient Rome to the Present*, edited by Christopher H. Johnson, Bernhard Jussen, David Warren Sabean, and Simon Teuscher, 244–65. New York: Berghahn.

Weston, Kath. 2017. *Animate Planet: Making Visceral Sense of Living in a High-Tech Ecologically Damaged World*. Durham, NC: Duke University Press.

Whyte, Fiona, and Malone Seán. 2017. *Without a Doubt: An Irish Couple's Journey through IVF, Adoption and Surrogacy*. Kildare, Ireland: Merrion.

Williams, Patricia. 1988. "On Being the Object of Property." *Signs: Journal of Women in Culture and Society* 14, no. 1: 5–24.

Williams, Patricia. 1991. *The Alchemy of Race and Rights: Diary of a Law Professor*. Cambridge, MA: Harvard University Press.

Williams, Patricia. 2016. "Babies, Bodies, and Buyers." *Columbia Journal of Law* 33, no. 1: 11–24.

Williams, Patricia J. 2018. "Governing Bodies." Reading Matters Workshop, UC Berkeley, September 14, 2018.

"The Witnessing and Blessing of a Marriage." 2015. *The Witnessing and Blessing of a Marriage*. New York: Church Publishing.

Wolfe, Patrick. 2006. "Settler Colonialism and the Elimination of the Native." *Journal of Genocide Research* 8, no. 4: 387–409.

Wolfson, Susan, and Marshall Brown, eds. 2006. *Reading for Form*. Seattle: University of Washington Press.

Wordsworth, William. 1807. *Poems, in Two Volumes*. London: Longman, Hurst, Rees, and Orme.

Work in Progress. 2019–2021. Created by Abby McEnany and Tim Mason. Showtime.

Yanagisako, Sylvia J. 1985. *Transforming the Past: Kinship and Tradition among Japanese Americans*. Palo Alto, CA: Stanford University Press.

Yanagisako, Sylvia Junko. 2002. *Producing Culture and Capital: Family Firms in Italy*. Princeton, NJ: Princeton University Press.

Yang, Qiu. 2005. "The 'Zhishu' Custom in Guangzhou Area and Its Manifestations in the Modern Period." *Collection of Women's Studies* 3: 52–57.

Yazzie, Melanie. 2017. "#NOBANSTOLENLAND: Towards a Politics of Radical Relationality." Presentation at the National Women's Studies Association annual meeting, Baltimore, Maryland, November 17.

Yuhas, Alan. 2020. "Don't Expect a Quarantine Baby Boom." *New York Times*, April 8, 2020. https://www.nytimes.com/2020/04/08/us/coronavirus-baby-boom.html.

Zang, Ma 臧马. 2002. "Zhuming nu geming jia Qiujin beihai muhou gushi" 著名女革命家秋瑾被害幕后故事 [The Behind-the-Scenes Story of the Death of the Famous Female Revolutionary Qiujin]. Wenshi Chunqiu 文史春秋 [Spring-Autumn Literature and History], November: 18–22.

Zelizer, Viviana. 1981. *Pricing the Priceless Child: The Changing Social Value of Children*. New York: Basic.

Zengin, Asli. 2016. "Violent Intimacies: Tactile State Power, Sex/Gender Transgression, and the Politics of Touch in Contemporary Turkey." *Journal of Middle East Women's Studies* 12, no. 2: 225–45.

Zhang, Xin-lu. 2018. "Cross-Dressing, Sworn Sisters and Compatriots: Qiu Jin's Feminist Revolution." *Journal of Chinese Women's Studies* 2: 102–20.

Zhou, Lijun 周立军. 2012. "Qiujin zhisi yu wanqing shehui yulun" 秋瑾之死与晚清社会舆论 [The Death of Qiujin and Public Opinion in Late-Qing]. *Wenshi Tiandi* 文史天地 [The World of Literature and History] (October): 46–49.

Zitkala-Ša. 1900. "An Indian Teacher among Indians." *Atlantic Monthly* 85: 381–86.

Zitkala-Ša. 1902. "Why I Am a Pagan." *Atlantic Monthly* 90: 801–3.

Contributors

Aqdas Aftab is an assistant professor of English at Loyola University Chicago, working at the intersections of trans studies, queer of color critique, postcolonial literatures, decolonial studies, and Black diaspora studies. They are currently writing a book on decolonial trans interiority in Black and Dalit diasporic literatures. They teach courses on decoloniality, postcolonialism, queer and trans theories, and race and migration. Aqdas is also a creative writer, and they have written speculative fiction and poetry for venues such as *Strange Horizons* and *The World That Belongs to Us: An Anthology of Queer Poetry from South Asia*. As a community activist, they are the co-creator of Transform Gender Collective, a transformative-justice collective for transmasculine people of color.

Leah Claire Allen is an assistant professor in gender, women's, and sexuality studies and English at Grinnell College, where she teaches courses on queer and trans literatures, LGBTQ studies, and feminist histories. She has published articles in *Signs*, *Criticism*, *Parallax*, and the *American Review of Canadian Studies*. Her article describing Andrea Dworkin as an unexpected ancestor of queer theory won the MLA Women's Caucus Florence Howe Award for outstanding feminist scholarship. Her current book project, *Evisceration as Feminist Method*, is a critical history of feminism's abiding commitment to obliterating its objects through scathing critique.

Tyler Bradway is an associate professor of English at SUNY Cortland. He is the author of *Queer Experimental Literature: The Affective Politics of Bad Reading* (2017). He is coeditor (with E. L. McCallum) of *After Queer Studies: Literature, Theory, and Sexuality in the 21st Century* (2019) and editor of "Lively Words: The Politics and Poetics of Experimental Writing" (2019), a special issue of *College Literature*. His articles have appeared or are forthcoming in PMLA, GLQ, *Mosaic, Textual Practice, Studies in the Fantastic, Stanford Arcade, American Literature in Transition 1980–1990, The Comics of Alison Bechdel: From the Outside In*, and the *Routledge Companion to Queer Theory and Modernist Studies*. He is currently writing a book titled *Group Work: Queer Relationality and Social Narration*.

Juliana Demartini Brito is a Gates Scholar and doctoral candidate in multidisciplinary gender studies in the Department of Politics and International Studies at the University of Cambridge. Her current research examines how Brazilian cultural production and activism offer alternative lenses to interpret the future for queer and racialized populations in the country. Brito also supervises undergraduate students in the sociology and modern and medieval languages departments at Cambridge. Her interests lie in Latin American culture and politics, queer theory, and decolonial approaches to gender and sexuality.

Judith Butler is Maxine Elliot Professor Emeritus in the Department of Comparative Literature and the Program of Critical Theory at the University of California, Berkeley. They received their PhD in philosophy from Yale University in 1984. They are the author of several books: *Subjects of Desire: Hegelian Reflections in Twentieth-Century France* (1987); *Gender Trouble: Feminism and the Subversion of Identity* (1990); *Bodies That Matter: On the Discursive Limits of "Sex"* (1993); *The Psychic Life of Power: Theories of Subjection* (1997); *Excitable Speech* (1997); *Antigone's Claim: Kinship between Life and Death* (2000); *Precarious Life: Powers of Violence and Mourning* (2004); *Undoing Gender* (2004); *Frames of War: When Is Life Grievable?* (2009); *Parting Ways: Jewishness and the Critique of Zionism* (2012); *Toward a Performative Theory of Assembly* (2015); and *The Force of Nonviolence* (2020). Their co-authored works include *Who Sings the Nation-State? Language, Politics, Belonging* (written with Gayatri Chakravorty Spivak, 2008); *Critique Secular?* (written with Talal Asad, Wendy Brown, and Saba Mahmood, 2009); *Sois Mon Corps* (written with Catherine Malabou, 2011); *Dispossession: The Performative in the Political* (written with Athena Athanasiou, 2013); and *Vulnerability in Resistance* (coedited with Zeynep Gambetti and Leticia Sabsay, 2016). Their books have been translated into more than twenty languages.

Dilara Çalışkan is an LGBTI+ rights activist in Turkey and a PhD candidate in socio-cultural anthropology at the University of Illinois. She is also a graduate student fellow of the Center for the Study of Social Difference at Columbia University. In 2014 she graduated from Sabancı University's Cultural Studies master's program with a thesis titled "Queer Mothers and Daughters: The Role of Queer Kinship in the Everyday Lives of Trans Sex Worker Women in Istanbul." Her reviews and essays have been published in *American Ethnologist, European Journal of Women's Studies*, and *Women Mobilizing Memory*.

Christopher Chamberlin is a fellow at the ICI Berlin (Institute for Cultural Inquiry). From 2018 to 2020, he was the UC President's Postdoctoral Fellow in English at the University of California, Berkeley. His work broadly examines psychoanalytic theory and practice in the aftermath of racial slavery. He currently serves as an editor for both *Psychoanalysis, Culture & Society* and *European Journal of Psychoanalysis* and has writing published in *Studies in Gender and Sexuality, Journal of Medical Humanities, Discourse: Journal for Theoretical Studies in Media and Culture, Postmodern Culture*, and *Hypatia*.

Aobo Dong is a PhD candidate in women's, gender, and sexuality studies (WGSS) at Emory University. Dong earned his BA from the College of Social Studies of Wesleyan University and his MTS from Harvard University, where he held dual research fellowships studying the intersections of religion, ethics, and politics at Harvard Divinity School and Harvard Law School. As part of his doctoral research, Dong is interested in how queer kinship and queer filial debt in the Chinese diaspora subvert and reinvent Western-centric queer theory and normative epistemes. His academic interests in WGSS also extend to how queer and gender theories translate into and interact with legal epistemologies in East Asia, the United States, and international human rights regimes.

Brigitte Fielder is an associate professor at the University of Wisconsin–Madison. She is the author of *Relative Races: Genealogies of Interracial Kinship in Nineteenth-Century America* (Duke University Press, 2020) and coeditor of *Against a Sharp White Background: Infrastructures of African American Print* (2019). She is currently writing a book about racialized human-animal relationships in the long nineteenth century, which shows how childhood becomes a key site for (often simultaneous) humanization and racialization.

Elizabeth Freeman is a professor of English at University of California, Davis. She specializes in American literature and gender/sexuality/queer studies, and her articles have appeared in numerous scholarly journals. She has written three books: *The Wedding Complex: Forms of Belonging in Modern American Culture* (Duke University Press, 2002); *Time Binds: Queer Temporalities, Queer Histories* (Duke University Press, 2010); and *Beside You in Time: Sense-Methods and Queer Sociabilities in the American Nineteenth-Century* (Duke University Press, 2019). She was also the editor of a special issue of GLQ, "Queer Temporalities" (2007), and coeditor, with Ellen Samuels, of a special issue of *South Atlantic*

Quarterly, "Crip Temporalities" (2021). Between 2011 and 2017 she served as co-editor of GLQ: *A Journal of Lesbian and Gay Studies.*

John S. Garrison is a professor of English at Grinnell College, where he teaches courses on early modern literature and culture. He is coeditor of three essay collections: *Sexuality and Memory in Early Modern England: Literature and the Erotics of Recollection* (2015); *Ovid and Masculinity in English Renaissance Literature* (2020); and *Making Milton: Print, Authorship, Afterlives* (2021). His books include *Friendship and Queer Theory in the Renaissance* (2014); *Glass* (2015); *Shakespeare at Peace* (with Kyle Pivetti, 2018); *Shakespeare and the Afterlife* (2019); and *The Pleasures of Shakespeare's Sonnets* (forthcoming).

Natasha Hurley is an associate professor in the Department of English and Film Studies at the University of Alberta in Edmonton, where she also currently serves as associate director of the Intersections of Gender Signature Area and director of Media and Technology Studies. She is the author of *Circulating Queerness: Before the Gay and Lesbian Novel* (2018), editor of a special double issue of *ESC: English Studies in Canada* on "Childhood and Its Discontents," and coeditor (with Steven Bruhm) of *Curiouser: On the Queerness of Children* (2004). She won the Hennig-Cohen Prize from the Melville Society (2018) and the Priestley Prize from the Association of Canadian College and University Teachers of English (2012). She was also co-winner of the Foerster Prize from *American Literature* (2003). Her contribution to this volume is drawn from "Kidless Lit: Children, Childhood, and Minor Kinship Forms," a research project funded by the Social Sciences and Humanities Research Council of Canada. She is also completing a book on psychoanalytic approaches to sexuality and children's literature titled *Sexuality Afterwards: Children's Literature as Enigmatic Signifier.*

Joseph M. Pierce is an associate professor in the Department of Hispanic Languages and Literature at Stony Brook University. His research focuses on the intersections of kinship, gender, sexuality, and race in Latin America, nineteenth-century literature and culture, queer studies, Indigenous studies, and hemispheric approaches to citizenship and belonging. He is the author of *Argentine Intimacies: Queer Kinship in an Age of Splendor, 1890–1910* (2019) and coeditor of *Políticas del amor: Derechos sexuales y escrituras disidentes en el Cono Sur* (2018) as well as the 2021 special issue of GLQ, "Queer/Cuir Américas: Translation, Decoloniality, and the Incommensurable." His work has been published recently in *Revista Hispánica Moderna*, *Critical Ethnic Studies*, and LARR, and it has also been featured in *Indian Country Today*. Along with S.J Norman (Koori of Wiradjuri descent), he is co-curator of the performance series Knowledge of Wounds. He is a citizen of the Cherokee Nation.

Mark Rifkin is the Linda Arnold Carlisle Distinguished Excellence Professor of women's, gender, and sexuality studies and professor of English at UNC Greensboro. He is the author of seven books, including *Speaking for the People: Native Writing and the Question of Political Form* (2021); *Fictions of Land and Flesh: Blackness, Indigeneity, Speculation* (2019); *Beyond Settler Time: Temporal Sovereignty and Indigenous Self-Determination* (2017); and *When Did Indians Become Straight? Kinship, the History of Sexuality, and Native Sovereignty* (2011). He also co-edited "Sexuality, Nationality, Indigeneity" (a special issue of GLQ) with Daniel Heath Justice and Bethany Schneider, and he has served as president of the Native American and Indigenous Studies Association.

Poulomi Saha is an associate professor of English at the University of California, Berkeley. Her research and teaching interests span eastward and forward from the late-nineteenth-century decline of British colonial rule in the Indian Ocean through to the Pacific and the rise of American global power and domestic race relations in the twentieth century, with a particular investment in psychoanalysis, critical theory, and feminist and queer studies. Her first book, *An Empire of Touch: Women's Political Labor and the Fabrication of East Bengal* (2019), was awarded the Harry Levin Prize for outstanding first book by the American Comparative Literature Association in 2020. Saha is currently at work on two new projects. The first is a book titled *Fascination: America's "Hindu" Cults*, which inquires into the figures, ideas, and social forms seemingly imported from India, but are in fact homegrown, that so enthrall an America public and that continue to shape its racial and spiritual self-conception. Saha's work has appeared in *differences*, *qui parle*, *Signs*, and *Interventions*, among other places.

Kath Weston is a professor of anthropology at the University of Virginia and British Academy Global Professor at the University of Edinburgh. Her current work focuses on visceral engagement, drawing on political economy, political ecology, kinship, historical anthropology, and science and technology studies. She has also published widely on how gender, class, race, and sexuality compound. Weston has conducted fieldwork and archival research in North America, India, Japan, and the United Kingdom. She is the author of numerous books, including *Families We Choose: Lesbians, Gays, Kinship* (2nd ed., 1997); *Gender in Real Time: Power and Transience in a Visual Age* (2002); *Traveling Light: On the Road with America's Poor* (2008); and *Animate Planet: Making Visceral Sense of Living in a High-Tech Ecologically Damaged World* (Duke University Press, 2017).

Index

60s scoop, 98
80'lerde Lubunya Olmak, 84

Abani, Chris, 177
Abdur-Rahman, Aliyyah, 163
ableism, 56, 91, 127
abolishing the family, 297–98
accountability, 96, 151, 154–56, 279
Achilles, 230
ACT UP, 231
Adams, Katherine, 48, 69n2
adjacency, 251–55, 258, 260, 263. *See also* social refraction
adoption, 41, 46, 88, 121, 129, 166, 172, 298; adoption law, 31, 122, 127–28; and family separation, 30, 32–33; of Indigenous children, 16, 19, 98–99, 103–6, 108–13
Adoptive Couple v. Baby Girl (Baby Veronica case, 2013), 104
affective labor, 132, 137n7
affinities, 9, 142, 181–82, 185, 193, 196–98, 299; and aesthetics, 5, 58; and bachelor communities, 17; and Black kinship, 15; and blood oaths, 270–71, 278, 282–83; and cannibalism, 183, 188; deployment of, 12; and Indigenous kinship, 10, 157; and roll calling, 190–91
African American literature, 48–69
Afro-fabulation, 37, 168, 172–73, 176
Afropessimism, 20
Aftab, Aqdas, 13–14, 20
Agamben, Giorgio, 231
Agard-Jones, Vanessa, 294
Ahmed, Sara, 147, 149, 156, 187, 238, 246n12
Airbnb, 7
Akanksha Infertility Clinic, 119, 136n4
akinship, 20, 203–25

Allen, Jafari S., 187
Allen, Leah, 13, 21
alliance, 131, 183, 288n4, 292, 299; and blood oaths, 271; deployments of, 1, 5, 12; and friendship, 227–32, 238, 244–45; love-based, 246n12; without exchange, 225
allotment, 16, 99, 100–101, 103, 112, 116–17n9
alterlife, 252–53, 268n4
altruism, 119, 124, 128, 131–36. *See also* gift economy
Alves, Jaime, 195
American Civil Liberties Union, 218
Amin, Kadji, 90, 234, 268n5
amity, 228, 230–31, 235
Ammons, Elizabeth, 50, 69n5
ancestry, 3, 15, 45, 129, 141, 168, 176, 268n4; ancestral futurity, 97, 116n4; ancestral kin, 19, 99; blood-based, 12, 157n3, 172; and Indigenous kinship, 19, 96–97, 99, 107–8, 113, 116, 116–17n9, 118n23
anchor babies discourse, 7, 17
ancient Greece, 230
Angel Island, 269, 287
anthrocentrism, 96, 107
anthropology, 5, 12, 97, 99, 114, 117n18, 131, 186, 295–96; cultural, 21, 26, 34, 36, 291; feminist, 27–28, 34, 123, 209–12; queer, 34; studies of Indigenous communities, 118n23, 138; studies of kinship, 17–19, 21, 25–28, 34–36, 41, 118n23, 138–39, 148, 151, 205–6, 224, 291–93; studies of slavery, 203, 214, 222; studies of the exchange of women, 209–14. *See also* ethnography
anthropophagy (cannibalism), 39, 183–85, 187–90, 191, 193

anti-Blackness, 14–15, 52, 54–55, 161, 168,
172–73, 195, 222, 270; and state violence,
9, 20–21
anti-Cartesianism, 208–9
anticolonialism/anti-imperialism, 174,
269–88. *See also* decolonization
antifeminism, 37
anti-social thesis, 11, 20–21, 41, 192, 225,
229, 241–42, 245, 260
Anzaldúa, Gloria, 1, 186, 190
apartheid, 43. *See also* Jim Crow
Aristotle, 229–31, 237, 246n6
asexuality, 243
Asian Americans, 17
askesis, 237, 246n5
assisted-reproductive technologies (ARTs),
120; IVF, 125, 136n4; surrogacy, 19, 30,
119–36, 256–57, 292
Association of American Indian Affairs
(AAIA), 104
aunties, 15, 259
aunts, 39, 134, 167, 260, 273
Australia, 9

Baby Veronica case. *See Adoptive Couple v.
Baby Girl* (Baby Veronica case, 2013)
Bachelard, Gaston, 77
bachelors, 17, 245, 260, 275, 287
bad kin, 8
Bahloul, Joëlle, 75, 79
Bailey, Marlon, 19, 75
Baldwin, James, 240, 296
bare life, 271, 277, 279, 284, 286–87
Barker, Joanne, 116–17n9
BDSM, 233–34
becoming Native, 109–10
being-in-good-relations, 99
Belcourt, Billy-Ray, 97
Benicio, Monica, 181, 194–98
Benjamin, Walter, 218
Bentley, Nancy, 17
Bento, Berenice, 185
Berlant, Lauren, 77, 147, 192, 229, 235
Bersani, Leo, 4–5, 192, 229, 234, 243–44
Bey, Marquis, 162

Beyoğlu Police Department, 85
Bhabha, Homi, 179n16
Bharatiya Janata Party (BJP), 128–30
biopolitics, 10, 104, 121, 122, 128, 225, 270,
272, 277, 279, 283; biopolitical racism,
275; of kinship, 12, 18, 22; and settler
colonialism, 104, 146; of slavery, 121
birth control, 251
birthrates, 249–50, 252
birthright citizenship, 7
Birth Strike, 267n2
bisexual people, 7
Black diaspora studies, 165
Black feminism, 70n10, 163, 205
Black kinship, 15, 20, 46, 159, 165, 171,
205–25. *See also* akinship
Black Lives Matter, 6, 9
Black Pink Triangle Izmir Association,
84
Black Power movement, 295
Black Renaissance, 51–52
Black studies, 163, 178n9
Black Trans Lives Matter, 9
Blevins, Wade, 118n22
blood, 9, 12, 109, 157n3, 236, 269–70, 301;
blood oaths, 3, 21, 270, 276–83, 287;
blood quantum, 100–101, 116–17n9; and
chosen family, 233, 297; and econom-
ics, 294–95, 300; menstrual, 177; and
racialized kinship, 18, 25–47; and trans
kinship, 169–73
boarding schools, 16, 99, 101–4, 106,
108–9, 113, 117n12
Boas, Franz, 153
body finance, 300–301
Bolick, Kate, 253
Bolsonaro, Jair, 180–81, 187, 191, 193, 195,
199n4
boomerang babies, 6
bourgeois kinship, 1, 143, 146, 148, 256
Boxer Rebellion (1889–1901), 288n3
Boysan's House (Boysan'ın Evi), 86
Bradway, Tyler, 91, 267
Braithwaite, William Stanley, 69
Brazil, 18, 20, 180, 182–86, 188–92, 194,

196, 198, 199n4; Rio de Janeiro, 181, 193, 195, 197; São Paulo, 187, 195

Briggs, Laura, 103

Brito, Juliana Demartini, 20

Britzman, Deborah, 259

Brooks, Kristina, 69n5

brotherhood, 21, 232, 271–86

Brown, William Wells, 55

Buddhism, 129, 288n1

Buggery Act (1533), 125

Burke Act (1906), 100

Butler, Judith, 21, 197, 224, 226; on embodiment, 189, 210–12; on kinship, 1–3, 5, 11–13, 19, 22n2, 190, 207; on performativity, 257

Butler, Octavia, 43–46; *Kindred*, 35

Çağdaş, Eylem, 86

California, 29, 43–44, 289n8; Chinatown (San Francisco), 274–75, 287; San Francisco Bay Area, 269, 292

Çalışkan, Dilara, 13–14, 19–20

Canada, 98, 112, 249, 267, 298

Canadian River, 112

cannibalism. *See* anthropophagy (cannibalism)

capitalism, 156, 165, 223, 243, 268n4, 268n7; bio-, 124; emotional, 137n7; and the exchange of women, 207, 214–15; and gay identity, 301; and kidless lit, 248, 251–53, 258, 260; late, 8; racial, 9, 161, 225; and settler colonialism, 96, 100, 252. *See also* liberalism; neoliberalism

cárdenas, micha, 82–83

Carlisle Indian School, 102, 106, 117n17

Carroll, Clint, 118n22

Carruthers, Charlene A., 138, 150, 156

Carsten, Janet, 28, 77, 292–93

Catholic Church, 187

Cavarero, Adriana, 189

Çelik, Belgin, 84–85

Cetinic, Marija, 256

Chama, 193

Chamberlin, Christopher, 9, 20

Channel 4, 245n2

Chen, Jian Neo, 82–83

Cherokee Nation, 17, 95–96, 99–101, 108–9, 110, 111–15, 118n22

Chesnutt, Charles, 50, 55–56, 69

Cheyenne People, 118n23

Chickasaw Nation, 100

Child, Lydia Maria, 55

children, 7, 10, 45, 114, 118n23, 142–43, 236, 289n8; and adoption, 16, 31, 98–99, 103–6, 109, 113; and anti-social thesis, 11, 192; in ballroom life, 10; bearing vs. raising, 70n10; and boarding schools, 99, 101–4, 108, 113; childlessness, 21, 248–67, 280; and family separation, 6, 29–30, 32–33; and kinship theory, 27; and nuclear family, 17, 120, 141; and queerness, 40, 87, 230, 232–33, 268n5; and race, 15, 19, 46, 48–69, 195, 204, 208, 215–17; and slavery, 15, 46, 208, 215–17; as strangers, 253; and surrogacy, 120, 124, 126–29, 131–33; and trans kinship, 82

Chile, 188–89

China, 18, 21, 212, 270, 289n8; Chengdu, 284; Eastern Han dynasty, 277, 288n4; Eastern Zhou dynasty, 271; Ming dynasty, 272–74, 282; Qing dynasty, 271–87; Sichuan Province, 284

Chinese Exclusion Act (1882), 269, 274, 288n5

Chinese party-state, 271

Chinese people, 7, 17, 21, 29, 59, 269–88; Han, 273; Manchu, 273

Choctaw Nation, 100

chosen family, 32, 172, 245n45; critiques of, 227–29, 231–34, 239–41, 243–44; racialized, 13, 172, 227–28; Weston on, 12, 21, 291–92, 294, 297, 300

Christian, Shawn Anthony, 67

Christianity, 101, 129, 270, 288n3. *See also* Catholic Church

chrononormativity, 7–8, 80, 169, 179n13, 236, 238, 246n9

Chu, Andrea Long, 247n16

Çiçek (interviewee), 88

Clarke, Adele E., 1, 250

Clastres, Pierre, 27

Cohen, Cathy, 178n10
Cohen, Ed, 302
Colen, Shellee, 250
Collier, Jane, 12, 27–28
colonialism/imperialism, 122, 223, 252–53;
    and Blackness, 160–64, 168, 169, 175–77,
    188; British, 128, 215, 275; kinship's role
    in, 1, 18–21, 35–36, 139, 143, 206; and In-
    digenous kinship, 16, 96–113, 116–17n9,
    152, 156, 259; resistance to, 14, 174,
    269–88; US, 34. *See also* anticolonialism/
    anti-imperialism; decolonization; post-
    colonialism; settler colonialism
Colorado: Denver, 116n8
Colored American Magazine, 69
colorism, 55–56. *See also* racism
Combahee River Collective, 231
commodification, 32, 121, 134, 207, 214–15,
    217
community hamlets, 293–94
compulsory maternity, 254–55
comradeship, 229
Confucianism, 272–74, 276, 278–79
consanguinity, 142–44, 157nn2–3
consent, 122, 124, 130, 204, 231, 233
Cooper, Melinda, 131
cosmology, 75, 97–98, 111
Costa, Petra: *The Edge of Democracy*, 180–81
COVID-19 pandemic, 6, 8–9, 249, 267n1,
    299–300
Coviello, Peter, 17
Cramblett, Jennifer, 30
Cree Nation, 96–98, 100
Creoles, 58, 61, 69n5
criminalization, 73, 86, 126, 204, 275
critical race studies/theory, 1, 7, 14–15, 121,
    258–59
Cuba, 186
Cultural Revolution (1966–76), 271
cultures of relatedness, 293
Curtis Act (1898), 100
Cvetkovich, Ann, 231

daddy play, 233–34
Dakota People, 152–55

DaMatta, Roberto, 186
Danticat, Edwidge, 177
Daoism, 270, 288n1
daughters, 19, 71–91, 107, 129
Daum, Megan, 253–54, 260
Davidson, Judy, 267
Dean, Jodi, 229
Dean, Tim, 242
death drive, 21, 136
de Certeau, Michel, 41
decolonization, 19–20, 96, 98, 109, 112,
    159, 162–64, 168, 173, 184, 253. *See also*
    anticolonialism/anti-imperialism
Deer, Sarah, 102
Delany, Samuel R., 239
DeLarverie, Stormé, 246n3
Delhi High Court, 125
Deloria, Ella, 153–55
D'Emilio, John, 9, 301–2
Derrida, Jacques, 135, 231, 239, 246n6,
    246n13
Descartes, René, 208
desexualization, 222–23
desocialization, 223
detention, 6–7, 32, 40, 269–70, 287
Dhritarashtra, King, 128
Dickinson, Emily, 70n6
Dinshaw, Carolyn, 246n10
disability, 9, 56, 70n7, 127, 158n5, 280. *See
    also* ableism
disciplining reproduction, 250
disidentification, 106, 164, 184, 258
disinheritance, 208
distributed reproduction, 250
distributive justice, 298
Dixon, Dustin, 246n11
DNA, 12, 30–31, 33
domestic couple, 7
domestic labor, 102, 122
domestic sphere, 28
domestic violence, 220–22, 253, 260,
    265–67, 298
Dong, Aobo, 21
D'Orsi, Lorenzo, 84
Douglas, Mary, 77

Du Bois, W. E. B., 164
Dunbar-Nelson, Alice, 19, 70n10; "The Child Is Father to the Man," 48–69, 70n6
durability, 3, 6, 13, 231
dysphoria, 20, 165, 178

ecstasy, 3, 14, 119, 220, 239; and Black trans representation, 159–78
Edelman, Lee, 21, 192, 229–30, 235, 250, 256, 263–64, 280
Ellison, Treva, 178n2
embedded theory, 297
empathy, 58, 261–63
empiricism, 12, 14, 44
enfamilyment, 140, 145–57
Eng, David L., 1, 106, 110, 117n18, 120, 149, 178n10, 204, 238
Engels, Friedrich, 1
England, 9, 215, 217. See also Great Britain; United Kingdom
Enlightenment, 121, 173
entre-lugar, 190
epigenetics, 30–33
Erll, Astrid, 87
erotic maroonage, 148
Ersoy, Bülent, 85
essentialism, 57, 59, 65, 161, 172, 283, 285
Estes, Nick, 102
ethnicity, 2, 28, 104, 186, 273
ethnographic stopgap, 296
ethnography, 19, 25, 36, 73, 123, 132, 134, 136n2, 176, 212, 292–96
Eubanks, Robert, 218, 220–21
eugenics, 70n7, 128, 136n5
Euro-Americans, 16, 119, 125, 139, 141
Eurocentrism, 186
Europe, 16, 18, 73, 141–42, 184, 186; and kinship models, 19, 27, 213; surrogacy in, 120
exchange of women, 206–7, 211–15
ex loco parentis, 251, 263

Facebook, 12
Fahs, Breanne, 243, 247n16

fairy tales, 263
fake families discourse, 29, 32, 34
familial time, 72, 75
family reunification policies, 7, 29, 33
family separation policies, 6, 10, 32–33
family trees, 4, 97, 172
Fanon, Frantz, 164, 176
Farah, Nuruddin, 177
Feel Good, 245n2
Feinberg, Leslie, 240–41
femininity, 79
feminism, 206, 232, 251, 255, 281, 297; Black, 70n10, 163, 205; and bloodlines, 31; Chinese, 285–86; feminist anthropology, 27–28, 34, 123, 209–10; Indigenous, 96, 105; Marxist, 250, 256–57; queer-of-color, 98; South Asian, 120; and surrogacy, 119–20, 123, 135; white, 231. See also antifeminism; women's liberation
feminist studies, 1
fetishism, 5, 32, 52, 55, 59; of Black trans bodies, 20, 159–60, 163, 166–67; and the exchange of women, 213; of the family form, 297, 299
feudalism, 285
fictive kinship, 18, 25, 35, 46–47, 97, 138, 165, 225, 284
Fielder, Brigitte, 5, 15, 19
figuration, 4, 6, 11, 13, 122, 134, 151, 156, 245, 268n4
filius nullius, 217
filius vulgi, 217
Five Civilized Tribes, 100
flesh (Spillers), 165, 171, 175
Florida: Fort Marion, 101–2
Floyd, George, 9
Floyd, Kevin, 268n7
formalism, 4–6
Forster, E. M., 230
Fortier, Anne-Marie, 82
foster care, 103, 108, 253, 260
Foucault, Michel, 1, 11–12, 21, 227, 239, 244, 246, 260
France, 33, 227

Franco, Marielle, 20, 180–83, 188–98

Franklin, Sarah, 12, 28–29, 249–50, 292

fraternity, 246n6

Free Brazil Movement (MBL), 187

Freeman, Elizabeth, 1, 39–40, 80, 91, 134, 179n13, 194–95, 246n9, 259, 267

Freud, Sigmund, 1, 3, 12, 238, 265–66

Freyre, Gilberto, 186

friendship, 2, 22n2, 26, 32, 38, 59–61, 73, 87–88, 204, 286–87; anonymous, 228, 234–40, 245; and blood oaths, 277, 281; critiques of, 13, 21, 227–46

fugitivity, 45, 97, 162, 176, 178, 205, 224

fungibility, 7, 10, 121–22, 173–74, 255

Gai Pied, 227

Gamze (interviewee), 87–88

Garner, Darrell, 203

Garner, Eric, 176

Garner, Tyrone, 203–5, 218–23

Garrison, John, 13, 21

gay liberation, 297

Gebhard, Caroline, 52, 58, 61

Gelaohui (Society of Brothers and Elders), 284

genealogical imperative, 165

General Allotment Act (Dawes Act, 1887), 16, 100

Genet, Jean, 234

genetics, 26, 28, 30–34, 47, 63, 256; testing, 29. *See also* DNA; epigenetics

genocide, 40, 42, 100, 136n3, 152, 241

George, Rosemary, 77

ghost in the machine of kinship, 34–35, 42–43, 124, 205–9, 217–18, 222

gift economy, 5, 107, 131–36. *See also* altruism

gifts, 60–61, 95, 122, 124; and the exchange of women, 211–15

Gill-Peterson, Jules, 178n1

Ginsburg, Faye, 292

Glissant, Édouard, 179n17

global North, 120–21, 126

global South, 126

Goeman, Mishuana, 117–18n19, 153

Goldwater Institute, 104

Gomes, Anderson, 181, 198nn1–2

Google Baby, 119

Gordon, Avery, 245

Gornick, Vivian, 253

governmentality, 4, 20, 275, 279

Great Britain, 18, 254, 267n2, 300; British colonialism, 128, 215, 275. *See also* England; Scotland; United Kingdom

Green, Kai M., 162

growing sideways, 8, 255

Gugu (interviewee), 78

Gutman, Herbert, 15

Han, Shinhee, 106, 110, 117n18

Han, Sora, 220

handkerchief sisters, 282

Haraway, Donna, 1, 22n1, 41

Harlem Renaissance, 19, 67

Harper, Frances, 55

Harper's Magazine, 253

Harpo Studios, 119

Hartman, Saidiya, 16, 42, 124, 167, 205, 207–8, 214, 222

Harvard University, 49

Haudenosaunee Confederacy, 115

Hayt, Ezra, 102

Heath, Terrance, 203

hermeneutics, 20, 159–68, 176–77

heterocentrism, 16

heteropatriarchy, 20, 50, 96, 111, 138, 140–41, 148, 156, 179n13, 225

heterosexism, 96, 259

heterosexuality, 147, 165, 198, 207, 225, 297, 300; and friendship, 227, 229–30, 232–33; heterosexual matrix, 278; and the incest taboo, 210–11; and marriage, 16, 120, 282; and mestiço kinship model, 186–87; and reproduction, 41, 60, 120, 127, 182

Heti, Sheila, 253

Hickman, Jared, 17

High Times, 243

Hill, Christina Gish, 118n23

Hinduism, 131; Arya Samaj, 129; Brahmo

Samaj, 129; Hindu nationalism, 128–29, 134, 136n3

Hindu Marriage Act (1955), 129

Hirsch, Marianne, 87

HIV/AIDS, 9, 231–32, 292

Hobson, Brandon: *Where the Dead Sit Talking*, 108–12, 115, 117–18n19

Hochschild, Arlie, 137n7

Hogan, Linda, 117–18n19

Holiday, Fernando, 187

Holland, Sharon P., 1

Holmes, Eugene C., 67

homo economicus, 120

homonationalism, 6, 161

homonormativity, 7, 146, 161, 165, 187

homophobia, 37, 72–73, 85, 180–81, 187, 246n7, 270

homo sacer, 279, 283–84, 286

homosexuality, 124, 180, 186–87, 227, 273; and anti-social thesis, 192; criminalization of, 203, 219–21; and surrogacy, 124–26. *See also* sinthomosexual

Hopkins, Pauline, 50, 69

Howard University, 163

Huffington Post, 126

huiguans, 275

Hull, Akasha (Gloria), 69n5

Human (Man2), 168

Human Rights Campaign, 40

Hurley, Natasha, 5, 21

hypodescent, 55

Ihanktowan (Yankton Sioux) People, 106

ILGA-Europe, 73

Illinois: Chicago, 119

imago, 4

immigration, 6–7, 14, 17, 29, 148, 249, 270, 287, 288n5

incest taboo, 210–11, 214, 216–17, 224–25, 281

India, 18–19, 212; Gujarat, 119, 128, 132; surrogacy in, 119–36

Indian Adoption Project, 103

Indian Child Welfare Act (ICWA, 1978), 104, 117n15, 117n18

Indian Country, 118n23

Indian Lok Sabha, 124–27

Indian Penal Code: Section 377, 125–26, 136n3

Indian Supreme Court, 126

Indian Territory, 100–101

Indigenous epistemologies, 96

Indigenous kinship, 16, 19–20, 95–118, 138–57, 258–59

Indigenous peoples, 2, 7–8, 18, 128, 183, 188, 249; and settler kinship, 10, 16. *See also* Native Americans; *individual nations and communities*

Indrani (interviewee), 132–33

in loco parentis, 253

insurgent ground, 165, 171

interdependency, 3, 8, 26, 33, 37, 182, 183, 189–90, 192, 299; and Indigenous kinship, 140, 149, 151, 154, 156–57

intergenerationality, 9, 19, 63, 84, 87, 105, 121, 129, 148, 165, 178n11, 227

intersectionality, 15–16, 37, 70n7. *See also* queer-of-color critique

Ipek (interviewee), 78–79, 85

Ireland, 120

Islam, 84. *See also* Muslims

Islas, Arturo, 296

Israel, 126, 136n3

IVF, 125, 136n4

Jacobs, Margaret D., 105

Jains, 129

Japanese internment, 7

Jaquet, Chantal, 257–58

jazz, 160, 166–74, 176–77

Jewish people, 129

Jim Crow, 52

Jinlan/Zishu Sisters, 282, 286

Jin Qiguang, 273

Johnson, Emily, 98, 116n5

Johnson, Marsha P., 246n3

Jordan, June, 163

jouissance, 19, 121, 174

joy, 3, 33, 163, 194, 228

Joy, Eileen, 239

The Joy of Gay Sex, 228
Justice, Daniel Heath, 96, 154

Kaminsky, Amy, 188
Kanazawa, Satoshi, 250
Kashmir, 136
Kay, Jackie: *Trumpet*, 20, 159–78
Kazanjian, David, 238
Keeling, Kara, 51–52, 236
Kellogg, Catherine, 267
kidless lit, 21, 248–67
Kılıç, Şevval, 86
Kimmerer, Robin Wall, 107
kin-aesthetics, 4–6, 10, 18
kincoherence, 3, 6, 10–11, 14–15, 17–18
kinematics, 13–14, 17–19
kinetics, 4–5, 97
kinfullness, 15
kinlessness, 6, 14–15, 17, 223
kinship as verb, 98–99, 154
kinship chains, 29
kinship idealism, 5, 40
kinship of memory, 72, 82, 89
kinship studies, 12, 15, 28, 34, 292–94
kinship theory, 1–7, 12, 14, 17–18, 21, 205, 224
kinstillations, 19, 95–116
Kiowa People, 108
Kipnis, Laura, 254, 260
Klein, Melanie, 40, 106
Koori People, 116n4
Korean adoptees, 106
Kurds, 83

Lacan, Jacques, 12, 225, 235
Lake Eufala, 112
Lakota Nation, 102
Lambda Legal Defense and Education Fund, 203, 219
Lan, Dingyuan, 274
Lane-McKinley, Madeline, 256
La Raza, 295
Latin America, 181–86, 188–89, 193
Latin American studies, 20
Latinx people, 17, 182, 184–85, 188

Lau, Jacob, 116n4
Lawrence, John, 203, 218–19
Lawrence v. Texas, 203–6, 218–22
Lee, Summer Kim, 238
Le Guin, Ursula K., 261–62
Lesbian Friendship: For Ourselves and for Each Other, 232
Lévi-Strauss, Claude, 3, 12, 20, 27, 206, 209, 211–14
Lewin, Ellen, 292
Lewis, Sophie, 136n1, 256
liberalism, 136n3, 139, 140–43, 145–57, 160, 163, 165, 173, 193; and chosen family, 13, 122–23; liberal empathy, 261, 263; queer, 120, 157n4, 204; and settler colonialism, 16
Lindsey, Karen, 233
lineage, 18, 171–72, 271, 274, 278–79, 288n4; intellectual, 293; matrilineage, 15–16, 50, 101, 111, 117n10, 208, 215–17; patrilineage, 59–60, 66, 172, 215, 217, 276, 285; and slavery, 35, 42, 208, 215–17
Livingston, Jennie, 10
Li Zhongyue, 286
Locke, Alain, 67
Lomawaima, K. Tsianina, 103
Lorde, Audre, 51–52, 169, 179n14, 231, 240–41
Love, Heather, 12
Loveless, Natalie, 267
Luhmann, Susanne, 267
luto é verbo, 181, 195, 197
lynching, 52

Macharia, Keguro, 165
Mackey, Nathaniel, 165
Made in India, 119
Mahabharata, 128
Manalansan, Martin, IV, 89
Marielle effect, 196
marriage, 6, 49, 59–62, 121, 140, 142–44, 206, 229, 241, 281, 298–99; companionate, 13; as the exchange of women, 206, 212–14; and friendship, 229, 236, 240; heterosexual, 16, 120, 124, 127, 282; mar-

riage equality, 204; monogamous, 16, 143, 148; plural, 152; same-sex, 6–7, 10, 27, 40, 121, 126, 149, 204, 234, 292; and slavery, 15; and surrogacy, 120–21, 123, 126–27, 129. *See also* exchange of women

Martí, José, 186

Martinique, 294

martyrdom, 21, 284–87, 288n7

Marxism, 209, 222, 268n7; Marxist feminism, 250, 256–57

Maryland, 44

masculinity, 179n15, 234; Black, 50–52, 171–73, 198n2, 221–23; Chinese, 271; mixed-race, 50–52, 60–61, 66–69; white, 67, 221

Massachusetts: Boston, 49, 61, 69

matrilineage, 15–16, 50, 101, 111, 117n10, 208, 215–17. See also *partus sequitur ventrem*

Mauss, Marcel, 133, 135

Mbembe, Achille, 285

McCaskill, Barbara, 52

McKinnon, Susan, 12, 28–29, 292

Meillassoux, Claude, 203, 214, 222–24

melancholia, 14, 108, 110, 238; racial, 106

Melanesia, 212

Melike (interviewee), 83

memory of kinship, 72, 82, 89

Menke, Pamela Glenn, 69n5

mestiçagem, 183, 186–88, 190, 199n5

mestizaje, 183, 186, 190

Mexico, 34, 186; Mexico City, 188

Michi Saagig Nishnaabeg People, 112, 154–55

midwives, 67

Mikdashi, Maya, 136n3

Ming Restoration thesis, 272

minor kinship, 21, 248–67

miscegenation, 28, 46

Mississippi River, 102

Missouri River, 106, 118n23

mixed-race identity, 15, 19, 48–69. *See also* miscegenation; one-drop rule

model minority discourse, 17

Modi, Narendra, 128–29

monogamy, 7, 16, 141, 143–44, 148, 187, 252; monogamish-ness, 12; white settler, 258

Montaigne, Michel de, 229–30

Mooney, James, 114

more-than-human kin, 95–96, 101, 103, 105–6, 108, 112, 115

Morgan, Jennifer, 215

Morgan, Louis Henry, 16, 139–45, 149, 156, 157nn1–2

Mormons, 17

Morrison, Toni, 35

Moten, Fred, 165, 173

Moynihan Report, 34, 50, 178n9

Mullings, Leith, 292

Muñoz, José Esteban, 40, 148, 164, 169, 181–82, 184, 193, 195, 235–36, 242, 246n10, 258, 285

Murphy, Michelle, 250, 252–53, 259, 268n4

Muscogee (Cree) People, 100

Muslims, 128–29. *See also* Islam

Musser, Amber Jamilla, 9

mutual aid, 272, 275, 277, 282

Nash, Jennifer, 163

natal alienation, 46. See also *partus sequitur ventrem*

natalism, 25

National Guidelines for the Accreditation, Supervision, and Regulation of ART Clinics in India, 130

National Post, 249

Native Americans, 16, 104, 186. *See also* Indigenous peoples; *individual nations and communities*

natrans people, 73, 91

Naz Foundation v. Govt. of NCT of Delhi, 125–26

necropolitics, 166, 168–69, 270, 278, 285, 288

neoliberalism, 6–8, 10, 20–21, 31, 148, 271, 283, 298; and chosen family, 228, 233; and friendship, 236, 243; neoliberal jouissance, 19, 121; and racialization of intimacy, 204; and surrogacy, 121–22, 125–26, 129

Nepal, 125; Kathmandu, 126

Neruda, Pablo, 189

New Guinea, 36

New Mexico: Albuquerque, 117n12

New York City, 246n3

The New Yorker, 239

New York Times, 249, 253

Nineteenth Annual National Conference
    of Charities and Correction (1892), 116n8

Niyogi pratha (paternal surrogacy), 128

nonmonogamy, 16, 148, 234, 259

nonreproduction, 257–60, 262, 264

Norman, S.J, 116n4

North America, 16, 248–49, 268n5, 297

North American Man-Boy Love Associa-
    tion, 268n5

nuestra América mestiza, 186

Nyong'o, Tavia, 172

Obergefell v. Hodges, 6

Occupation of Alcatraz, 295

Oedipal family, 1, 60

O'Hara, Frank, 236

Okiji, Fumi, 176–77

Oklahoma, 100, 108, 112

one-drop rule, 15; *See also* miscegenation;
    mixed-race identity

Oprah, 119

optimism, 11, 186, 197, 228–29, 240, 267n1

othermothers, 15, 70n10

Outlaws of the Marsh, 276

Overall, Christine, 248

Ownby, David, 272, 276–77, 279

paganism, 106–7

Page Act (1875), 17, 288n5

Palestine, 136n3, 285

Pande, Amrita, 123, 136n5

paper children, 289n8

Parker, William, 169

partus sequitur ventrem, 15, 215–17. *See also*
    matrilineage; miscegenation; mixed-
    race identity; natal alienation

Passarelli, Matheusa, 197

Patel, Nayana, 119

paternity, 16, 29, 32, 35, 46, 66, 127, 143

patriarchy, 1, 10, 47, 67, 130, 209, 241–43,
    266, 282–83, 285; and the exchange of
    women, 209, 212–15, 281; and friend-
    ship, 231; hetero-, 20, 50, 96, 111, 138,
    140–41, 148, 156, 179n13, 225; and settler
    colonialism, 96, 100–101, 104, 111–12,
    140–41; and slavery, 35, 215, 225

patrilineage, 59–60, 66, 172, 215, 217, 276,
    285

Patroclus, 230

Patterson, Orlando, 14–15, 35, 46, 171

Pearce, Ruth, 89

Pegg, Jerine, 267

Pelin (interviewee), 74, 81, 85

Penang riots (1867), 280

Pennsylvania, 102

Perdue, Theda, 117n10

performativity, 10, 41, 161, 181, 194, 211, 257,
    259, 270, 277, 280

Perreau, Bruno, 33

Perrone, Charles, 184

pessimism, 11, 20

Peter Pan millennials, 8

Peterson, Dawn, 104–5

phallocentrism, 231, 246n6

phenomenology, 4, 77–78

Philadelphia (film), 227

Phillips, Caryl, 178n11

Piepzna-Samarasinha, Leah Lakshmi, 9

Pierce, Joseph M., 16, 19–20

Pine Ridge Agency, 102

pinkwashing, 125

Plains Indian Wars, 101

Plato, 39, 230

podding, 299

political ecology, 291

polygamy, 17, 213

Polynesia, 36

pornotrope, 159, 163, 178n7

postcolonialism, 19, 122–23, 125–26, 128,
    164–65, 177

poststructuralism, 2, 12, 14

Potawatomi People, 107

Povinelli, Elizabeth, 10, 146, 261

Power, Nina, 264
Pratt, Mary Louise, 295
Pratt, Richard Henry, 101–2, 109, 116n8
pregnancy, 30, 32, 46, 132. *See also* surrogacy
Preston, John, 233
private sphere, 81, 134, 139, 141, 143, 150
prosopopoeia, 237
psychoanalysis, 1, 13, 33, 39–40, 117n18, 209; object relations, 106
Puar, Jasbir, 136n3, 204, 285
public sphere, 22n1, 130, 184
Purple (interviewee), 74, 81

Qiu Jin, 285
Quakers, 106
Quashie, Kevin, 164, 178n8
queer assemblages, 285
queer belonging, 2, 11, 20, 40–41, 180, 183
queer bonds, 83
queer domesticity, 274, 287
queer hypersociability, 11
queer Indigenous studies, 14
queer latinoamericanidad, 182
queer liberalism, 120, 149, 157n4, 204
queer-of-color critique, 14, 16–17, 98, 161–63, 191, 197
queer post-memory, 87
queer studies, 162, 182, 185, 204, 235, 270, 293, 301; kinship in, 1, 147, 151, 165
queer temporalities, 3, 6, 51, 236, 285, 287
queer theory, 5, 20, 21, 185, 243, 268n7; anti-social thesis, 11, 20–21, 41, 192, 225, 229, 241–42, 245, 260; belonging in, 40–41; and Indigenous kinship, 16, 19; kinship in, 1–3, 6, 206, 226n2; and kinship theory, 6, 10–13; and lineage, 18–19; and race, 14, 16–17, 245; stranger sociability in, 258–59; and structuralism, 211; and transness, 161; trauma in, 194. *See also* queer-of-color critique
Quinlan, Susan, 184

race, 4, 81, 91, 231–32, 245–46nn2–3, 246n12, 262, 300; and blood, 18, 25–47,
100–101, 116–17n9; and children, 15, 19, 46, 48–69, 195, 204, 208, 215–17; and chosen family, 13, 172, 227–28; and colonialism, 101–6, 109–10, 117n15, 116, 139–57, 160–64, 168, 169, 175–77, 188; and disability, 70n7; and fetishism, 20, 159–60, 163, 166–67; and gender, 20, 159–78, 179n12; and immigration, 17, 275; and kinship, 2, 12–13, 15, 20, 46, 159, 165, 171, 205–25, 250; and masculinity, 50–52, 60–61, 66–69; and national identity, 181, 185–90, 194–96; and queer theory, 14, 16–17, 245; racial capitalism, 9, 161, 225; racial democracy, 186–88; racialization of intimacy, 120, 204; racial melancholia, 106; racial passing, 56; and slavery, 15, 122, 124, 205–25. *See also* anti-Blackness; critical race studies/theory; *filius nullius*; *filius vulgi*; miscegenation; mixed-race identity; natal alienation; one-drop rule; *partus sequitur ventrem*; slavery; white supremacy
racism, 7, 17, 37, 41, 169, 189–90, 231, 246n7; biopolitical, 275; anti-Black, 9, 14–15, 20–21, 52, 54–55, 161, 168, 172–73, 195, 222, 270; and immigration, 7, 17; and genetics, 30–31; and mixed-race identity, 50, 56, 59; in Moynihan report, 34; resistance to, 14, 298; scientific, 56; Trump's, 6. *See also* anchor babies discourse; apartheid; colorism; Japanese internment; Jim Crow; lynching; slavery; white supremacy
radical kinship, 256
Rapp, Rayna, 292
Raymond, Walter, 275
raza cósmica, 186
Rechy, John, 239
Recollet, Karyn, 96, 116n5; "Kinstillatory Gathering," 97–98
Reeves, Roger, 236
Reid-Pharr, Robert, 60, 63, 70n9
reproductive futurism, 21, 256, 264
reproductive labor, 32, 119, 122, 124, 129, 136n1

reproductive rights, 255

reproductive tourism, 119, 123, 125

reproductive turn, 250

Rich, Adrienne, 1

Richardson, Matt, 167, 171, 179n12, 179n15

Rifkin, Mark, 1, 16, 19–20, 80

Rio de Janeiro City Council, 193

Rivera, Sylvia, 246n3

Roach, Tom, 231

Roberts, Dorothy, 121

Rocha, Luciane, 195

Rodríguez, Juana María, 1, 148, 182, 187

Rodríguez, Richard T., 1

Roebuck, Christopher, 27, 41

Rohy, Valerie, 80, 230

Rojda (interviewee), 74, 82

roll calling, 188, 190–92, 197–98

Romance of the Three Kingdoms, 276

Rosaldo, Renato, 295

Roscoe, Will, 117n12

Rosebud Agency, 102

Ross, Marlon, 67

Rowe, Desireé, 247n16

Rubin, Gayle, 1–2, 11–13, 209–10, 212

Rudrappa, Sharmila, 123, 132

Ryle, Gilbert, 207–8

Saha, Poulomi, 19

Sahlins, Marshall, 12, 36, 38–40

Sainte-Marie, Buffy, 98

Sandler, Lauren, 248

Santiago, Silviano, 182–85, 190

savings glut, 300

Schneider, David, 12, 25, 26–28, 34, 46, 139, 293

Schulman, Sarah, 136n3

Scotland, 18, 160, 166, 171–74. *See also* Great Britain

Sedgwick, Eve Kosofsky, 1, 164, 246n7, 259–60

Selek, Pınar, 85

self-begetting, 19, 51, 53, 65–69

Selin (interviewee), 86

Seminole People, 100

settler colonialism, 117–18n19; and blood quantum, 116–17n9; and kinship, 7, 14, 16, 19, 98–113, 151–52, 155, 252–53, 258–59; and patriarchy, 96, 100–101, 104, 111–12, 140–41

seven generations, 96

sex/gender system, 209, 225

sexuality studies, 1

sexual violence, 102, 220–22, 282; in Indigenous boarding schools, 102; and kinship, 40, 46, 208; and slavery, 15, 46, 208

sex work, 17, 72–76, 78, 80–81, 85–87, 281

Shah, Nayan, 17, 274

Sharpe, Christina, 42

Shaye, Amaryah, 174

Showtime, 245n2

Sikhs, 129

Silveira, Daniel, 193

Silverman, Kaja, 5

Simpson, Leanne Betasamosake, 112–13, 154–55

sinthomosexual, 264, 280

sisterhood, 75, 231–32, 281–83, 286

slavery, 7, 17, 40, 47, 55, 70n9, 174; and akinship, 20, 204–5, 217, 222–25; anthropological studies of, 203, 214, 222; as ghost in the machine of kinship, 34–35, 42–43, 124, 205–9, 217–18, 222; and kincoherence, 14–15; in *Kindred*, 43–46; and maternity, 208, 214–17; and paternity, 65, 208; and property relations, 31; and surrogacy, 121–22, 124; and ungendering, 135, 165, 167, 171. See also *filius nullius*; *filius vulgi*; natal alienation; *partus sequitur ventrem*

Snorton, C. Riley, 165, 171

Snyder, Meredith, 267

social death, 14–15, 35, 168, 223

social refraction, 252, 255–57, 260, 267

social reproduction, 46, 153, 156, 222, 250, 252, 255–57, 259

Social Sciences Research Council of Canada, 267

sodomy, 125, 204, 218–20
Solanas, Valerie: SCUM Manifesto, 228–29, 241–45; Up Your Ass, 241, 244, 247n16
Solnit, Rebecca, 253–54, 268n6
South Africa, 43
Spillers, Hortense, 1, 15, 34–35, 50, 65, 135, 165, 171, 223
Spindelman, Marc, 220–21
Stack, Carol, 15
Stallings, L. H., 148, 164
Statistics Canada, 249
stepparenting, 3, 253–55, 260, 263
Stockton, Kathryn Bond, 80, 255
Stonewall (film), 246n3
Stowe, Harriet Beecher, 55
Straits Settlements (1826–1946), 275
stranger relationality, 22n1, 263
stranger sociability, 21, 258–59
Strathern, Marilyn, 212, 292
stratified reproduction, 250
Stremlau, Rose, 100, 105
structuralism, 1, 14, 18, 26–27, 42, 205–7, 209–12
Strychacz, Thomas, 69n5
Subramaniam, Banu, 128–29
suicide, 109, 259, 270, 282, 285, 287
Sun Yat-sen, 284
Suppression of Dangerous Societies Act (1890), 275
surrogacy, 19, 30, 256–57, 292; altruistic, 131–35; commercial, 120–36; full, 256; gestational, 119–21, 125, 132, 136n2; Niyogi pratha (paternal surrogacy), 128
Surrogacy Bill (2018), 120–33
survivance, 96, 113
Swaraj, Sushma, 124, 126, 133

Taiwan, 273–74
TallBear, Kim, 116–17n9, 151–52, 253, 258
Taşcıoğlu, Ezgi, 73
Teuton, Christopher B.: Cherokee Stories of the Turtle Island Liars' Club, 114–15
Texas, 204, 206, 220; Houston, 203, 218

Tiandihui (Heaven and Earth Society), 280
Time magazine, 126, 248–49, 253
tiospaye, 152, 154
Tipton, Billy, 166
traffic in women, 206, 209, 212, 281. See also exchange of women
Trail Where They Cried (Trail of Tears), 112
trans*, 162
trans class, 257, 263, 267
Trans Day of Remembrance, 161
trans hermeneutics, 20, 159–68, 176–77
transing, 162–64
trans-interior, 159–61, 163–66, 168, 176–77
trans of color theory, 13, 20, 162
transphobia, 37, 72–73, 85–86, 169, 270
trans studies, 160, 178n1
transtemporality, 97, 106, 116n3
trans theory, 7, 13
trans time, 81
transviad@, 185
trauma, 14, 33, 84, 102, 110, 117–18n19, 172, 177, 227, 245, 259; in queer theory, 194–95
Troester, Rosalie Riegle, 70n10
Troy, 230
Trump, Donald, 6, 29, 32–33
Tsalagi (Cherokee language), 111–12, 118n22
Tupi People, 184
Türkan (interviewee), 76
Turkey, 18–19, 72, 76–82, 84, 86–91; Ankara, 74, 84, 85; Antalya, 74; Istanbul, 71, 73–75, 83, 85; Izmir, 74
Turtle Island, 107, 114–15
Twitter, 194–96

Ulusoy, Süleyman "Süleyman the Hose," 85–86, 88
uncles, 39, 260
ungendering, 135, 159, 165, 167, 171–72, 221
United Kingdom, 120. See also England; Great Britain

United Nations, 249, 267n2

United States, 50, 55, 67, 105, 141, 147, 153, 157, 244, 289n8, 293–94; birthrates in, 249; citizenship in, 34, 100–101; civil rights in, 43; immigrants in, 29, 33, 270, 274, 287; Indigenous boarding schools in, 99, 102–4; kinship in, 8, 18; marriage in, 6; racism in, 275, 279; slavery in, 14–15, 121, 122, 208; state violence in, 9; US colonialism, 34

University of Delaware Library: Alice Dunbar-Nelson Papers, 48, 69n1, 70n6

US Army, 117n12

US Border Patrol, 10

US Bureau of Indian Affairs, 102–4

US Constitution, 31, 104; Fourteenth Amendment, 7, 204

US Supreme Court, 10, 105

Utah, 17

utopia, 13, 19, 37, 119, 121, 134, 169, 181, 242–43, 261

Vasconcelos, José, 186

Vietnam War, 295

Virginia, 15, 215

Viveiros de Castro, Eduardo, 38

Vizenor, Gerald, 113

Vora, Kalindi, 122

Vuong, Ocean, 245; "Someday I'll Love Ocean Vuong," 228, 236–39

Wali, Alaka, 292

Warner, Michael, 147, 230, 258

Warner, Sara, 247n16

War on Terror, 291

Watkins, Frances Ellen, 50

Watts, Mary Jo, 247n16

Weinbaum, Alys Eve, 124

Weiner, Joshua J., 83

West, Elizabeth, 69n5

Weston, Kath, 1, 27, 227, 233–34, 245n1, 298, 299; *Animate Planet*, 291, 295–96,

299, 301; *Families We Choose* (FWC), 12, 21, 291–95, 297, 300

White House, 29, 33

white supremacy, 1–2, 8–9, 14, 30, 104, 164, 294; and mixed-race identity, 51, 55–56. *See also* anti-Blackness; apartheid; Japanese internment; Jim Crow; lynching; slavery

Williams, Patricia, 30–31, 35

Wilson, Sheena, 267

Winfrey, Oprah, 119, 135

Winnicott, D. W., 110

Wiradjuri People, 116n4

Wojnarowicz, David, 234

Wolfe, Patrick, 99

women's liberation, 209–10. *See also* feminism

Wordsworth, William, 48, 51, 53, 65

Worker's Party, 187, 199n4

Work in Progress, 245n2

world making, 19–20, 72, 138, 147–48, 258

World War II, 103–4

Wynter, Sylvia, 168

xenophobia, 6, 188. *See also* Chinese Exclusion Act (1882); Japanese internment; Page Act (1875)

xiedou, 274, 279, 288n4

Xinhai Revolution (1911), 286

Yanagisako, Sylvia, 12, 27–28, 292, 295

Yankton Sioux People, 153

Yazzie, Melanie, 155

Yıldız (interviewee), 82, 91

Yılmaz, Sevda, 86

Young, Damon, 83

Yup'ik People, 98

Zagarell, Sandra, 69n2

Zelizer, Viviana, 131

Zengin, Aslı, 73

Zitkala-Ša, 106–7, 117n17

Zuni Pueblo People, 117n12